Excel® 2007 Advanced Report Development

Excel® 2007 Advanced Report Development

Timothy Zapawa

Wiley Publishing, Inc.

Excel® 2007 Advanced Report Development

Published by
Wiley Publishing, Inc.
10475 Crosspoint Boulevard
Indianapolis, IN 46256
www.wiley.com

Published by Wiley Publishing, Inc., Indianapolis, Indiana

Published simultaneously in Canada

ISBN: 978-0-470-04644-9

Manufactured in the United States of America

10 9 8 7 6 5 4 3 2 1

Limit of Liability/Disclaimer of Warranty: The publisher and the author make no representations or warranties with respect to the accuracy or completeness of the contents of this work and specifically disclaim all warranties, including without limitation warranties of fitness for a particular purpose. No warranty may be created or extended by sales or promotional materials. The advice and strategies contained herein may not be suitable for every situation. This work is sold with the understanding that the publisher is not engaged in rendering legal, accounting, or other professional services. If professional assistance is required, the services of a competent professional person should be sought. Neither the publisher nor the author shall be liable for damages arising herefrom. The fact that an organization or Website is referred to in this work as a citation and/or a potential source of further information does not mean that the author or the publisher endorses the information the organization or Website may provide or recommendations it may make. Further, readers should be aware that Internet Websites listed in this work may have changed or disappeared between when this work was written and when it is read.

For general information on our other products and services or to obtain technical support, please contact our Customer Care Department within the U.S. at (800) 762-2974, outside the U.S. at (317) 572-3993 or fax (317) 572-4002.

Library of Congress Cataloging-in-Publication Data

Zapawa, Timothy, 1970-
   Excel 2007 advanced report development / Timothy Zapawa.
      p. cm.
   Includes index.
   ISBN-13: 978-0-470-04644-9 (paper/website)
   ISBN-10: 0-470-04644-9 (paper/website)
 1. Microsoft Excel (Computer file)   2. Business report writing--Computer programs.   I. Title.
   HF5548.4.M523Z367 2007
   005.54--dc22

                                                      2006101345

Wiley also publishes its books in a variety of electronic formats. Some content that appears in print may not be available in electronic books.

For Lisa

About the Author

Timothy Zapawa (Saline, Michigan) obtained a baccalaureate in Accounting and Arabic from the University of Michigan in Ann Arbor in 1997. Prior to that, he served four years in the United States Navy, specializing in electronic communications. He has completed several certifications and professional examinations in a variety of financial and technical fields, including the Certified Public Accountant (CPA), Certified Management Accountant (CMA), Certified Financial Manager (CFM), Project Manager Professional (PMP), Microsoft Certified Systems Engineer (MCSE), and Microsoft Certified Database Administrator (MCDBA). Tim is currently an implementation director at Advantage Computing Systems, Inc. (www.advantagecs.com), a company that produces enterprise software for publishing companies and service bureaus. He leads teams of engineers, developers, and managers through software implementation projects. He has also developed several technical training courses for his company's clients, including modules on Business Intelligence, Crystal Reports, SQL programming for Oracle and SQL Server, and Excel PivotTable Reporting.

Credits

Acquisitions Editor
Katie Mohr

Development Editor
Kelly Talbot

Technical Editor
Todd Meister

Production Editor
Angela Smith

Copy Editor
Kim Cofer

Editorial Manager
Mary Beth Wakefield

Production Manager
Tim Tate

Vice President and Executive Group Publisher
Richard Swadley

Vice President and Executive Publisher
Joseph B. Wikert

Project Coordinator
Lynsey Osborn

Graphics and Production Specialists
Sean Decker
Denny Hager
Stephanie D. Jumper
Jennifer Mayberry

Quality Control Technician
Jessica Kramer
Brian H. Walls

Proofreading and Indexing
Aptara

Anniversary Logo Design
Richard Pacifico

Contents

Acknowledgments

I'd like to express my deep gratitude to Katie Mohr, my acquisition editor, who initiated this project and ensured that I received all the support I needed while working with the beta versions of Excel 2007. I'd also like to thank Kelly Talbot, my development editor, for all his excellent work in helping me organize these chapters, and Todd Meister, my technical editor, who performed an outstanding job on the technical verification of these materials.

My understanding of the reporting tools throughout this book is based on my 10 years of experience at Advantage Computing Systems (ACS), where I have been able to work with numerous organizations throughout the United States and England in developing reporting solutions. I'd like to thank the principals of ACS for fostering a first-rate business culture and a challenging work environment, and Tom Burbeck in particular for his valuable mentoring.

I'd also like to take this opportunity to give special thanks to my mom, who has always worked very hard to ensure that I've had the opportunity to succeed, and to my father-in-law, David Wu, for his ongoing encouragement and support.

Last, but most importantly, I'd like to again thank my wife, Lisa, for her continued support of the many late nights and weekends that went into this book.

Introduction

If you are a SQL programmer, report developer, or sophisticated Excel user and want to learn more about Excel's reporting capabilities, this book is for you. In the pages that follow, I provide comprehensive information on both the technical and strategic areas of Excel report development—paying special attention to online transactional processing (OLTP) databases.

By reading this book and following the practice exercises scattered liberally throughout the chapters, you can learn to develop powerful and innovative reporting solutions using Microsoft Excel 2007. This book's step-by-step approach can help you steadily gain confidence in your ability to use Excel's reporting functions as you enhance your skills by working through the hands-on examples. Many of the examples offer an accompanying video on the book's companion web site that you can watch to ensure that you fully understand every step (see the section "On the Web Site" later in this Introduction).

Highlights

This book covers a broad range of topics having to do with report development with Excel. Here are some of the highlights:

- Single-source coverage of Excel's report development features with notes, tips, warnings, and real-world examples at the end of each chapter

- Extensive and in-depth information on PivotTable and Spreadsheet report features, functions, and capabilities

- Thorough documentation of the Microsoft Query program included with Excel

- Comprehensive information on Excel's client-based OLAP cube tools for processing very large data sets from OLTP data sources

In addition, this book helps you thoroughly understand these main features of Excel's reporting technology:

- PivotTable reports: A powerful and dynamic reporting tool that allows users to analyze data sets by dragging-and-dropping fields into various report sections. Numerical data can be aggregated and summarized into a myriad of products and forms. Using this technology, you can rapidly move fields in and out of the report, change aggregations, and customize filters. Drill down on any subtotal or total cell to reveal the underlying data—and simply click the mouse button to refresh your report with the most up-to-date information from OLTP databases and other external data sources.

- Spreadsheet reports: A reporting tool that allows users to import data into a more traditional columnar-type format. After the data is in the Spreadsheet report, users have numerous options and powerful functions at their fingertips, such as filters, advanced sorts, conditional formatting, lists, and fill-down formulas. As is the case with PivotTables, Spreadsheet report data can be immediately refreshed with a click of a button.

- Parameter queries: One of the most powerful, overlooked, and undocumented areas of Excel reporting, parameter queries allow users to dynamically specify filters each time a Spreadsheet report or PivotTable list is updated. Using this feature, you can restrict the number of records returned from a data source before the data is even imported into Excel. This results in faster report run-times and more concentrated focus of report information. Parameter queries are frequently used in conjunction with SQL stored procedures, views, and queries to target a specific range of data such as a date range, product line, region, or division.

What You Need to Know

You don't have to know Structured Query Language (SQL) to get real value from this book. However, readers who are familiar with SQL programming will probably get the most out of it. Indeed, many SQL programmers find that Excel report development is the next logical progression in their technology education. Still, even if you are only an experienced user of Excel, you will learn a substantial amount about Excel reporting, especially in the earlier chapters where the graphical Excel tools are used to build SQL queries that run against external data sources such as delimited files, spreadsheets, and databases.

What You Need to Have

To make the best use of this book, you need the following software installed on your computer:

- **Excel 2007:** Microsoft has made several enhancements to both the graphical display and report development features in this latest Excel release. If you are using an earlier version of Excel, you should purchase my first book entitled Excel Advanced Report Development (ISBN: 0764588117).

- **Microsoft SQL Server 2005:** Much of the material in this book is focused on report development using OLTP databases. Many exercises require access to the SQL Server AdventureWorksDW database that is included as part of a default installation of SQL Server 2005.

- **Microsoft SQL Server Analysis Services 2005:** This program is included on the Microsoft SQL Server 2005 CD-ROM. It should be installed so that you can follow along with the online chapter on Online Analytical Processing (OLAP) cubes.

How This Book Is Organized

Because there are so many enterprise software systems in the marketplace, it's impractical to include report examples for each one of them. Instead, for most of the exercises and examples I've used Microsoft SQL Server's AdventureWorksDW database that is included as part of a default installation of SQL Server 2005.) This database provides an excellent example of how a data mart or data warehouse database might be organized. Using this database program, I think you can obtain a useful and informed perspective on how you might go about developing comparable reports for your enterprise systems.

I've organized this book to help readers of all skill levels. If you're new to Excel reports, you should start with Part I of the book. Advanced users who are already familiar with Excel's reporting features and with external data sources can skip to Part II, where the core features, functions, and components of Excel reports are covered. The appendixes in Part III provide references for installing the NorthwindCS database, configuring your Windows operating system to display extensions for known file types, and using basic SQL.

Part I – Report Basics

This part consists of three chapters. Chapter 1 provides an introduction and orientation to the major types of Excel reports and reporting components. Chapter 2 introduces PivotTable report technology, providing a conceptual overview of how PivotTable report data is organized. Here, I demonstrate how data is summarized and presented in a PivotTable report. Chapter 3 provides an overview of the components and essential elements of an Excel 2007 PivotTable report.

Part II – External Data

This section of the book includes six chapters – all covering external data from various perspectives. Chapter 4 provides an overview on accessing external data sources, including the various types of ways that data can be accessed from Excel. In Chapter 5, I cover the five buttons of the Get External Data group that can be used to access data from text files, Access databases, web sites, OLAP cubes, and SQL/Oracle databases. Chapters 6-8 provide comprehensive coverage of the Microsoft Query program that can be used to build and/or process sophisticated SQL queries.

Part III – PivotTable Reporting

The principal topics of Excel PivotTable reports are covered in Chapters 10-13. Chapter 10 includes material on PivotTable report design. Here you learn about the enhanced filtering, tools included in Excel 2007 along with the core PivotTable functions for sorting and grouping data, creating custom formulas, and working with inner and outer fields. Chapter 11 includes a comprehensive review of conditional formatting tools, report style template, and report layout options. I describe how data can be managed in Chapter 12 and then cover the graphical options available in PivotCharts in Chapter 13.

Part IV– Spreadsheet Reporting

The principal topics of Excel Spreadsheet reports are covered in this part of the book, Chapters 14-16. I cover the core features and tools of Spreadsheet reports in Chapter 14, including filtering, navigation, and report management tools. Taking Excel reports to the next level, I demonstrate how several Spreadsheet reports can be linked to one another to develop a larger, automated report solution in Chapter 15. And in Chapter 16 I provide detailed information on Spreadsheet report formatting.

Part V– Appendices

Appendix A includes an SQL reference. Here, basic and sophisticated query structures are dissected and reviewed in detailed. This appendix includes a review of string and mathematical operators, aggregate functions, and Case logic. Finally, a review of the clicking actions, pop-up menus, and tab functions of PivotTable reports are summarized into Appendix B.

Conventions

To help you get the most from the text of this book and keep track of what's happening, I've used a number of conventions throughout the book.

NOTE In text formatted like this you will find important "extra" information that is directly relevant to the surrounding text. By reading these Notes, Tips, Warnings, Cross-References, On the Web, and Watch the Video text boxes, you can get additional help and learn some special tips.

These special styles are used in the text throughout the book:

- Important words are highlighted in *italics* when they are first introduced.

- Text you are being asked to type is shown in **bold**.

- URLs and portions of SQL queries or statements shown within the text are shown in a special `monofont` typeface.

A Note on SQL

I use the abbreviation SQL numerous times throughout this book. I pronounce the word as "Sequel" and say it that way in conversations, even though it is an acronym for Structured Query Language. Since it is technically an abbreviation, you'll often see "an SQL ..." instead of "a SQL". You should realize that this abbreviation is in transition and that it appears to be gaining some traction in being recognized as a word by itself.

On the Web Site

This book's companion web site contains some valuable information that will help you on your journey to becoming an Excel 2007 report development guru. Included are sample query files and report examples that you can download to your computer. All the real world examples throughout each chapter are captured in online videos available for you to watch. If you find any of the material difficult to understand or you just want to see how it's done without trying to follow each step, simply connect to the web site and watch the video. Lastly, while materials on Online Analytical Processing (OLAP) were not ready in time for this book's publication date, the chapter will be available on the web site for you to review by the time this book goes to print. Click over to it and download the PDF version for more information about using Excel 2007's OLAP reporting tools.

Getting Sample Files

As you work through the examples in this book, you will run into special text boxes that remind you to go to the book's companion web site to download example files. These boxes look like this

ON THE WEB You can download the Expense Data.csv document to your computer from this book's companion web site at `www.wiley.com/go/excelreporting/2007`. **Look for this document in either the Chap03.zip file or the Chap03 directory.**

Be sure to take advantage of the provided files so that you can follow along seamlessly with the step-by-step examples used in the chapters.

All the files you need are available for download at `www.wiley.com/go/excel-reporting`. When you get to that page, you can choose to:

- Download all the files for a single chapter (Chap01.zip, for example)
- Download one large zip file that includes the files for all the chapters (Excel Reporting.zip) and that will create a folder structure on your hard drive with directories for each chapter
- Click one of the listed .avi files to watch a video of a particular exercise

Watching Videos

When you see a box like the following after an exercise, it's telling you that an accompanying video is available on the web site:

WATCH THE VIDEO **To see how to convert a PivotTable report to a PivotTable list, click the Ch12vid01.avi file at** `www.wiley.com/go/excelreporting/2007` **to watch the video.**

So watch for these notes in the text that steer you to a plethora of available—and helpful—files on the web site.

Downloading the Online Analytical Processing (OLAP) Chapter

When you're ready to download the OLAP chapter, click over to this book's companion web site and download the PDH version at: www.wiley.com/go/excelreporting/2007.

Getting More Information About Excel 2007 Reporting Tools

If you're interested in learning about how to leverage Excel 2007's reporting tools, check out my web site blog at www.excelreportsolutions.com. I'm also a big fan of Charley Kyd's web site, www.exceluser.com, which provides excellent articles on business applications of Excel. There are all sorts of archived newsletters, real-world perspectives, examples, and links on developing dashboards, reports, and business solutions.

As you will discover throughout this book, Excel 2007 provides a robust suite of powerful reporting tools. I tried to cover them from my own experience and provide perspective on how they can be used in the real world. I wish you the best of luck in your own report development endeavors, and I welcome any comments or suggestions for improvement. Please feel free to send me email at `excelreports@earthlink.net`.

Why I Wrote This Book

For the last 10 years, I have helped lead several prominent organizations through implementations of our proprietary enterprise software. Like many enterprise systems, our software affects many departments within a particular company. In order to implement our system, department managers assign staff to ensure that their particular needs are properly handled. One of the many needs usually involves replacing reports that managers and personnel rely on to identify problems, track productivity, show profitability, and summarize results.

Replacing reports that may have been used for several years can be difficult. Depending on the number of reports and the size of the organization, this activity can become both expensive and time-consuming. Just picture interviewing numerous users of hundreds, or even thousands, of reports across various departments in hopes of trying to understand what data is being summarized. Not only are the two systems much different, but report-users may also use terminology that only their peers who are familiar with the system being replaced can understand. Trying to decipher field meanings, determine what data needs to be summarized—and when—is only the beginning. Breaks, sorts, totals, and filters also need to be identified, documented, and programmed. After that, the report still needs to undergo rigorous testing to ensure that the data is accurate and properly formatted. This process may be repeated several times before the new report is fully approved as an acceptable replacement.

As a project manager, I found that reports were consuming more money, time, and resources than the project had been allocated. Beyond just eliminating some of the reports, I had to find a faster, cheaper, and more effective method of replacing them. First, I started using Crystal Reports. I liked Crystal's reporting features, graphical tools, and tight integration with Microsoft SQL Server's stored procedures. Getting the report to look just right, however, took substantially more time than simply using our native application report development utilities. Sure, the report looked a lot better than a traditional columnar report, but I didn't get any closer to achieving my goals of developing reports faster and cheaper.

Around the same time, I also started using Excel reports. Being new to this technology, I didn't immediately grasp its full potential and capabilities. Eventually, things clicked. With some experience, I learned how a single PivotTable could replace dozens of existing reports. I also discovered that most report users could easily be trained to run, maintain, and modify the report once the underlying data was extracted for them. I no longer had to spend unnecessary time trying to understand sorts, breaks, totals, and filters. Instead, I simply had to focus on the main purpose of the report, and then simply develop an SQL query that extracted the data. Once a basic report shell was created with the fields from the SQL query, report users could shape and format the report as they saw fit. Often, a single Excel report replaced numerous existing reports. On many implementation projects, we not only reduced the time and expense involved in replacing the reports, we also provided the report users with increased data analysis capabilities. In finding a better reporting tool that also reduced project costs, you can probably see why it didn't take long for this technology to quickly take hold at our company, and throughout our user community. PivotTable reporting became—and still is—a real buzzword among our clients.

Excel® 2007 Advanced Report Development

Report Basics

Taking a First Look at Excel's Reporting Tools

This chapter provides you with an overview of Excel's reporting features. It shows you the principal types of Excel reports and how you can use them to satisfy many of the business requirements you may face. It covers some of the benefits of using Excel reports, including real-time access, simplified report updates, and reduced cost of ownership.

In this first chapter, I try to give you a snapshot overview of PivotTable and Pivot-Chart reports, Spreadsheet reports, parameter queries (how you can map parameters to stored procedure variables), and web queries, along with a quick look at some of the new features available in Excel 2007.

Keep in mind that this chapter just helps you get started with the basics. As you work your way through the other chapters, you have the opportunity to dive into these topics in a lot more detail. So let's begin!

Why Use Excel for Reports?

Companies produce reports from enterprise software systems using numerous methods. A report might be generated from the native enterprise software program or from a standalone report development software program such as Business Objects (formerly Crystal Reports). In other scenarios, the report data may be extracted to a delimited file that is loaded into a program such as Excel or Access. The number of enterprise software applications, the amount and level of internal expertise, and the degree of organizational leadership are just a few factors that can determine how reports are managed within a company.

NOTE You might be asking yourself, "What is an enterprise software system, anyway?" Some popular enterprise software systems include SAP, PeopleSoft, Siebel, and Baan. These systems are used in all types of organizations to run the business more efficiently and effectively. Hospitals use medical information systems to track a patient's vital data and health care history. Companies such as Amazon.com or Barnes & Noble use warehouse management systems to reduce the time and labor expenses for shipping products to customers. The company I work for produces enterprise software for magazine and book publishers. More than 35 modules are available to perform business functions from advertising, billing, inventory, circulation, and payroll to conference management, web access, and customer relationship management.

Although report development tools are often bundled with enterprise software applications, many organizations use a separate report development software application for creating and running reports. So why would an organization spend additional funds to purchase reporting software if it is already included as part of its enterprise software system? Learning and supporting the report development tools included with an enterprise software application can be both difficult and expensive. Furthermore, many organizations have numerous enterprise applications, so that work and cost can be magnified several times. Enhanced performance and standardization to a single system are major benefits for organizations seeking to reduce costs and maintain their report development skills. Instead of paying six employees to develop and manage reports using the report development tools in a few enterprise software applications, it may take only two employees to develop and manage equivalent reports for the same enterprise systems using a single report development software program.

Initially, information technology (IT) professionals and business managers unfamiliar with Excel's reporting capabilities are often skeptical about using Excel to produce reports from an enterprise system. However, even the most skeptical of IT decision-makers are generally convinced once they

- See Excel's powerful reporting tools in action.

- Receive superb feedback from report users.

- Understand how much less software licensing feed, support costs, and maintenance is involved with Microsoft Excel compared to other software reporting packages.

Here are some of the top considerations for using Excel reports over competing report development software programs:

- **Excel reports can retrieve data from an enterprise software application's OLTP database in real time.** Many systems require reports to be run by first launching the application and then requesting it. If the report is exported to Excel, a second step is likely involved for actually importing and formatting the data. (Many software systems build interfaces to Excel.) In comparison, by using native Excel reporting functionality, you can accomplish all of this in a fraction of the time. With hardly more than a mouse click, data can be fetched directly from one or more databases to update an Excel report with the most up-to-date information.

▪ **Sorts, breaks, and totals can easily be applied, modified, and removed.** With only limited training, even a novice Excel user can add or remove subtotals, apply complex sorts, and insert page breaks or lines between various report groups. It can take days or weeks of training to be able to understand and perform this same type of task with competing report development software programs and enterprise reporting tools.

▪ **Some Excel report types, such as PivotTable reports, are very dynamic and powerful.** One report can replace dozens of traditional columnar reports. A PivotTable report can contain many more fields than what is actually displayed in a single view of the report. Inserting and removing fields, changing field locations, and applying filters are easily and readily performed.

▪ **Excel reports are cost effective.** Running and modifying reports from an enterprise software application or report development software program usually requires that the application be installed. This can add a considerable burden to support, training, and software licensing costs. In contrast, most computers already have Excel installed and users are often familiar with the basics of how this program works.

▪ **Report development time is often much faster than with competing reporting software applications.** Enterprise reporting tools and report development software programs can be very intricate and complex. Organizations regularly hire report programmers or consultants to help develop many of their reports. In contrast, learning and using Excel report development tools is simple. Reports can frequently be developed more quickly, and at a lesser cost, than competing report development software programs and enterprise reporting tools.

▪ **Excel reports are integrated with related Microsoft products.** The integration among the various Office programs becomes more seamless and feature-rich with each new release of Microsoft Office, allowing you to develop ever more powerful and innovative reporting solutions.

PivotTable Reports

With PivotTable reports, you can interactively create and build cross-tabular reports from a list of available fields. These fields can be derived from another worksheet tab, an SQL or Oracle database, a text file, an OLAP cube, or some other external data source. After the PivotTable shape is created, users can move fields to different locations in the report, change the type of aggregation (for example, calculate an average amount instead of a total amount), apply filters to determine which items in a report field are displayed, and apply complex sorts based on aggregated values or other field items in the report.

Using PivotTable technology, report users can do the following:

- Produce a number of different views and reports by simply dragging fields from a field list to different locations in the PivotTable.

- Apply simple or advanced filters to determine which items should be displayed in a field.

- Conditionally add icons, data bars, color scales, and other formats to highlight critical report information.

- Aggregate numeric fields in a variety of ways.

- Group and sort data, toggle subtotals, and apply report format styles.

- Access and refresh data from external data sources using nothing more than a simple click of the mouse.

- Drill down on numeric data to reveal the underlying dataset detail.

- Use basic and advanced sorting tools to sort date, text, and numeric data in a variety of different ways.

With a PivotTable, you can drag fields from within the PivotTable Field List dialog box to different areas in the report. Using this technology, you can dynamically shape and format reports using the simple but powerful functions of Excel. Adding or removing a field, changing a filter, or modifying a sort order is easy. If you're not happy with the current report view, you can drag fields on or off the PivotTable, modify filter settings, and change how numerical data is aggregated to completely transform the look, meaning, and shape of the report.

The PivotTable in Figure 1-1 shows Total Revenue by Month within Payment Method and Type of Service. Notice that State is a field at the top of the PivotTable. With just a few clicks and moves of the mouse, the report can instantly be changed to instead show Average Revenue by Month and State (see Figure 1-2).

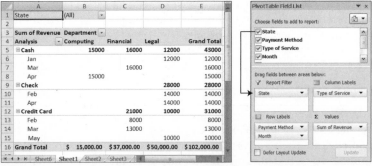

Figure 1-1: A PivotTable report is developed by simply dragging fields from the top of the PivotTable Field List dialog box to one of the areas in the bottom half of the dialog box.

Average revenue instead of total revenue   Field no longer on report

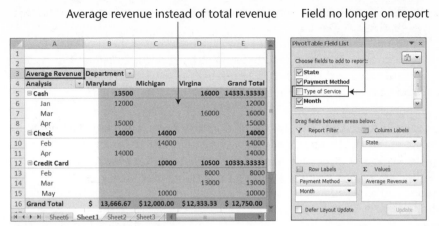

Figure 1-2: Now the report shows Average Revenue instead of Total Revenue, and State is now in the Column Labels area.

TIP You can create PivotTable reports that have numerous fields which do not necessarily have to be dragged to a report location (notice that Type of Service in Figure 1-2 no longer appears in the report). Using this type of approach, a PivotTable report can replace several regular reports, because fields can simply be dragged to locations in the report when they are needed.

Perhaps you might want to display data for a few of the months. To do so, just click the drop-down arrow on Month to deselect the values Jan and Feb, as shown in Figure 1-3.

Check or uncheck items to display in the report

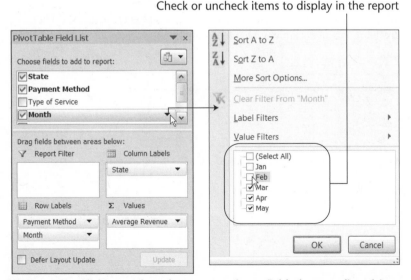

Figure 1-3: Clicking a drop-down arrow for a field shows a list of items that can be displayed (checked) or not displayed (unchecked).

After the filter is applied, the report is automatically resized to show only Mar, Apr, and May, as shown in Figure 1-4.

One of the most powerful utilities of PivotTable reports is the capability to drill down on the summarized report data to the underlying detail. In Figure 1-4, double-clicking any cell value in the range B5:E13 creates a new worksheet with the dataset that makes up that cell. Figure 1-5 shows the underlying data for cell B13.

CROSS-REFERENCE Be sure to read Chapters 2 and 3 to learn more about the basics of PivotTable reports, and then turn to Chapter 10 for a more complete analysis of PivotTable functionality, Chapter 11 for PivotTable formatting information, and Chapter 12 for PivotTable data management.

Filter icon appears to signify
that a filter is applied

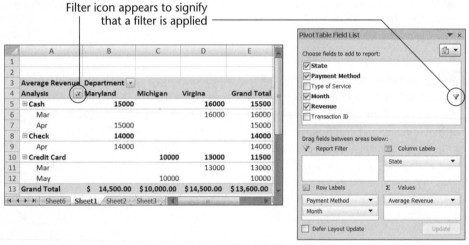

Figure 1-4: PivotTable reports are automatically resized once a filter is applied. Additionally, helpful filter icons let report users know which fields are being filtered.

	A	B	C	D	E
1	State ▾	Payment Method ▾	Type of Service ▾	Month ▾	Revenue ▾
2	Maryland	Cash	Computing	Apr	15000
3	Maryland	Check	Legal	Apr	14000

Figure 1-5: The supporting dataset that makes up cell B13 in Figure 1-4.

PivotChart Reports

PivotCharts enable you to visually view and analyze trends in data by linking to a Pivot-Table report. This link provides you with all the capabilities of a PivotTable report while also providing similar design and features in the graphical PivotChart that can be displayed on a different worksheet or right alongside the PivotTable report. Using a PivotChart, you see the data represented in a chart format, rather than summarized numerically, as is the case for a PivotTable report.

PivotCharts have much the same functionality as PivotTables and are organized in almost the same way. Using PivotChart technology, report users can do the following:

- Produce a number of different types of charts by simply dragging fields from a field list to different locations in the PivotChart.

- Apply simple or advanced filters to determine which items should be displayed in a field.

- Graphically represent numerical aggregations in many different ways using a variety of chart types.

- Use filters to control which items are charted.

- Link to a PivotTable report on the same worksheet or a different worksheet.

Figure 1-6 shows a sample PivotChart report linked to a PivotTable.

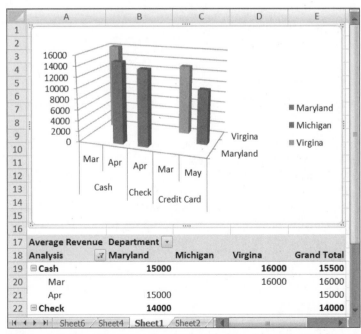

Figure 1-6: PivotCharts can be displayed alongside a PivotTable report (shown here) or on their own worksheet tab.

Several types of charts are available with PivotCharts. You can choose from a simple two-dimensional bar, column, or pie chart, to a more complex three-dimensional area, bubble, or radar chart. There are also numerous functions for controlling how the data is displayed for each data element in the series.

CROSS-REFERENCE To find out the details of creating and using PivotCharts, see Chapter 13.

Spreadsheet Reports

Instead of the cross-tabular format of PivotTable reports, Spreadsheet reports organize data into a columnar format. You can use this type of report to extract non-numeric data, such as customer address data or a list of product titles. You can also use this data to extract a mix of alphanumeric and numeric data, such as order line details or product inventory counts. And, as with PivotTable reports, the external data is easily loaded into the report, requiring only a simple click of the mouse button to refresh.

As with most columnar reporting packages, you can apply sorts, filters, breaks, and totals. Unlike other traditional report development software, however, Spreadsheet reports enable you to use all the powerful tools and functions built into Excel. In addition, Spreadsheet reports

- Give you clear-cut functions for applying sorts, breaks, and totals.
- Provide simple and advanced filtering tools to determine which items should be displayed.
- Include a robust suite of tools for applying conditional formatting, including data bars, icon sets, and graded color scales.
- Update report data automatically at predefined intervals or when the report is opened.

Figure 1-7 shows how a Spreadsheet report might extract and format data from an external database system. Notice that this report contains the same data as the Pivot-Table reports in the previous section of this chapter. It is, however, in a more columnar format. Don't be fooled by the simplicity of the report layout. It offers many powerful features for calculated fields, applying conditional field formats, and refreshing data at predefined intervals. Additionally, once the data is in the report, you are able to leverage the robust suite of Excel tools and functions to manipulate and analyze the report data.

All that's required to apply a filter is to click the drop-down arrow next to a field. Additionally, once a filter is applied, a helpful icon appears next to the field to indicate that the field is being filtered, as shown in Figure 1-8.

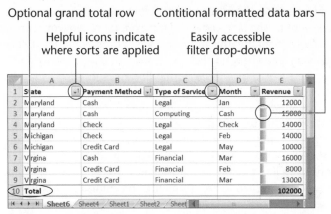

Optional grand total row   Contitional formatted data bars

Helpful icons indicate   Easily accessible
where sorts are applied   filter drop-downs

Figure 1-7: Spreadsheet reports display data in a columnar format.

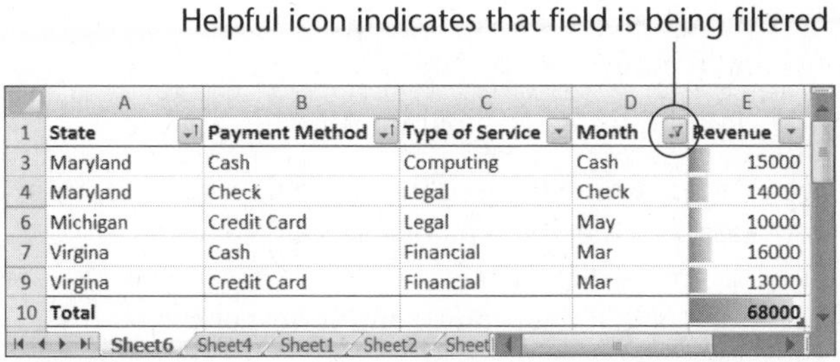

Helpful icon indicates that field is being filtered

Figure 1-8: Filter icons appear next to fields that have a filter applied to them.

CROSS-REFERENCE To find out the details of creating and using
Spreadsheet reports, read Chapters 14–16. Chapter 14 covers building and
using Spreadsheet reports, Chapter 15 covers reporting solutions (a group of
linked Spreadsheet reports designed to deliver a more robust report solution),
and Chapter 16 covers Spreadsheet report formatting.

Parameter Queries

Filters can be applied before or after the data is imported into the report. However, filtering data on a client machine running Excel is much slower than filtering data on a
powerful server with substantial memory and processing resources. There are also
numerous other reasons to filter data prior to loading it into the report (see Chapters 11
and 14); thus the data is typically filtered prior to loading it into Excel. This filtering is
usually performed by specifying a constraint in the underlying SQL query. However,
unless the user can enter a different value each time the report is run, the constraint is
static and cannot be specified by the report user.

Static constraints might filter data to a particular product line, region, company division, or period of time (for example, the last 30 days). However, if the report user has to define the product line, region, company division, or period of time before the report is run, the underlying SQL query must be modified. Because most report users do not have the technical skills or the security privileges to modify an SQL query, another solution is required. Parameter queries can fill this gap.

Parameter queries act as dynamic constraints, allowing the user to specify a value (or values) each time the report is run. Instead of importing a huge dataset into Excel, parameter queries apply a filter to return only a subset of the records from the data source. With a smaller dataset, the report can run much quicker because it uses fewer server resources. It also consumes less memory and disk space on the computer running the report, enhancing report manipulation performance and computer processing speed. Using parameter queries, you can

- Limit the amount of data that is displayed in a report before the data is imported into the report.

- Integrate the parameters with SQL stored procedure arguments and/or SQL queries to restrict the type and amount of data that is returned.

- Automatically re-query the data source when a parameter value is changed.

Figure 1-9 shows how a parameter query can be used in conjunction with a Spreadsheet report to restrict the report data to a specific type of service. When the Color or the Product Category is changed from the drop-down boxes in cells D3 or D4, the Spreadsheet report automatically queries that data source and refreshes the report.

CROSS-REFERENCE To find out the details of creating and using parameter queries, see Chapter 15.

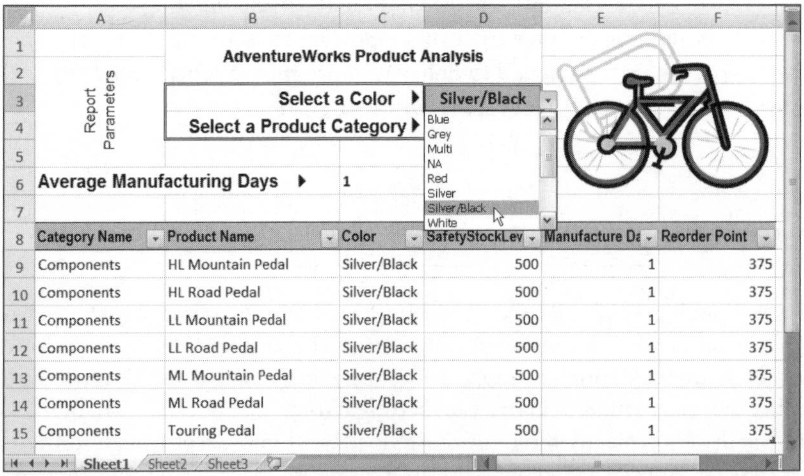

Figure 1-9: Parameter queries can automatically refresh the report as different values are selected.

Web Queries

The web query feature is another exciting and novel reporting tool included as part of Microsoft Excel. Imagine getting the latest currency exchange rates or mortgage interest rates imported directly from the web into your Spreadsheet report. It's as easy as navigating to the web page within Excel and selecting the table (or tables) that you want to import. By simply clicking the report and selecting the Refresh function, you can automatically refresh the report at predefined intervals.

Using this technology, you can

- Import data from the Internet and Intranet web sites.
- Integrate parameters to pull only the data for a specified query.
- Update report data automatically at predefined intervals or when the report is opened.

Figure 1-10 shows how a web query pulls the Historical Mortgage Rate Report information from the Freddie Mac web site. Note that this report uses the `http://www.freddiemac.com/pmms/pmms30.htm` link at the Freddie Mac web site.

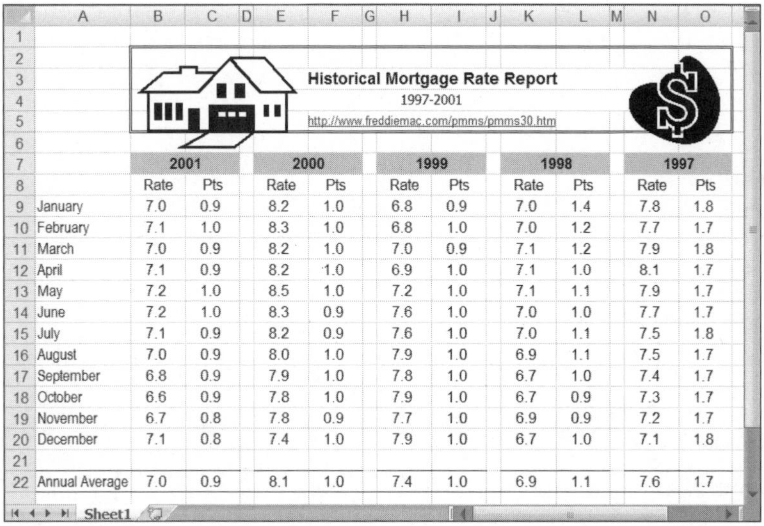

Historical Mortgage Rate Report
1997-2001
http://www.freddiemac.com/pmms/pmms30.htm

	2001		2000		1999		1998		1997	
	Rate	Pts	Rate	Pts	Rate	Pts	Rate	Pts	Rate	Pts
January	7.0	0.9	8.2	1.0	6.8	0.9	7.0	1.4	7.8	1.8
February	7.1	1.0	8.3	1.0	6.8	1.0	7.0	1.2	7.7	1.7
March	7.0	0.9	8.2	1.0	7.0	0.9	7.1	1.2	7.9	1.8
April	7.1	0.9	8.2	1.0	6.9	1.0	7.1	1.0	8.1	1.7
May	7.2	1.0	8.5	1.0	7.2	1.0	7.1	1.1	7.9	1.7
June	7.2	1.0	8.3	0.9	7.6	1.0	7.0	1.0	7.7	1.7
July	7.1	0.9	8.2	0.9	7.6	1.0	7.0	1.1	7.5	1.8
August	7.0	0.9	8.0	1.0	7.9	1.0	6.9	1.1	7.5	1.7
September	6.8	0.9	7.9	1.0	7.8	1.0	6.7	1.0	7.4	1.7
October	6.6	0.9	7.8	1.0	7.9	1.0	6.7	0.9	7.3	1.7
November	6.7	0.8	7.8	0.9	7.7	1.0	6.9	0.9	7.2	1.7
December	7.1	0.8	7.4	1.0	7.9	1.0	6.7	1.0	7.1	1.8
Annual Average	7.0	0.9	8.1	1.0	7.4	1.0	6.9	1.1	7.6	1.7

Figure 1-10: Web queries can access data from Intranet and Internet web sites.

Chapter Review

This chapter provided an introduction to some of the principal types of Excel reports and highlighted some of the innovative tools and features included with each report type. It highlighted some of the features available in the numerous types of Excel reporting tools, including PivotTable reports, PivotChart reports, Spreadsheet reports, parameter queries, and web queries.

The next two chapters provide a more comprehensive look at PivotTable reports. In Chapter 2, I provide a conceptual overview on how PivotTable reports work and how the data is summarized. In Chapter 3, I provide a more detailed review of the Pivot-Table components and describe the purpose and use of each area in the PivotTable report.

Getting Started with PivotTable Reports

If you aren't familiar with PivotTables and how they work, it's important to read this chapter. Here, I cover the concepts, terminology, and basic functions of PivotTables. Even if you are experienced with this technology, I recommend at least skimming this chapter, because you may need an orientation to the vastly redesigned Excel 2007 menu structure and tools for PivotTable reports.

I start by providing you with a basic framework of how data is summarized in a Pivot-Table report and how you can change the report shape by moving fields to different areas in the PivotTable. Here, you create your first PivotTable and learn about the purpose and use of each area in the report. I also introduce the essential components of a PivotTable report and familiarize you with some of the terminology. At the end of this chapter, I've included a hands-on exercise where you can practice what you've learned using a real-world business example.

Understanding PivotTable Data Organization

It's important for you to know that a PivotTable displays only the unique values in a dataset in a cross-tabular format. (See the note that follows if you are not familiar with the term *dataset*.) An aggregate function, such as a count, an average, or a total of some other field, is then calculated against these unique values. The following example illustrates how this works.

NOTE A *dataset* can also be referred to as a *recordset*. This term refers to the data included in a table or returned from an SQL query. In the Travel Expenses example used here, the dataset includes the information in the rows and columns of Table 2-1.

Taking the sample list of travel expenses shown in Table 2-1, you can see that many of the transactions have a duplicate Category or Month.

Table 2-2 shows how this data would be organized into a PivotTable report of Amount by Month. Note that only the unique values of Month are displayed. Jan, Feb, and Mar are listed only once, not multiple times, as they are in Table 2-1. In this example, Amount is summed for each value of Month.

Table 2-1: Sample List of Travel Expenses

MONTH	TYPE	CATEGORY	AMOUNT
Jan	Personal	Restaurant	35
Jan	Business	Taxi	42
Jan	Business	Restaurant	64
Jan	Personal	Restaurant	22
Jan	Business	Tips	12
Feb	Personal	Restaurant	32
Feb	Personal	Entertainment	24
Feb	Business	Entertainment	45
Feb	Business	Lodging	98
Mar	Business	Airfare	250
Mar	Personal	Restaurant	24
Mar	Business	Restaurant	45
Mar	Business	Lodging	160
Mar	Business	Tolls	8

Table 2-2: Total Amount by Month

MONTH	AMOUNT
Jan	175
Feb	199
Mar	487

If you'd rather display the Sum of Amount by Category, the PivotTable calculates the total Amount for each unique value of Category, as shown in Table 2-3.

As you discovered in Chapter 1, PivotTables are a very flexible reporting tool. With only a few clicks of the mouse, you could also analyze the total Amount by Month and Category. In this case, the data would look like Table 2-4.

You could just as easily count the number of records instead of summing Amount. In that case, the PivotTable report would display the data as shown in Table 2-5.

And, finally, instead of calculating a sum or a count of Amount, you could do both. Table 2-6 shows a count and a sum of Amount by Month and Category.

Table 2-3: Total Amount by Category

CATEGORY	AMOUNT
Airfare	250
Entertainment	69
Lodging	258
Restaurant	222
Taxi	42
Tips	12
Tolls	8

Table 2-4: Total Amount by Month and Category

CATEGORY	JAN	FEB	MAR
Airfare			250
Entertainment		69	
Lodging		98	160
Restaurant	121	32	69
Taxi	42		
Tips	12		
Tolls			8

Table 2-5: Count of Expenses by Month and Category

CATEGORY	JAN	FEB	MAR
Airfare			1
Entertainment		2	
Lodging		1	1
Restaurant	3	1	2
Taxi	1		
Tips	1		
Tolls			1

Table 2-6: Count and Total of Amount by Month and Category

CATEGORY	JAN COUNT	AMOUNT	FEB COUNT	AMOUNT	MAR COUNT	AMOUNT
Airfare					1	250
Entertainment			2	69		
Lodging			1	98	1	160
Restaurant	3	121	1	32	2	69
Taxi	1	42				
Tips	1	12				
Tolls					1	8

PivotTable reports enable you to do much more than just count or sum data against unique values. You can also calculate averages, maximum or minimum values, standard deviations, and running totals, and perform many other mathematical and statistical functions. What data is displayed and how you display it is completely up to you. It's easy to turn the data around and around while performing different functions and calculations against it.

Creating Your First PivotTable

Now that you know the basics of how data is organized in a PivotTable, you're ready to create your first one.

WATCH THE VIDEO To see how to create a PivotTable, watch the `ch0201_video.avi` **video file on this book's companion web site at** www.wiley.com/go/excelreporting/2007.

To create a PivotTable, follow these steps:

1. Type the field headings and values shown earlier in Table 2-1 into Excel (see Figure 2-1).

TIP Before you click the PivotTable button, make sure you have selected one of the cells containing data. In this example, I selected cell A1, but any cell in the range A1:D15 will do. In the real world, you may want to highlight Columns A–D prior to inserting a PivotTable, because the defined range for this PivotTable report example is only A1:D15. Selecting all the columns sets the much larger range of A:D and ensures that any new rows added to the defined column range will be included in the report when the PivotTable is refreshed. This tip is demonstrated in the "Trying It Out in the Real World" section of this chapter.

2. When you have finished entering the data, click cell A1 and choose Insert → PivotTable, as shown in Figure 2-2. Note that you should click the PivotTable button and not the PivotTable drop-down arrow (located right below the button), because it isn't necessary to access the drop-down menu to create a Pivot-Table report. You only need to access this menu when creating a PivotChart.

NOTE Previous versions of Excel required that you select Data → PivotTable and PivotChart Report to bring up the PivotTable and PivotChart Wizard program, which included three steps. Microsoft simplified this task by adding a PivotTable button under the Insert menu.

	A	B	C	D
1	Month	Type	Category	Amount
2	Jan	Personal	Restaurant	35
3	Jan	Business	Taxi	42
4	Jan	Business	Restaurant	64
5	Jan	Personal	Restaurant	22
6	Jan	Business	Tips	12
7	Feb	Personal	Restaurant	32
8	Feb	Personal	Entertainment	24
9	Feb	Business	Entertainment	45
10	Feb	Business	Lodging	98
11	Mar	Business	Airfare	250
12	Mar	Personal	Restaurant	24
13	Mar	Business	Restaurant	45
14	Mar	Business	Lodging	160
15	Mar	Business	Tolls	8

Figure 2-1: Type the data from Table 2-1 into Excel.

Click on the button—not the
drop-down arrow under the button

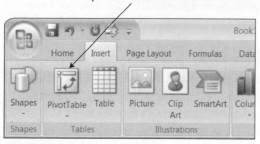

Figure 2-2: Click the PivotTable button to create a PivotTable report from the data you entered in the first step.

3. When the Create PivotTable dialog box appears, as shown in Figure 2-3, click OK to confirm the range and create the PivotTable report on a new worksheet.

4. Verify that a PivotTable icon and PivotTable Field List dialog box are created, as shown in Figure 2-4.

   The Report Layout area in Figure 2-4 appears in the worksheet with the name of the PivotTable report shown inside a rectangular box. Notice also that there are two sections of the PivotTable Field List dialog box. The top-half of the dialog box is called the Fields section. This is where all the available fields are displayed. Here, you can add fields to the report, modify filters, change labels, and perform sorts. The bottom-half of the dialog box is called the Areas section. In this section, you can change field settings, configure subtotals, arrange field hierarchies, and set layout options. You can also drag fields from one area to another. In short, most PivotTable functions can be managed from the PivotTable Field List dialog box.

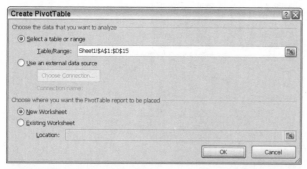

Figure 2-3: Click OK to tell Excel to create a PivotTable.

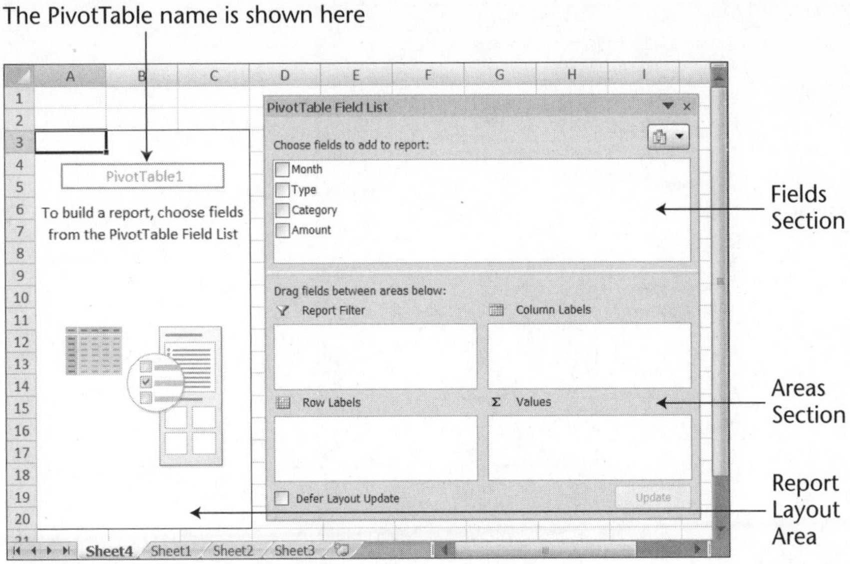

The PivotTable name is shown here

Figure 2-4: The Report Layout area with the name of the PivotTable (PivotTable1 in this example) is displayed when no fields are added to the report.

NEW FEATURE Previous versions of Excel displayed a PivotTable layout area instead of a PivotTable icon. Fields from the PivotTable Field List could then be dragged to different sections of the layout area. With Excel 2007, you can do all this and much more — all from within the PivotTable Field List dialog box. You no longer need to drag fields from the PivotTable Field List dialog box all the way over to the PivotTable report. Of course, if you prefer to use the older (and slower) method, you can still do that by checking the Classic PivotTable Layout box under the Display tab in the PivotTable Options dialog box.

5. Drag the Month field to the Row Labels area in the PivotTable Field List dialog box and then verify that your PivotTable report looks like Figure 2-5.

NOTE Notice that the location of the shading on the icon changes as you drag a field from the Fields section over a particular area in the Areas section of the PivotTable Field List dialog box.

6. Instead of dragging the field, you can also move it into the report by right-clicking it and selecting an area from the pop-up menu. Right-click Amount in the PivotTable Field List and choose Add to Values from the pop-up menu (see Figure 2-6).

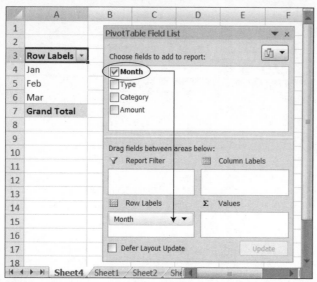

Figure 2-5: Fields can be dragged to an area in the PivotTable by selecting a field in the Fields section and dragging it to an area in the Areas section.

Figure 2-6: Right-clicking a field enables you to add it to a PivotTable area.

NOTE The PivotTable Field List window appears only when you have selected a cell in the PivotTable. Clicking off the PivotTable automatically hides the window.

The PivotTable now looks like Figure 2-7.

	A	B
1		
2		
3	Row Labels ▾	Sum of Amount
4	Jan	175
5	Feb	199
6	Mar	487
7	**Grand Total**	**861**

Figure 2-7: PivotTable of Expenses by Month that shows the same data as Table 2-2.

Notice that the PivotTable has changed shape again. It also displays the same data that was shown in Table 2-2 (with the exception that a Grand Total is displayed by default in a PivotTable).

Checking the box next to any field in the Fields section (top-half of the PivotTable Field List dialog box) of the PivotTable Field List dialog box adds it to the report. Keep in mind that alphanumeric fields are automatically added to the Row Labels area, whereas numeric fields are automatically added to the Values area. If you want to add a field to the Column Labels or Report Filter areas, you'll either need to drag it to that area (see Figure 2-5) or you'll need to right-click it and then select the area where you wish to add the field (see Figure 2-6).

You've now learned how to move data into the PivotTable report using three methods:

■ Dragging a field from the Fields section to an area in the Areas section of the PivotTable Field List dialog box.

■ Right-clicking a field in the Fields section of the PivotTable Field List dialog box and choosing an area from the pop-up menu to move the field to the selected area.

■ Clicking the check box in the Fields section to add an alphanumeric field to the Row Labels area or a numeric field to the Values area.

CROSS-REFERENCE Read Chapter 11 to learn how to enable the Classic PivotTable setting that enables you to also drag fields from the PivotTable Field List dialog box to the PivotTable.

Modifying the PivotTable

You've successfully created your first PivotTable report, hopefully with ease. As you have learned so far, creating a PivotTable is simple. And, it's just as easy to modify one that's already created. This section covers some of the basic functions that you can use to customize or *shape* your PivotTable report.

NOTE Moving fields into and out of a PivotTable report results in the shape of the PivotTable being changed. Look at the difference between Figure 2-4 and Figure 2-5 if you forgot how that works. PivotTable experts often refer to the act of customizing a PivotTable as "shaping" the report.

Removing a Field from a PivotTable

What if you need to remove a field from the PivotTable report? You shouldn't be surprised to learn it's just as easy as moving fields to the report. Simply click the field in the Areas section of the PivotTable Field List dialog box that you want to move and drag it off the dialog box or back to the Fields section of the dialog box.

In the PivotTable you created in the preceding section, for example, select Month in the Row Labels section and drag it off the report as shown in Figure 2-8. Notice the icon's appearance as you "pick up" a field and drag it off an area.

If you prefer to use the pop-up menus instead of dragging, just left-click the field and choose Remove Field from the pop-up menu. Of course, the simplest way to remove the field from the report is to just uncheck the box next to the field in the Fields section of the PivotTable Field List dialog box. Figure 2-9 shows the PivotTable report after Month has been removed.

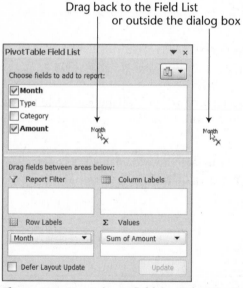

Figure 2-8: Removing a field from the PivotTable is easy: just drag it back to the Fields section or off the PivotTable Field List dialog box.

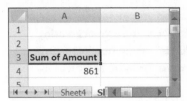

Figure 2-9: PivotTable with only the Amount field remaining in the Values area.

Changing the Summary Type

When you added Amount to the Values area of the PivotTable report, the data in this field was summed to derive the total Amount by Month. (See step 6 and Figure 2-6 in the previous section if you want to review how this was done.) How can you *count* the number of expense transactions instead of calculating a *sum* of the expense amount? You do that by changing how the data is aggregated.

NOTE By default, numerical fields are *summed* and alphanumeric fields are *counted* when they are dragged into the Values area of a PivotTable.

To *count* the number of expenses instead of *totaling* expenses, follow these steps:

1. Drag Category to the Row Labels area. The PivotTable report should now look like Figure 2-10.

2. Modify the PivotTable to *count* the number of expenses instead of calculating the *sum* of expenses. To do this, left-click the Sum of Amount field in the Values area of the PivotTable Field List dialog box and choose Field Settings from the pop-up menu. The Data Field Settings dialog box appears, as shown in Figure 2-11.

	A	B
1		
2		
3	**Row Labels** ▾	Sum of Amount
4	Airfare	250
5	Entertainment	69
6	Lodging	258
7	Restaurant	222
8	Taxi	42
9	Tips	12
10	Tolls	8
11	**Grand Total**	**861**

Figure 2-10: The PivotTable of total Amount by Category that matches the information from Table 2-3.

NEW FEATURE   Previous versions of Excel required you to access the Field
Settings dialog box from the PivotTable report. With Excel 2007, you can bring
up this dialog box directly from the PivotTable Field List dialog box. Also, notice
that the Field Settings dialog box has been reorganized for more intuitive
access to display options and field settings.

3. Select Count on the Summarize By tab (see Figure 2-12) and click OK.

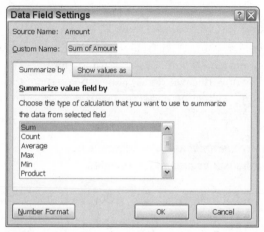

Figure 2-11: This dialog box opens when you left-click the Sum of Amount field in the
Values area of the PivotTable Field List dialog box.

Figure 2-12: Change Amount to be *counted* instead of *summed*.

4. The PivotTable now counts the number of entries for each Category. Compare the total and number of entries by Category in Figure 2-13 to what is displayed in Figure 2-1. Notice that the Grand Total count of 14 records in cell B11 of Figure 2-13 is equal to the 14 records that you typed into the Excel worksheet in the first step of the previous exercise (see Figure 2-1).

NOTE Observe that Sum of Amount in cell B3 of Figure 2-10 was changed to Count of Amount in cell B3 of Figure 2-13 when the summary type was changed from Sum to Count.

5. Add Month into the Column Labels area and verify that your PivotTable reports look like Figure 2-14.

Figure 2-13: Count of Expenses by Expense Category.

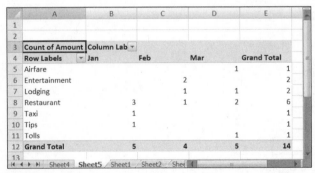

Figure 2-14: Count of Expenses by Expense Category and Month that matches the information from Table 2-4.

6. By now, you're probably getting quite adept with using a PivotTable report. Try adding a field into the report twice. Drag Amount into the Values area of the PivotTable. Notice that once this field is dropped, a new field — *Values* — is automatically added below the Month field in the Column Labels area, as shown in Figure 2-15.

7. Drag the Values field in the Column Labels area under the Category field in the Row Labels area of the PivotTable Field List to shape the PivotTable report like Figure 2-16.

NOTE With the exception of the Values area (where fields are aggregated into new data elements), fields can appear in only one location of the PivotTable report at any one time. Dragging a field from the Fields section to the Areas section of the PivotTable Field List dialog box, when it is already in the Areas section, results in that field being *moved* to the selected area of the report. Try it and see.

The Values field is automatically added

Figure 2-15: Drag Amount into the Values area for a second time.

	A	B	C	D	E	F	G
1							
2							
3		Column Labels					
4	Row Labels	Jan	Feb	Mar	Grand Total		
5	Airfare						
6	Count of Amount			1	1		
7	Sum of Amount			250	250		
8	Entertainment						
9	Count of Amount		2		2		
10	Sum of Amount		69		69		
11	Lodging						
12	Count of Amount		1	1	2		
13	Sum of Amount		98	160	258		
14	Restaurant						
15	Count of Amount	3	1	2	6		
16	Sum of Amount	121	32	69	222		
17	Taxi						
18	Count of Amount	1			1		
19	Sum of Amount	42			42		
20	Tips						
21	Count of Amount	1			1		
22	Sum of Amount	12			12		
23	Tolls						
24	Count of Amount			1	1		
25	Sum of Amount			8	8		
26	Total Count of Amount	5	4	5	14		
27	Total Sum of Amount	175	199	487	861		
28							
29							

Sheet4 | **Sheet5** | Sheet1 | Sheet2 | Sheet3

Figure 2-16: The Count of Amount and Sum of Amount by Category and Month that summarizes information similar to Table 2-6.

Refreshing Report Data

You might find that the underlying source data is changed or that you need to modify it. Don't worry if that happens. You don't need to re-create the entire PivotTable report from scratch. After the source data is updated, all you need to do is just right-click the PivotTable and select Refresh from the pop-up menu to update the report with the new data.

To refresh the report data, follow these steps:

1. Click the worksheet tab you created in Figure 2-1, and then change the Amount for Lodging in cell D14 from 160 to **120**, as shown in Figure 2-17.

2. Refer to the PivotTable report on the preceding Excel worksheet (the one shown in Figure 2-16). Right-click the PivotTable and select Refresh from the pop-up menu, as shown in Figure 2-18.

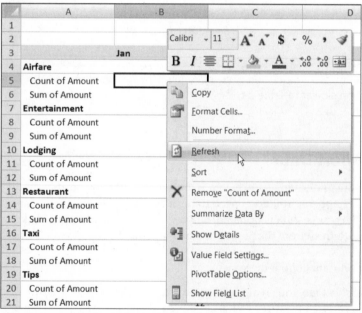

	A	B	C	D
1	Month	Type	Category	Amount
2	Jan	Personal	Restaurant	35
3	Jan	Business	Taxi	42
4	Jan	Business	Restaurant	64
5	Jan	Personal	Restaurant	22
6	Jan	Business	Tips	12
7	Feb	Personal	Restaurant	32
8	Feb	Personal	Entertainment	24
9	Feb	Business	Entertainment	45
10	Feb	Business	Lodging	98
11	Mar	Business	Airfare	250
12	Mar	Personal	Restaurant	24
13	Mar	Business	Restaurant	45
14	Mar	Business	Lodging	120
15	Mar	Business	Tolls	8

Sheet4　Sheet5　**Sheet1**　Sheet2

Figure 2-17: Change the amount for Lodging in Mar from 160 to 120.

	A	B	C	D
1				
2		Calibri ▾ 11 ▾ A A $ ▾ % ,		
3		**Jan** B I ≡ ⊞ ▾ A ▾		
4	**Airfare**			
5	Count of Amount			
6	Sum of Amount	Copy		
7	**Entertainment**	Format Cells...		
8	Count of Amount	Number Format...		
9	Sum of Amount			
10	**Lodging**	Refresh		
11	Count of Amount			
12	Sum of Amount	Sort ▸		
13	**Restaurant**	Remove "Count of Amount"		
14	Count of Amount			
15	Sum of Amount	Summarize Data By ▸		
16	**Taxi**	Show Details		
17	Count of Amount			
18	Sum of Amount	Value Field Settings...		
19	**Tips**	PivotTable Options...		
20	Count of Amount	Show Field List		
21	Sum of Amount			

Figure 2-18: Use the Refresh command to update the PivotTable report data from the data entered into the Excel worksheet.

When the Refresh command is selected, Excel accesses the original data source, in this case the Excel worksheet in Figure 2-17, and refreshes the PivotTable report with the updated data. In this example, the only cell updated was the Amount for Lodging in Mar. If you did everything right, your report should now look like Figure 2-19.

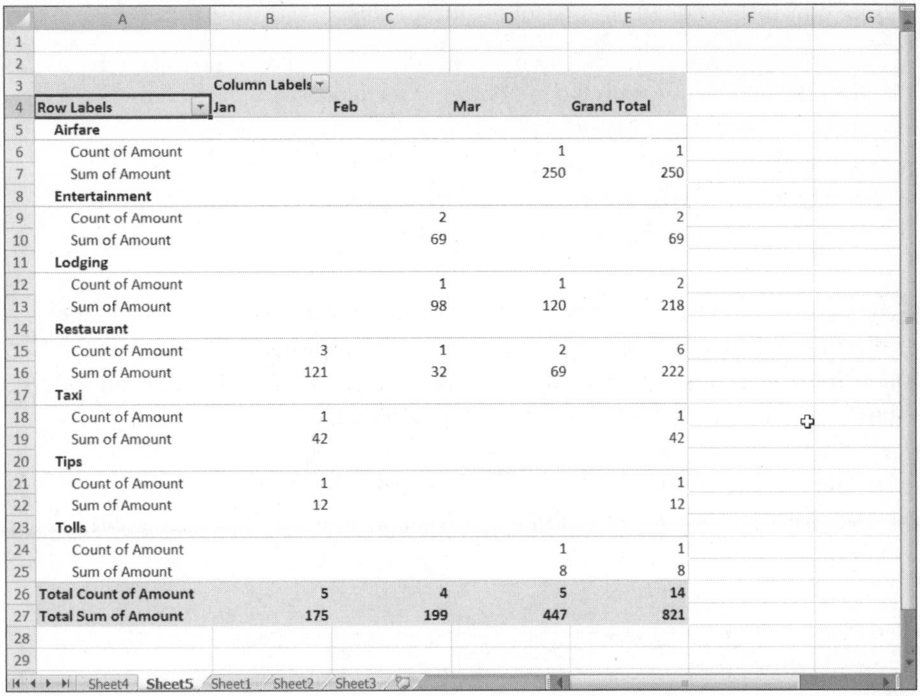

	Column Labels					
Row Labels	Jan	Feb	Mar	Grand Total		
Airfare						
Count of Amount			1	1		
Sum of Amount			250	250		
Entertainment						
Count of Amount		2		2		
Sum of Amount		69		69		
Lodging						
Count of Amount		1	1	2		
Sum of Amount		98	120	218		
Restaurant						
Count of Amount	3	1	2	6		
Sum of Amount	121	32	69	222		
Taxi						
Count of Amount	1			1		
Sum of Amount	42			42		
Tips						
Count of Amount	1			1		
Sum of Amount	12			12		
Tolls						
Count of Amount			1	1		
Sum of Amount			8	8		
Total Count of Amount	5	4	5	14		
Total Sum of Amount	175	199	447	821		

Figure 2-19: The PivotTable report is updated with the new Lodging expense of $120 when the Refresh function is selected from the pop-up menu.

CROSS-REFERENCE In this example, the data source is just another worksheet tab in the Excel workbook. The true power of the Excel PivotTable is the capability to fetch the source data from an external data source, such as an online transaction processing (OLTP) database. Imagine getting critical business data about marketing campaigns, sales information, or operating expenses with barely more than a click of a mouse button. Read Chapter 12 for more information about connecting to an SQL database from an Excel PivotTable report.

Drilling Down on Report Data

Did you ever look at a report and find that some of the figures are difficult to accept? I know from experience it can take a long time to determine whether it's an error or a legitimate figure. You might have to track down several people in an organization or run database queries to determine what actually happened. PivotTables can make this investigation process much easier. You can *drill down* on any numerical value in the Values area of the PivotTable report to reveal the underlying data that makes up a particular cell value.

To see how drilling down works, follow these steps:

1. Double-click any of the cells in the Values area (defined as the cell range B5–E27) to drill down on the full dataset that makes up a particular cell. In Figure 2-20, I've double-clicked cell B15.

   A new Excel worksheet is created with the underlying data (see Figure 2-21). Notice that all the columns in the underlying row set (including the column headings) are included in the new worksheet.

NOTE The same worksheet in Figure 2-21 is produced, regardless of whether cell B15 or cell B16 in Figure 2-20 are double-clicked. Why? Because, even though the data is being counted (B15) and summed (B16) in different cells of the PivotTable, it is still the same underlying dataset.

2. When you're finished looking at the data, right-click the active worksheet tab and choose Delete from the pop-up menu to return to the PivotTable report shown in Figure 2-20.

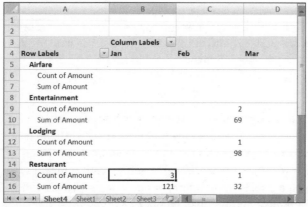

Figure 2-20: Double-clicking cell B15 reveals the underlying table data that makes up the count of three expense entries for the Restaurant category.

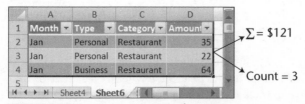

Figure 2-21: A new Excel worksheet with three restaurant expense entries.

The next section covers the basic terminology of PivotTable reports. First, review what you've learned so far in this chapter:

- You can convert data entered into an Excel spreadsheet with field headings into a PivotTable by clicking any cell in the data range, choosing Insert → Pivot-Table, and then clicking the OK button.

- When source data changes, you can update a PivotTable by right-clicking any-where in the report and selecting Refresh from the pop-up menu.

- You can drag fields or right-click them to add them to the report — all from within the PivotTable Field List dialog box.

- You can perform many types of functions on items in the Values area of a Pivot-Table report. A couple of the functions used here were Count and Sum.

- You can double-click cells in the Values area of a PivotTable to produce a new Excel worksheet that reveals the underlying data that comprises the cell's value.

Terminology

By this point, I hope you are finding that PivotTable reports are understandable and easy to use. As you can probably tell, these reports can be a powerful reporting solution. You can dynamically drag fields on or off the report, apply filters in the Row Labels, Column Labels, or Report Filter areas, and change the type of aggregation using easy-to-learn functions that you can control from your mouse. These tremendous capabilities make this technology very popular with several Microsoft programs. When used within these different applications, the terminology and icons are sometimes different. I cover these differences in more detail as these new topics are introduced. For now, here's a brief review of a few of the terms you've learned so far in this chapter:

- **Dataset:** Also called a *recordset*. This term refers to the rows and columns in a data source.

- **Data source:** The location of the source data. It could be an Excel worksheet, a delimited file, or an SQL query extract. In this chapter, the data source for the PivotTable was simply an Excel worksheet.

- **Drilling down:** The act of double-clicking cell values in the Values area of a PivotTable report to create a new worksheet that shows the underlying data.

- **Area:** The PivotTable area where fields are dropped. It includes the Report Fil-ter, Row Labels, Column Labels, and Values areas.

- **Shaping the report:** The act of customizing the PivotTable report. This includes moving fields into or out of the PivotTable, changing the area where fields are located, or applying a filter against a field in the report.

- **Summary type:** Also called an *aggregation type,* this is the kind of function applied to a group of data in the Values area. The functions covered in this chapter include Sum and Count.

CROSS-REFERENCE Now that you're familiar with the PivotTable basics and terminology, you're ready to read Chapter 3 to learn more about the PivotTable components.

You're now ready to try a real-world example that demonstrates how you can import data from an external software application into Excel to create a PivotTable report.

Trying It Out in the Real World

You've just been hired as a new data analyst at AdventureWorks, and your first assignment is to start learning about PivotTable report technology. You start on this assignment by following along and completing all the examples in this chapter. You then decide to add the rows in Table 2-7 to the dataset in Figure 2-1 in order to calculate the average expense amount by month and category for business type expenses. You figure that completing this exercise will help ensure that you've got a good handle on the basics of PivotTable reporting.

Getting Down to Business

In order to complete this exercise, you'll need to do the following:

- Add the rows in Table 2-7 to the Excel worksheet that you have already modified in Figure 2-17.

- From the existing PivotTable report on Sheet4 (see Figure 2-20), redefine the PivotTable data source range to A:D instead of A1:D15.

- Shape the PivotTable report to look like Figure 2-24.

- Apply a filter to Type, such that only Business expenses are displayed in the PivotTable report.

Table 2-7: Additional List of Travel Expenses for Real-World Example

MONTH	TYPE	CATEGORY	AMOUNT
Jan	Business	Taxi	38
Jan	Business	Lodging	127
Feb	Business	Restaurant	64
Mar	Business	Airfare	422
Apr	Business	Tolls	12
Apr	Business	Entertainment	70

Now that you have added the entries in Table 2-7 to the worksheet in Figure 2-17, follow these steps:

1. Click the PivotTable you created on Sheet4 to select it and click the PivotTable Tools button located just above the Excel drop-down menus, as shown in Figure 2-22.

2. Click the Change Data Source button (located right below the PivotTable Tools button in Figure 2-22) to bring up the Change Data Source dialog box.

3. Click in the Table/Range field of the Choose Data Source dialog box and then highlight columns A–D in Sheet1. Verify that the dialog box name changes to Move PivotTable and looks like Figure 2-23 and then click OK to continue.

4. Verify that the PivotTable Tools tab is displayed and choose Clear → Clear All to clear all the fields and filters from the PivotTable report.

5. Drag Type to the Report Filter area, Month to the Column Labels area, Category to the Row Labels area, and Amount to the Values area. Notice that Count of Amount is displayed instead of Sum of Amount in the Values area of the PivotTable Field List dialog box. This is because the data source range of A:D includes blank cells, so Excel treats this as an alphanumeric field.

6. Left-click the Count of Amount drop-down arrow in the PivotTable Field List dialog box and select Field Settings from the pop-up menu to bring up the Data Field Setting dialog box.

7. Left-click Average in the Summarize Value Field By section and then click OK to calculate the average expense amount for each month and category combination.

Click this button to display the PivotTable Tools toolbar

Figure 2-22: The PivotTable Tools button appears when the PivotTable is selected.

Figure 2-23: The data source range for the PivotTable report now includes all the cells in Columns A–D of Sheet1.

8. Left-click Type in the Fields section of the PivotTable Field List dialog box and choose Business from the drop-down menu.

9. Verify that your PivotTable report looks like Figure 2-24.

WATCH THE VIDEO **To see how to do this exercise, watch the** `ch0202_video.avi` **video on the companion web site at** `www.wiley.com/go/excelreporting/2007`**.**

Due to space constraints, I don't show a screenshot for every step in this exercise, or for the exercises in other chapters. I'm confident that you can complete most of the steps without a visual aid. If you do get stuck on a step, however, don't forget that you can reference this book's companion web site at `www.wiley.com/go/excelreporting/2007` and watch a video showing how many of the tasks are done.

Reviewing What You Did

This example demonstrates how you can add new rows to your source data and configure the PivotTable to bring in these new rows. In the real world, it's likely that data will be appended and modified — regardless of whether it is derived from an Excel worksheet, a text file, a database, or an OLAP cube. In the case of an Excel worksheet, setting a larger data range like A:D enables new rows to automatically be loaded into the PivotTable report whenever the PivotTable is refreshed. Of course, it's easy to forget or not plan for that step when you first create the PivotTable. However, as I just demonstrated in this example, it's easy to handle that situation by just redefining the data source range. Similar functions exist for other types of data sources and are covered in Chapter 12 in more depth.

	A	B	C	D	E	F
1	Type	Business				
2						
3	Average of Amount	Column Labels				
4	Row Labels	Jan		Feb	Mar	Apr	Grand Total
5	Airfare			336			336
6	Entertainment			45		70	57.5
7	Lodging	127	98	120			115
8	Restaurant	64	64	45		57.66666667
9	Taxi	40					40
10	Tips	12					12
11	Tolls			8	12		10
12	Grand Total	56.6	69	169	41	94.46666667

Figure 2-24: If you did everything right, your PivotTable report should look like this.

Chapter Review

In this chapter, you learned about the basic components and functions of a PivotTable report. It showed you how data is summarized in a PivotTable report and how you can move fields to different locations of the report by dragging fields or using the Pivot-Table Field List. It illustrated how columnar formatted data can be aggregated into the cross-tabular format of a PivotTable, and it demonstrated how you can interactively change the PivotTable report view to design several different types of reports from a list of available fields.

CHAPTER 3

PivotTable Essentials and Components

This chapter focuses on the essential elements and components of PivotTable reports. I start this chapter with an overview of the three primary PivotTable components. Following that, I review each component in more depth, starting with the Report Layout area, where I cover the use and available features of each PivotTable area. Next, I briefly cover the PivotTable Report tab and describe how it can be accessed. After that, I review the PivotTable Field List dialog box. All three of these components have been significantly enhanced over prior Excel versions. If you're just starting out with Excel 2007, you'll want to review this chapter to get a better feel of the new organization, features, and tools of PivotTable reports in this latest version of Excel. I conclude this chapter with a real-world example that utilizes many of the concepts that I cover throughout the chapter.

Before You Begin

The dataset shown in Figure 2-1 of Chapter 2 is used throughout the various sections of this chapter. If you want to follow along with the examples and see the same data that I show in the various screen captures of this chapter, you should complete these steps:

1. Create a PivotTable report using the dataset shown in Figure 2-1 of Chapter 2.

2. Drag Month to the Report Filter area, Category to the Row Labels area, Type to the Column Labels area, and Amount to the Values area.

3. Verify that your PivotTable report looks like Figure 3-1.

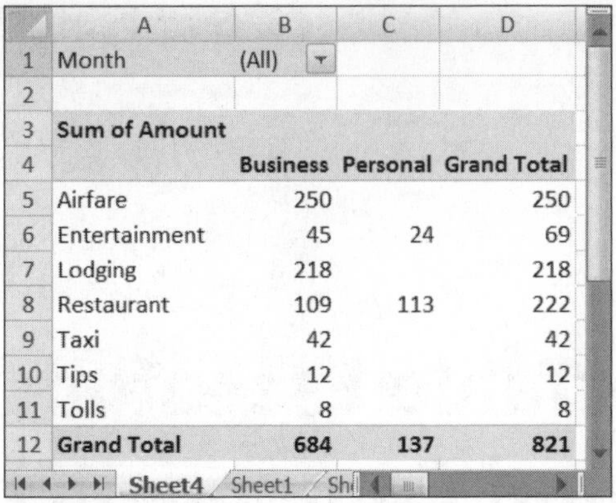

	A	B	C	D
1	Month	(All) ▾		
2				
3	**Sum of Amount**			
4		**Business**	**Personal**	**Grand Total**
5	Airfare	250		250
6	Entertainment	45	24	69
7	Lodging	218		218
8	Restaurant	109	113	222
9	Taxi	42		42
10	Tips	12		12
11	Tolls	8		8
12	**Grand Total**	**684**	**137**	**821**

Sheet4 / Sheet1 / Sh

Figure 3-1: Shape your PivotTable as shown here to follow along with the examples in this chapter.

PivotTable Components

There are three components that control the operation, design, and management of PivotTable reports. I informally introduced each one of them in Chapter 2, as I familiarized you with the basic use, organization, and operation of a PivotTable report. In the next three sections of this chapter, I take a closer look at each of the three components listed here:

- Report Layout area
- PivotTable Field List dialog box
- PivotTable Tools tab

All three of these components have been overhauled from earlier versions of Excel. The PivotTable report area names have been changed and the features and capabilities in each area of the PivotTable have been significantly enhanced. The PivotTable Tools tab also has many new functions, buttons, and tools that will help you manage and operate PivotTable reports more efficiently. The PivotTable Field List dialog box looks completely different, and it now includes several tools for designing and shaping your PivotTable report. All of these components are shown in Figure 3-2.

PivotTable Field List Dialog Box

PivotTable Report

PivotTable1

PivotTable Tab

Figure 3-2: The primary components of a PivotTable include the Report Layout area, the PivotTable Field List Dialog Box, and the PivotTable Tools tab.

Working in the Report Layout Area

The Report Layout area is the primary component of a PivotTable report. Most functions and report operations can be controlled from here. It is made up of four areas (described later in this section) and several types of pop-up menus that are accessible by right-clicking different areas of the PivotTable report.

In this section, I take you through a brief tour of the Report Layout area component, starting with a closer look at each PivotTable report area.

Looking at the PivotTable Areas

A PivotTable report is comprised of four *areas,* or *drop zones*:

- **Report Filter Area:** Used for displaying data as if it were on separate pages
- **Row Labels Area:** Used for displaying data for fields that have a large number of unique items

- **Column Labels Area:** Used for displaying data for fields that have a small number of unique items
- **Values Area:** Used for summarizing or aggregating numerical data — typically against items in the Row Labels or Column Labels areas of the PivotTable

NOTE I use the terms drop zone and area interchangeably. The term *drop zone* is most often referred to as an *area*, but either term is understood to be the same by Excel report developers.

The names of the areas have varied based on the type of application being used (Excel, Microsoft Analysis Services, FrontPage, and so on) and the version of Excel that is running. I believe that Microsoft has tried to both standardize and simplify the names of these areas in this latest release of Excel. I consistently use these new area names throughout this book. I've also summarized the old and new names, along with some of the major changes for each area in Table 3-1.

As you can see from Table 3-1, the name changes are easy enough to understand. The Row and Column areas are now simply referred to as Row Labels and Column Labels areas, respectively. And because there are some nice enhancements to the graphical tools of these two areas (explained later in this book), the term *label* is very appropriate. The other name changes for the Data area (now Values area) and the Page area (now Report Filter area) are more representative of the area's purpose, so these new names should also be easy to remember.

Table 3-1: Excel 2007 Name Changes and Enhancements

EXCEL 1995–2003 NAME	EXCEL 2007 NEW NAME	MAJOR ENHANCEMENTS AVAILABLE WITH EXCEL 2007
Page Area	Report Filter Area	Multiple items can now be selected from the drop-down Report Filter menu. Filter icons appear next to fields that are being filtered.
Row Area	Row Labels Area	There are now 1,048,576 available rows (previously 65,536). More advanced filters and graphical icons are available for managing report operations.
Column Area	Column Labels Area	There are now 16,385 available columns (previously 256). More advanced filters and graphical icons are available for managing report operations.
Data Area	Values Area	More flexible options and tools for displaying aggregated data, including icons and shading tools that can be based on conditional logic.

I cover the purpose and use of each area in the following sections, along with some of the Excel 2007 changes that are outlined in Table 3-1.

Report Filter Area

Fields in the Report Filter area can be used to display data as if it were on separate pages. Filters applied in this area control what's displayed in the PivotTable (positioned directly below the Report Filter area). In earlier versions of Excel, you were only able to select either a single item or all of the items from the drop-down list. Now, with Excel 2007, you can choose multiple items by clicking the Select Multiple Items box shown in Figure 3-3.

Notice that only three items for Category are displayed in Figure 3-4 when Jan is selected from the Month field in Figure 3-3. This is because other transaction categories, such as Airfare and Entertainment, were not incurred during that month. The expenses in Jan had a Type of both Business and Personal, so the Column Labels area was not automatically resized. Had all the expenses in Jan had a Type of Business, the Column field would have been resized to display only Business.

CROSS-REFERENCE Read Chapter 10 to learn how to always display all of the items in the Column Labels and Row Labels areas, regardless of whether a Report Filter area filter is applied.

Click this box
to enable multiple
item selection

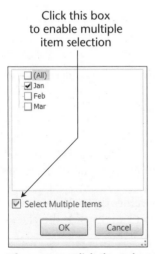

Figure 3-3: Click the Select Multiple Items box to enable selection of multiple items from the Report Filter area.

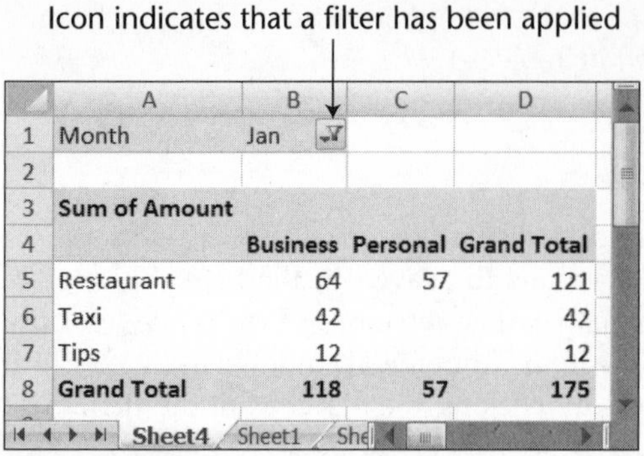

Icon indicates that a filter has been applied

Figure 3-4: Changing the Report Filter area field — Month — to filter only those records that have a Month of Jan results in the shape of the PivotTable being changed to display only the unique items of Category and Type incurred during Jan.

Notice also that once you select only Jan from the Month field, filter icons appear next to Month in both the PivotTable report and in the Fields section of the PivotTable Fields dialog box. Additionally, Jan is displayed next to Month in cell B1 of Figure 3-4. If a filter isn't applied to a Report Filter area field, then All is displayed in this cell. If multiple items are selected for a Report Filter area field, then Multiple Items is displayed.

Try selecting a few different combinations of months to see how different items in a Report Filter area field affect the shape and look of the PivotTable report. When you're finished, reset the PivotTable to look like Figure 3-1.

Row Labels Area

You can drag fields to the Row Labels area to vertically display unique fields, one item per row. You should use this area for fields that have several unique items. Earlier versions of Excel limited the display to 32,000 unique items, but Excel 2007 has extended that limit to more than one million.

As you can see in Figure 3-5, when you click the drop-down arrow in a Row Labels area field, the drop-down box is separated into three sections. In the first section, you can apply a simple alphabetical or reverse-alphabetical sort or define more advanced sorting of Row Labels items by clicking More Sort Options. In the second section, you can define filters against the items in the selected field or the values (in the Values area) that are associated with each item. In the third section, you simply click the check boxes to choose to display a single item, multiple items, or all items.

CROSS-REFERENCE Read Chapter 10 to learn more about advanced filters and sorting options.

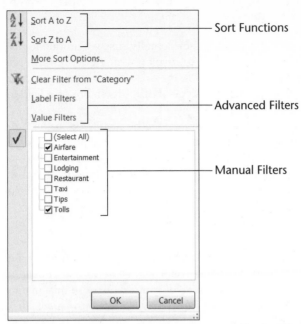

Sort Functions

Advanced Filters

Manual Filters

Figure 3-5: Clicking an item in the Row Labels or Column Labels areas brings up a drop-down box where you can sort, change labels, and apply filters.

Selecting only Airfare and Tolls resizes the Column Labels area as shown in Figure 3-6. Why? That's because these expense Categories all have a Type of Business, so Personal data is not displayed. Be sure to carefully review the dataset in Figure 2-1 of Chapter 2 if you're not completely sure about how this works.

Try selecting a few different combinations of Category to see how different items in a Row Labels area field affect the shape of the PivotTable. When you're finished, reset the PivotTable report to appear as shown in Figure 3-1.

	A	B	C
1	Month	(All)	
2			
3	**Sum of Amount**		
4		**Business**	**Grand Total**
5	Airfare	250	250
6	Tolls	8	8
7	**Grand Total**	**258**	**258**

Sheet4 / Sheet1

Figure 3-6: Selecting Airfare and Tolls results in the Column Labels area being resized because all the expenses for Airfare and Tolls had a Type of Business.

Column Labels Area

You can drag fields to the Column Labels area to horizontally display unique items, one item per column. Here, you can also choose to display a single item, multiple items, or all the unique items in the dataset. Clicking the drop-down arrow next to a field in the Column Labels area brings up the same type of drop-down box as a field in the Row Labels area (see Figure 3-4).

Although Excel 2007 allows up to 16,384 unique items to be displayed in the Column Labels area, you should generally drop fields in this area for which there are only a few unique items. This is because report users are typically more accustomed to viewing, managing, and printing PivotTable reports where the unique items scroll down, rather than across.

Values Area

You can drag fields into the Values area to perform some type of aggregate function on them. Here you can choose to count, sum, or average data against items that appear in Row Labels and Column Labels areas of the PivotTable. You can also use this area to find a minimum or maximum value for item in a Row Labels, a Column Labels, or a Row Labels and Column Labels combination.

When there is only one field being summarized in the Values area of the PivotTable report, the summarized field is labeled as the field name preceded with a description of the aggregation type. In Figure 3-7, it's Sum of Amount. If you were to change the summary type to Count, then Count of Amount would instead be displayed in cell A3 of Figure 3-7.

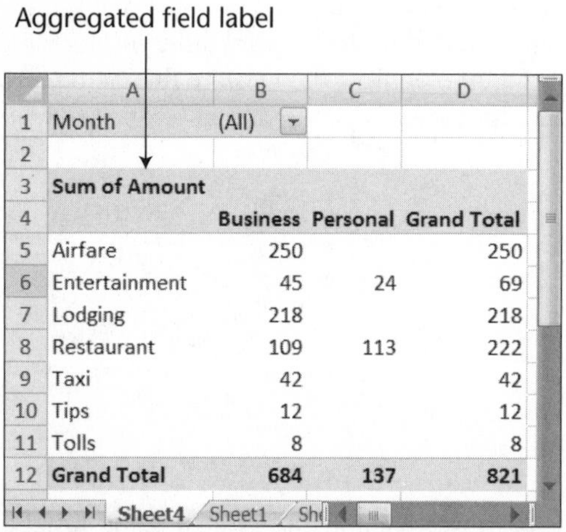

Aggregated field label

	A	B	C	D
1	Month	(All) ▾		
2				
3	**Sum of Amount**			
4		**Business**	**Personal**	**Grand Total**
5	Airfare	250		250
6	Entertainment	45	24	69
7	Lodging	218		218
8	Restaurant	109	113	222
9	Taxi	42		42
10	Tips	12		12
11	Tolls	8		8
12	**Grand Total**	684	137	821

Sheet4 / Sheet1 / Sh

Figure 3-7: The aggregation type and field are shown where the Row Labels and Column Labels field headings meet when only a single value is being summarized.

NOTE You don't have to have fields in the Row Labels or Column Labels area to summarize a field(s) in the Values area. However, it usually makes sense to have one or more fields in these areas to provide some context to the aggregated field.

If you drag Amount into the Values area of the report a second time, the aggregation field label in cell A3 is removed and the summary types are listed as separate items in the Column Labels area, as shown in Figure 3-8.

Whenever there are two or more fields being summarized in the Values area of a PivotTable report, Excel displays a Values field in the PivotTable Field List dialog box. This Values field represents all the fields (two or more) being summarized in the Values area of a PivotTable report. You can move this field up or down in the hierarchy of fields displayed in either the Row Labels or Column Labels area. Keep in mind that while the various summarized fields in the Values area can be added, removed, and modified, the displays of the summarized fields are always bound together in the Values field.

NOTE Adding a second field to the Values area results in a Values field being added to the lowest level of the hierarchy in the Column Labels area. Though it's possible to move this field to any level of the hierarchy in either the Row Labels or Column Labels areas, there are no options for customizing the default placement of the Values field when it is first added to the PivotTable report.

Multiple items in the Value area
are displayed in the Column Labels area

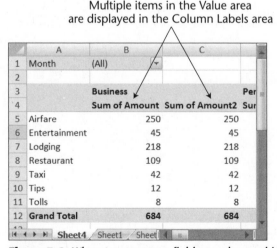

	A	B	C
1	Month	(All)	
2			
3		Business	Per
4		Sum of Amount	Sum of Amount2	Sur
5	Airfare	250	250
6	Entertainment	45	45
7	Lodging	218	218
8	Restaurant	109	109
9	Taxi	42	42
10	Tips	12	12
11	Tolls	8	8
12	Grand Total	684	684

Figure 3-8: When two or more fields are dropped in the Values area, the aggregated field label is no longer displayed.

Follow these steps to see how multiple summarized fields can be displayed in a Pivot-Table report:

1. Starting with the PivotTable report in Figure 3-1, drag Amount into the Values area a second time to shape the PivotTable like Figure 3-8.

2. Left-click Sum of Amount2 in the Areas section of the PivotTable Field List dialog box and choose Field Settings from the pop-up menu to bring up the Data Field Settings dialog box. When the dialog box opens, change the summary type to Average in the Summarize Value Field By pane, type **Average Amount** in the Custom Name field, and then click OK to apply the changes and close the dialog box.

3. Drag the Values field in the Column Labels area underneath Category in the Row Labels area of the PivotTable Field List dialog box. Verify that Sum of Amount and Average Amount are repeated for each Row Labels item, as shown in Figure 3-9.

4. Drag Average Amount to the top of the hierarchy in the Values area of the Pivot-Table Field List dialog box.

5. Drag Values above Category in the Row Labels area of the PivotTable Field List dialog box.

6. Verify that your PivotTable report and PivotTable Field List dialog box look like Figure 3-10.

If you compare Figures 3-9 and 3-10, you'll notice that either the aggregated fields can be summarized under each Row Labels item (Figure 3-9) or each Row Labels item can be summarized under each type of aggregation (Figure 3-10). The type of report being produced, the information being provided, and the preference of the user are all factors that you should evaluate when deciding how to organize this information into the PivotTable.

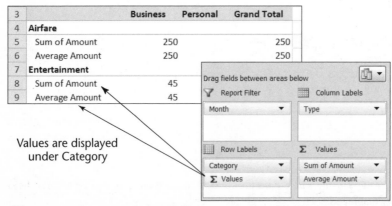

Figure 3-9: When two or more fields are summarized in the Values area, the Values field is added to the PivotTable list where it can be dragged to other report areas.

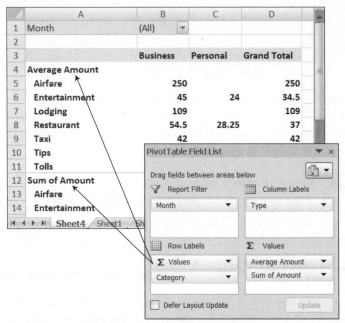

Figure 3-10: Hierarchies for Row Labels and Values areas for the PivotTable report can be controlled from the PivotTable Field List dialog box.

CROSS-REFERENCE Read the "Working with Inner and Outer Fields" section of Chapter 10 for more information about using multiple fields in the Row Labels or Column Labels area of a PivotTable report.

Shaping the Report

In earlier versions of Excel, you could simply drag fields from the PivotTable report to the Report Layout area. With Excel 2007, this feature is only enabled when you check the Classic PivotTable Layout option under the Display tab in the PivotTable Options dialog box (read Chapter 11 for more information about enabling this option). Using the new Excel 2007 methodology, fields are now dragged to different areas of the Pivot-Table — all from within the PivotTable Field List dialog box (described later in this chapter). This is more efficient than the previous method, but if you're accustomed to working with earlier Excel versions, it may take some time before you're comfortable with this new technique.

Using the Pop-Up Menus

Excel 2007 provides contextual pop-up menus for different areas of a PivotTable report. There are four kinds of pop-up menus, which can be accessed by right-clicking the following report areas:

- Report Filter area
- Values area
- Row Labels or Column Labels areas
- Items in the Row Labels, Column Labels, or Values areas

Commonly used functions that are relevant to the selected PivotTable area appear in these various pop-up menus. Keep in mind that though numerous functions appear in the pop-up menu, you'll still need to use the PivotTable Tools tab to execute some functions, such as inserting a Calculated Field or a Calculated Item.

CROSS-REFERENCE Read Appendix B for graphical examples and explanations of functions in the pop-up menus and the PivotTable Tools tab.

Looking at the PivotTable Tools Tab

Several functions for managing your PivotTable report are accessible from the Pivot-Table Tools tab. This tab provides you with a handy means of performing many Pivot-Table functions and operations. Buttons are readily accessible for refreshing and sorting data, generating PivotCharts, toggling display options, clearing filters, and launching PivotTable report dialog boxes.

You can access the PivotTable Tools tab by clicking the PivotTable Tools tab that appears above the Options tab, as shown in Figure 3-11. Keep in mind that this special tab only appears when you click a PivotTable report in the Excel workbook.

Once you click the PivotTable Tools tab, the PivotTable Tools tab is revealed, as shown in Figure 3-12.

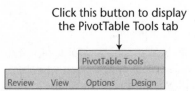

Click this button to display
the PivotTable Tools tab

Figure 3-11: The PivotTable Tools tab appears above the Options tab and is enabled only when a PivotTable report is selected.

Figure 3-12: The PivotTable Tools tab is used to manage many PivotTable operations.

Notice that the buttons in the PivotTable Tools tab are organized into eight groups. These various groups and a short description of available functions are summarized in Table 3-2.

Because these buttons perform a variety of functions, I cover the use of them in more detail under their relevant sections of this book.

CROSS-REFERENCE Read Appendix B for a detailed explanation of each button of the PivotTable Tools tab.

Table 3-2: Summary of PivotTable Tools Tab Groups

TAB GROUP	PURPOSE
PivotTable	Accessing the PivotTable Options dialog box, changing the PivotTable report name, showing Report Filter pages, and toggling the Generate Get PivotTable option.
Active Field	Access the Field Settings dialog boxes, expand and collapse fields in the Row Labels or Column Labels area.
Group	Group and ungroup items in the Row Labels or Column Labels areas of the PivotTable.
Sort	Sort data and items in the PivotTable.
Data	Refresh the PivotTable report, change the data source, and access the Connection Properties dialog box.
Actions	Clearing filters, removing all fields from the PivotTable report, selecting PivotTable areas, and moving the PivotTable report.
Tools	Create PivotCharts, manage Calculated Fields and Calculated Items, and access OLAP tools.
Show/Hide	Toggle the display of the PivotTable Field List dialog box, report expansion indicators, and field headers.

Using the PivotTable Field List Dialog Box

The third and last component of a PivotTable is the PivotTable Field List dialog box. This dialog box supports most PivotTable functions related to report design. It's separated into two sections: the Fields section and the Areas section. All the available fields that can be used in the PivotTable are displayed in the Fields section (the top half of the PivotTable Field List dialog box of Figure 3-13). The fields in this section of the dialog box can be dragged to different areas (drop zones) in the Areas section (the bottom half of the PivotTable Field List dialog box of Figure 3-13). Looking at Figure 3-13, you can see that Month is in the Report Filter area, Category is in the Row Labels area, and Sum of Amount is in the Values area of the Areas section.

The Fields and Areas sections of the dialog box each provide a unique set of functions. The Fields section includes functions for sorting data, configuring filters, and setting field locations. The Areas section includes tools for moving fields up or down in the hierarchy, switching field locations, and accessing the Field Settings dialog box, where more advanced tools and options can be used. Right-clicking and left-clicking fields in each of these two sections of the PivotTable Field List dialog box brings up different pop-up menus where you can access these commonly used functions for managing the PivotTable report. I've summarized the functions and pop-up menus in Table 3-3.

CROSS-REFERENCE Read Appendix B to review the graphical pop-up menus and a brief description of each item in the pop-up menu, and read Chapter 10 for more information about the Field Settings dialog box.

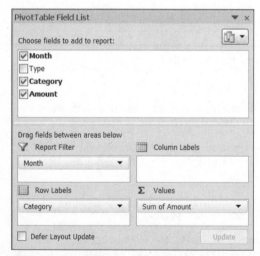

Figure 3-13: Fields are bolded and checked when they are being utilized in the PivotTable report.

Table 3-3: Left- and Right-Click Functions in the PivotTable Field List Dialog Box

ACTION	FIELDS SECTION	AREAS SECTION
Right-click field	Brings up a pop-up menu where the field can be added or moved to a selected PivotTable report area.	No action.
Left-click check box	Adds (checked) or removes (unchecked) the field from the PivotTable.	Not applicable as fields in the Areas section do not have a check box.
Left-click drop-down arrow next to field	Brings up the filter dialog boxes shown in Figure 3-3 (Report Filter area) or Figure 3-5 (Column Labels and Row Labels fields).	Brings up a pop-up menu where the field can be moved to a different report area, removed from the report, or moved up or down in the hierarchy of fields in the selected area. The Field Settings dialog box can also be launched from here.

Working in the Fields Section

The fields being utilized in the PivotTable report are bolded and checked in the Fields section of the PivotTable Field List dialog box. In Figure 3-13, Type is the only field that is not being utilized in the report and is therefore not checked or bolded. Unchecking a field in the Fields section removes the field from the PivotTable report.

Dragging your mouse pointer over a field name highlights it and also reveals a drop-down arrow at the far right of the field, as shown in Figure 3-14. Left-clicking this drop-down arrow brings up a Filter dialog box; Report Filter area filters look like Figure 3-3 and Column Labels or Row Labels filters look like Figure 3-5.

If you choose to filter a field to show only particular item, a Filter icon appears next to the field in both the PivotTable Field List and the PivotTable report. This Filter icon helps ensure that the report user can readily see that a filter is applied on the field. Figure 3-15 shows the filter icon after I opted to display only Jan and Mar in the Month field.

NOTE Because the Report Filter area cannot show unique items like a Column Labels field (across) or a Row Labels field (down), "Multiple Items" instead appears in the field value (cell B1 of Figure 3-15) when multiple items are selected. If you choose only a single item, then that item name is displayed (selecting Jan displays "Jan"). Choosing to display all the items in a Report Filter area field shows "All".

Click the drop-down arrow to bring up the Filter dialog box

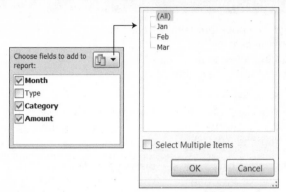

Figure 3-14: Dragging your mouse over a field reveals a field drop-down arrow, which can be clicked to bring up a Filter dialog box, such as the one shown here.

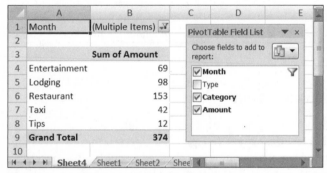

Figure 3-15: Filter icons in the PivotTable report and PivotTable Field List dialog box show you which fields have filters applied.

Working in the Areas Section

The Areas section of the PivotTable Field List dialog box shows where each field in the PivotTable report is being displayed in the Report Layout area of the PivotTable. Left-clicking a field in the Areas section brings up a pop-up menu that is separated into four sections, as shown in Figure 3-16. The first section of this pop-up menu enables you to move the field up or down in the hierarchy of fields being displayed in the selected area (drop zone) of the PivotTable. The second section shows a list of areas where the field can be moved. The third section includes only one item (Remove), which when selected removes the selected field from the PivotTable report. The fourth and last section also lists one item (Field Settings). Clicking this menu item in the pop-up menu brings up the Field Settings dialog box, where you can access more advanced tools.

CROSS-REFERENCE Read Chapter 10 for more information about the Field Settings dialog box.

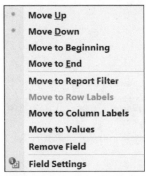

Figure 3-16: Left-clicking a field in the Areas section brings up this pop-up menu where you can rearrange the field location or remove it from the PivotTable.

TIP You can simply left-click a field in the Areas section, instead of moving all the way to the right of the field and clicking the field's drop-down arrow.

Setting Display Options

The PivotTable Field List dialog box in Figure 3-17 displays Fields and Areas side by side. This is the default display setting. You can change this display configuration by clicking the Display Setting button to bring up a pop-up menu that enables you to change the PivotTable Field List display to any of the following:

- Fields Section and Areas Section Stacked
- Fields Section and Areas Section Side-By-Side
- Fields Section Only
- Areas Section Only (2 by 2)
- Areas Section Only (1 by 4)

Displaying both the Fields and Areas sections of this dialog box (either of the first two options in the pop-up menu of Figure 3-17) is useful when you are initially shaping the PivotTable report or when you know that frequent changes will be necessary. Earlier versions of Excel were limited to displaying only the Fields section (the third option in Figure 3-17). If you prefer using the earlier method of dragging fields to the PivotTable from the PivotTable Field List dialog box, choose this display setting. The last two options for displaying only the areas are best used when fields are only rearranged, but not added to or removed from the PivotTable.

I've summarized the display configurations in Table 3-4 and provided a brief description and graphical example of each display configuration in the next few sections.

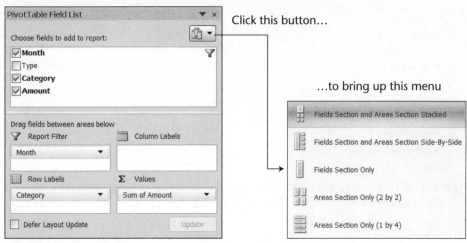

Click this button...

...to bring up this menu

Figure 3-17: Click the Display Setting button (top right of the PivotTable Field List dialog box) to bring-up the pop-up menu where the display configuration can be changed.

Fields Section and Areas Section Stacked

This is the default display setting shown in Figure 3-18. It is optimized for displaying fields with long names. This configuration enables you to easily move fields from one area to another and from the Field section to the Areas section. Clicking the line in the center of the dialog box enables you to customize the size of the PivotTable Fields section. This display setting provides the most flexibility and ease of use for most reports, thus the reason for it being the default setting.

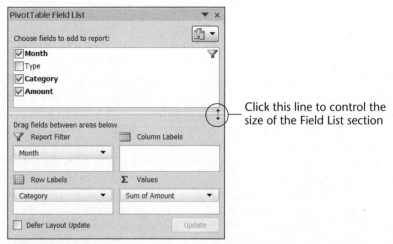

Click this line to control the size of the Field List section

Figure 3-18: The default display configuration that provides readily available access to fields and areas.

Table 3-4: PivotTable Fields Display Configurations

DISPLAY CONFIGURATION	NUMBER OF FIELDS	FIELD LENGTH	FIELDS DISPLAYED?	DROP AREAS DISPLAYED?	USE WHEN
Fields Section and Areas Section Stacked	Small number of fields for fast retrieval without a scroll bar.	Optimized for long field names.	Yes	Yes	Active shaping, sorting, and filtering of the PivotTable. Works best for small number of fields with long field names.
Fields Section and Areas Section Side-By-Side	Large number of fields can be shown before a scroll bar is required.	Optimized for short to medium field names.	Yes	Yes	Active shaping, sorting, and filtering of the PivotTable. Works best for large number of fields with short field names.
Fields Section Only	Any number of fields.	Optimized for field names of any length.	Yes	No	Using the PivotTable Classic layout (dragging fields from the PivotTable Field List to the Report Layout Area).
Areas Section Only (2 by 2)	Small number of fields for fast retrieval without a scroll bar.	Optimized for short to medium field names.	No	Yes	Report fields are rearranged, but not added or removed. Best for small number of fields with long field names.
Areas Section Only (1 by 4)	Large number of fields can be shown before a scroll bar is required.	Optimized for long field names.	No	Yes	Report fields are rearranged, but not added or removed. Best for large number of fields with short field names.

Fields Section and Areas Section Side-By-Side

This display setting shown in Figure 3-19 is useful when you have a large number of report fields that you want to readily access without a user having to click a scroll bar to locate a particular field. Because both the Areas and the Field sections are displayed, you still have the capability to readily move fields on and off the report. This display setting doesn't work as well for long field names, because the side-by-side display configuration results in a shorter viewable width for reading the names.

Fields Only

This display setting shown in Figure 3-20 most closely mimics prior Excel versions where only the list of available fields is displayed. Select this display option if you prefer using the earlier method of dragging fields from the PivotTable Fields section to the Report Layout area.

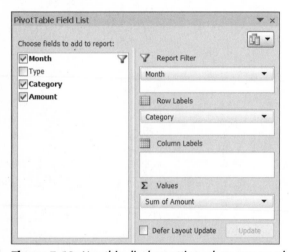

Figure 3-19: Use this display setting when you need to readily access fields from a large number of available ones.

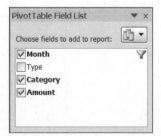

Figure 3-20: Choose this display configuration when using the PivotTable Classic Layout, where fields are dragged on and off the Report Layout area.

Areas Section Only (2 by 2)

This display setting (shown in Figure 3-21) is best used when fields are not moved on or off the report, but rather to different areas of the PivotTable. Under this configuration, the Report Filter area may be used as a parking lot for storing fields that are not used in the PivotTable, but need to be accessible to the report user.

Areas Section Only (1 by 4)

This is the same as the 2 by 2 display setting in Figure 3-21, except that it provides a better display of long field names and a poorer display of large numbers of fields. It is shown in Figure 3-22.

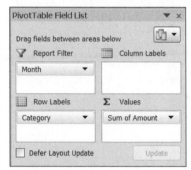

Figure 3-21: Use this display configuration when fields are only rearranged — not added or removed from the PivotTable.

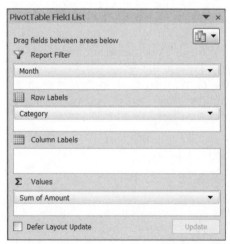

Figure 3-22: An alternative display of Figure 3-21 providing better display of long field names.

CROSS-REFERENCE Read Chapter 11 for more information about how to enable the PivotTable Classic setting to enable dragging fields from the PivotTable Field List dialog box to the PivotTable report.

Deferring Updates

The Defer Layout Update box, located at the bottom left of the PivotTable Field List dialog box (see Figures 3-18 through 3-22), is enabled for all the display configurations listed in Table 3-4, except the Field List Only setting (see Figure 3-20). Checking this box simply defers changes to the PivotTable until the Update button (at the bottom right of the dialog box) is clicked. So, for example, if you checked the Defer Layout Update box and then moved a field in the Fields section to a different report area in the Areas section of the PivotTable Field List dialog box, the changes would not be applied to the PivotTable report until you click the Update button. You should use this option when performance is slow (usually due to importing large datasets) and several changes to the report are required. Instead of waiting for each report change to complete before moving on to the next, you can make several changes at once and then click the Update button to apply all the changes at once.

Trying It Out in the Real World

Jean Trenary, the Information Services Manager at AdventureWorks, has asked you to provide a brief demonstration to the Information Services department on the new features of PivotTables in Excel 2007. Jean would like to see more about how multiple summarized fields in the Values area and how the PivotTable Field List dialog box can be configured where fields can be rearranged on the report with the idea that fields would likely not be added or removed.

You decide to use the dataset in Figure 2-1 for the demonstration and configure the PivotTable report to summarize the minimum and maximum expense amount by Category and Month. You decide to show the minimum expenses in the first part of the report and the maximum expenses in the second part of the report. You also configure the PivotTable Field List dialog box to show only the areas in a 2 by 2 format.

Getting Down to Business

Follow these steps to complete this exercise:

1. Create a PivotTable report using the dataset shown in Figure 2-1 of Chapter 2.

2. Drag Type to the Report Filter area, Category to the Row Labels area, Month to the Column Labels area, and Amount to the Values area.

3. Left-click Sum of Amount in the Values area of the PivotTable Field List dialog box and choose Field Setting from the pop-up menu.

4. Select Min in the Summarize Value Field By pane and type **Minimum Amount** in the Custom Name field. Click OK to close the dialog box.

5. Drag Amount under Minimum Amount in the Values area of the PivotTable Field List dialog box.

6. Left-click Sum of Amount in the Values area of the PivotTable Field List dialog box and choose Field Setting from the pop-up menu.

7. Select Max in the Summarize Value Field By pane and type **Maximum Amount** in the Custom Name field. Click OK to close the dialog box.

8. Drag Values in the Column Labels area above Category in the Row Labels area.

9. Left-click the Display Settings button in the PivotTable Field List dialog box and choose Areas Section Only (2 by 2) from the pop-up menu.

10. Verify that your PivotTable report and PivotTable Field List dialog box look like Figure 3-23.

WATCH THE VIDEO To see how to do this exercise, watch the
`ch0301_video.avi` **video on the companion web site at**
`www.wiley.com/go/excelreporting/2007`.

Figure 3-23: If you did everything right, your report and dialog box should appear as shown here.

Reviewing What You Did

This example provided you with some additional practice with using just the Pivot-Table Field List dialog box to perform most report design operations. It also highlighted the new Values field that binds multiple fields in the Values area to an icon that can be dragged to different levels of a hierarchy in the Row Labels or Column Labels area. A real-world scenario also required that you change the PivotTable Field List display configuration.

Chapter Review

This chapter included a review of the three primary PivotTable components. I started with a review of the Report Layout area component, describing how each area of a PivotTable is used. After that, I introduced you to the PivotTable Tools tab component and showed you how it is accessed from Excel. I then moved on to the last Pivot-Table Field List dialog box component, describing how it can be customized and used to manage most report design operations. I concluded with a real-world example that tied together several concepts that I covered throughout the chapter.

PART

II

External Data

Working with External Data Sources

In this chapter I provide an overview on how you can access, connect to, and manage data that is external to your Excel workbook. Learning and understanding this material is essential to developing Excel reports that retrieve important business data from your enterprise databases, data warehouse OLAP cubes, and Intranet and Internet web tables.

I start this chapter with an overview of external data sources. Next, I review the essential components required to access a data source. After that, I cover the various ways of connecting to external data sources from Excel. Here, I describe the various connection options, helping you understand how to choose the best option for your reporting needs. Next, I review the tools and available features for managing external data source connections within your workbook. I follow that with an explanation of how to change your data source connections. I conclude with a real-world example that helps tie together the material covered throughout this chapter.

Understanding External Data

External data comes in a variety of electronic formats for an almost infinite number of uses. It could be something as simple as a text file of your credit card transactions to something as complicated as a human genome database.

In Chapter 2, you keyed data into an Excel workbook. Although that may work for a few credit card transactions, it certainly wouldn't work well for a human genome database that contains more than 10 terabytes of data. In this chapter, I explain how you can connect to an external data source from Excel. By doing this, instead of manually keying information into the workbook, you can simply click the report to load the data from an external source directly into your workbook.

Accessing External Data

When you create a connection to an external data source for your Excel report, you must supply Excel with some information about the type of data that you are accessing, where it is located, your security credentials for accessing the data, and the name of the specific object that you want to access. Specifically, there are four elements that are either specified or obtained from the user's account when setting up a connection to an external data source. These elements are usually supplied in the following order:

- Type of external data
- Location of the data source
- Security credentials for accessing the data source
- Name of the object in the external data source

The ordering of these elements is important, because each new element builds on the last. For example, you can't specify a data source location without first specifying the type of data that you want to access. That's because the meaning of a location can be much different from one type of data source to the next. A location for a text file might be a Windows directory, whereas a location for an SQL database is a Microsoft database server. Similarly, security credentials can also vary from one type of data source and location to the next. You may have access to a test database on a development server, but not to a marketing database on a production server.

The first element, type of external data, is specified by selecting a data source driver (discussed in the next section). The second element, the location of the data source, identifies where the data resides. Locations can be local to the computer you are working on, a server in your organization, a remote server in another location, or even a File Transfer Protocol (FTP) site. And, depending on the *type* of data that you are accessing, the location might be a database server, a web site, a file directory, or even an Analysis Server. The third element, security credentials, must be supplied in order for you to see what objects are available and whether you can access them. Security credentials may be a login and password, or an access token that is associated with a user's Windows login account. The last element, the object name, is simply the target data source being accessed; it might be a text file, a database table, or an OLAP cube.

Understanding Data Source Drivers

External data is accessed by selecting a *data source driver*, which is simply a program designed to connect to a specific type of data source and extract data from it. For example, if the data source is a text file, the data driver instructs Excel to prompt for elements such as the file directory and file format. If, instead, the data source is an SQL database, the data source driver instructs Excel to prompt for elements such as the database server and database name.

A default installation of Microsoft Excel includes drivers for the following types of data sources:

- Microsoft SQL Server database
- Microsoft OLAP cube
- Microsoft Access database
- Microsoft FoxPro database
- Microsoft Paradox database
- dBase database
- XML file
- Microsoft Excel workbook
- Oracle database
- Delimited or fixed-width files

You can also access other types of applications and database systems if you have the appropriate drivers installed on your computer.

TIP If the source system you want to access is not supported by one of these drivers, you can try using Microsoft's generic ODBC driver or contact the software program's manufacturer to see if one is available.

Authenticating to External Data Sources

External data sources are typically protected by multiple layers of security. A user must have sufficient security privileges to access the domain and computer on which the data source resides. There may also be share-level and/or file-level security requirements on particular directories that limit access. All these requirements must first be satisfied before the user can even see the data source, let alone authenticate to it. So, for example, before you can authenticate to a Microsoft Access database that is protected by a login and password, you'll need sufficient security credentials to first see the database file on the network.

The second component for authenticating to a data source is providing the proper security credentials to the data source itself. Some types of data sources require a user login and password for access, whereas other data sources look at the user's Windows account to determine if access will be granted.

CROSS-REFERENCE Read Chapter 6 for more information about authenticating to specific types of data sources.

Connecting to External Data Sources

In earlier versions of Excel, connections to external data sources were set up as part of creating a Spreadsheet or PivotTable report. Though you can still create the report and external data source connection at the same time, Excel 2007 provides you with the ability to add workbook connections to external data sources without associating them with a report. Using this model, you can:

- Set up external data source connections to easily switch back and forth between production and test servers.

- Facilitate regional display differences by adding multiple workbook connections where particular fields are uniquely formatted (such as when using £ or € instead of $) and fields with different languages are referenced (such as when pulling a French product title instead of an English product title).

- Easily share connections among multiple PivotTable reports.

- Set up and save template workbook(s) with the external data source connections already defined to a network location that report developers can utilize for building reports.

Throughout the next few sections, I demonstrate some of these examples in more depth. Whether you're a seasoned report developer or a report neophyte, I suggest that you read this material carefully, because many tools and methods are available for connecting to external data sources in Excel.

Using the Get External Data Group

Connections to external data sources are made from the Get External Data group, which is accessed from the Data menu. This toolbar, shown in Figure 4-1, has five buttons for connecting external data sources to the workbook. The first three buttons provide a quick means of setting up connections to Access, Web, and Text data sources. Clicking the fourth button, From Other Sources, reveals a drop-down menu where SQL Server database tables, Analysis Server cubes, and XML files can be accessed. There are also buttons for importing data using the Data Connection Wizard and the Microsoft Query program; the latter being an old but trusted friend of many Excel report developers. The Existing Connections button provides access to the Existing Connections dialog box, where all the connections in the workbook, network, and local computer are displayed.

I provide a brief description of each button in the Get External Data group in Table 4-1.

Figure 4-1: The Get External Data group is accessed from the Data menu.

Table 4-1: Get External Data Group Button Descriptions

BUTTON	DESCRIPTION
From Access	Brings up the Select Data Source dialog box where a connection to an Access database can be made.
From Web	Brings up the New Web Query dialog box where a connection to an Intranet or Internet table can be made.
From Text	Brings up the Import Text File dialog box where a connection to a text file(s) can be made.
From Other Sources	Reveals a drop-down menu for connecting to other data sources such as an Analysis Server, a database server, an XML file, or an unlisted data source. The Microsoft Query program is also accessed from this drop-down menu.
Existing Connections	Brings up the Existing Connections dialog box where connection files in the My Data Sources folder are displayed.

Selecting a Method to Get External Data

Excel 2007 provides many new ways to access and manage external data source connections. Regardless of whether you're accustomed to developing reports in earlier versions of Excel, or you're just now starting to develop reports using this latest Excel release, you may be perplexed by all the available options. For example, you might be asking yourself whether you should use the From Text button or the Microsoft Query program to connect a text file to your Excel report.

In order to help you understand which connection option to select, I've listed the various methods for connecting to external data sources in Table 4-2. This table has five columns. In the first column, I identify the data source type and the toolbar button that can access it. Some data sources can be accessed by multiple buttons. When this is the case, each button has its own row in the table. The second column in the table, When to Use, identifies when you should select a particular method. The last three columns identify what features and types of Excel reports are supported. Keep in mind that I only provide an overview of the various options in this table and throughout this chapter. For more detailed information about connecting to a particular type of data source and method, read Chapter 5.

TIP The Microsoft Query program still provides the most flexibility and support for text files and databases. Although the From Access and From Text buttons are more readily accessible than the MS Query program, they do not provide support for SQL queries or parameters.

Table 4-2: External Data Source Button Explanations

DATA TYPE SOURCE BUTTON	WHEN TO USE	QUERY SUPPORT	SUPPORTED REPORTS	PARAMETERS
Access database Data → From Access	* Connecting to a single database table or query in the Access database where all the data is loaded into the Excel report.	No	PivotTable PivotChart Spreadsheet	No
Access database Data → From Other Sources → From Microsoft Query	* Connecting to a single database table or view where a filter is applied prior to loading the data into the Excel report. * Connecting to multiple database tables and/or views. * Parameters must be used in the Excel report.	Yes	PivotTable PivotChart Spreadsheet	Yes[†]
OLAP Cube Data → From Other Sources → From Analysis Services	* Connecting to an Analysis Server cube. * Connecting to an Analysis Server cube or a SharePoint server.	N/A	PivotTable PivotChart	N/A
Data → From Other Sources → From Microsoft Query				
SQL Database Data → From Other Sources → From SQL Server	* Connecting to a single database table or view in the SQL database where all the data is loaded into the Excel report.	No	PivotTable PivotChart Spreadsheet	No

Table 4-2 *(continued)*

DATA TYPE SOURCE BUTTON	WHEN TO USE	QUERY SUPPORT	SUPPORTED REPORTS	PARAMETERS
SQL Database Data → From Other Sources → From Microsoft Query	* Connecting to a single database table or view where a filter is applied prior to loading the data into the Excel report. * Accessing multiple database tables and/or views. * A stored procedure is used to access the source data. * Parameters must be used in the Excel report. * Using the Query Wizard program.	Yes	PivotTable PivotChart Spreadsheet	Yes†
Text File Data → From Text	* Connecting to a single text file where a filter is not applied prior to loading the data into the Excel report. * A PivotTable or PivotChart report is NOT required.	No	Spreadsheet	No
Text File Data → From Other Sources → From Microsoft Query	* Connecting to a single file where a filter is applied prior to loading the data into the Excel report. * Accessing multiple database files where file relationships are required. * A PivotTable or PivotChart report is required.	Yes‡	PivotTable PivotChart Spreadsheet	Yes†
Web Query Data → From Web	Connecting to a table on an Intranet or Internet web site.	No	Spreadsheet	No

† Parameters are only in Spreadsheet reports.

‡Only limited query features are available for text files; fields can only be selected, but there is no support for SQL functions.

USING MICROSOFT QUERY TO ACCESS EXTERNAL DATA

I've read and received a lot of correspondence about the Microsoft Query program not being updated for such a long period of time. When I initially looked at the new Get External Data group in Excel 2007, I was excited about what improvements lay ahead with external data sources. With all the new buttons and design changes, I wondered whether the Microsoft Query program was finally updated with better query design tools and improved support of parameters, stored procedures, and client-side OLAP.

Unfortunately, I was disappointed to learn that the new toolbar buttons provided only a subset of what was already available with older data source driver programs. And instead of updating the Microsoft Query program, features were instead removed. I, like many other report developers, continue to look forward to an overhauled Microsoft Query program. Perhaps we'll see that soon!

Managing External Data Sources

Connections to external data sources are primarily managed from the Workbook Connections dialog box that is accessible by choosing Data → Connections. This dialog box, shown in Figure 4-2, provides numerous tools for managing external data source workbook connections. From the Workbook Connections dialog box, you can:

- Add and remove connections to external data sources
- Locate where external data sources are being utilized in a workbook
- Identify when external data sources were last refreshed
- Refresh one or more data sources
- Monitor and cancel refresh operations
- Access the Connection Properties dialog box
- Add or modify descriptions of workbook connections

The Workbook Connections dialog box is separated into two panes. At the top half is the Connection pane, where all the external data source connections for the workbook are displayed. At the bottom half is the Location pane, which can be used to view where a selected data source in the top half of the dialog box is being utilized in the workbook.

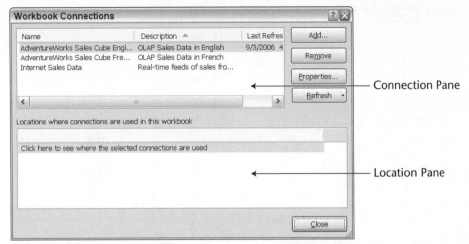

Figure 4-2: Use this Workbook Connections dialog box to locate where external data sources are being utilized in the workbook and when they were last refreshed.

Viewing Where Connections Are Used in the Workbook

You can view where an external data connection is being used in the workbook by clicking the external data connection in the Connection pane (located in the top half of the Workbook Connections dialog box) and then clicking the Click Here to See Where the Selected Connections Are Used hyperlink in the Location pane (located in the bottom half of the Workbook Connections dialog box). Note that this hyperlink is replaced with the report locations once it is clicked (as is the case in Figure 4-3). Also, if the external data source is being utilized by one or more reports, you'll see all the locations in the Location pane. If the data source is not being utilized in the workbook, an Excel Message box appears stating that the connections are not used anywhere in the workbook. Notice that Figure 4-3 shows the AdventureWorks Sales Cube English data source being utilized by two PivotTable reports that each display a different view.

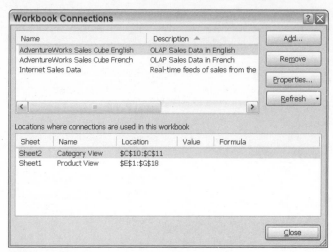

Figure 4-3: You can view where external data source connections are being utilized in the workbook in the bottom part of this dialog box.

Adding an External Data Source Connection to the Workbook

External data source connections can be added to the Excel workbook by clicking the Add button in the Workbook Connections dialog box. When you click this button, the Existing Connections dialog box shown in Figure 4-4 appears. This dialog box displays external data source connections in the current workbook, connection files on the network, and connection files on the local computer. The Show field at the top of the dialog box can be used to filter selections to display only one or all of these locations. Clicking the Browse for More button at the bottom left of the dialog box enables you to browse other locations or create a new data source file. Double-clicking a connection or selecting it and clicking the Open button enables you to create a new Excel report using the selected data source. Clicking the Cancel button closes the dialog box.

The following locations are queried to produce the full list of available connection files in the Existing Connections dialog box:

```
C:\Program Files\Common Files\ODBC\Data Sources
C:\Program Files\Microsoft Office\Office12\QUERIES
C:\Documents and Settings\User\Application Data\Microsoft\Queries
C:\Documents and Settings\User\My Documents\My Data Sources
```

TIP Dragging your mouse pointer over a connection object in the Existing Connections dialog box reveals the full path name for where the connection file is stored.

Figure 4-4: Connection files and existing workbook connections can be accessed from this dialog box for building new Excel reports.

You can make new connections to the workbook by double-clicking an existing connection under the Connections in This Workbook, Connection Files on the Network, or Connection Files on This Computer sections of the Existing Connections dialog box. Clicking the Browse for More button opens the Select Data Source dialog box shown in Figure 4-5, where you can view existing connections in the My Data Sources folder and create new connections using the Data Connection Wizard.

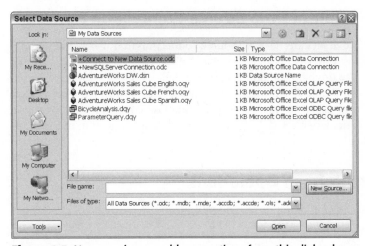

Figure 4-5: You can view or add connections from this dialog box.

Clicking the New Source button toward the bottom right of the Select Data Source dialog box starts the Data Connection Wizard program. From this dialog box, you can:

- Create an SQL Server connection to a single table or view
- Create a new OLAP Services connection
- Create a connection to a dBase, Excel, or Access file using an ODBC driver
- Create a Microsoft Data Access connection to an Oracle database
- Create a data link file connection to an external data source

NOTE You should only add a new data source from this dialog box when you want to connect to a specific database table, a specific file, or to an Analysis Server cube. If you want to use an SQL query in your external data source connection (either to a text file or to a database), the query must already be created and saved.

Removing External Data Source Connections

Connections to external data sources in the workbook can be removed by selecting a connection in the Connection pane of the Workbook Connections dialog box and clicking the Remove button. For Spreadsheet reports (not PivotTable reports), you also have the option of disconnecting an external data source from the report by clicking the Unlink button in the External Data toolbar, which is accessed from the Table Tools toolbar.

Reconnecting External Data Source Connections

If you accidentally remove an external data source connection that was being used by one or more reports in your workbook, you may still be able to reconnect it to the report without having to develop the report from scratch. By simply adding the connection back to the workbook, the report and external data source are reconnected. This works for OLAP cubes, saved query files, and database tables. However, keep in mind that this only works when the data source is linked to a connection in the Existing Connections dialog box.

Managing Data Refresh Operations

There are several tools for managing refresh operations in the Workbook Connections dialog box. From this dialog box, you can:

- Refresh one or more external data source connections
- View when an external data source connection was last refreshed
- View the status of refresh operations
- Cancel a refresh operation

You can also view when a data source was last refreshed from the Last Refreshed column, located in the top pane of the Workbook Connections dialog box. Refer back to Figure 4-2 to see that column in the dialog box. Note that the last refresh information does not appear for web queries or Spreadsheet reports.

TIP If the Last Refreshed column does not appear in your dialog box, right-click the header row and verify that the Last Refreshed field is checked.

Refreshing Data

You can refresh data from an external data source connection from either the Excel report or from the Workbook Connections dialog box. Refreshing external data sources from the Workbook Connections dialog box provides some additional flexibility in that you are able to choose multiple external data source connections to refresh (more than one connection, but not all connections), while also obtaining quick access to current refresh operations.

NOTE An external data source connection can only be refreshed when it is used in an Excel report. That's because the data is only loaded into Excel when the connection is tied to a report.

Clicking the drop-down arrow next to the Refresh button in the Workbook Connections dialog box reveals a drop-down menu with the following items:

- Refresh
- Refresh All
- Refresh Status
- Cancel Refresh

Choosing Refresh triggers a refresh operation for the selected connection in the Connection pane. You can refresh multiple connections at once by first holding down the Control key and then clicking each connection. Once you have highlighted the connections that you want to update, click the Refresh button.

Selecting Refresh All updates the data for all the external data source connections that are associated with a report in the workbook. Note that this item is also available in the PivotTable and Spreadsheet toolbars.

Monitoring Refresh Operations

Select Refresh Status from the Refresh drop-down button in the Workbook Connections dialog box to bring up the External Data Refresh Status dialog box shown in Figure 4-6. Here, you can view how long background queries have been running, the number of rows that have been fetched from the external data source, and what reports are being refreshed.

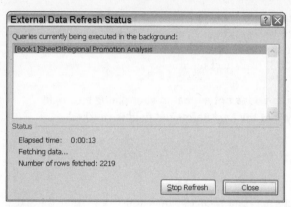

Figure 4-6: You can monitor the status of one or more background refresh operations from this dialog box.

WARNING In order to monitor refresh operations — or to even be able to continue working in the Excel workbook — the report query must be configured to run in the background. This setting is enabled by default for Spreadsheet reports. However, for PivotTable reports, you'll need to check the Enable Background Refresh option in the Connection Properties dialog box. Also, keep in mind that this option can only be enabled for PivotTable reports that access OLTP data sources; OLAP data sources freeze the Excel session until the refresh operation is complete.

Canceling a Refresh Operation

If the report is taking too much time to refresh, you can cancel the refresh operation by selecting the external data source connection and clicking the Stop Refresh button in the External Data Refresh Status dialog box, shown in Figure 4-6. It's also possible to cancel the refresh operations of all external data sources by holding down the Esc key.

Changing External Data Source Connections

You may find it necessary to change the external data source location for your Excel report. This might be because the external data source is being relocated to a different server, or perhaps the report is accessing a test or development server, and now it needs to be pointed to a production database.

Changing data source connections is much easier to do for PivotTable reports than it is for Spreadsheet reports. This is because there is a new Change Data Source button available for PivotTable reports that automates the process of changing data sources — for any type of data source, including OLAP cubes. For Spreadsheet reports, you'll need to either plan ahead by using an SQL login to access the external data source or to edit the connection string from the report's Connection Properties dialog box.

Using the Change Data Source Button for PivotTable Reports

The Change Data Source button that is located on the PivotTable toolbar can be used to change the external data source for a PivotTable report to utilize a new or different data source. Clicking this button brings up the Change PivotTable Data Source dialog box. Notice that in Figure 4-7, this dialog box shows that the report is connected to the AdventureWorks Sales Cube English.

Clicking the Choose Connection button brings up the Existing Connections dialog box (refer back to Figure 4-4 to see an example of this dialog box), where you can select an existing connection file or create a new one.

As you can probably surmise, it's very easy to switch external data source locations for your PivotTable reports. Using the AdventureWorks example, you could easily switch between a Sales cube that uses English descriptions, a U.S. ($) currency symbol, and an American date format (MM/DD/YY) to a Sales cube that uses French descriptions, a Euro (€) currency symbol, and a European date format (DD/MM/YY).

NEW FEATURE Read the online OLAP chapter to learn more about how the new features in Excel 2007 can support formatting defined on the Analysis Server cube.

When you change the external data source for a PivotTable report, the new data source can utilize a completely different query or table. You can even change the type of data that you're accessing; for example, from a text file to an SQL database or from an offline cube file to an online Analysis Server cube. The only limitation is that you cannot switch from OLTP data sources to OLAP data sources or vice versa. This is due to the underlying connection properties that are initially created when these data sources are first added to the PivotTable report.

Figure 4-7: Clicking the Change Data Source button brings up this dialog box, which enables you to choose a different connection.

Changing an External Data Source Connection for a Spreadsheet Report

There is no Change Data Source button for a Spreadsheet report (Microsoft included this button only for PivotTable reports), so you'll need to utilize one of the following two methods to change the data source for Spreadsheet reports that access an SQL database:

- Uncheck the Save Password box
- Edit the connection properties

The first method, unchecking the Save Password box, is the simplest and fastest method to change the data source to a different server. It does, however, assume that you used an SQL login to access the external data source. If you connected to the report using a trusted connection (or Windows Authentication), you'll need to edit the connection properties to point to the new external data source.

Unchecking the Save Password Button

If you are using an SQL login account and password to access an SQL database for your Spreadsheet report, follow these steps to change the data source:

1. Click the Spreadsheet Report to select it, click the Table Tools button to display the Table Tools menu, and then choose Refresh → Connection Properties to open the Connection Properties dialog box.

2. Click the Definition tab of the Connection Properties dialog box and uncheck the Save Password box, as shown in Figure 4-8.

3. Click OK to close the Connection Properties dialog box.

4. Right-click the Spreadsheet report and select Refresh from the pop-up menu.

5. When the SQL Server Login dialog box in Figure 4-9 appears, click the Options button to expand the dialog box and enter in your password and the new connection information. This new connection information could be a different server, a different database, or both.

6. Click OK to apply the changes.

NOTE The Save Password option is unchecked when a new Spreadsheet report is added. If this box hasn't been checked since the report was initially created, you can skip directly to step 4.

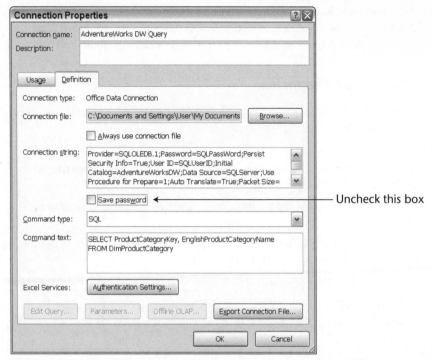

Figure 4-8: Uncheck Save Password in the Connection Properties dialog box to enable the external data source connection to be changed.

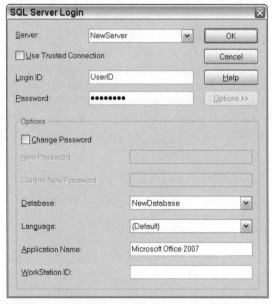

Figure 4-9: Enter the updated server and database information for the Spreadsheet report in this dialog box.

It's also possible to change the authentication type to Windows Authentication Mode by checking the Use Trusted Connection box in the SQL Server Login dialog box. This might be necessary if the new server does not support an SQL login account.

Editing Connection Properties

If you are using a trusted connection to access an SQL database for your Spreadsheet report, follow these steps to change the data source:

1. Click the Spreadsheet Report to select it, click the Table Tools button to display the Table Tools menu, and then choose Refresh → Connection Properties to open the Connection Properties dialog box.

2. Click the Definition tab of the Connection Properties dialog box, as shown in Figure 4-8.

3. Replace the database and/or server with the updated connection information in the Connection String pane of the dialog box.

4. Click OK to close the Connection Properties dialog box and refresh the report.

Here's an example of a sample ODBC connection string (note that I added cursor returns and line numbers, so that it could be more easily understood):

```
1. DRIVER=SQL Server;
2. SERVER=SQLServerName;
3. UID=UserID;
4. APP=Microsoft Office 2007;
5. WSID=ComputerName;
6. DATABASE=AdventureWorksDW;
7. Trusted_Connection=Yes
```

Line 1 shows that the connection is to an SQL Server database. The SQL Server name is stored in the second line. The Windows account for the user, the application name, and the computer name are stored in lines 3–5. The database is stored in line 6, and line 7 confirms that this connection uses Windows Authentication or trusted security.

If the query was created using an OLEDB driver, it will be slightly longer and the terms will be a little different, as shown here:

```
1. Provider=SQLOLEDB.1;
2. Integrated Security=SSPI;
3. Persist Security Info=True;
4. Initial Catalog=AdventureWorksDW;
5. Data Source=SQLServerName;
6. Use Procedure for Prepare=1;
7. Auto Translate=True;Packet
8. Size=4096;
9. Workstation ID=ComputerName;
10. Use Encryption for Data=False;
11. Tag with column
```

Many of the lines in this file are note required for the connection string to function. However, there are some important lines that you should know about. For example, the Initial Catalog in line 4 represents the database name and the Data Source in line 5 represents the SQL Server name. You can simply enter the new names directly into this pane.

If the connection was added through the Existing Connections dialog box, you'll get a warning message that says the link to the file will be removed. Just click the OK button to acknowledge the message. It basically means that your report is no longer linked to the connection file. The only real impact here is that you will not be able to restore your connection should you remove it from the workbook.

Trying It Out in the Real World

Jean Trenary, the information services manager at AdventureWorks, has requested your assistance in rolling out an Excel-based reporting solution for the information services department. Jean wants you to demonstrate the following Excel 2007 features to the team:

- Making connections to external data sources without associating them to a specific report

- Switching connections in a PivotTable report to pull English, Spanish, and French product titles from the unified AdventureWorks DW database

- Viewing where connections to external data sources are being utilized in an Excel workbook

Jean has already obtained three sample SQL queries for each product title language from Dan Wilson, a database administrator at AdventureWorks. She has asked that you use these queries for your demonstration.

Use this SQL query for the English connection:

```
SELECT EnglishProductName AS [Product Name],
       Color              AS [Color],
       SUM(OrderQuantity) AS [Qty Ordered],
       SUM(UnitPrice)     AS [Unit Price]
FROM DimProduct Prod
INNER JOIN FactInternetSales Sales ON Prod.ProductKey = Sales.ProductKey
WHERE FinishedGoodsFlag = 1
GROUP BY EnglishProductName,
         Color
```

Use this SQL query for the Spanish connection:

```
SELECT SpanishProductName AS [Product Name],
       Color              AS [Color],
       SUM(OrderQuantity) AS [Qty Ordered],
       SUM(UnitPrice)     AS [Unity Price]
```

```
FROM DimProduct Prod
INNER JOIN FactInternetSales Sales ON Prod.ProductKey = Sales.ProductKey
WHERE FinishedGoodsFlag = 1
GROUP BY SpanishProductName,
         Color
```

Use this SQL query for the French connection:

```
SELECT FrenchProductName  AS [Product Name],
       Color              AS [Color],
       SUM(OrderQuantity) AS [Qty Ordered],
       SUM(UnitPrice)     AS [Unity Price]
FROM DimProduct Prod
INNER JOIN FactInternetSales Sales ON Prod.ProductKey = Sales.ProductKey
WHERE FinishedGoodsFlag = 1
GROUP BY FrenchProductName,
         Color
```

ON THE WEB You can download the Ch04_English.sql, Ch04_Spanish.sql, and Ch04_French.sql files to your computer from the web site www.wiley.com/go/excelreporting/2007.

Getting Down to Business

After you download the files to your computer, follow these steps to complete the exercise:

1. From Excel, choose Data → From Other Sources → From Microsoft Query to bring up the Choose Data Source dialog box.

2. When the Choose Data Source dialog box appears, select <New Data Source> and click OK to bring up the Create New Data Source dialog box.

3. Type **AdventureWorks DW** into the data source name field, select SQL Server Native Client as the type of data driver, and click Connect to bring up the SQL Server Login dialog box.

4. In the Server field, type the name of the SQL Server that you will access; select an authentication type, and then click the Options button to reveal the bottom half of the SQL Server Login dialog box. In the bottom half of this dialog box, set the default database to AdventureWorksDW, and click OK.

5. When you are returned to the Create New Data Source dialog box, leave the default table field blank. Verify that your dialog box looks like Figure 4-10 and click OK.

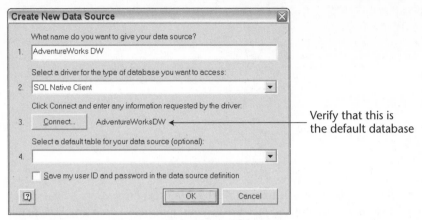

Figure 4-10: Leave the default table field blank when you are using SQL queries to create a PivotTable report.

6. When you are returned to the Choose Data Source dialog box, uncheck the Use the Query Wizard to Create/Edit Queries option.

7. Verify that your dialog box looks like Figure 4-11 and click OK to continue.

8. The Microsoft Query program is started, and the Add Tables dialog box shown in Figure 4-12 appears. Click Close in this box, because you will be pasting an SQL query into the report. (Manually adding tables is not necessary.)

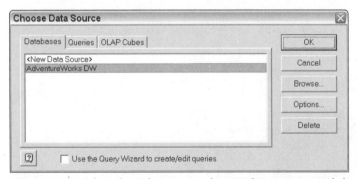

Figure 4-11: Select the AdventureWorks DW data source, and then uncheck the Use the Query Wizard to Create/Edit Queries option to bypass the Query Wizard.

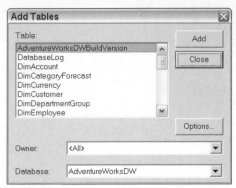

Figure 4-12: When a default table is not specified in the Create New Data Source dialog box (refer back to Figure 4-10), the Add Tables dialog box appears. You can simply close this box if you are using an SQL query for the report.

9. In the Microsoft Query dialog box shown in Figure 4-13, click the SQL button to open the SQL dialog box where you can paste a query.

10. Copy and then paste the English SQL query into the SQL dialog box, as shown in Figure 4-14, and click OK.

11. Click OK when the Microsoft Query dialog box appears, warning you that the query cannot be displayed graphically.

NOTE Microsoft Query attempts to display queries graphically, showing the table names, fields, and relationships. Complex SQL queries often cannot be displayed graphically — and that's ok. Just ignore this warning.

SQL button

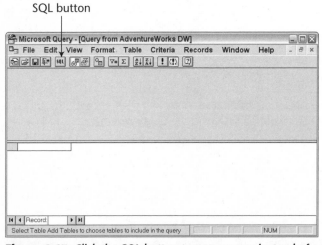

Figure 4-13: Click the SQL button to use a query instead of a table or a view.

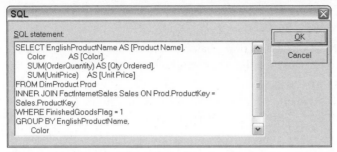

Figure 4-14: The SQL dialog box allows you to paste an SQL query that identifies the fields, field names, tables, and conditions of your report.

12. Choose File → Save As to bring up the Save As dialog box. Type **Sample Query – English** in the File Name field and click Save to save the query and close the dialog box.

13. In the Microsoft Query dialog box shown in Figure 4-13, click the SQL button to open the SQL dialog box and then delete the English query.

14. Copy and then paste the Spanish SQL query into the SQL dialog box and click OK.

15. Click OK when the Microsoft Query dialog box appears, warning you that the query cannot be displayed graphically.

16. Choose File → Save As to bring up the Save As dialog box. Type **Sample Query – Spanish** in the File Name field and click Save to save the query and close the dialog box.

17. In the Microsoft Query dialog box shown in Figure 4-13, click the SQL button to open the SQL dialog box and then delete the Spanish query.

18. Copy and then paste the French SQL query into the SQL dialog box and click OK.

19. Click OK when the Microsoft Query dialog box appears, warning you that the query cannot be displayed graphically.

20. Choose File → Save As to bring up the Save As dialog box. Type **Sample Query – French** in the File Name field and click Save to save the query and close the dialog box.

21. Choose File → Cancel and Return to Microsoft Office Excel to close the Microsoft Query program and return to Excel.

22. Choose Data → Connections to bring up the Workbook Connections dialog box.

23. Click the Add button to bring up the Existing Connections dialog box shown in Figure 4-15.

24. Select Sample Query – English and click Open to add this query as a workbook connection.

25. Click the Add button to bring up the Existing Connections dialog box again and add the French query. Repeat this process again for the Spanish query.

26. Verify that your Workbook Connections dialog box looks like Figure 4-16 and click the Close button to close the dialog box and return to Excel.

27. Choose Insert → PivotTable to bring up the Create PivotTable dialog box. Click the Use an External Data Source button and then click the Choose Connection button to bring up the Existing Connections dialog box.

28. Select Sample Query – English under the Connections in This Workbook section and then click Open to select this query and return to the Create Pivot-Table dialog box.

29. Click OK to create the PivotTable report using the Sample Query – English query.

30. Drag Product Name to the Row Labels area, Color to the Column Labels area, and Qty Ordered to the Values area of the PivotTable report.

31. Click the PivotTable Tools button and then click the Change Data Source button to bring up the Change PivotTable Data Source dialog box.

32. Click the Choose Connection button to open the Existing Connections dialog box, select Sample Query – French, and click Open.

33. Click the OK button in the Change PivotTable Data Source dialog box to close the dialog box and switch from pulling English product names to pulling French product names.

Figure 4-15: The AdventureWorks DW connection file and the saved queries from earlier steps now appear in the Existing Connections dialog box.

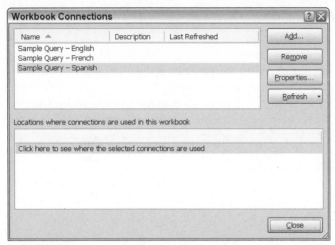

Figure 4-16: The three SQL queries are now connected to your Excel workbook.

WATCH THE VIDEO **Watch the ch0401_video.avi video on how the external data sources are added and associated with PivotTable reports at** www.wiley.com/go/excelreporting/2007.

Reviewing What You Did

I used this exercise to review how external data source connections have been restructured in Excel. I started by saving the three SQL queries in Microsoft Query. Queries must be saved from this program in order for them to be accessed from the Existing Connections dialog box. This is because you can only add new connections to single database table from the Existing Connections dialog box; SQL queries are not supported.

After the queries were saved, I showed how they could be added as connections to the workbook without tying them to a report. Once all the connections were added, I demonstrated how you could associate an existing connection to a report. I concluded the example with switching the data source of the report using the new Change Data Source button. For this example, I pulled French descriptions instead of English descriptions. In the real world, you might choose to switch between development and test servers, or use completely different queries.

Before you move on to other chapters, I suggest that you try using some of the others features and tools that I covered in this chapter. For example, add another Pivot-Table report using the same connection — and then use the Workbook Connections dialog box to locate where the data sources are being used in the workbook.

Chapter Review

This chapter provided you with an overview of external data sources and how they can be accessed from Excel. I started this chapter by describing the four elements that must be supplied for accessing external data. After that, I outlined the different methods for accessing external data sources from Excel. Next, I reviewed the Workbook Connections dialog box that is used for managing external data source connections in Excel. Following that, I identified the steps for changing external data source connections for PivotTable and Spreadsheet reports. I concluded with real-world example that tied together the material covered throughout this chapter.

CHAPTER 5

Looking at the Get External Data Tab

In this chapter, I show you how to connect to external data sources using the buttons and menu items in the Get External Data tab. This tab provides quick access to several types of external data sources, including text files, databases, and web sites. I conduct a comprehensive review of each tab button and menu item, providing recommendations on when to use the tab button and when to use the Microsoft Query program (covered in the next chapter).

I start this chapter by demonstrating how you can connect to delimited and fixed-width files using the From Text tab button. After that, I cover intranet and Internet web site connections. Next, I show you how to set up connections to Access and SQL Server database tables. Following that, I cover Analysis Server cube connections. I conclude with a real-world example where I show you how to create and connect to an SQL Server database view for your Excel report.

Connecting to Text Files

Many software programs include tools to export data to a text file that can in turn be imported into Microsoft Excel for further analysis or reporting. Some examples of personal software programs include Quicken, Microsoft Money, and Access. There are also many middle-tier and enterprise-level software packages in the marketplace that provide similar functionality. And if you are still stuck on a mainframe system, it's usually not too difficult to create an extract file that can be imported into Excel. Figure 5-1 shows how a mainframe application produces a text file that is saved to a network file server and is subsequently imported into Excel to produce a report.

Typically, a mainframe's database is not accessible from Excel, so a text file of the data is instead produced. Depending on the size of the text file, it may be saved to a network file server (as shown in Figure 5-1) or simply emailed to the report user. Once the text file is produced, it can then be imported into Excel to produce some type of report. The data is exported to the text file in one of two ways:

- **Delimited:** Each field in the file is delimited by a special character, such as a comma, tab, or pipe symbol (|).

- **Fixed-width:** Each field is delimited by its relative column position in the file.

Once the data is exported to either a delimited or fixed-width format, you can load that data into Excel using either the From Text button or the Microsoft Query program; accessed from the Get External Data group, under the Data tab. In the next few sections I cover both importing options, demonstrating how you can import both delimited and fixed-width files into Excel.

Using the From Text Button

The From Text button is ideal for quickly importing the data from a delimited or fixed-width file into Excel as a table (or Spreadsheet report). You can use this button when the text file will be loaded into Excel only once or even when you expect that the text file will regularly be updated and subsequently loaded into Excel. Some examples include a regular marketing feed from a mainframe system, a download of your monthly credit card transactions, or an extract of financial data from some type of middle-tier software package.

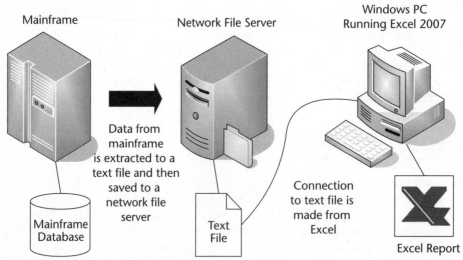

Figure 5-1: Data exported to a text file from a mainframe system can be imported into Excel to produce a report.

When you use the From Text button, the connection information to the text file is stored in Excel. This includes the following:

- Name and extension of the imported file
- Location where the file is stored
- Columns imported and not imported
- Position number and length of columns (for fixed-width files)
- Column data types

You can remove this link by unchecking the Save Query Definition option in the Data Range Properties dialog box (covered in the "Removing the Connection Information" section of this chapter), ignore it, or use it for refreshing the report when updated text files become available.

Using Microsoft Query

The Microsoft Query program can also be used to import text files, and there is better support of reporting functions; it just takes a little longer than the From Text button to get through all the steps. If you're unsure about which method to use, refer back to Table 4-2 and keep in mind that the principal drawbacks of the From Text button are:

- Files cannot be imported into a PivotTable report.
- Only one file can be linked to the Spreadsheet report.

If you need to import multiple text files into a single Excel report or you want to import the file(s) directly into a PivotTable report, skip to Chapter 6 and read the "Using MS Query to Import Text Files" section, where I describe how you can join multiple text files together for your Excel report as if they were database tables.

Importing Delimited Files

In order to distinguish each column or field in a file, fields are delimited with a special character, usually a comma or a tab. This allows programs such as Excel to identify and separate the data into individual fields as the data is being imported.

In this next example, I modified the file used in the "Trying It Out in the Real World" section at the end of Chapter 2 by adding a new column, AuthCode. This column is comprised of a two-position code, 01 for Personal expenses and 02 for Business expenses, followed by a transaction code that indicates the type of expense. This kind of coding scheme is frequently used in marketing and financial systems to analyze data. If this is at all confusing, don't worry about trying to understand the coding scheme, because it really isn't important. I've simply included it here so that you can see how Excel handles text fields that have numerical values.

To import a delimited file into Excel, follow these steps:

1. Download the ExpenseData.csv file from the web site or type the data in manually and save it as ExpenseData.csv.

ON THE WEB You can download the ExpenseData.csv **file to your computer from this book's companion web site at** www.wiley.com/go/ excelreporting/2007. **Look for the file in the** Chap05.zip **file or the Chap05 directory (depending on which file you choose to download from the site).**

```
Month,Type,Category,Amount,AuthCode
Jan,Personal,Restaurant,35,01.200
Jan,Business,Taxi,42,02.350
Jan,Business,Restaurant,64,02.200
Jan,Personal,Restaurant,22,01.200
Jan,Business,Tips,12,02.900
Feb,Personal,Restaurant,32,01.200
Feb,Personal,Entertainment,24,01.700
Feb,Business,Entertainment,45,02.700
Feb,Business,Lodging,98,02.320
Mar,Business,Airfare,250,02.300
Mar,Personal,Restaurant,24,01.200
Mar,Business,Restaurant,45,02.200
Mar,Business,Lodging,120,02.320
Mar,Business,Tolls,8,02.360
Jan,Business,Taxi,38,02.350
Jan,Business,Lodging,127,02.320
Feb,Business,Restaurant,64,02.200
Mar,Business,Airfare,422,02.300
Apr,Business,Tolls,12,02.360
Apr,Business,Entertainment,70,02.700
```

2. From Excel, choose Data → From Text to bring up the Import Text File dialog box.
3. When the Import Text File dialog box appears, locate the directory where you saved the file (see Figure 5-2), select it, and click Import.

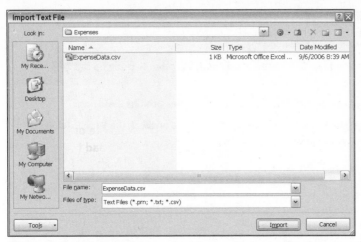

Figure 5-2: Locate and open the ExpenseData.csv file that was downloaded from this book's companion web site.

4. Select the file and click Open. The data should appear in the Text Import Wizard, as shown in Figure 5-3.

NOTE If you don't see the file extension, your computer is configured to automatically hide file extensions for known file types. Read the sidebar "Displaying File Extensions" to configure Windows to show .csv file extensions.

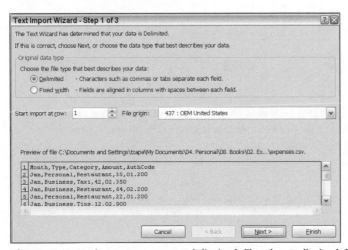

Figure 5-3: To import a comma-delimited file, the Delimited file type button must be selected.

DISPLAYING FILE EXTENSIONS

To display file extensions for known file types, follow these steps:

1. **Right-click the Windows Start button and choose Explore to bring up the Windows Explorer program.**

2. **Choose Tools → Folder Options to bring up the Folder Options dialog box.**

3. **In the Folders Options dialog box, click the View tab, uncheck the Hide Extensions For Known File Types option, and click OK.**

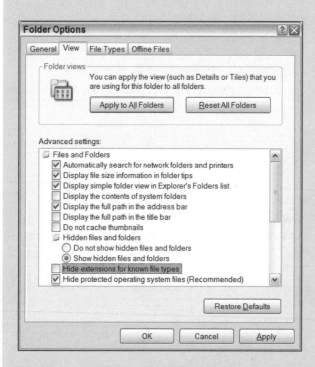

With this option set, you can readily view file extensions for files that are already assigned to an installed program (for example, .xls is assigned to Microsoft Excel and .doc is assigned to Microsoft Word).

5. Verify that the Delimited button is selected and click Next to continue. You should now see the second view of the Text Import Wizard, step 2 of 3, shown in Figure 5-4.

6. Uncheck the Tab delimiter and check the Comma delimiter as shown in Figure 5-5. Notice how the text in the Data Preview window changes when the Comma delimiter is selected. Click Next to continue.

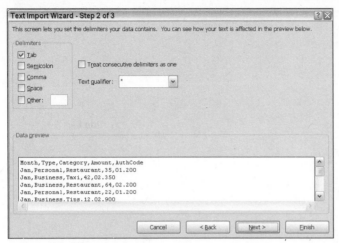

Figure 5-4: The data appears as one column with four commas in this figure, because the delimiter is set to Tab.

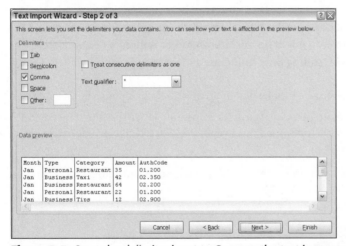

Figure 5-5: Once the delimiter is set to Comma, the text is separated into five columns.

7. In the final Text Import Wizard box (step 3 of 3, as shown in Figure 5-6), you assign a data format to each field. Set the column data format to Text for the fields Month, Type, Category, and AuthCode by selecting each column and clicking the Text button. Leave the Amount column with a data format of General.

TIP If you do not want to import a column into Excel, select the column and click the Do Not Import Column (Skip) button.

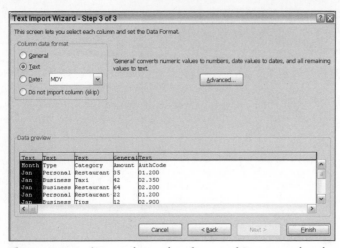

Figure 5-6: Assign a column data format of Text to each column except Amount, which should remain set as General.

TIP From a practical perspective, the column data format has to be set only for fields in which the data might be misinterpreted or require a certain date format. In this example, setting only AuthCode to text is sufficient.

8. Verify that your dialog box looks like Figure 5-6 and click Finish.

9. The Import Data dialog box in Figure 5-7 appears. Notice that the data can only be imported as a table (or Spreadsheet report). Click OK to close the dialog box and import the data.

If you did everything right, the data should now be imported into Excel, as shown in Figure 5-8.

Figure 5-7: Data can only be imported as a Table when the Text button is used to connect to the text file.

	A	B	C	D	E
1	Month	Type	Category	Amount	AuthCode
2	Jan	Personal	Restaurant	35	01.200
3	Jan	Business	Taxi	42	02.350
4	Jan	Business	Restaurant	64	02.200
5	Jan	Personal	Restaurant	22	01.200
6	Jan	Business	Tips	12	02.900
7	Feb	Personal	Restaurant	32	01.200
8	Feb	Personal	Entertainment	24	01.700
9	Feb	Business	Entertainment	45	02.700

Sheet1 Sheet2 Sheet3

Figure 5-8: AuthCode is converted as a Text data type, maintaining the data's integrity.

Importing Fixed-Width Files

Fixed-width files are not delimited with any type of special character, such as a comma or a tab. Instead, the position of the data represents a particular field. Here's how the Expense Data file looks in a fixed-width format:

```
MonthType     Category     AmountAuthCode
Jan  Personal Restaurant   35    01.200
Jan  Business Taxi         42    02.350
Jan  Business Restaurant   64    02.200
Jan  Personal Restaurant   22    01.200
Jan  Business Tips         12    02.900
Feb  Personal Restaurant   32    01.200
Feb  Personal Entertainment24    01.700
Feb  Business Entertainment45    02.700
Feb  Business Lodging      98    02.320
Mar  Business Airfare      250   02.300
Mar  Personal Restaurant   24    01.200
Mar  Business Restaurant   45    02.200
Mar  Business Lodging      120   02.320
Mar  Business Tolls        8     02.360
Jan  Business Taxi         38    02.350
Jan  Business Lodging      127   02.320
Feb  Business Restaurant   64    02.200
Mar  Business Airfare      422   02.300
Apr  Business Tolls        12    02.360
Apr  Business Entertainment70    02.700
```

The fields are position-delimited with each position being counted as the number of characters at which each column begins within the code, as outlined in Table 5-1.

Table 5-1: Field Positions for ExpenseData.txt

FIELD	START POSITION	NUMBER OF POSITIONS	END POSITION
Month	1	5	5
Type	6	9	14
Category	15	13	27
Amount	28	6	33
AuthCode	34	8	41

ON THE WEB **You can download the** `ExpenseData.txt` **file to your computer from the companion web site at** `www.wiley.com/go/ excelreporting/2007`**.**

Follow these steps to import a fixed-width file into Excel:

1. Download the file from the web site or type the data in manually and save it as ExpenseData.txt.

2. From Excel, choose Data → From Text to bring up the Import Text File dialog box.

3. When the Import Text File dialog box appears, locate the directory where you saved the file, select the file, and then click Open. You should see the Text Import Wizard – Step 1 of 3 dialog box shown in Figure 5-9.

4. Verify that the Fixed Width button is selected and click Next to continue. You should see the next view of the Text Import Wizard, as shown in Figure 5-10.

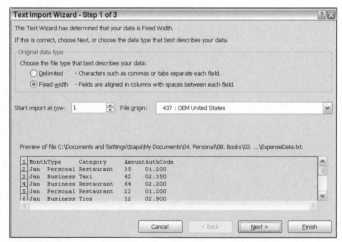

Figure 5-9: To import a fixed-width file, you must select the Fixed Width file type button.

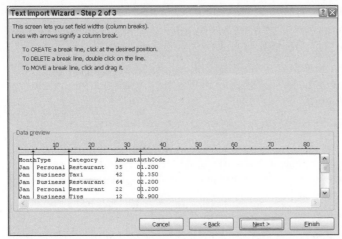

Figure 5-10: Excel automatically generates break lines that define the fields created when a file is imported.

Notice that Excel has automatically created break lines for the data. These break lines define the various columns — or fields — that will be created as the data is imported into Excel. Often, the break lines are incorrect and require adjustment, as is the case for this example. Figure 5-10 shows that Month is cut off (*Mont* instead of *Month*) and Category and Amount are being interpreted as one field instead of two fields.

5. Select the first break line for Month and drag it over one position to the right, just before the "T" in Type. Notice that the solid arrow changes to a dotted line as you move it (see Figure 5-11).

TIP Don't worry if you accidentally create a break line in the wrong position or you add one too many break lines. Just drag the line to the correct position if it's not properly aligned, or double-click the break line to remove it.

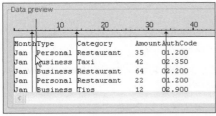

Figure 5-11: Click the first break line and drag it over one position to the right.

6. Verify that the Data Preview window looks like Figure 5-12.

7. Aim the mouse pointer at the 27 mark on the ruler and click once to create a break line between Category and Amount.

8. Select the break line after the "A" in AuthCode at the 34 mark on the ruler and drag it one position to the left, just before the "A" in "AuthCode" and right after the "t" in "Amount."

9. Verify that the Data Preview window looks like Figure 5-13 and click Next to continue.

10. Set the column data format to Text for the fields Month, Type, Category, and AuthCode by selecting each column and choosing Text. Leave Amount set as General.

11. Verify that your dialog box looks like Figure 5-14 and click Finish.

12. The Import Data dialog box in Figure 5-7 appears. Notice that the data can only be imported as a table (Spreadsheet report). Click OK to close the dialog box and import the data.

If you did everything right, the data should now be imported into Excel, as shown in Figure 5-15.

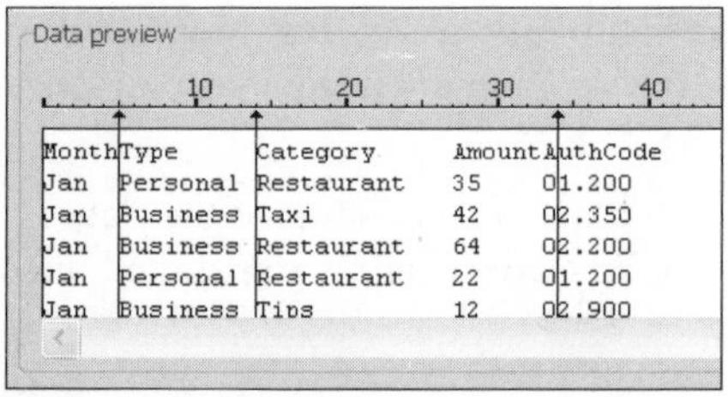

Figure 5-12: The dotted line reverts back to a solid arrow when you drop it in place.

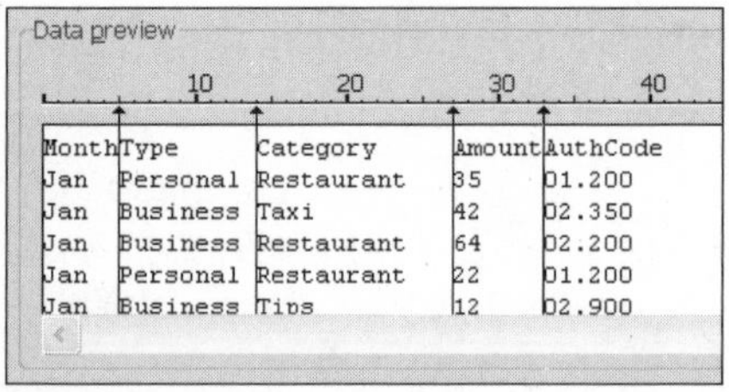

Figure 5-13: With the break lines added and properly positioned, you're ready to proceed to the next step of defining the data types for each column.

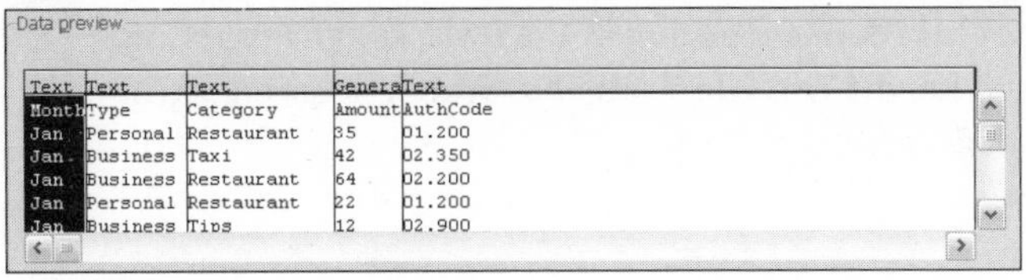

Figure 5-14: Set the Column data format to Text for all columns except Amount.

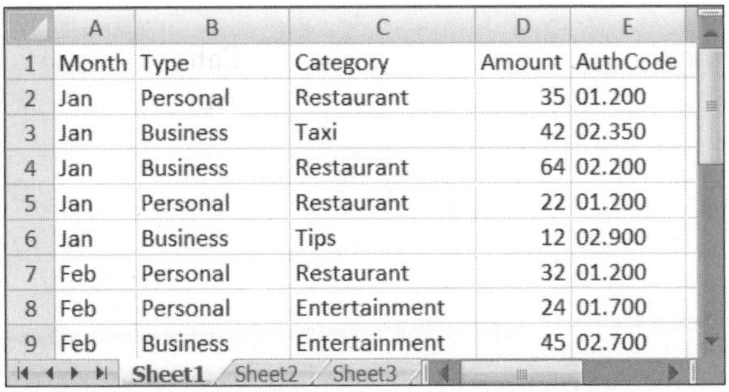

	A	B	C	D	E
1	Month	Type	Category	Amount	AuthCode
2	Jan	Personal	Restaurant	35	01.200
3	Jan	Business	Taxi	42	02.350
4	Jan	Business	Restaurant	64	02.200
5	Jan	Personal	Restaurant	22	01.200
6	Jan	Business	Tips	12	02.900
7	Feb	Personal	Restaurant	32	01.200
8	Feb	Personal	Entertainment	24	01.700
9	Feb	Business	Entertainment	45	02.700

Figure 5-15: AuthCode is converted as a data type of Text, maintaining the data integrity of the values in that field.

Looking at the Imported Data

Regardless of how the data was imported (for example,. delimited format from Figure 5-8 or fixed-width format from Figure 5-15), you can see that the values under AuthCode are left-aligned, indicating that they were imported as text. Had AuthCode not been set to a data type of Text, the values would be right-aligned, as are the ones under Amount with the leading and trailing zeros removed (for example, in cell E2 of Figure 5-15, 01.200 would appear as 1.2).

Refreshing Data

Because the file format and location are stored with the imported data, you can simply right-click anywhere on the Spreadsheet report and select Refresh from the pop-up menu to update the report with the most recent information in the text file. If you decide to maintain the link for report refreshes, keep in mind that the structure of the data file must not change (meaning it must use the same number and ordering of fields) for the data to be imported properly. However, if the structure or format of the file does change, right-click the Spreadsheet report and select Edit Text Import from the pop-up menu. This restarts the Text Import Wizard, where you can repeat the process of picking a file, selecting a file format, choosing columns to import, and assigning column data formats.

TIP Uncheck the Prompt for Filename option in the Data Range Properties dialog box to suppress the Import Text File dialog box from appearing each time the report is refreshed.

Removing the Connection Information

You may want to remove this information for security reasons; for example, perhaps you do not want anyone to know where specific files are stored on your computer. You can disable the report from being refreshed and remove the connection information by removing the query definition from the report.

To remove the query definition from the Spreadsheet report, follow these steps:

1. Right-click the Spreadsheet report and choose Data Range Properties from the pop-up menu to bring up the Data Range Properties dialog box.

2. Uncheck Save Query Definition in the Data Range Properties dialog box. This brings up a Microsoft Office Excel message box that warns you that the connection information will permanently be removed from the report. Click OK to acknowledge the warning.

3. Click OK to close the External Data Range Properties dialog box.

4. Save the report with the updated changes.

Once the Save Query Definition option is unchecked and the Data Range Properties dialog box is closed, the connection information is removed. If you right-click the report again, you'll notice that there are no longer any options for refreshing the report data. Don't forget to resave the Excel workbook; otherwise the changes will not be permanently saved.

Connecting to Web Data Sources

It's very easy to create web queries that retrieve information posted on Internet and intranet web sites. And the process is very simple; there is no complex programming involved. Merely clicking the From Web button on the Get External Data tab brings up a mini web browser that you can use to surf the web. Each web page is brought up with the borders and tables surrounded by a yellow box. All you need to do is click the check box in the top left of a particular table or frame and drag it into your report.

Using this technology, you can import:

- Web tables posted on intranet and Internet web sites

- Formatted text, but not graphics, icons, or pictures

- Hyperlinks that access web pages or generate an email message ("Mail To" function)

Though this is cutting-edge technology, there are some limitations. For example, whereas you can use a web query to pull in several tables or frames, a single query can access only a single web page. Also, there is no facility for storing and passing user logins and passwords in Excel to access the web page (like a user login and password for your credit card statement).

Accessing data from Internet and Intranet web sites for your Spreadsheet reports can be accomplished using the From Web button on the Get External Data tab. This process is similar to extracting data from other sources; it's just that the location is a Uniform Resource Locator (URL) instead of a Windows directory or database.

In Figure 5-16, I illustrate how a PC running Excel 2007 might access data from a server connected to the World Wide Web (WWW).

To try a web query, follow these steps:

1. From Excel, choose Data → From Web to bring up the New Web Query dialog box.

2. Type **www.wiley.com/go/excelreporting/sample_web_table** in the Address field, and click Go to open the sample web site that shows the first six months of 2004 stock performance for Wiley Publishing, Inc.

3. Click the yellow arrow icon next to the Prices Table to select it (the icon changes from a yellow arrow to a green check mark).

4. Verify that your New Web Query dialog box looks like Figure 5-17 and click the Import button to import the finance data into Excel.

5. When the Import Data dialog box in Figure 5-18 appears, click OK to import the Prices Table into a Spreadsheet report.

6. Verify that your Spreadsheet report looks like Figure 5-19.

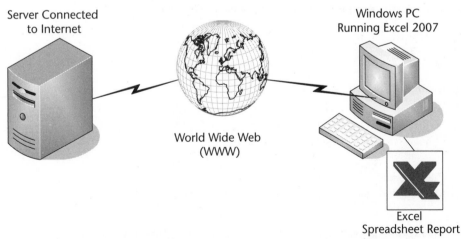

Figure 5-16: Excel Spreadsheet reports can access data posted on Internet web sites.

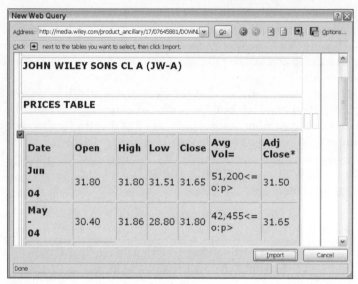

Figure 5-17: Import tables and frames from web sites into Excel by clicking a yellow arrow icon to change it to a green check mark.

Figure 5-18: Web queries can only be imported into Spreadsheet reports.

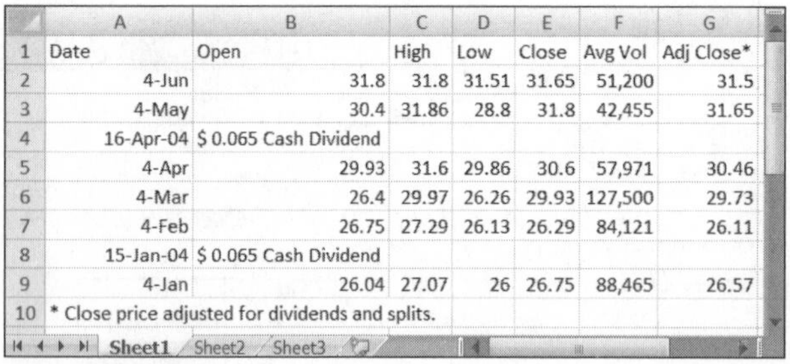

	A	B	C	D	E	F	G
1	Date	Open	High	Low	Close	Avg Vol	Adj Close*
2	4-Jun	31.8	31.8	31.51	31.65	51,200	31.5
3	4-May	30.4	31.86	28.8	31.8	42,455	31.65
4	16-Apr-04	$ 0.065 Cash Dividend					
5	4-Apr	29.93	31.6	29.86	30.6	57,971	30.46
6	4-Mar	26.4	29.97	26.26	29.93	127,500	29.73
7	4-Feb	26.75	27.29	26.13	26.29	84,121	26.11
8	15-Jan-04	$ 0.065 Cash Dividend					
9	4-Jan	26.04	27.07	26	26.75	88,465	26.57
10	* Close price adjusted for dividends and splits.						

Figure 5-19: The data from the web site in a Spreadsheet report.

Once the data is loaded into Excel, you can simply right-click the report and select Refresh from the pop-up menu to update the Spreadsheet report with the most recent data on the web site.

In the next three sections, I provide some additional information about the Web Query dialog box, the Web Query tab, and the Web Query Options dialog box. Review the information in these sections to learn more about advanced connection options that are available for your web queries.

Working in the Web Query Dialog Box

The Web Query dialog box works just like a web browser, although you may notice that the performance is a little slow because the tables and frames must be identified as each new web page is loaded. The Address drop-down feature does not use the auto-complete function that's standard in Microsoft Internet Explorer. However, all your saved web addresses in Internet Explorer are still available in the Address drop-down field. You can either select a previously saved web address or type in a new one, and then click Go or press Return to open the web page for the specified address.

There are a couple of things to keep in mind with web queries. First, web queries do not import graphics, icons, or pictures. Second, web queries can only extract data from a single web address. This means that you cannot access data protected by a login and password that directs you to another web address. You can, however, access web sites that use an NTLM style of authentication.

Using the Web Query Tab

The Web Query tab, accessed from the Web Query dialog box, is shown in Figure 5-20 and is similar to the Internet tab. It includes functions for moving back and forward to previously viewed web pages, refreshing the currently viewed web page, and stopping the current web page from loading. There are also options for toggling the display of the table/frame icon, saving the web query, and setting query options.

Table 5-2 provides an explanation of the tab buttons available in the Web Query tab.

Table 5-2: Web Query Tab Buttons and Descriptions

NUMBER	BUTTON	DESCRIPTION
	Back	Loads the web page of the next previously viewed URL address in memory.
	Forward	Loads the web page of the last previously viewed URL address in memory.
	Stop	Stops the current web page from loading.

(continued)

Table 15-2 (continued)

NUMBER	BUTTON	DESCRIPTION
	Refresh	Refreshes the web page for the selected URL address in the Address field.
	Hide Icons	Toggles the display of icons for frames and tables.
	Save Query	Saves the current URL as a web query using an .iqy file extension. The query can be accessed from the Select Data Source dialog box by choosing Data → Import External Data → Import Data.
	Options	Launches the Web Query options dialog box for customizing how the web page information is loaded into Excel.

Figure 5-20: The Web Query tab includes functions for navigating the web, saving queries, and setting query options.

Customizing Web Query Options

You can open the Web Query Options dialog box (see Figure 5-21) by clicking the Options button on the Web Query tab. In this dialog box, you configure how data is imported and formatted in the Spreadsheet report.

Table 5-3 provides a description of each option in the Web Query Options dialog box.

Figure 5-21: Formatting and import options for web queries are configured in this dialog box.

Table 5-3: Web Query Options Dialog Box

OPTION NAME	DESCRIPTION
Formatting	Imports the web site text as plain text, rich text, or HTML. Selecting Plain Text Formatting removes all formatting for the imported text. Selecting Rich Text Formatting maintains the formatting, but discards hyperlinks. The Full HTML Formatting option maintains the formatting and the hyperlinks.
Import <PRE> Blocks into Columns	Separates the data in the preformatted sections into columns. Uncheck this option to load the data into a single cell.
Treat Consecutive Delimiters as One	Ignores additional delimiters between data fields. Only available when the Import <PRE> Blocks into Columns option is checked.
Use the Same Import Settings for the Entire Selection	Imports preformatted sections using the same settings for all selections. Uncheck this option to have Excel determine the best settings. Only available when the Import <PRE> Blocks into Columns option is checked.
Disable Date Recognition	Disables date or text data from being formatted as a Date field in the Spreadsheet report.
Disable Web Query Redirections	Disables automatic web query redirections within the Web Query dialog box.

Connecting to Access Database Tables and Views

There are two ways to connect to an Access database. You can either use the From Access button or the Microsoft Query program. The From Access button is conveniently located on the Get External Data tab, whereas the Microsoft Query program is positioned in a slightly less convenient location, as a menu item under the From Other Sources button. The From Access button enables you to create either a Spreadsheet report or a PivotTable report from a single table or view in a selected Access database. However, unlike the Microsoft Query program, the From Access button does not provide support for querying multiple tables, using parameters, or running SQL queries. So, unless you have very simple requirements (such as pulling all the records from a single table in an Access database), you'll need to use the Microsoft Query program to connect to the Access database (which is covered in Chapter 6).

TIP If you are not skilled with developing SQL queries outside of the Microsoft Access program but need to query multiple tables for your Excel report, you could also create a view within the Access database that pulls only selected fields and records from a specified set of tables.

To connect to a single database table or view for your Excel report, follow these steps:

1. From Excel, choose Data → From Access to open the Select Data Source dialog box. Locate the file that you want to connect to for your report. In Figure 5-22, I located the Access database Marketing Analysis.

2. Click the file to select it and then click Open to connect to the database.

3. If the database is protected by a password, the Database Password dialog box in Figure 5-23 appears. Enter the password here and click OK to continue.

4. When the Select Table dialog box in Figure 5-24 appears, click a table or query to select it, and then click the OK button to connect to that database table or query.

5. When the Import Data dialog box in Figure 5-25 appears, select the type of report that you want to create and click the OK button.

Figure 5-22: Locate the Access database that you want to open from this dialog box.

Figure 5-23: If the Access database is protected by a password, it must be entered here.

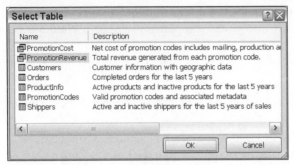

Figure 5-24: You can connect to a table or a view from this dialog box.

Figure 5-25: The last step in connecting to an Access database is choosing what type of report to use for the selected table or view.

That's all there is to connecting to Access databases using the From Access button. Like the other types of external data sources in this chapter, you can right-click the report and select Refresh from the pop-up menu to update the report with the most recent information in the selected Access database table.

Connecting to SQL Database Tables and Views

There are two ways to connect to an SQL database. You can either use the From SQL Server menu item or the Microsoft Query program, both of which are located under the From Other Sources button in the Get External Data tab. The From SQL Server button is designed for very simple operations; anything beyond connecting to and extracting all the data from a single database table or view must be performed using the Microsoft Query program.

CROSS-REFERENCE Read Chapter 6 to learn more about advanced SQL database connection options where you can import data from multiple tables, use stored procedures, set up parameter queries, and filter data from one or more tables.

In Figure 5-26, I illustrate how the From SQL Server connection option extracts data from a single database table or view into an Excel report running on a Windows PC with Excel 2007.

To connect to a single database table or view for your Excel report, follow these steps:

1. From Excel, choose Data → From Other Sources → From Microsoft SQL Server to bring up the Data Connection Wizard.

2. Enter in the name of the SQL Server that you want to connect to in the Server Name field and then enter the security credentials in the Log On Credentials section, as shown in Figure 5-27.

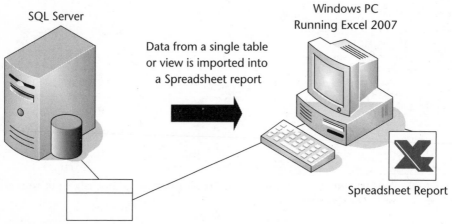

Figure 5-26: The From SQL Server menu item under the From Other Sources button imports all the data from a single database table or view.

Figure 5-27: Enter in the name of the SQL Server and select either Windows Authentication or enter in an SQL login and password to connect to the SQL Server.

3. After the SQL Server name and security credentials have been input, click the Next button.

4. When the Select Database and Table view of the Data Connection Wizard dialog box appears, choose a database from the database drop-down field at the top of the dialog box. Once you select a database from the drop-down list, notice that the tables in that database appear in the Tables pane of the dialog box. In Figure 5-28, I selected the AdventureWorksDW database and the Dim-ProductCategory table.

TIP Unchecking the Connect to a Specific Table option can significantly reduce the number of connection files that are required and enable you to skip the process of setting up a new connection file each time a new table or view is added to the database. When there is no default table, the report user is simply prompted to select a table or view when the data source connection file is used for an Excel report.

5. Click Next to continue to the Save Data Connection File and Finish dialog box view of the Data Connection Wizard or click Finish to automatically save the ODC file with the default connection information.

The Save Data Connection File and Finish dialog box view can be a valuable tool for storing additional information about the connection file. This might include a description of the data and where it resides. There are also fields for storing a friendly name and search keywords, which could be very useful in an organization where there are numerous types of software systems, databases, and connection files.

6. When the Import Data dialog box appears, select the type of report that you want to create and click OK.

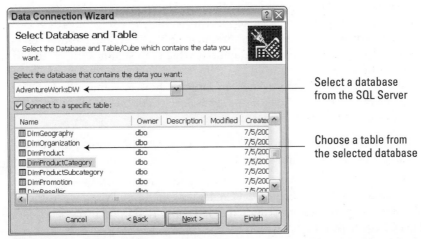

Figure 5-28: Choose a database and then a cube from this view of the Data Connection Wizard dialog box.

That's all there is to connecting to a single table or view from an SQL database. As I outlined at the beginning of this section, the principal drawbacks of this connection option are the inability to query more than a single table or even to restrict the number of rows or columns in a single table.

Creating a Data Source for an OLAP Cube

Accessing data from an Online Transaction Processing (OLTP) database is useful when Excel report updates need to be rapidly processed without numerous procedures. However, when a dataset becomes very large, you may encounter some problems, including the following:

- Long periods of time to import data into Excel
- Processing delays when the report is modified
- Database locking that interferes with normal operations of the enterprise system
- Adverse performance impact on users accessing the OLTP database or enterprise system

When any of these problems arise, you can either reduce the size of the dataset or build an Offline Analytical Processing (OLAP) cube of the data. An OLAP cube usually resolves all the performance, locking, and processing issues. However, setting up and maintaining an Analysis Server, where all the OLAP cubes are stored, can cost a lot of time and money.

CROSS-REFERENCE Read the online OLAP chapter available on this book's companion site at www.wiley.com/go/excelreporting/2007.

Like many of the options in this chapter, you can connect to an OLAP cube from either the Get External Data tab or from the Microsoft Query program. However, only the Microsoft Query program provides support for connecting to offline data cube files. The principal advantage of using the From Analysis Services option is that you do not have to specify a default cube for the database, which can significantly reduce the number of connection files that you need.

The following is a detailed, step-by-step example on how to connect to an OLAP cube from Microsoft Excel using the From Analysis Services option.

To connect to an OLAP cube, follow these steps:

1. From Excel, choose Data → From Other Sources → From Analysis Services to bring up the Data Connection Wizard.

2. Enter in the name of the Analysis Server that you want to connect to in the Server Name field. Leave the Log On Credentials set to use Windows Authentication (this is the only authentication method supported in Analysis Services) and click Next to continue.

3. When the Select Database and Table view of the Data Connection Wizard dialog box appears, choose a database from the database drop-down fields at the top of the dialog box. Once you select a database from the drop-down list, notice that the cubes in the database appear in the Tables pane of the dialog box. In Figure 5-29, I selected the AdventureWorks DW database and the AdventureWorks cube.

TIP Unchecking the Connect to a Specific Cube or Table option can significantly reduce the number of connection files that are required and enable you to skip the process of setting up a new connection file each time a new cube is added to the database. When there is no default cube, the report user is simply prompted to select a cube when the data source connection file is used for an Excel report.

4. Click Next to continue to the Save Data Connection File and Finish dialog box view of the Data Connection Wizard or click Finish to automatically save the ODC file with the default connection information.

   You can store information about the connection in the Save Data Connection File and Finish dialog box view. This might include a description of the data and where it resides. This dialog box also has fields for storing a friendly name and search keywords. If you work in an organization with numerous types of software system, database, and connection files, this information might be very valuable for helping other personnel to locate and recognize the purpose of connection files.

5. When the Import Data dialog box appears, select the type of report that you want to create and click OK.

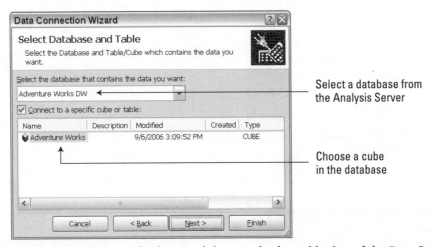

Figure 5-29: Choose a database and then a cube from this view of the Data Connection Wizard dialog box.

You'll notice in the last step (selecting the type of report) that you can only choose from a PivotTable report or a PivotTable and PivotChart report. The Table option (Spreadsheet report) is not available, because the data in the cube has been summarized to show only the aggregates. Read the online chapter on OLAP for more information about OLAP data cubes.

Trying It Out in the Real World

Jean Trenary, the information services manager at AdventureWorks, was very impressed with your demonstration on connecting to external data sources from Excel. Although Jean is doing quite well with rolling out the Excel-based reporting solution, she's concerned that non-technical managers may have a difficult time in setting up their own connections to the AdventureWorksDW database. And because there isn't an OLAP-based solution in place yet, Jean has asked Dan Wilson to create several new SQL database views that users can connect to for their own reports. You are charged with showing the non-technical team how to connect to these views to build PivotTable reports. Dan has already provided you with a sample query that creates the View-ProductSoldProfile database view that you should use for your demonstration.

```
CREATE VIEW ViewProductSoldProfile AS
SELECT EnglishProductName             AS 'ProductName',
       Color                          AS 'Color',
       Status                         AS 'Status',
       EnglishProductSubcategoryName  AS 'Subcategory',
       EnglishProductCategoryName     AS 'Category',
       OrderQuantity                  AS 'Qty Ordered'
FROM FactInternetSales fact
INNER JOIN DimProduct prod
       ON fact.ProductKey =
          prod.ProductKey
INNER JOIN DimProductSubcategory subc
       ON prod.ProductSubcategoryKey =
          subc.ProductSubcategoryKey
INNER JOIN DimProductCategory catg
       ON subc.ProductCategoryKey =
          catg.ProductCategoryKey
```

ON THE WEB   You can download the **ViewProductSoldProfile.sql file to your computer from the web site** www.wiley.com/go/excelreporting/2007.

Getting Down to Business

After you download the ViewProductSoldProfile.sql file to your computer, follow these steps to complete the exercise:

1. Create the view in the AdventureWorksDW database by opening and running the file from Microsoft SQL Server Management Studio. If you don't have access to this program, you can also use the Execute SQL dialog box in the Microsoft Query program (see Chapter 9 for more information about using this dialog box).

2. From Excel, choose Data → From Other Sources → From SQLServer to bring up the Data Connection Wizard.

3. Enter in the name of the SQL Server and security credentials and click Next to continue.

4. When the Select Database and Table view of the Data Connection Wizard dialog box appears, choose the AdventureWorksDW database from the Database drop-down field. After that, select the ViewProductSoldProfile view in the Tables pane, as shown in Figure 5-30. Click Finish to continue.

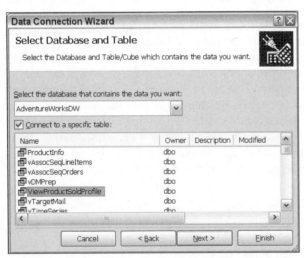

Figure 5-30: Select the ViewProductSoldProfile view from the list of available tables and views.

5. When the Import Data dialog box appears, select PivotTable and click OK to import the data into a new PivotTable report.

WATCH THE VIDEO Watch the ch0501_video.avi video to see how the SQL database view is created from Excel and how the data is imported into a PivotTable report using the From SQL Server option at www.wiley.com/go/ excelreporting/2007.

Reviewing What You Did

I used this exercise to demonstrate how SQL database views could be used to get data that would normally require report users to join tables or build SQL queries. The database views can be a neat alternative to training non-technical users (who probably aren't all that interested in learning SQL anyway). As you can see from this example, it's very easy for users to connect to the table for their reports. They could also use the Microsoft Query Wizard (covered in Chapter 7) to add simple filters on the table.

For more technical users, Chapters 8 and 9 are where I cover how to use the Microsoft Query program to connect to external data sources. This program provides many more robust functions and features for getting external data into your Excel report.

Chapter Review

This chapter outlined the various methods for getting source data into an Excel report using the buttons and menu items on the Get External Data tab. I started by showing you how Excel can connect to and import delimited and fixed-width files, while explaining how to define the data types of fields in a text file to ensure that the data is properly imported. After that, I covered how you can import data from Intranet and Internet web sources into a Spreadsheet report. Next, I covered how connections to Access and SQL Server database tables can be created. Following that, I provided some background and examples on connecting to OLAP cubes. I concluded with a real-world example that demonstrated how a database view could be created and subsequently used in a report using the From SQL Server menu item on the Get External Data tab.

CHAPTER 6

Retrieving External Data Using Microsoft Query

In this chapter, I show you how to connect to external data sources using Microsoft Query. This program provides powerful tools for accessing and importing external data into your Excel reports. Using Microsoft Query, you can simultaneously query multiple text files, execute sophisticated queries against Oracle, SQL Server, and Access databases, and connect to OLAP cubes (both Analysis Server cubes and offline cube files).

I start this chapter with a conceptual overview of the Microsoft Query program and its components. After that, I show you how to configure a connection that can simultaneously query multiple text files, as if the files were tables in a database. Next, I cover how to set up connections to Access and SQL Server databases. Following that, I review the procedures for connecting to offline and Analysis Server cubes. I conclude with a real-world example that provides some practice with querying multiple text files.

Looking at the Microsoft Query Program

Although the Microsoft Query program hasn't truly been updated in more than a decade, it still provides the most powerful tools for connecting external data sources to Excel reports. The program has numerous features and tools for making connections and building queries; enough for four chapters in this book. This chapter covers the how you can create connections using Microsoft Query. Chapter 7 covers the Query Wizard component, and Chapters 8 and 9 cover the main Microsoft Query program.

In Figure 6-1, I show a conceptual view of how the program components are separated, as well as the program body flow. Note the chapter number under the program components.

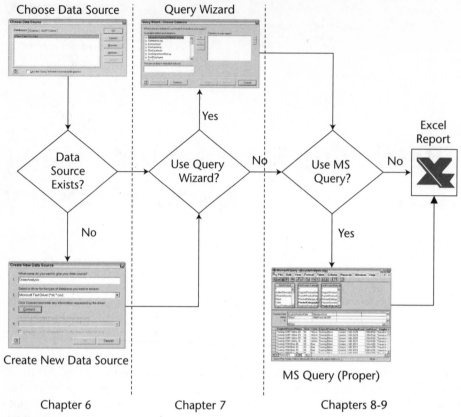

Figure 6-1: Conceptual diagram of the Microsoft Query program components with program flow.

The general flow of using the program can be described like this:

1. The Microsoft Query program is started by choosing Data → From Other Sources → From Microsoft Query.

2. Upon starting, the Choose Data Source dialog box appears. Here, you can either select an existing external data source connection or create a new one.

   ▪ If you decide to create a new connection by choosing <New Data Source> under the Databases or the OLAP Cubes tabs, the Create New Data Source dialog box is brought up. Here, you input the data driver, location, security credentials, and default object.

   ▪ If you decide to select an existing data source connection, then you just select one from the list under the Databases, Queries, or OLAP Cubes tabs.

3. Once the data connection is set up, you can use the Query Wizard program to build an SQL query or skip directly to the Microsoft Query program proper (note that the Microsoft Query program only works with OLTP sources, so

selection of a data source under the OLAP Cubes tab brings you to the Excel report step at the end of the diagram in Figure 6-1).

■ The Query Wizard provides some rudimentary tools for creating basic SQL queries, which can then be edited in the Microsoft Query program or used, as is, for the Excel report.

■ The main Microsoft Query program provides numerous tools for building and executing advanced queries. Here, you can also customize the query created in the Query Wizard program.

Once the SQL query is created, the returned dataset can be used in the Excel report.

Creating and Accessing Connections

In order to access the Microsoft Query program proper, you must first specify some type of data source to use in Microsoft Query. There are two ways to accomplish this. One is to select an existing data source in the Databases tab or an existing query in the Queries tab of the Choose Data Source dialog box (see Figure 6-2). The other is to create a new data source connection under the Databases tab.

NOTE You might see about six to eight additional data sources below <New Data Source> in your view of the Choose Data Source dialog box. These data sources are created when this feature is initially installed.

The connection information in the Choose Data Source dialog box is similar to what was set up in Chapter 5 using the Get External Data tab. The same connection elements (type of data, location, credentials, and object) are supplied, and new connections are automatically saved for future reports. The principal difference is that the Microsoft Query program provides a more robust toolkit for getting external data. And, unlike most of the buttons on the Get External Data tab, you are not limited to pulling all the rows and columns from only a single table or view.

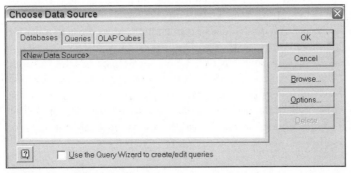

Figure 6-2: Before you can access the core Microsoft Query program, you must first choose an external data source to use.

Notice that there are three tabs at the top of the Choose Data Source dialog box in Figure 6-2. The first tab, Databases, provides tools for connecting to OLTP data sources, which include text files, databases, and Excel spreadsheets. The second tab, Queries, displays saved query files that you can bring up in the Microsoft Query program. The third tab, OLAP Cubes, provides tools for connecting to offline cube files and Analysis Server cubes. You can only create new connections from the Databases and OLAP Cube tabs; saved queries can only be opened from the Queries tab.

CROSS-REFERENCE Read Chapter 9 to learn more about building and saving queries in the Microsoft Query program.

In this chapter, I review how to add connections for the following types of data sources:

- Text files
- Access databases
- SQL databases
- OLAP cubes

Keep in mind that the Microsoft Query program proper can only be used with OLTP data sources; it is not possible to build SQL queries against OLAP data sources. This is because the data in an OLAP cube has already been aggregated and is stored in a completely different format. You can, however, build multidimensional (MDX) queries using SQL Server Analysis Services (SSAS) tools, such as the SQL Server Business Intelligence Development Studio program. This is outside the scope of this book, but you might want to pick up a copy of *Professional SQL Server Analysis Services 2005 With MDX* by Sivakumar Harinath and Stephen R. Quinn (ISBN: 0-7645-7918-5) if you want to learn more about this topic.

Data Source Name Connection Files

When you create an Excel report that accesses an external data source, the connection information is stored in the Excel report. This enables any user who has connectivity to the data source and sufficient security privileges to refresh that report data. In addition to storing the connection information in the Excel report, a copy of the connection information is also saved to a *Data Source Name* (DSN) file. This DSN file is what appears in the Choose Data Source dialog box each time you create an Excel report using the From Microsoft Query option. Thus, if you are regularly writing reports against the AdventureWorks DW database, you only have to set up the connection information one time. Once the connection file is created, you can just select it from the Choose Data Source dialog box.

WARNING Creating numerous external data sources can lead to confusion, especially if you have multiple environments for testing, development, and production that all use the same type of data source. Be sure to develop a smart naming convention that considers all these potential variables.

The connection information in the connection files is easy to interpret and can be modified through a simple text editor, such as Notepad. These files are covered individually, under each data source.

Using MS Query to Import Text Files

If you are regularly accessing a text file (or set of text files) that is created from an enterprise software program or some other type of software package, you do not have to manually import it into Excel each time a new file is available. In this situation, the connection information (filenames and location) can be stored in the Excel report. The updated data in the text files can be automatically imported *on-demand*, using a simple click of the mouse button, or *scheduled*, using a refresh interval that you define.

Querying Multiple Text Files

Unlike with the From Text button, you can query multiple text files and join them together as if they were tables in a database. As an example, in Figure 6-3, I show how the Orders.csv file could be joined to the Customers.csv and Products.csv files.

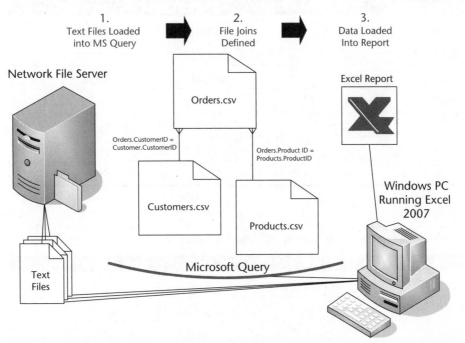

Figure 6-3: Multiple text files can be loaded into MS Query and joined as if they were database tables for use in a PivotTable or Spreadsheet report.

I've included a detailed, step-by-step example of how this works. However, before you start on the example, take a quick look at the structure and data of each file.

NOTE Whereas text files can be queried from Microsoft Query, there is no support of database functions. Remember, you're not accessing an SQL database, where these functions are defined and parsed by the query engine.

Table 6-1 shows the Orders.csv file. This file stores the order transactions with references to customer numbers and product numbers. The total order amount is stored in the Amount column. Notice that the customer and product names cannot be derived from this table alone. Like a normalized database, this file has foreign keys; valid customer numbers are maintained in the Customers.csv file and valid product numbers are maintained in the Products.csv file.

The structure and contents of the Customers.csv file are stored in Table 6-2. Notice that this file contains much more detailed information about the customer than the Order file. Also notice that there are some customers in this table that are not in the Orders table.

Table 6-1: Structure and Contents of the Orders.csv File

ORDERNUM	CUSTOMERNUM	PRODUCTNUM	AMOUNT
3200	951	WDG01	121.45
3201	2073	GDG03	312.12
3202	89	WDG06	98.76
3203	97	RTH08	10.22
3204	1047	RTH02	13.88
3205	951	RTH02	13.88
3206	89	GSG03	312.12

Table 6-2: Structure and Contents of the Customers.csv File

CUSTOMERNUM	NAME	CITY	STATE
89	Tom Hermans	Naples	FL
97	Jane Wu	San Mateo	CA
108	Megan Gignac	Hickory	NC
951	Mike Miklosovic	Kansas City	MO
1023	Marty Ryerson	Vienna	WV
1047	Vanessa Sevigny	Boston	MA
2073	John Sheehy	Kalamazoo	MI

In Table 6-3, I show the contents of the Products.csv file, where the product numbers and product descriptions are maintained.

ON THE WEB You can download the Orders.csv, Customers.csv, and Products.csv files to your computer from www.wiley.com/go/ excelreporting/2007.

To create a connection file for these text files, follow these steps:

1. Create a folder called OrderAnalysis in the root directory of your C drive.

2. Download and save the Orders.csv, Customers.csv, and Products.csv files to the OrderAnalysis directory you created in step 1.

3. Starting with a new workbook in Excel, choose Data → From Other Sources → From Microsoft Query to bring up Choose Data Source dialog box.

4. Select <New Data Source> under the Databases tab in the Choose Data Source dialog box and click OK.

5. Type **OrderAnalysis** into the data source name field, select Microsoft Text Driver (*.txt, *.csv) as the driver for the type of database you are accessing, and click the Connect button (see Figure 6-4).

WARNING You must select the Microsoft Text Driver (*.txt, *.csv) and not another driver, such as the "Text" driver to import the data through the Microsoft Query program.

Make sure that the name you choose for the connection file in the Create New Data Source dialog box is meaningful. It will appear in the Choose Data Source dialog box each time a new Excel report is created from an external data source.

Table 6-3: Structure and Contents of the Products.csv File

PRODUCTNUM	PRODUCTDESC
GDG02	Green gadget
GDG03	Red gadget
RTH02	Nickel ratchet
RTH08	Chrome ratchet
WDG01	Standard widget

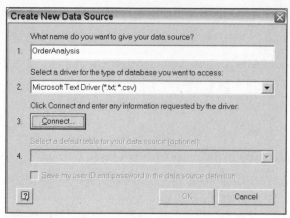

Figure 6-4: Select the Microsoft Text data driver and enter a meaningful description for the type of text file data being accessed.

Setting the Directory

When you click the Connect button in the Create New Data Source dialog box, the ODBC Text Setup dialog box appears, as shown in Figure 6-5. Here, you can opt to use the My Documents default directory or choose a specific location that should be searched for importing one or more files into Excel. The location can be a local directory, a network share, or even an FTP site.

When determining the directory to use, keep in mind that you can configure the connection to import a single file from that location or prompt for a choice of files. Various types of text file types (fixed-width, comma-delimited, tab-delimited, and so on) can be stored in a single directory along with the column and data type definitions of each file.

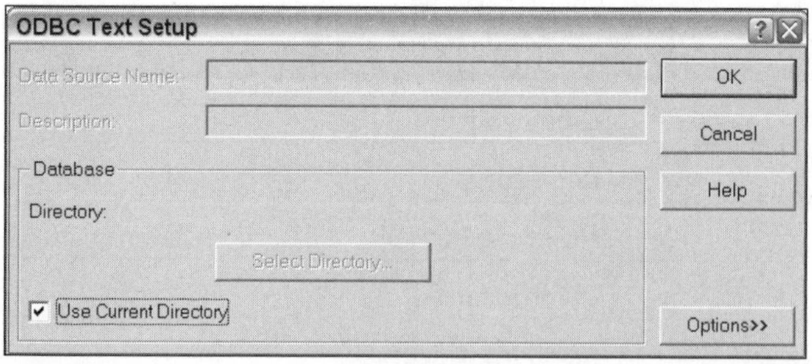

Figure 6-5: Uncheck the Use Current Directory box to specify a location for the text files.

WARNING Once a connection file is created it cannot be modified from Excel. If you want to change the location of the text files, you must either create a new connection or edit the DSN file from Windows using Notepad (covered later in this section).

To configure the connection to use the file directory for this example to C:\Order-Analysis, follow these steps:

1. In the ODBC Text Setup dialog box, uncheck Use Current Directory and click the Select Directory button to choose a specific location for importing the file.

2. When the Select Directory dialog box shown in Figure 6-6 appears, change the directory to C:\OrderAnalysis and click OK.

TIP You can also specify a Universal Naming Convention (UNC) share by clicking the Network button in the Select Directory dialog box.

3. In the ODBC Text Setup dialog box, click the Options button to reveal the bottom half of the ODBC Text Setup dialog box shown in Figure 6-7.

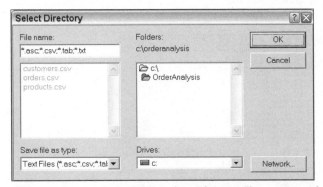

Figure 6-6: Locate the folder where the text files are stored and click OK.

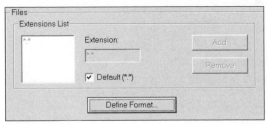

Figure 6-7: The file definitions for each file are defined here.

The extensions for files that will be scanned in a directory can be customized by unchecking Default (*.*). Once this box is unchecked, the Extension field opens, where you can type in new file extensions to look for in the Define Text Format dialog box (see Figure 6-8). You can also remove extensions by selecting them in the Extensions List pane and clicking Remove.

4. Click the Define Format button in Figure 6-7 to open the Define Text Format dialog box in Figure 6-8.

Defining the File Format

After a directory has been selected for importing the text files, the next optional step is to define the valid file formats. This step is optional, because all the files in the directory will appear as available in the Microsoft Query program when this data source is selected. If you only want files with particular extensions to be displayed, however, you can complete this step to read only the files with the extensions that you define.

The Tables pane in Figure 6-8 shows all the files in this directory for which a format file can be defined. If multiple files are saved in this directory, you can define formats for all of them from this dialog box. The file formats are saved to a Schema.ini file that is created in that same directory. The next section, "Supporting Files of Text File Connections," shows you what's stored in that file.

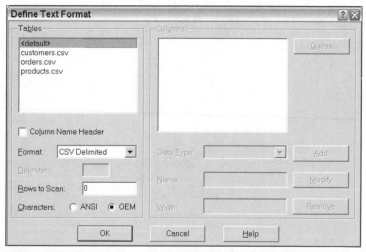

Figure 6-8: The column names and data types for each file in the Tables pane can be defined in this dialog box. These definitions are saved to a Schema.ini file, located in the same directory as the text files.

TIP Only files that have extensions displayed in the Extensions List pane in the ODBC Text Setup dialog box (refer to Figure 6-7) appear in the left Tables pane of Figure 6-8. You can remove these file extensions or create custom extensions using the Add and Remove buttons in the ODBC Text Setup dialog box. (Note that custom extensions cannot be more than three positions in length.)

The Column Name Header option box is checked when the field headings are included in the first row of the data. Use the Format field to select a file format for each file in the directory. You can choose from four types of formats from the Format drop-down list:

- **CSV Delimited:** Select this option when the data is comma-delimited.
- **Tab Delimited:** Select this option when the data is tab-delimited.
- **Custom Delimited:** Select this option when the data is delimited by something other than a tab or comma. If this option is selected, the Delimiter Character field is enabled, allowing you to enter a 1–5 position delimiter.
- **Fixed Length:** Select this option when the field is a fixed-width file (note that this option only appears when a file is selected in the Define Text Format dialog box).

The Rows to Scan field controls the number of fields scanned when previewing the data. I suggest leaving it set to the default of 25. ANSI and OEM determine the character set that is used for reading the data. In most cases, this shouldn't matter and you can ignore it.

The Guess function is similar to the Import Wizard you saw in the last section. Basically, it guesses at field information, including the data type and length of each field. This button can be a real time-saver, but be sure to carefully review the calculated data types and field lengths.

NOTE Guess can be used only for delimited files. Fixed-width files require that you define the data type, field width, and field name for each field in the file.

Follow these steps to define field formats for the Orders.csv, Customers.csv, and Products.csv files:

1. Select Orders.csv, check the Column Name Header, and click the Guess button.
2. Change the data type from Char to LongChar for the first three fields: Order-Num, CustomerNum, and ProductNum. Set the data type of Amount to Float.

WARNING A software bug in Microsoft Excel requires that fields with a data type of Char be set to LongChar. Note that not all users have this software bug, so it's likely a characteristic of how other programs are installed or whether the Microsoft Excel program was installed new or upgraded from a previous release. You might want to try using the Char data type, and if it doesn't work then try setting the data type to LongChar. Also, be sure to verify that you click Modify after each field is changed from Char to LongChar; otherwise the change is not processed. For this example, you must click Modify *four* times (one time for each column), not just once. You can verify the change is completed by checking that the Width field is blank and disabled, as shown in Figure 6-9 for the Month field. If you do want to use the Char data type, you'll need to edit the Schema.ini file (explained in the "Understanding the Schema.ini File" section of this chapter).

3. Select Customers.csv, check the Column Name Header, and click the Guess button. Change the data type from Char to LongChar for all four fields: CustomerNum, Name, City, and State.

4. Select Products.csv, check the Column Name Header, and click the Guess button. Change the data type from Char to LongChar for ProductNum and ProductDesc.

5. After the fields have been updated, click OK in this dialog box and OK again when you are returned to the ODBC Text Setup dialog box.

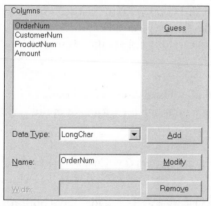

Figure 6-9: Ensure that the file format is accepted by changing the data type of the fields Month, Type, Category, and AuthCode from Char to LongChar.

TIP To ensure that the source data has been properly configured, click Define Format again and verify that the field formatting settings are still present. If you see an error message, you did something wrong and you'll need to repeat steps 1–5.

6. The Create New Data Source dialog box appears as shown in Figure 6-10. Notice that the file directory of C:\OrderAnalysis is shown next to Connect.

TIP If Select a Default Table for Your Data Source is set to blank in Figure 6-10, the Microsoft Query and the Query Wizard programs will both display a dialog box that shows a list of all the text files in that directory whenever that connection is selected for an Excel report. This can be useful when you want to join multiple text files together and query them, as if they were tables in a database.

You have now created a data source connection that scans the files in the Order-Analysis directory at the root of your C drive. You can now use it for an Excel report. Note that it will also continue to appear in the Choose Data Source dialog box as a valid external data source connection for future reports (see Figure 6-11). When you no longer plan to use this data source, you can use the Delete button to remove it.

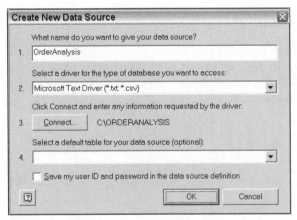

Figure 6-10: Leave the default table blank to use a file directory for the connection, or select a file to associate the connection to a specific text file.

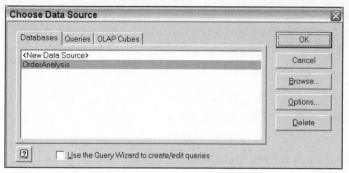

Figure 6-11: The new DSN file appears for this text file as a valid selection in this dialog box each time an Excel report is created from an external data source.

Supporting Files of Text File Connections

A Schema.ini file and a connection file are created for text file connections. This is unlike most other data sources where only a connection file is created. The Schema.ini file is necessary because text files cannot store field information such as field data type and field width. In this section, I review both the Schema.ini and the connection files contents, providing a brief description of each line.

Understanding the Schema.ini File

Each time Excel connects to the external text file data source, it reads the Schema.ini file that is saved in that same directory to determine the data type and name of each field. You can add or edit the values in this file using Notepad. Here is the Schema.ini file for the text files example used earlier in this section:

```
 1. [customers.csv]
 2. ColNameHeader=True
 3. Format=CSVDelimited
 4. MaxScanRows=0
 5. CharacterSet=OEM
 6. Col1=CUSTOMERNUM LongChar
 7. Col2=NAME LongChar
 8. Col3=CITY LongChar
 9. Col4=STATE LongChar
10. [orders.csv]
11. ColNameHeader=True
12. Format=CSVDelimited
13. MaxScanRows=0
14. CharacterSet=OEM
```

```
15. Col1=ORDERNUM LongChar
16. Col2=CUSTOMERNUM LongChar
17. Col3=PRODUCTNUM LongChar
18. Col4=AMOUNT Float
19. [products.csv]
20. ColNameHeader=True
21. Format=CSVDelimited
22. MaxScanRows=0
23. CharacterSet=OEM
23. Col1=PRODUCTNUM LongChar
25. Col2="PRODUCT DESC" LongChar
```

As you can see, many of the lines are similar to the information you entered in the various connection dialog boxes. Line 1 identifies that the first text file data source is for the Customers.csv file. Line 2 indicates that the first row of the data in the Customers.csv file contains column headings. The next line defines the file format, comma-delimited. Line 4 defines the number of preview rows, and line 5 defines the character set as OEM. Lines 6–9 define the various columns, names, and data types. The same type of information is repeated for the Orders.csv file in lines 10–18 and for the Products.csv file in lines 19–25.

Any file in the selected directory with a valid extension type can appear in the Define Text Format dialog box. If you were to define file formats for additional files in the OrderAnalysis directory, all of these settings would be stored in the same Schema.ini file that you see here. An entry is simply created for the new text file with the corresponding formatting and field options listed below it.

NOTE Changing the Schema.ini file has an immediate effect on the next refresh of an Excel report. For example, if you change the data type of Amount to Integer, save the updated Schema.ini, and then refresh the PivotTable report, Amount is treated as an integer and decimals will no longer appear in that column.

CUSTOMIZING THE SCHEMA.INI FILE

I've received several reports of a software bug in the Define Text Format dialog box (see Figure 6-8) that prevents columns from being defined with a Character (Char) data type; thus, I recommend setting the data type of fields to LongChar instead of Char. Keep in mind that not all users seem to have this problem, so by all means you should use the Char data type if it works okay for you. You can also edit the Schema.ini file to use a Character data type (thanks to Marty Ryerson for his help in figuring this out) by replacing LongChar with Char Width n, where n represents the number of characters for the character field.

Viewing the Connection File for a Text File

The DSN connection file stores the connection information used to access the external data source. It is used only for creating new reports and appears in the Choose Data Source dialog box each time you create an Excel report from an external data source. Deleting the connection file has no effect on existing reports that initially used it for connecting to an external data source. Remember, connection information is saved in the Excel report; the DSN file is there as a convenience for you. You can simply select it instead of re-entering all the connection information each time you create a report using that data source.

Text file DSNs are stored in this directory:

C:\Program Files\Common Files\ODBC\Data Sources

Many of the lines in the connection file correspond to options that were selected when the data source was defined. Here is connection file for the OrderAnalysis example that used earlier in this section:

```
1. [ODBC]
2. DBQ=C:\ORDERANALYSIS
3. DefaultDir=C:\ORDERANALYSIS
4. Driver={Microsoft Text Driver (*.txt; *.csv)}
5. DriverId=27
6. FIL=text
7. MaxBufferSize=2048
8. MaxScanRows=8
9. PageTimeout=5
10. SafeTransactions=0
11. Threads=3
12. UserCommitSync=Yes
```

Just like the Schema.ini file, many of the lines in this file correspond to options and fields selected when you initially set up the data source. There are a couple of lines that are worth highlighting. First, line 3 controls the default directory that is searched when this connection file is selected. Line 4 shows the data driver that is used with this data source. Had a default file been selected in the last field of the Create New Data Source dialog box (see Figure 6-10), it would be stored in the last line of this file.

NOTE Remember that you are not able to change any lines in this connection file from Excel. However, you can edit the file using a program, such as Notepad.

Connecting to Access Databases

The Microsoft Query program provides a robust toolkit for connecting to Access databases. Unlike the From Access button, this program provides tools for applying filters to a single table, querying multiple database tables, and creating parameter queries.

To create a connection to an Access database, follow these steps:

1. From Excel, choose Data → From Other Sources → From Microsoft Query to bring up the Choose Data Source dialog box.

2. When the Choose Data Source dialog box appears, select <New Data Source> and click OK.

3. Type a meaningful name into data source name field, select Microsoft Access 12.0 Driver (*.mdb, *accdb) as the data driver type, and click Connect.

   If the connection to the Access database is not to a specific table or view, then the name of the database is probably sufficient for the data source name. In Figure 6-12, I entered Marketing Database as the data source name.

   After you click Connect in Figure 6-12, the ODBC Microsoft Access Setup dialog box in Figure 6-13 appears.

The ODBC Microsoft Access Setup dialog box shown in Figure 6-13 provides tools for selecting, creating, repairing, and compacting Access databases. Clicking the Select button opens the Select Database dialog box (see Figure 6-15), where you can browse your local computer or network for an Access database to select as your external data source. Clicking Create brings up the Create Database dialog box, where you can create a new Access database. I can't envision any scenario where one might want to create an Access database from this dialog box — or at this juncture — so I suggest that you ignore that button. The Repair and Compact buttons do just what they say; they repair and compact Access databases. Again, this type of function is probably best handled through the Access program and not from this dialog box.

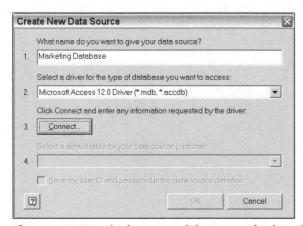

Figure 6-12: Type in the name of the Access database in the data source name field and choose Microsoft Access 12.0 for the type of driver when creating a connection to an Access 2007 database.

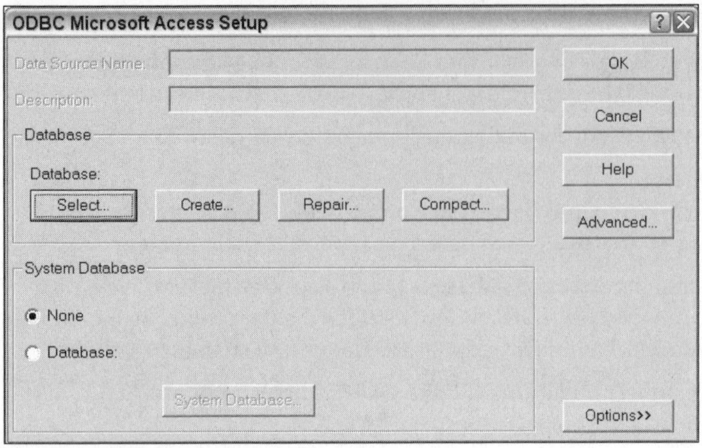

Figure 6-13: Click Select in this dialog box to connect to a specific Access database.

Clicking the Advanced button brings up the Set Advanced Options dialog box (see Figure 6-14) where you can specify a user login and password for the connection. There are also other advanced connection options, such as the maximum buffer size, page timeout, and default threads that be modified from this dialog box. If the Access database is protected by a user login and password, enter that information here in the Default Authorization section.

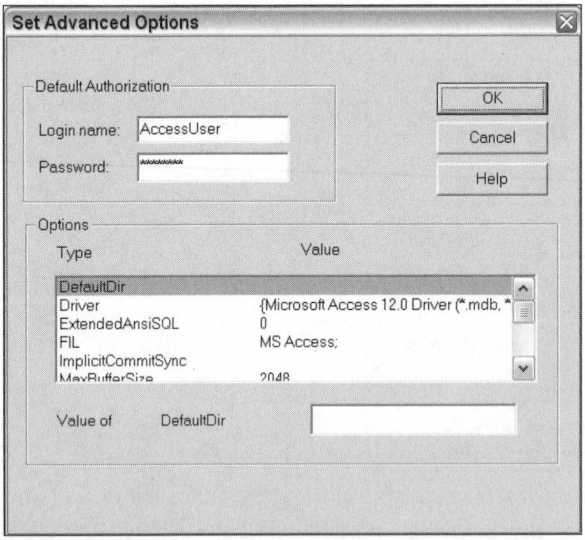

Figure 6-14: If the Access database is protected by a login and password, enter that information into the Login Name and Password fields of this dialog box.

NOTE A Microsoft Access 12.0 database can be protected by both a database password and a login account and password. This driver program only uses one of these methods for authenticating to the Access database. If both of these security elements are in place, enter in the Access user login and password. If only the database password is being used, enter Admin in the login name and enter the database password in the Password field.

To select an Access database and complete the setup of the external data source connection, follow these steps:

1. From the ODBC Microsoft Access Setup dialog box, click Select to open the Select Database dialog box. Browse your local computer or network for the Access database that you want to open. Click the Access database file to select it and then click OK to open it. In Figure 6-15, I selected the Marketing Database.

2. If the database requires a user login and password or a database password, click the Advanced button and enter in the user login and password for the Access database in the Default Authorization section of the Set Advanced Options dialog box.

3. Click OK to close the ODBC Microsoft Access Setup dialog box and return to the Create New Data Source dialog box.

4. If there is a default table or view that will be associated with this connection, select it in the Select a Default Table for Your Data Source drop-down field and click OK to close the close the Create New Data Source dialog box.

You have now created a connection to an Access database. The connection will continue to appear in the Choose Data Source dialog box as a valid external data source connection for future reports. When you no longer plan to use this data source, you can use the Delete button to remove it.

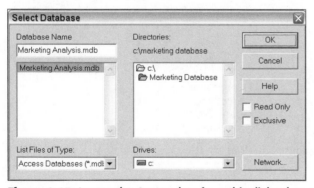

Figure 6-15: Locate the Access data from this dialog box and click OK to select it as your external data source.

Connecting to SQL Databases

Many enterprise software programs use SQL Server and Oracle databases to store critical business information. These programs sometimes have reporting and query tools for extracting data. However, as the database and reporting technology advances, many of these enterprise software publishers are unable to stay competitive with the cutting-edge report-development software applications in the marketplace. As a result of this and several other reasons identified in the Introduction, many organizations access the database directly, using more innovative and powerful reporting tools such as Excel Reports.

Figure 6-16 illustrates how Excel can access information from an enterprise system's OLTP database to instantaneously update reports. In this situation, the data can be pulled directly from the database and instantly imported into the report.

This section tells you how you can create connections to SQL databases using the Microsoft Query program. It provides a step-by-step example on how to create a connection to the AdventureWorks DW database that is included with Microsoft SQL Server 2005.

Establishing a Connection to an SQL Server

When you create a connection to an SQL database, you must specify the server and default database. After that, you can also assign a default database table or view to the data source. This option can be useful if you are not familiar with SQL programming or you want to use the Query Wizard to generate basic SQL statements.

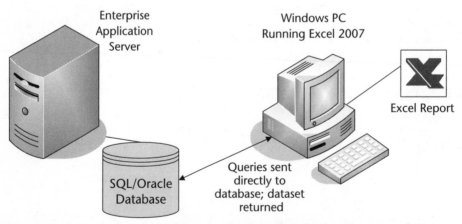

Figure 6-16: Excel can extract information from an OLTP database in near real-time.

CROSS-REFERENCE If you want to pull all the rows and columns from an SQL database, you might want to use the From SQL Server option, located under the From Other Data Source button on the Get External Data Tab. Read the section "Connecting to SQL Database Tables and Views" in Chapter 5 for more information about using this method.

To create a connection to an SQL Server database, follow these steps:

1. From Excel, choose Data → From Other Sources → From Microsoft Query to bring up the Choose Data Source dialog box.

2. When the Create New Data Source dialog box appears, select <New Data Source> and click OK.

3. Type **AdventureWorks Data Warehouse** into the data source name field, select SQL Native Client as the data driver, and click the Connect button (see Figure 6-17).

Be sure to enter a meaningful name, because it will appear in the Choose Data Source dialog box each time a new Excel report is created from an external data source. Here are some of the data elements you might want to include in the name:

- SQL Server
- Default database
- Default database table or view

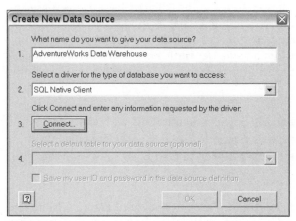

Figure 6-17: Type a meaningful name for the data source and choose SQL Server for the type of driver.

Authenticating to the Database

After selecting an SQL Server driver and clicking the Connect button, the SQL Server Login dialog box appears. Here, you enter in the name of the SQL server and the authentication credentials.

> **NOTE** In order to determine whether a particular user or SQL login can access a database or database object, authentication to the server is performed first.

You can choose from two types of authentication methods:

- **Trusted Security:** The Windows domain user account or group and password of the user is used to authenticate to the SQL server.

- **SQL Login Account and Password:** A specific user account and password is specified to authenticate to the SQL server.

> **NOTE** The SQL Server must be configured to SQL Server and Windows Authentication Mode (also referred to as Mixed Mode) in order for an SQL login to be accepted. You can enable this mode in the Security page of the Server Properties dialog box.

In a general sense, one authentication method isn't better than another, although Windows Authentication is more secure. The SQL Server authentication mode can be useful in some situations, because it's easier to distribute PivotTable reports without having to worry about getting each user access to the SQL database. However, using this method is less secure. Of course, determining what method is best for your organization requires an evaluation of security policies and the existing network, operating system, and database security already in force. Depending on the results of this analysis and future goals, one of these authentication methods might be preferable over the other.

> **WARNING** If you opt to use an SQL login authentication method, I recommend that you do not use the sa account. Instead, consider setting up and using an SQL login account that is assigned to the db_datareader role on the applicable databases.

When the SQL Server Login dialog box appears, as shown in Figure 6-18, follow these steps to connect to the SQL server and set the default database to Adventure-WorksDW:

1. In the Server field, type the SQL Server name or click the drop-down arrow to select an SQL Server from the list.

NEW FEATURE If you are using SQL Server Authentication, you are now able to change the password for the account from this dialog box. Just click Change Password and enter the new password in the New Password and Confirm New Password fields.

2. Select an authentication method by either clicking the Use Trusted Connection check box or providing an SQL Server Login ID and Password.

3. Click the Options button to display the Options section of the SQL Server Login dialog box, and then select the AdventureWorksDW database from the Database drop-down box.

4. Verify that your dialog box looks similar to the one shown in Figure 6-18 and click OK.

   You should now be returned to the Create New Data Source dialog box shown in Figure 6-19. Notice that the default database now appears next to the Connect button. You can select a default table or view from the Select a Default Table for Your Data Source drop-down box.

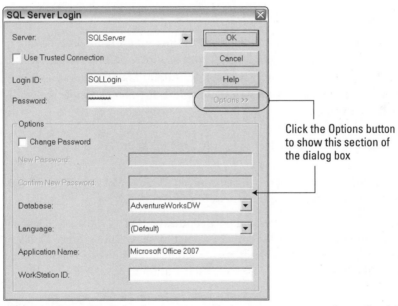

Figure 6-18: In this dialog box, you specify the SQL server, security credentials, and default database for the DSN file.

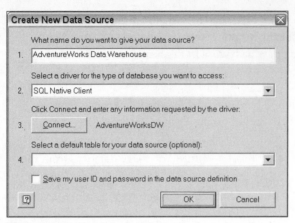

Figure 6-19: The default database selected earlier now appears next to Connect.

If you plan to extract data from the database using an SQL query, leave the Select a Default Table for Your Data Source drop-down box blank. Otherwise, select the default database table or view that should be used for this data source.

WARNING Object owners are not displayed in the Default Table drop-down box. Thus, the object owner (usually "dbo") is not explicitly defined. Rather, it is implicitly set by selecting an object. For example, if there are two database tables that have the same name but different owners, the names simply appear twice in the drop-down box.

5. For this example, leave the Select a Default Table for Your Data Source box blank.

6. If you are using an SQL Server login account, check Save My User ID and Password in the Data Source Definition check box and click OK.

You have now created a connection to the AdventureWorksDW database. The connection will appear in the Choose Data Source dialog box shown in Figure 6-20 whenever you create an Excel report that has an external data source. When you no longer plan to use this data source, you can click the Delete button to remove it from the list of valid data sources.

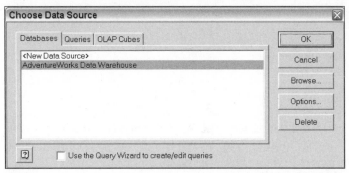

Figure 6-20: The new DSN file appears for this SQL database as a valid selection in this dialog box each time an Excel report is created from an external data source.

CROSS-REFERENCE Read Chapter 9 to learn how Excel reports can extract data from multiple SQL databases located on multiple SQL servers.

Looking at Database Connection Files

The connection information for accessing a particular database on a particular database server is stored in the connection file. This connection file is used only for creating new reports and appears in the Choose Data Source dialog box each time that you create a new Excel report from an external data source. Deleting the connection file has no effect on existing reports that initially used it to connect to an SQL database. Remember, connection information is saved in the Excel report; the connection file is only used to save you time by not having to re-enter the connection information each time you create a new report for the same data source.

Database connection files are stored in this directory:

C:\Program Files\Common Files\ODBC\Data Sources

This section provides examples of connection files for both types of authentication methods for the AdventureWorks Data Warehouse example.

Viewing the DSN File for a Trusted Connection

Many of the lines correspond to options that were selected when the data source was defined. Here is the AdventureWorks Data Warehouse file that uses a Trusted Connection authentication method:

```
1. [ODBC]
2. DRIVER=SQL Native Client
3. SERVER=SQLServerName
4. Trusted_Connection=Yes
5. APP=Microsoft Office 2007
6. WSID=WorkStationComputerName
7. DATABASE=AdventureWorksDW
```

Lines 1 and 2 define the ODBC data driver. The SQL Server and database name you specified in Figure 6-18 appear in lines 3 and 7, respectively. If you opted to use a Trusted Connection, line 4 is set to Yes.

Viewing the DSN File for an SQL Login

The connection file for an SQL Server authentication method is similar to a Trusted Connection authentication method. The main difference is that the Trusted Connection line is removed. Also, if the Save My User ID and Password in the Data Source Definition option is checked, the SQL login and password are also stored in the last two lines of this file.

```
1. [ODBC]
2. DRIVER=SQL Native Client
3. SERVER=SQLServerName
4. APP=Microsoft Office 2007
5. WSID=WorkStationComputerName
6. DATABASE=AdventureWorksDW
7. [Microsoft Office]
8. UID=SQLLoginAccount
9. PWD=Password
```

Lines 1 and 2 define the ODBC data driver. The SQL Server and database name you specified in the SQL Server Login dialog box appear in lines 3 and 6, respectively. Lines 8–9 appear only when the Save My User ID and Password option is checked.

> **WARNING** If you are using an SQL Authentication method, you can see how easy it is to locate the User ID and password in the text file. If security is a concern, do not save these credentials to the DSN file.

Creating a Data Source for an OLAP Cube

Accessing data from an Online Transaction Processing (OLTP) database is useful when Excel report updates need to be rapidly processed without numerous procedures. However, when a dataset becomes very large, you may encounter some problems, including the following:

- Long periods of time to import the data into Excel
- Processing delays when the report is modified
- Database locking that interferes with normal operations of the enterprise system
- Adverse performance impact on users accessing the OLTP database or enterprise system

When any of these problems arise, you can either reduce the size of the data set or build an Offline Analytical Processing (OLAP) cube of the data. An OLAP cube usually resolves all the performance, locking, and processing issues. However, setting up and maintaining an Analysis Server, where all the OLAP cubes are stored, can cost a lot of time and money.

Establishing a Connection to an Analysis Server

When you connect to an OLAP cube using the Microsoft Query program, you must specify an Analysis Server, a database, and a target cube. This is a bit different than the From Analysis Server option on the Get External Data tab, where a target cube is not required. If you have several OLAP cubes, choose Data → From Other Sources → From Analysis Server for creating your connection files, because this method enables you to reduce the number of connection files that must be set up; report users can simply select a cube when the connection file is used, instead of having to set up a connection file for each cube.

One advantage of the Microsoft Query program over the From Analysis Services option is that you can connect to offline data cube files. Note that Microsoft Excel can create offline data cube files from online Analysis Server cubes.

CROSS-REFERENCE Read the online OLAP chapter for information on creating offline cube files.

The following is a detailed, step-by-step example on how to connect to the AdventureWorks OLAP cube using the AdventureWorks DW database that is available with Microsoft SQL Server 2005.

To create a connection to the AdventureWorks cube, follow these steps:

1. From Excel, choose Data → From Other Sources → From Microsoft Query to bring up the Choose Data Source dialog box.

2. When the Create New Data Source dialog box appears, click the OLAP Cubes tab toward the top of the dialog box, select <New Data Source>, and click OK.

3. Type **AdventureWorks Cube** into the data source name field, select Microsoft OLE DB Provider for Analysis Services 9.0 as the data driver, and click the Connect button (see Figure 6-21).

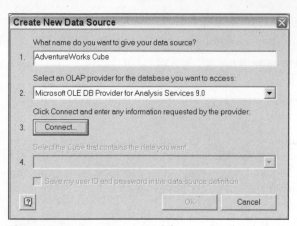

Figure 6-21: Type a meaningful name for the data source and choose SQL Server for the type of driver.

You choose the type of data driver and provide a name for the DSN in the Create New Data Source dialog box. The name should be meaningful because it will appear in the dialog box each time a new Excel report is created from an OLAP cube or cube file. Here are some of the data elements you might want to include in the name:

- Analysis Server
- Database
- Cube

NOTE Select the OLAP 8.0 driver for an SQL Server 2000 data cube and the OLAP 9.0 driver for SQL Server 2005 data cube.

Accessing the OLAP Cube

After you click the Connect button in the Create New Data Source dialog box, you are presented with the Multidimensional Connection dialog box. In this dialog box, you can choose to connect to an Analysis Server or browse for an OLAP cube file. Cube files can be created from an Analysis Server or from Microsoft Excel (as explained in the online OLAP chapter). Unless you are establishing an HTTP connection, you can leave the User ID and Password fields blank

NOTE Accessing an OLAP cube requires that the Windows login or Windows group be granted access to the cube in Analysis Services.

Follow these steps to connect to an Analysis Server and select the AdventureWorks cube in the AdventureWorks DW database:

1. Type the name of the Analysis Server that you want to access in the Server field and click Next, as shown in Figure 6-22.

2. The next view of the dialog box appears, showing all the valid databases on the Analysis Server. Select Adventure Works DW and click Finish, as shown in Figure 6-23.

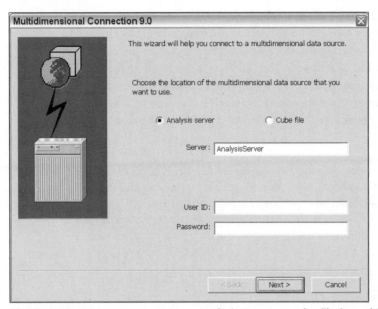

Figure 6-22: You can connect to an Analysis Server or cube file from this dialog box.

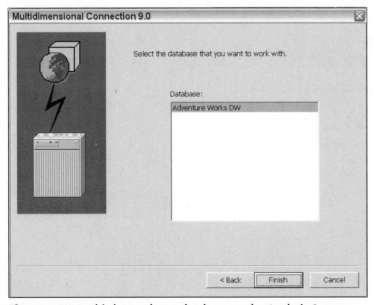

Figure 6-23: In this box, select a database on the Analysis Server.

You should now be returned to the Create New Data Source dialog box, as shown in Figure 6-24. Notice that the database you selected appears next to the Connect button.

3. Select the Adventure Works cube from the Select the Cube That Contains the Data You Want drop-down box and click OK.

WARNING You must select a cube from the drop-down box shown in Figure 6-24, otherwise the connection will fail. If you have numerous cubes and databases, consider using the From Analysis Server option under the Get External Data group described in the "Creating a Data Source for an OLAP Cube" section of Chapter 5, because this type of connection enables the user to specify a cube when the data source is selected. This can significantly reduce the number of connection files and the amount of time it takes to connect to an OLAP cube.

You have now created a connection for the AdventureWorks cube in the Adventure-Works DW database. The connection will appear under the OLAP Cubes tab in the Choose Data Source dialog box (as shown in Figure 6-25) whenever you create an Excel report that uses an OLAP cube. If you no longer plan to reference this data source, you can click the Delete button to remove it from the list of valid data sources.

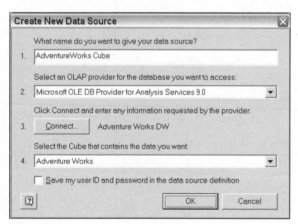

Figure 6-24: You must select a cube to create this connection.

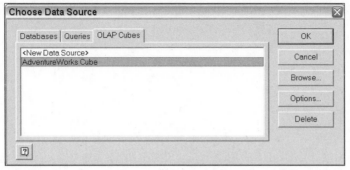

Figure 6-25: The new DSN file for this OLAP cube appears as a valid selection in this dialog box each time an Excel report is created from an external data source.

Supporting Files of OLAP Cube Connections

The DSN connection file stores the connection information for accessing a particular OLAP cube in a specified OLAP database and Analysis Server. It is only used for creating new reports and appears in the Choose Data Source dialog box each time you create a new Excel report with an OLAP cube data source. Deleting the connection file has no effect on existing reports that initially used it to connect to an external data source. Remember, connection information is saved in the Excel report; the connection file is only used to keep you from having to re-enter the connection information each time you create a new report with the same data source.

OLAP cube connection files are stored in this directory:

C:\Documents and Settings\{User}\Application Data\Microsoft\Queries

Viewing the Connection File for an OLAP Cube

Many of the lines in the connection file correspond to options that were selected when the data source was defined. Here is the connection file for the AdventureWorks cube in the AdventureWorks DW database:

```
 1. QueryType=OLEDB
 2. Version=1
 3. CommandType=Cube
 4. Connection=Provider=MSOLAP.3;
 5. Cache Authentication=False;
 6. User ID="";
 7. Initial Catalog=Adventure Works DW;
 8. Data Source=SQLServerName;
 9. Impersonation Level=Impersonate;
10. Location=WorkStationID;
```

```
11. Mode=ReadWrite;
12. Protection Level=Pkt Privacy;
13. Auto Synch Period=20000;
14. Default Isolation Mode=0;
15. Default MDX Visual Mode=0;
16. MDX Compatibility=0;
17. MDX Unique Name Style=0;
18. Non Empty Threshold=0;
19. SQLQueryMode=Calculated;
20. Safety Options=1;
21. Secured Cell Value=0;
22. SQL Compatibility=0;
23. Compression Level=0;
24. Real Time Olap=False;
25. Packet Size=4096
26. CommandText=Adventure Works
```

Lines 7–8 store the database and server names, respectively. The computer that created the connection is stored in line 10. The default cube from Figure 6-24 is stored in line 26. The remaining lines are basically assigned by the connection, and there are no options for customizing them from Excel.

Trying It Out in the Real World

David Bradley, the marketing manager at AdventureWorks, has requested your assistance in looking at some historical marketing data that is stored on an old mainframe system. David realizes that you're very busy these days showing off your PivotTable reporting skills to the organization and has thus assigned Karen Berg, an application specialist, to help you with the project. Basically, David wants several text files extracted from the mainframe system to be joined together and imported into a single PivotTable report.

Karen has already read up on PivotTable reporting and has asked that you simply demonstrate how multiple text files can be joined together and imported into a PivotTable report. You decide to show her how this works using the OrderAnalysis example earlier in this chapter.

Getting Down to Business

Follow these steps to complete this exercise:

1. Verify that the OrderAnalysis data source has been successfully created, as outlined in the "Using MS Query to Import Text Files" section.

2. From Excel, choose Data → From Other Sources → From Microsoft Query to bring up the Choose Data Source dialog box.

3. Select the OrderAnalysis data source from the Choose Data Source dialog box and click OK to open the Microsoft Query program.

4. When the Add Tables dialog box appears, double-click Customers.csv, Orders.csv, and Products.csv to add these files as tables in the Microsoft Query program.

5. Click Close to close the Add Tables dialog box.

6. Drag CustomerNum from Orders on top of CustomerNum in Customers in the Tables section of the Microsoft Query program.

7. Drag ProductNum from Orders on top of ProductNum in Products in the Tables section of the Microsoft Query program.

8. Double-click the following fields in the following tables to add them to the Result section of the Microsoft Query program:

   - OrderNum from Orders
   - ProductDesc from Products
   - CustomerNum from Customers
   - Name from Customers
   - City from Customers
   - State from Customers
   - Amount from Orders

9. Verify that your Microsoft Query windows looks like Figure 6-26 and click the Open Door button (fourth button from the left) to return the data to Excel.

10. When the Import Data dialog box appears, click the PivotTable Report and then OK to import the data into a new PivotTable report.

11. Drag ProductDesc into the Row Labels area and Amount into the Values area of the PivotTable report.

12. Verify that your PivotTable report looks like Figure 6-27.

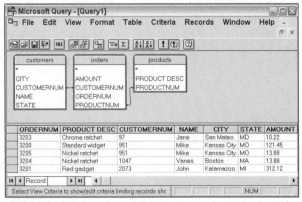

Figure 6-26: The three text files have been joined together as if they were tables in a database.

	A	B
1	Row Labels	Sum of AMOUNT
2	Chrome ratchet	10.22
3	Nickel ratchet	27.76
4	Red gadget	312.12
5	Standard widget	121.45
6	Grand Total	471.55

Sheet1 She

Figure 6-27: If you did everything right, your PivotTable report should utilize three joined text files from the OrderAnalysis directory and look like this.

WATCH THE VIDEO **To see how to do this exercise, watch the ch0601_video.avi video on the companion web site at** www.wiley.com/go/excelreporting/2007.

Reviewing What You Did

This example demonstrated how multiple text files could be joined together and then imported into an Excel PivotTable report. This technology can be useful for organizations that have their data on a mainframe system or in a text file database. You can learn more about using the Microsoft Query program to build queries by reading Chapters 8 and 9.

Chapter Review

This chapter outlined the various methods for getting source data into an Excel report using the Microsoft Query program. You started by learning how you could import and string together multiple text files, treating them as if they were database tables. After that you reviewed the procedures for setting up connections to Access and SQL Server databases. You concluded with a real-world example on importing multiple text files into an Excel report.

Using the Query Wizard

This chapter focuses on the Query Wizard program that is integrated into Microsoft Excel. Using this wizard, users can choose fields, apply filters, and add sort instructions using simple and easy-to-use graphical screens. This program can be especially helpful for organizations with a very limited supply of SQL knowledge, because the Query Wizard enables users to build basic SQL queries from existing database tables and views.

In this chapter, I cover all four dialog boxes of the Query Wizard. I use a single example for building the query from the wizard, and I show you how that query is saved and accessed. This discussion includes a detailed explanation of the query itself, similar to Chapter 6, where I reviewed the DSN file. I finish this chapter with another real-world example that you can use for additional practice.

Overview of the Query Wizard

The Query Wizard guides you through four different dialog boxes where you define the key components for building an SQL query. In the first dialog box, you start by choosing the fields you want to include in your Excel report. Here, you can even arrange the order in which fields are displayed (left to right) in the query. In the second dialog box of the wizard, you can apply filters to any of the fields you selected in the first dialog box. You define the filters by first selecting a string or mathematical operator from a drop-down list of available ones and then specifying a value. In the third dialog box, you can sort the result set by choosing an ascending or descending sort order for one or more columns. You finish in the fourth and last dialog box by choosing either to return the data to Excel or launch the Microsoft Query program (covered in Chapters 8 and 9) to further tweak the SQL query.

Table 7-1 lists each dialog box with a brief explanation of its purpose and an explanation of what part of the query is being generated. Notice that only the first three dialog boxes actually build the query; the fourth dialog box is used as a bridge to either return the data to Excel or to launch the Microsoft Query program. Keep in mind that you only have to complete the information in the first dialog box shown in Figure 7-2; filtering (the second dialog box) and sorting (the third dialog box) are not mandatory steps.

The wizard is capable of generating only basic SQL queries. Field concatenation, aggregate functions, conditional logic, and sub-queries are beyond the scope of what can be accomplished with the Query Wizard program.

Table 7-1: Explanation of the Query Wizard Dialog Boxes

DIALOG BOX	PART OF SQL QUERY	PURPOSE
1 - Choose Columns	`Select <Columns>` `From <Objects>`	Choose the fields, the order of the fields in the query, and the objects from which these fields are selected.
2 - Filter Data	`Where <Conditions>`	Specify the conditions for data to be extracted from its data source. Note that you can specify conditions only on fields or columns selected in the first dialog box.
3 - Sort Order	`Order By`	Define how the resulting dataset is sorted. An ascending or descending sort order can only be defined on fields that were selected in the first dialog box.
4 – Finish	This area is not applicable to the SQL query, because it only acts as a bridge to either return the query created in the first three steps to Excel or edit the query in the Microsoft Query program.	Optionally save the query for future use on another report and then choose to either Return the Data to Excel or View and/or edit the Data in the Microsoft Query program.

TIP Some organizations have succeeded in creating SQL database views to solve multiple table joins, aggregate functions, and complex filter conditions. These views can also replace the database field names with more understandable names (CUSNUM could be CustomerNumber, for example) and eliminate fields that report users don't need. This enables novice report users to rely on the database views and easy-to-understand field headings to obtain their data.

The following sections describe how to start the wizard and explain in more detail what features and functions are available in each of the four dialog boxes.

Starting the Wizard

The wizard enables users who are unfamiliar with SQL programming to build basic SQL queries by specifying the query components in the first three graphical dialog boxes of the program. Using this wizard, you can

- Select specific columns or fields that should be included in the report
- Filter data using several types of mathematical and string operators
- Sort on columns or fields in ascending or descending order

In order to invoke the Query Wizard, you must access data from an external data source and connect to the data source using Microsoft Query. Follow these steps to start the Query Wizard:

1. From Excel, choose Data → From Other Sources → From Microsoft Query to bring up the Choose Data Source dialog box shown in Figure 7-1.

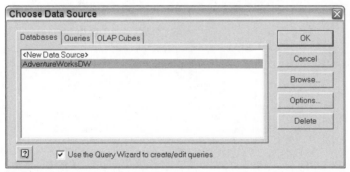

Figure 7-1: Check the Use the Query Wizard to Create/Edit Queries option to enable the Query Wizard for new Excel reports.

2. Verify that the Use the Query Wizard to Create/Edit Queries box is checked. Checking this box enables the Query Wizard to start when the data source is accessed by either double-clicking it or selecting it and then clicking OK. If this option is unchecked, the wizard is bypassed and you are routed directly to the Microsoft Query program.

If you click the various tabs at the top of this dialog box, you'll notice that the Query Wizard is only enabled for the Databases and Queries tabs. It is not used for OLAP Cubes, because the data has already been aggregated and typically filtered to meet a specific business need or purpose.

NOTE If you choose to save a query, it can be accessed from the Queries tab in Figure 7-1. Read the section "Opening a Saved Query" later in this chapter for more information about how this works.

Selecting Objects

Chapter 6 showed you how to create a Data Source Name (DSN) file for connecting to external data sources. After you create a DSN, you can select data from it using the Query Wizard (explained in this chapter) or the Microsoft Query program (covered in Chapters 8 and 9). For this example, select the AdventureWorksDW database you created in the Chapter 6. Make sure that you check the Use the Query Wizard to Create/Edit Queries option at the bottom of the Choose Data Source dialog box before clicking OK. This should bring up the Query Wizard – Choose Columns dialog box, shown in Figure 7-2.

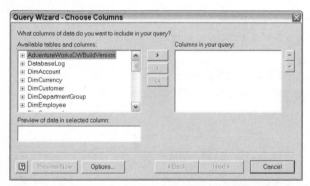

Figure 7-2: When the data source is a database, the first view of the Query Wizard shows the various tables, views, and synonyms in the database.

Figure 7-2 shows the first of the Query Wizard's four dialog boxes. Here, you choose the fields you want to include in your report. You select the fields from various types of objects in the external data source. Depending on how you have the Table Options set, you may see a list of different objects than the ones shown in Figure 7-2 for the AdventureWorksDW database. You can modify the view to match this dialog box by following the steps listed in the next section.

Using Table Options for Object Selection

The Table Options dialog box (see Figure 7-3) lets you choose whether tables, views, system tables, and/or synonyms are shown in the Available Tables and Columns pane of the Choose Columns dialog box. This dialog box also offers you a couple of other options. In the Owner field, you can opt to show only the objects for a particular database owner. And if you want your tables and columns displayed in alphabetical order, you can check the box near the bottom of the dialog box. I usually display objects in alphabetical order when I am not familiar with the database entities and need to locate specific columns and tables. If you are already familiar with the table layout, you may find that this option is more of a nuisance than a help.

NOTE Synonyms act as aliases for your objects, enabling you to simplify the naming of objects (including remote objects in another database or another schema). They are available only in Oracle databases.

The meaning of Tables, Views, and System Tables in Figure 7-3 varies with the type of external data source you are accessing. Table 7-2 includes a list of several external data sources, with a short explanation of what each corresponding Table Option value means.

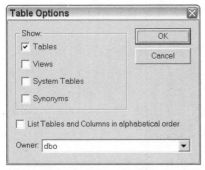

Figure 7-3: The objects displayed in Figure 7-2 can be filtered by object type and by object owner from this dialog box.

Table 7-2: Table Option Meanings Based on Data Source

TYPE	TABLES	VIEWS	SYSTEM TABLES	SYNONYMS	OWNER
Access database	Tables are shown as Tables	Queries are shown as Views	Hidden system tables are shown as System Tables		
Excel workbook	Used in conjunction with System Tables to show worksheet tabs and data		Used in conjunction with Tables to show worksheet tabs and data		
Oracle database	User tables are shown as Tables	Database views are shown as Views	Database system Tables are shown as System Tables	Public and private synonyms are shown as Synonyms	Database schemas are shown as Owners
SQL Server database	Database user tables are shown as Tables	Database views are shown as Views	Database system tables are shown as System Tables	SQL 2005 synonyms are not supported	Database owners are shown as Owners (usually dbo)
Text file or directory	Files are shown as Tables				

To set the Table Options to match the screen shown in Figure 7-2 and follow the example in this chapter, complete these steps:

1. Click the Options button in Figure 7-2 to bring up the Table Options dialog box in Figure 7-3.

2. Check Tables and uncheck Views, System Tables, and Synonyms.

3. Uncheck List Tables and Columns in Alphabetical Order.

4. Select **dbo** as the Owner.

5. Click OK to close the Table Options dialog box and return to the Query Wizard – Choose Columns dialog box.

6. Verify that your dialog box looks like Figure 7-2.

Choosing Fields

After you are returned to the first view of the wizard, you can choose the specific fields you want to include in your Excel report. The pane on the left shows the available objects and the fields in each object. The pane on the right shows the fields you have selected for your report.

From the dialog box shown in Figure 7-4, you can expand the tree to select fields from individual tables. Clicking a table name in the left pane and then clicking the right-pointing single arrow button moves all the fields from that table to the Columns in Your Query pane. You can select a single field in the Columns in Your Query pane and click the left-pointing arrow button to move it back to the Available Tables and Columns pane. Or you can click the double left-arrow button to move all the fields back. The up and down arrows to the right of the Columns in Your Query pane control the order of the columns in the query (explained in the "Adjusting Field Order" section of this chapter).

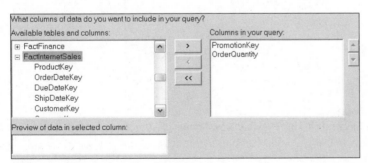

Figure 7-4: Choose the fields you want to include in your report from the available objects in this dialog box.

To follow along with the example used in this chapter, select these fields for your report:

- PromotionKey and OrderQuantity from the FactInternetSales table
- BirthDate, Marital Status, Gender, and NumberCarsOwned from the Dim-Customer table
- City, StateProvinceName, and EnglishCountryRegionName from the Dim-Geography table

Previewing Object Data

Selecting a field name from either the Available Tables and Columns or the Columns in Your Query window and clicking the Preview Now button shows a list of the unique values in the selected field. This feature is useful when you're unsure about the information that is stored in a particular field. Figure 7-5 shows how this works for the City field.

Adjusting Field Order

As you select the various fields for your report, you may find it necessary to adjust the order in which they are displayed. For PivotTable reports this means how the fields are ordered from top-to-bottom in the PivotTable field list. For Spreadsheet reports this means how fields are arranged from left to right in the worksheet. Keep in mind that you can also arrange the order of fields from the Microsoft Query program or from Excel (discussed in Chapters 8 and Chapter 14, respectively).

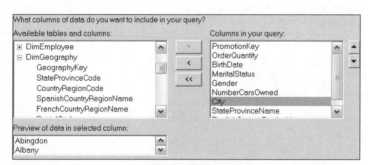

Figure 7-5: Selecting City and clicking Preview Now shows a list of items for that field to be displayed in the Preview of Data in Selected Column window.

TIP You might find it helpful to group the Values area fields (which are usually fields with a numeric data type) at the end of the selection while also grouping and organizing the Row Labels, Column Labels, and Report Filter area fields. For example, the geographical fields should be grouped together and then arranged from top to bottom as Country, State/Province, and City.

To follow along with this example, arrange the selected fields in the following order:

- PromotionKey
- EnglishCountryRegionName
- StateProvinceName
- City
- Marital Status
- Gender
- BirthDate
- OrderQuantity
- NumberCarsOwned

Once you have finished arranging the fields, verify that your dialog box looks like Figure 7-6.

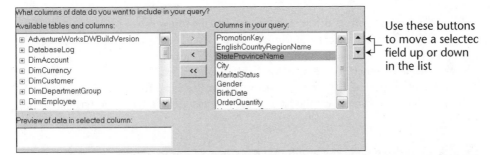

Figure 7-6: Adjust field order by clicking the up and down arrows to the right of the Columns in Your Query dialog box.

Filtering Data

Filters are used to limit the amount of data returned or displayed in a report. For example, a sales database might have 10 years of sales data, but only the last 3 years are applicable for revenue forecasting. So, if you are creating a sales forecast report from this data source, you might want to apply a filter against a field such as Order Date to extract only the transactions for the last 3 years. This filter can be applied in one of two ways:

- **Before the data is returned to Excel:** This method uses a condition specified in the Where clause of an SQL query. The wizard creates the Where clause from the operators and values you input into the fields of the Query Wizard's Filter Data dialog box.

- **After the data is returned to Excel:** This method uses the drop-down arrows in the Excel report to limit the data displayed. This option was demonstrated in Chapter 3.

CROSS-REFERENCE The first option for filtering described in the preceding list can be further classified into two categories: a filter applied as part of the query (for example, quantity > 10) or a filter specified each time the report is updated. The latter is called a *parameter query* and is covered in Chapter 15.

The first option controls the amount of data that is returned and displayed, and the second option controls only the amount of data displayed. In the first option, only the last three years of sales data are imported into the Excel report. Contrast that with the second option, in which 10 years are loaded into the report. Depending on the number of rows being imported, this could result in a significant performance difference. This section focuses exclusively on the first option because this is what the wizard accomplishes.

TIP Unless you need the additional data, use a filter to import only the necessary information you need. This results in faster report updates, improved performance, and reduced disk space requirements.

The wizard builds the Where clause in an SQL query by using the operators and values that you select in this second view of the dialog box. There are numerous operators in the drop-down list, but keep in mind that this is only a small subset of what is actually available to users who are knowledgeable about SQL programming. Nevertheless, the available options are a good start and usually sufficient for novice users who do not have complex requirements.

CROSS-REFERENCE See the SQL reference in Appendix A for a more complete list of operators and some examples of their use.

In order to simplify the organization of the available operators, I have classified them into a mathematical category for numeric data and into a string category for alphanumeric data. That is not to say that you cannot use a mathematical operator on a string field or vice versa, but just be sure to think about the results. For example, using "Greater than or Equal To" a "W" results in the values W, X, Y, and Z being returned.

Using the Wizard to Filter Data

In the second view of the Query Wizard, the Filter Data box, you can select fields and then apply a filter condition or conditions. In the left-most pane, Columns to Filter, a list of all the fields you selected in the previous dialog box is presented. After you select a field, you can choose an operator and enter a numeric or string value in the Filter Value field. Note that you can only select from the list of available operators. (Refer to Tables 7-3 and 7-4 later in this chapter for a complete list of mathematical and string operators.) The Filter Value field, which is a drop-down box next to the Operator field, shows a preview of data in the selected field. This can be helpful if you are selecting a particular value or just want to validate that the field data is correct. Unlike the Operator drop-down box, you do not have to select a particular value from the drop-down list and you may want to type in a completely new string or number into the field.

NOTE By the way, you won't see the Filter Value and Operator fields labeled as such in the Filter Data dialog box. I have assigned these names to the fields to help you better understand the figures and text in this chapter.

In the example shown in Figure 7-7, I have selected the EnglishCountryRegion-Name field and specified two conditions. The first is that the EnglishCountryRegion-Name begins with a U. The second condition is that this field is equal to Canada. In layman's terms, this means that only the records that have a country name that begins with a U (United States and United Kingdom) or a country name of Canada should be selected from the data source when this query is run.

NOTE You can get a full list of the items in EnglishCountryRegionName by clicking the drop-down arrow in the Filter Value field when EnglishCountryRegionName is selected.

Operator field   Filter Value field

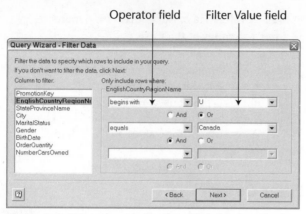

Figure 7-7: You can apply filters to fields by choosing an operator and entering a value.

NOTE Remember, you do not have to specify a filter. This is an optional step in the Query Wizard process.

When you specify multiple conditions for a particular field, as is the case in Figure 7-7, you must specify And or Or to evaluate them. If I had used And instead of Or, no records would have been selected.

Applying Multiple Filters

After you apply a filter to a field, the field name appears in bold in the Columns to Filter pane on the left side of the dialog box. You can apply multiple filters by simply selecting another field and defining the operator type and value. In Figure 7-8, I selected NumberCarsOwned and defined the filter criteria to be greater than 0.

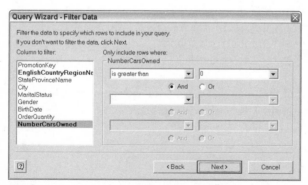

Figure 7-8: After you apply a filter, the field appears in bold, as is the case for English-CountryRegionName and NumberCarsOwned.

Mathematical Operators

Table 7-3 lists all the mathematical operators available from the Query Wizard, along with their SQL programming equivalents and a short explanation of what the operator is intended to accomplish.

CROSS-REFERENCE The SQL reference in Appendix A provides a more complete list of mathematical operators available with SQL programming.

String Operators

Table 7-4 lists all the string operators available from the Query Wizard, along with the SQL programming equivalent and a short explanation of what the operator is intended to accomplish. I use the letter A in the SQL Equivalent column to represent a string value. Replace A with the particular text you want to use with the string operator.

Table 7-3: Mathematical Operators and SQL Interpretations

OPERATOR	EXPLANATION	SQL EQUIVALENT
Equals	Equals the number or text specified in the Filter Value drop-down field	=
Does not equal	Does not equal the number or text specified in the Filter Value drop-down field	<>, !=
Is greater than	Is greater than the number specified in the Filter Value drop-down field	>
Is greater than or equal to	Is greater than or equal to the number in the Filter Value drop-down field	>=
Is less than	Is less than the number specified in the Filter Value drop-down field	<
Is less than or equal to	Is less than or equal to the number specified in the Filter Value drop-down field	<=

Table 7-4: String Operators and SQL Interpretations

OPERATOR	EXPLANATION	SQL EQUIVALENT
Begins with	Begins with the character or text specified in the Filter Value drop-down field	LIKE A%
Does not begin with	Does not begin with the character or text specified in the Filter Value drop-down field	NOT LIKE A%
Ends with	Ends with the character or text specified in the Filter Value drop-down field	LIKE %A
Does not end with	Does not end with the character or text specified in the Filter Value drop-down field	NOT LIKE %A
Contains	Contains the character or text specified in the Filter Value drop-down field	LIKE %A%
Does not contain	Does not contain the character or text specified in the Filter Value drop-down field	NOT LIKE %A%
Like	Contains the text specified in the Filter Value drop-down field	LIKE A%
Not Like	Does not contain the text specified in the Filter Value drop-down field	NOT LIKE A%
Is Null	Has a null value for the selected field	IS NULL
Is Not Null	Does not have a null value for the selected field	IS NOT NULL

CROSS-REFERENCE The SQL reference in Appendix A gives a more complete list of string filters available with SQL programming.

Viewing and Changing Filter Conditions

If you want to remove a filter or just a particular filter condition, simply select the bold field in the Column to Filter pane, and the filter conditions automatically appear on the right. You can then remove the filter conditions by selecting a blank operator in the Operator field. If there are multiple operators, be sure that the operators are all set to blank.

> **TIP** A blank operator is located at the top of the list in the Operator field drop-down box.

Now that you've seen how this works, try it for yourself. Complete these steps to practice filtering data and follow along with my example in this chapter:

1. Select EnglishCountryRegionName and apply the conditions Begins with U or Equals Canada.

2. Select NumberCarsOwned and apply the conditions Is Greater Than 0. (Refer back to Figure 7-8 if you want to see how I entered these filter conditions.)

3. Click Next to continue to the Sort Order dialog box of the wizard.

Sorting Data

After you click Next in the Filter Data dialog box, the Sort Order dialog box appears. Here, you define the sort order of the dataset that is returned from the data source. The dataset, as a whole, is sorted when you choose a field in the Sort By drop-down list and select an ascending or descending sort order. You should use this dialog box to sort records for Spreadsheet reports, not for PivotTable reports. Why? Because the unique field items in each column are automatically sorted as fields are dropped into a Pivot-Table report location. Thus, sorting the entire result set each time the report is updated serves no purpose.

> **NOTE** Remember, choosing a sort order is an optional step. You do not have to specify a sort.

In Figure 7-9, I first selected BirthDate and specified a descending sort order. Next, I selected NumberCarsOwned and specified an ascending sort order. If you want to remove a sort, simply select the field and choose the blank value in the drop-down list.

Figure 7-9: You sort the dataset by selecting fields and specifying an ascending or descending sort order.

NOTE In Figure 7-9, I demonstrate how to apply a sort order for a PivotTable report. This doesn't provide any useful utility and only serves to increase the amount of time it takes to execute the query. You should use this dialog box only when you are creating a Spreadsheet report. I've done this here just so you can see how this dialog box works and how the SQL statement is generated.

To practice choosing a sort order and continue with my example, follow these steps:

1. Select BirthDate and specify a Descending sort order.

2. Select NumberCarsOwned and specify an Ascending sort order.

3. Click Next to continue to the Finish dialog box of the wizard.

Finishing Up

After you click Next in the Sort Order dialog box of the Query Wizard, the Finish dialog box appears, as shown in Figure 7-10. This is the fourth and last dialog box of the wizard. Here, you can perform the following functions:

- Return Data to Microsoft Excel to finish creating the report
- View data or edit the query in the Microsoft Query program
- Save the query

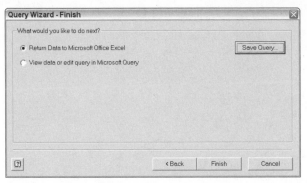

Figure 7-10: Use this last view of the wizard to return data to Excel, tweak the query in the Microsoft Query program, or save the query to a file directory.

If you want to modify the SQL query or view the data returned from the data source, select the second option, View Data or Edit Query in Microsoft Query, to start the Microsoft Query program. If no changes are required, you can select the first option, Return Data to Microsoft Office Excel. This option takes you back to the Excel program so that you can finish creating your Excel report.

Saving the Query

Queries created from the Query Wizard or from the Microsoft Query program can be saved and accessed whenever you create a new Spreadsheet or PivotTable report. Keep in mind that the query file stores both the connection information used to access the external data source and the SQL query used to extract the data. It is used only for creating new reports and appears in the Queries tab of the Choose Data Source dialog box each time you create an Excel report from an external data source. Deleting the query file has no effect on existing reports that initially used this query to connect to the external data source. Remember, connection information and query information are saved in the Excel report; the query is used only to keep you from having to re-enter the connection information and build the SQL query each time you create a new report.

By default, queries are saved to this location:

```
c:\documents and settings\user\application data\microsoft\queries
```

WARNING Saving a query to another location may require you to manually browse for that location when the query is accessed from Excel.

When you click the Save Query button in the final Query Wizard box to save the SQL query you created in the wizard, the Save As dialog box appears, as shown in Figure 7-11.

Figure 7-11: You can save the query that you created in the wizard for later access or use.

To continue following along with my example, complete these steps:

1. Click the Save Query button in the Query Wizard - Finish dialog box.

2. When the Save As dialog box appears, save the query with a meaningful name such as **EnglishPromoResponseWithCustomerDemographics**.

3. When you are returned to the Finish dialog box shown in Figure 7-10, select View Data or Edit Query in Microsoft Query and then click Finish to open the Microsoft Query program.

Viewing a Saved Query

When you look at the query you saved earlier, notice that many of the lines correspond to query parameters entered in the various dialog boxes of the Query Wizard. Here is the query file for the AdventureWorksDW database example covered in this chapter. Some of the lines are very long, so I split them apart and indented the code to make it easier for you to read. I also inserted the line number followed by a letter after the number (3a, 3b, 3c, and so on) to indicate the actual line in the file. In order for the query to be read by Excel, however, the format cannot be changed:

```
1a. XLODBC
2a. 1
3a. DRIVER=SQL Server;
3b. SERVER=SQLServerName;
3c. UID=WindowsUserLogin;
3d. APP=Microsoft Office 2007;
3e. WSID=ComputerName
```

```
3f. DATABASE=AdventureWorksDW;
3g. Trusted_Connection=Yes
4a. SELECT FactInternetSales.PromotionKey,
4b.        DimGeography.EnglishCountryRegionName,
4c.        DimGeography.StateProvinceName,
4d.        DimGeography.City,
4e.        DimCustomer.MaritalStatus,
4f.        DimCustomer.Gender,
4g.        DimCustomer.BirthDate,
4h.        FactInternetSales.OrderQuantity,
4i.        DimCustomer.NumberCarsOwned
4j. FROM AdventureWorksDW.dbo.DimCustomer DimCustomer,
4k.      AdventureWorksDW.dbo.DimGeography DimGeography,
4l.      AdventureWorksDW.dbo.FactInternetSales FactInternetSales
4m. WHERE DimCustomer.CustomerKey = FactInternetSales.CustomerKey
4n.   AND DimCustomer.GeographyKey = DimGeography.GeographyKey
4o.   AND ((DimGeography.EnglishCountryRegionName Like 'U%')
4p.   AND (DimCustomer.NumberCarsOwned>0)
4q.    OR (DimGeography.EnglishCountryRegionName='Canada')
4r.   AND (DimCustomer.NumberCarsOwned>0))
4s. ORDER BY DimCustomer.BirthDate DESC,
4t.          DimCustomer.NumberCarsOwned
5a. <cursor return>
6a. <cursor return>
7a. PromotionKey<tab>
7b. EnglishCountryRegionName<tab>
7c. StateProvinceName<tab>
7d. City<tab>
7e. MaritalStatus<tab>
7f. Gender<tab>
7g. BirthDate<tab>
7h. OrderQuantity<tab>
7i. NumberCarsOwned
8a. <Blank Line>
```

Lines 1–3 contain the connection information. Line 4 contains the SQL query that was created in the various dialog boxes of this chapter. Lines 4a–4i contain the fields and field objects specified in the first dialog box of the Query Wizard. Note that the database, the database owner, and the object are all specified in lines 4j–4l. Lines 4m and 4n contain the instructions for joining the FactInternetSales, DimCustomer, and DimGeography tables to one another. Lines 4o–4r contain the filter conditions that were entered in the second dialog box of the Query Wizard. Lines 4s and 4t contain the sort order specified in the third dialog box of the Query Wizard. Lines 5a–6a are just blank lines that separate the SQL query from the column heading names. Lines 7a–7i contain the field names for each column in the query. Each field name is separated by a <tab>. The blank line in line 8 is simply the end of file marker.

NOTE Looking carefully at the saved query reveals that the filter criteria on NumberCarsOwned is repeated twice (Figure 7-13 also shows this duplicate filter condition in a graphical format). This duplicate condition does not cause any actual problems, but it isn't required. As you've probably heard in the software development industry, it isn't a *software bug;* rather, it's just a program *feature*.

Opening a Saved Query

Although the query used in this chapter's example is very basic, it is possible to create more sophisticated queries (typically using external programs such as Microsoft Query Analyzer or Microsoft SQL Server Studio) and make them available to users for creating their Excel reports. This can be useful in organizations where the report users don't have an advanced knowledge of SQL or the database entities and relationships but are able to create Excel reports from the extracted data. Of course, don't forget that SQL views and stored procedures are also possible alternatives to a saved query.

Microsoft Excel looks for saved queries in two default locations:

```
c:\program files\common files\odbc\data sources
c:\documents and settings\user\application data\microsoft\queries
```

You can define additional browse locations by clicking the Options button in the Choose Data Source dialog box shown in Figure 7-12 to bring up the Data Source Options dialog box. Once this dialog box appears, type in a new search location in the Folders to Search for Data Sources field and click the Add button to include the new location. Keep in mind that this location can either be a file directory or a share name.

Follow these steps to access a saved query for a new Excel report:

1. From Excel, click Data → From Other Sources → From Microsoft Query to bring up the Choose Data Source dialog box.

2. Click the Queries tab when the Choose Data Source dialog box appears, as shown in Figure 7-12.

3. Open the saved query by double-clicking it or by highlighting it and then clicking the Open button.

NOTE Don't forget that the connection information is also saved along with the SQL query.

Click on the Queries tab
to open a saved query

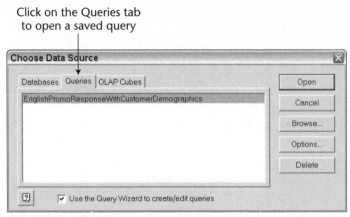

Figure 7-12: Click the Queries tab to access previously saved SQL queries for creating new Excel reports.

Viewing the Query Using the Microsoft Query Program

After you have created the basic SQL query from the Query Wizard, you can view and edit the query from the Microsoft Query program. Notice that the three tables — Dim-Customer, DimGeography, and FactInternetSales — selected in the first dialog box of the wizard all appear in the upper part of the program window shown in Figure 7-13. The fields that were selected in this first dialog box of the Query Wizard also appear in the bottom portion of the window. Notice that the fields are also arranged (left to right) in the same order as Figure 7-6. The filters that were applied in the second dialog box of the wizard appear in the Criteria Fields section displayed in the middle of the program window.

Criteria is repeated twice (nuance of the query builder)

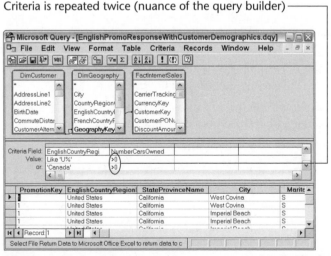

Figure 7-13: The Microsoft Query program graphically displays the SQL query that was created in the Query Wizard program.

You can close the program from Microsoft Query by choosing File → Cancel and Return Data to Microsoft Office Excel.

CROSS-REFERENCE Chapters 8 and 9 cover the Microsoft Query program.

Trying It Out in the Real World

Brian Welcker, the Vice President of Sales at AdventureWorks, wants to know more about what types of products are being purchased by new customers who are homeowners with at least one child at home. After some further discussion with Brian, you learn that a new customer is defined as someone who has a first purchase date that is no earlier than 2004. You also learn that Brian would like this report in a PivotTable format with the following fields:

- Order number, order line number, and the order quantity from the Internet sales table
- The English product name description
- The customer's occupation and education level (in English)

Getting Down to Business

Follow these steps to develop this PivotTable report for Brian:

1. From Excel, choose Data → From Other Sources → From Microsoft Query.

2. When the Choose Data Source dialog box appears, verify that Use the Query Wizard to Create/Edit Queries is checked; and then select the AdventureWorksDW database and click OK.

3. The Query Wizard - Choose Columns dialog box appears. Move the following fields from the Available Tables and Columns pane to the Columns in Your Query pane:

   - CustomerKey, SalesOrderNumber, SalesOrderLineNumber, and OrderQuantity from the FactInternetSales table
   - NumberChildrenAtHome, EnglishEducation, EnglishOccupation, HouseOwnerFlag, and DateFirstPurchase from the DimCustomer table
   - EnglishProductName from the DimProduct table

4. Verify that your dialog box looks like Figure 7-14 and click Next to continue.

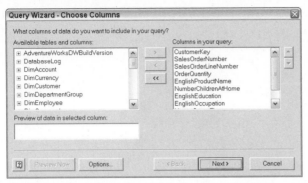

Figure 7-14: Select the fields for the PivotTable report from the FactInternetSales, DimCustomer, and DimProduct tables in the AdventureWorksDW database.

5. Click NumberChildrenAtHome in the Column to Filter pane; and then select Is Greater Than in the Operator drop-down list and type **0** in the Filter Value field, as shown in Figure 7-15.

6. Click DateFirstPurchase and select Is Greater Than or Equal To in the Operator drop-down list and type **1/1/2004** in the Filter Value field.

7. Click HouseOwnerFlag and select Equals in the Operator drop-down list and type **1** in the Filter Value field.

8. Verify that your dialog box looks like Figure 7-16 and click Next to continue.

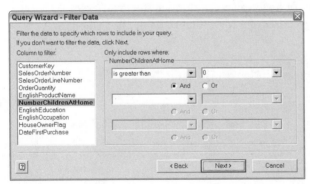

Figure 7-15: Define the three filter conditions for this exercise in the Filter Data dialog box of the Query Wizard.

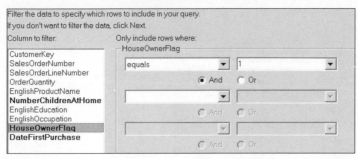

Figure 7-16: You should have three filters applied in this dialog box, indicated by bold text.

9. Click Next to bypass the Sort Order dialog box.

10. When the fourth and last dialog box of the wizard appears, verify that the Return Data to Microsoft Office Excel option is checked and click Finish.

11. Click Finish when the PivotTable and PivotChart Wizard dialog box appears.

12. Select PivotTable Report and click OK when the Import Data dialog box appears to return the data to Excel and create the PivotTable report.

13. When you are returned to Excel, drag EnglishProductName to the Report Filter area, EnglishEducation to the Column Labels area, EnglishOccupation to the Row Labels area, and OrderQuantity to the Values area.

> **NOTE** The fields HouseOwnerFlag, DateFirstPurchase, and NumberChildrenAtHome do not need to be displayed in the PivotTable. However, they must be selected in order for a filter to be applied when the Query Wizard is used.

14. Verify that your PivotTable report looks like Figure 7-17.

	A	B	C	D	E	F	G
1	EnglishProductName	(All)					
2							
3	Sum of OrderQuantity	Column Labels					
4	Row Labels	Bachelors	Graduate Degree	High School	Partial College	Partial High School	Grand Total
5	Clerical	36			438	152	626
6	Management	637	229	180	48	7	1101
7	Manual			386	114	114	614
8	Professional	579	151	527	1236	41	2534
9	Skilled Manual	729	94	127	83	143	1176
10	Grand Total	1981	474	1220	1919	457	6051
11							
12							
13							

Sheet1 / Sheet2 / Sheet3

Figure 7-17: If you did everything right, the PivotTable report should look like this.

Reviewing What You Did

This exercise provided you with some more practice with using the Query Wizard program while demonstrating a real-world scenario. Notice that while the wizard provides some useful functions, it is also very limiting and requires that you conform to a sometimes rigid template. For example, you didn't need to include the HouseOwnerFlag, the DateFirstPurchased, or the NumberChildrenAtHome fields in the report, but you were forced to select them in order to apply the filter.

Despite the limitations and the sometimes awkward interface, this Query Wizard can still be very helpful, especially for novice report users. You can use it to build a basic SQL query and then continue to the Microsoft Query program to make the necessary changes to fine-tune the query. This method can assist report users who are just beginning to learn SQL programming. Another option that I've found to be very successful in some organizations is for a savvy database administrator to create database views that several novice report users can access for creating their reports.

Don't forget to watch the video if you were not sure about any of the steps in this exercise or you just want to verify that you did everything right.

WATCH THE VIDEO Watch the ch0701_video.avi video on how to create this PivotTable report using the Query Wizard at www.wiley.com/go/excelreporting/2007.

Chapter Review

This chapter started by outlining the general purpose and use of each of the four dialog boxes of the Query Wizard program. It went on to describe how the wizard is started when Excel reports are created. It then walked you through the details of the four dialog boxes and showed you how to select fields from various objects, arrange the order of fields in the query, select the type of filter to apply, and change and remove filter conditions. This chapter also discussed why you should use the sort order only for Spreadsheet reports and showed you how to save, access, and interpret a saved query.

For readers who are not familiar with SQL programming, this chapter can be used as a bridge to the next chapter, which describes the various functions and features of the Microsoft Query program.

Getting Started with Microsoft Query

This chapter provides an overview of the Microsoft Query program that is integrated into Microsoft Excel and shows you how to start the program from new and existing Excel reports. It then takes you on a tour of the program environment, menu items, and the toolbar. I conclude with a real-world example that you can use as additional practice for some of the Microsoft Query program features that I cover in this chapter. This chapter covers the program environment and general functions, and the next provides more in-depth coverage of SQL query building.

Microsoft Query acts as an intermediary between an Excel report and an external data source. Novice users can use this program to build a new SQL query using the program's graphical tools, or even fine-tune one that was started from the Query Wizard. Advanced users can use this program to simply paste in an SQL query that was created from an external SQL development program or just type the SQL directly into an SQL window in the Microsoft Query program.

In a general sense, Microsoft Query is the next level up in complexity over the Query Wizard you learned about in Chapter 7. Although you are still constrained by some of the program's limitations for building SQL queries, it offers many new, powerful tools that are not available in the Query Wizard program. Using Microsoft Query, you can perform several types of table joins, design complex filter conditions, create formula fields, and insert parameters. There are also tools for managing database objects and editing table data.

Introducing the Microsoft Query Program

The Microsoft Query program acts as an intermediary between an Excel report and an external data source. You can use this program to tweak a query that was initially created from the Query Wizard (covered in Chapter 7), build a query from scratch using the program's graphical tools, or simply paste in an SQL query that was already created using SQL development programs such as:

- Query Analyzer (Microsoft SQL Server 7.0/2000 databases)
- SQL Server Management Studio (Microsoft SQL Sever 2005 databases)
- SQL*Plus (Oracle databases)
- Toad (Oracle databases)

The Microsoft Query program includes several graphical tools for building all the fundamental parts of an SQL query from the Select to the Order By parts, and it includes tools for creating aggregate functions, expressions, and even parameters. There is also an SQL window available for pasting or entering more complex SQL queries created from external SQL development programs.

If you choose to build a query using the program's graphical tools, an SQL query is generated in the background. Adding or removing a field, modifying a filter condition, or changing a sort order using the program's graphical tools produces a corresponding change to the background SQL query.

Although Microsoft Query has many more capabilities than the Query Wizard, it still has many limitations. For example, you can use Microsoft Query to perform single query operations only. Queries that produce more than one result set are problematic in the sense that Microsoft Query reads only the first result set. Some examples that involve multiple query operations include:

- Multiple queries separated by a GO statement
- Stored procedures that produce more than one result set
- Compute By statements

Additionally, although you can paste queries into the SQL dialog box that utilizes Case logic, subqueries, correlated subqueries, and union operators, there are no graphical tools for building these query components. Of course, these are more advanced programming topics and are probably best handled through a more robust development tool, anyway.

CROSS-REFERENCE Read Chapter 9 to learn more about using SQL queries in the Microsoft Query program and Appendix A for more information about SQL programming, including Case logic.

Beyond the tools included for building SQL queries, the Microsoft Query program also includes several other tools for analyzing data and managing database objects. Using this program, you can:

- Create, edit, and drop database tables and views
- Create, edit, and drop stored procedures
- Index fields on a database table or view
- Edit table data

Although these tools are not designed to replace a database management program, they can be useful in a pinch (for example, when you're supporting users who do not have database management programs installed on their computers). These tools are briefly covered in the next chapter.

Starting Microsoft Query

There isn't a hot-key or a menu item in Excel that launches the Microsoft Query program. The program can be started only when you create or modify an existing report that uses an external data source. Reports that can use Microsoft Query include the following:

- PivotTable reports
- PivotChart reports
- Spreadsheet reports

There are a few different methods for starting the Microsoft Query program that vary with the type of report you are using and whether it is a new report or an existing report. The various options are outlined here.

With New Reports

In earlier versions of Excel, the Microsoft Query program was started differently for PivotTable and Spreadsheet reports. With Excel 2007, Microsoft unified the procedures and moved the choice of report type (PivotTable, PivotChart with PivotTable, or Spreadsheet report) to the final step of the report creation process.

Of course, the Microsoft Query program can still only be launched when you create a new PivotTable or Spreadsheet report that utilizes an external data source. Follow these steps to start the Microsoft Query program:

1. From Excel, choose Data → From Other Sources → From Microsoft Query to bring up the Choose Data Source dialog box in Figure 8-1.

2. Verify that the Use the Query Wizard to Create/Edit Queries box is unchecked.

3. Create or choose an external data source in the Databases tab, or select a saved query file under the Queries tab.

CROSS-REFERENCE Read Chapter 4 to learn more about external data sources and how to create one from the Choose Data Source dialog box in Figure 8-1.

4. After selecting a query or data source connection, click OK to bring up the Microsoft Query program.

As demonstrated in Chapter 7, you can either start building a basic query using the Query Wizard or route directly to the Microsoft Query program by unchecking the Use the Query Wizard to Create/Edit Queries option, selecting a data source, and then clicking OK.

When the Microsoft Query program is launched for a new report, you are presented with the Add Tables dialog box shown in Figure 8-2. You can either close this dialog box to paste in or open a saved SQL query, or you can select the various objects (tables, views, and synonyms) to start building a query using the program's graphical tools. The "Trying It Out in the Real World" section of this chapter provides a brief demonstration of how this is done.

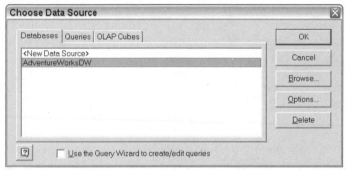

Figure 8-1: Make sure that Use the Query Wizard to Create/Edit Queries is unchecked to start Microsoft Query; otherwise, you have to first route through the four dialog boxes of the Query Wizard before getting to Microsoft Query.

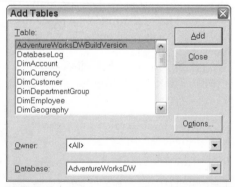

Figure 8-2: Select the various tables or views to build a query, or close the dialog box to either open or paste a saved query into the SQL dialog box.

With Existing Reports

Accessing the Microsoft Query program from an existing report is necessary when the underlying SQL query must be modified, as is the case for the following types of tasks:

- Adding or removing report fields
- Changing the filter conditions to adjust the amount of data being imported into the report
- Fixing errors or modifying formulas in the SQL query
- Adjusting, adding, or removing table joins in the query
- Inquiring on the query of an Excel report that uses an external data source for its report data

There are slightly different methods for starting the Microsoft Query program for the different types of Excel reports. PivotTable and PivotChart reports require that you first open the Connection Properties dialog box, whereas Spreadsheet reports provide a more immediate pathway.

PivotTable and PivotChart Reports

Follow these steps to start the Microsoft Query program from an existing PivotTable or PivotChart report:

1. Verify that the PivotTable or PivotChart report is selected by clicking it, and then click the PivotTable Tools button to display the PivotTable Tools toolbar.
2. Choose Change Data Source → Connection Properties to bring up the Connection Properties dialog box.
3. Click the Definition tab and then the Edit Query button at the lower left of the Connection Properties dialog box, as shown in Figure 8-3.

NOTE If the Query Wizard option is checked and the report can be edited by the Query Wizard, the Query Wizard appears before the Microsoft Query program can be launched. Just click Next to get to the Finish dialog box of the wizard. In that last dialog box, you can select View Data or Edit Query in Microsoft Query and then click Finish to start the program.

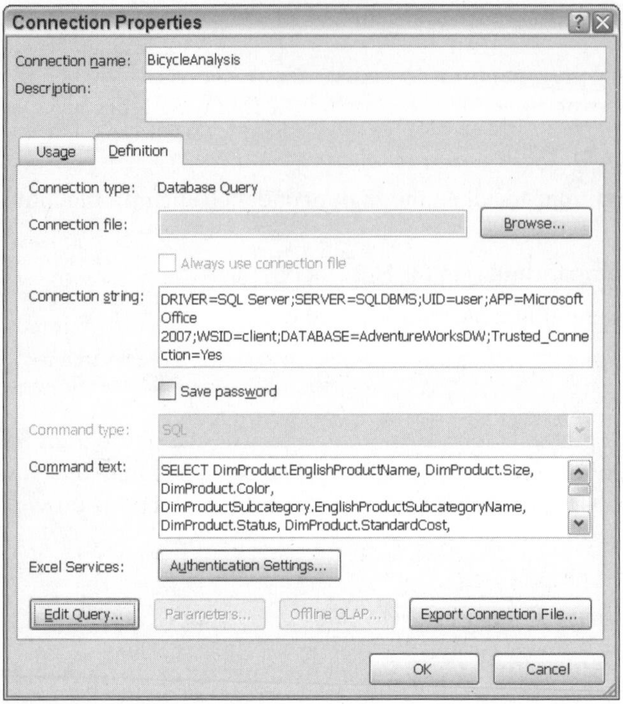

Figure 8-3: Click Edit Query in this dialog box to edit the SQL query from the Microsoft Query program.

Spreadsheet Reports

Launching the Microsoft Query program from an existing Spreadsheet report is more direct. Simply right-click the report and choose Table → Edit Query from the pop-up menu. Keep in mind that the Query Wizard appears first if the Use the Query Wizard to Create/Edit Queries option is checked in the Choose Data Source dialog box.

TURNING OFF THE QUERY WIZARD

If the Query Wizard option is checked and the report can be edited by the Query Wizard, the Query Wizard appears before the Microsoft Query program can be launched. If you want to bypass the Query Wizard, just follow these steps to quickly turn off the Query Wizard program:

1. Click off the Excel report and choose Data → From Other Data Sources → From Microsoft Query to bring up the Choose Data Source dialog box.

2. Uncheck the Use the Query Wizard to Create/Edit Queries box in the dialog box.

3. Click Cancel to return to Excel.

Understanding the Basics

The Microsoft Query program is a basic visual development program that you can use to build SQL queries. It's similar to the Visual Basic Editor available in most Office applications (and which is accessible by simultaneously pressing the <ALT> and <F11> keys). Microsoft Query, however, is used only for queries, and it is a much less robust development program than the Visual Basic Editor. Nevertheless, there's still a lot to take in the first time you see it, especially for those without a programming background. This section covers the basics of the program and familiarizes you with its various windows, toolbar buttons, and objects. It starts by reviewing the environment, briefly describing the purpose of each section, menu item, and toolbar button. Following this introduction, the section describes how you can customize the environment and configure query options to your own particular preference.

Getting to Know the Environment

When the Microsoft Query program starts, you see a few different sections. The menu and toolbar buttons are displayed at the top of the window, followed by the Table and Criteria sections. You can toggle the display of these last two sections, although they are suppressed when a query cannot be displayed graphically (which is explained later). The Results section is next. Here is where the selected fields in the query are displayed. If a query has been executed, the results are also displayed. The Status Bar section is the fifth and last section, where toolbar tips, keyboard settings, and the Record Box are displayed.

Take a closer look at the Microsoft Query program by opening the BicycleAnalysis.dqy file, which is available on this book's web site.

ON THE WEB **You can download the BicycleAnalysis.dqy file to your computer from this book's companion web site at** `www.wiley.com/go/excelreporting/2007.`

You can open this file from the Microsoft Query program by following these steps:

1. Download the Ch08_BicycleAnalysis.dqy file from the web site and save it to this location (be sure to replace *user* with your Windows login):

   `c:\documents and settings\`*user*`\application data\microsoft\queries`

2. From Excel, choose Data → From Other Sources → From Microsoft Query.

3. When the Choose Data Source dialog box appears, verify that the Use the Query Wizard to Create/Edit Queries box is unchecked and click the Queries tab at the top of the dialog box.

4. Select BicycleAnalysis, as shown in Figure 8-4, and click Open to bring up the saved query in the Microsoft Query program.

Click this tab to open a saved query

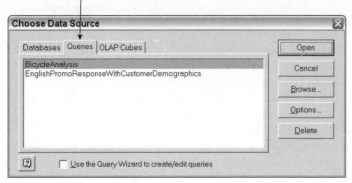

Figure 8-4: The saved query file appears under the Queries tab in the Choose Data Source dialog box.

5. Verify that your Microsoft Query window looks similar to the one shown in Figure 8-5.

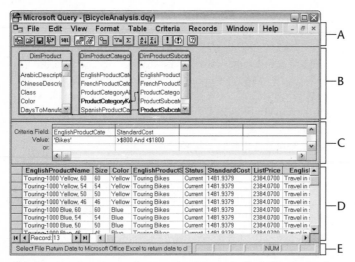

Figure 8-5: The Microsoft Query environment includes several areas for developing an SQL query using the program's graphical tools.

As you can see in Figure 8-5, each section of the Microsoft Query program is labeled with a letter. Table 8-1 identifies the section name and provides a brief description of its purpose.

You can toggle the display of the Tables and Criteria sections by using the relevant toolbar buttons (these buttons are described a little later in Table 8-2). If the query results do not appear in the Results section, you can press the F9 key to execute the SQL query.

Table 8-1: Explanation of the Microsoft Query Sections

ID	SECTION	PURPOSE
A	Menu and toolbar	Perform program functions; access utilities; configure options; and open, save, and run queries.
B	Tables	View tables and manage joins.
C	Criteria	View and manage filters.
D	Results	View, modify, delete, and add fields; view query results; sort columns; and arrange the order of fields in the query (left to right).
E	Status Bar and Record Box	The Record Box enables you to go to a particular record number and the Status Bar enables you to view toolbar button explanations and keyboard settings such as Num or Caps Lock.

Menu and Toolbar Section

You can use the menu and toolbar to perform all the functions for managing a query. Table 8-2 provides a brief description of all menu items and buttons. Many of these items are also covered in more detail throughout this chapter, under their relevant sections. I include them here because I think it provides a handy reference. Keep in mind that there are a few toolbar buttons that do not have an associated menu item. I have included a button name next to each toolbar button that I reference in various examples throughout this chapter.

Table 8-2: Microsoft Query Toolbar Menus and Associated Buttons

MENU	MENU ITEM OR BUTTON NAME	BUTTON	DESCRIPTION
File	New		Creates a new query.
	Open		Opens a saved query.
	Save		Saves the current query. If the file already exists, it is just overwritten with the updated one.
	Save As		Saves the current query as a different filename.

(continued)

Table 8-2 *(continued)*

MENU	MENU ITEM OR BUTTON NAME	BUTTON	DESCRIPTION
	Table Definition		Opens a dialog box to view, create, delete, or index a table.
	Execute SQL		Opens a dialog box to run an SQL query.
	Return Data		Exits the Microsoft Query program and returns the data to the Excel report.
	Cancel and Return to Microsoft Excel		Exits the Microsoft Query program without returning the data to the Excel report.
Edit	Undo/Redo		Redoes the last Undo operation.
	Cut		Cuts the selected data and copies it into memory.
	Copy		Copies selected data to the clipboard.
	Copy Special		Copies the selected data and optionally row numbers and column headings into the clipboard.
	Paste		Pastes the contents from the clipboard.
	Delete		Deletes selected data, object, or criteria.
	Options		Opens a dialog box to set Microsoft Query program options.
View	Show/Hide Tables		Toggles the display of the Tables section.
	Show/Hide Criteria		Toggles the display of the Criteria section.
	Zoom Field		Opens the Zoom dialog box to view data in the selected cell.
	Query Properties		Opens the Query Properties dialog box to extract only unique records or to group records.

Table 8-2 *(continued)*

MENU	MENU ITEM OR BUTTON NAME	BUTTON	DESCRIPTION
	Parameters		Opens the Parameter dialog box to edit Parameter prompts.
	SQL	[SQL]	Opens the SQL dialog box to view or edit the SQL query.
Format	Font		Opens the Font dialog box to set font type, font style, and font size for records in the Results section.
	Row Height		Opens the Row Height dialog box to configure the row height of cells in the Results section.
	Column Width		Opens the Column Width dialog box to configure the column width of cells in the Results section.
	Hide Columns		Hides the selected column or columns.
	Show Columns		Opens the Show Columns dialog box to hide or show columns.
Table	Add Tables	[icon]	Opens the Add Table dialog box to add tables, views, and synonyms to the query.
	Remove Table		Removes the selected table from the query.
	Joins		Opens the Joins dialog box to manage table joins.
Criteria	Add Criteria	[Y=]	Opens the Add Criteria dialog box to create an aggregate function and/or add a filter condition.
	Remove All Criteria		Removes all defined criteria.
Records	Add Column		Opens the Add Column dialog box to add an additional field to the query.

(continued)

Table 8-2 *(continued)*

MENU	MENU ITEM OR BUTTON NAME	BUTTON	DESCRIPTION
	Remove Column		Deletes the selected column or columns from the query.
	Edit Column		Opens the Edit Column dialog box to modify the field, field name, and/or aggregate function.
	Sort		Opens the Sort dialog box to add, view, modify, and remove existing sorts.
	Go To		Opens the Go To dialog box to route to a specific record number in the query result set.
	Allow Editing		Allows data to be edited in the result set of a single table.
	Query Now	▣	Executes the current SQL query.
	Automatic Query	▣	Toggles whether the SQL query is automatically executed.
Window	Tile		Tiles the display of multiple query windows.
	Cascade		Cascades the display of multiple query windows.
Help	Help	▣	Opens the Help dialog box to review online help.
	About Microsoft Query		Opens the About Query dialog box to review license and release information.
Not listed on any menu*	Cycle Through Totals	Σ	Applies an aggregate function to the selected field. Continued mouse clicks cycle through the aggregation functions Sum, Avg, Count, Min, Max, and <none>. There is no associated menu item for this toolbar button.

Table 8-2 *(continued)*

MENU	MENU ITEM OR BUTTON NAME	BUTTON	DESCRIPTION
	Sort Ascending	(A/Z↓)	Removes all existing sorts and then applies an ascending sort on the selected column or columns. There is no associated menu item for this toolbar button.
	Sort Descending	(Z/A↓)	Removes all existing sorts and then applies a descending sort on the selected column or columns. There is no associated menu item for this toolbar button.

*The last three buttons shown in this table are not associated with any menu in the Microsoft Query program.

Tables Section

You can toggle on the display of the Tables section by choosing View → Tables from the menu or by clicking the Show/Hide Tables toolbar button. Queries not created in the Microsoft Query program often cannot be displayed graphically in the Tables or Criteria sections. When this happens, several toolbar and menu functions are also disabled. A warning message is displayed that reads SQL Query can't be represented graphically. Continue Anyway? and requires you to acknowledge it by clicking OK. (Read the "Displaying Queries Graphically" section of this chapter for more information about the implications of not being able to graphically display an SQL query.)

NOTE The tables and the table joins of an SQL query are displayed in the Tables section of the Microsoft Query program. The fields in each table are listed in alphanumeric order. The primary key fields are shown in bold; table joins are represented by connection lines. An Inner Join is represented by a line with a ball on either side, whereas a Left or Right Join is represented by a ball on one side and an arrow on the other side.

The table and table joins for the BicycleAnalysis query example are shown in Figure 8-6. Double-clicking a connection line launches the Table Joins dialog box, where you can view all the table joins. Double-clicking a field in a table adds that field to the Results section of the Microsoft Query program and thus also as a selected field in the SQL query. Double-clicking the asterisk at the top of the table adds all the fields in that table to the SQL query.

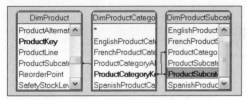

Figure 8-6: Table joins are represented by connection lines; primary key fields are displayed in bold.

Criteria Section

You can toggle on the display of the Criteria section by choosing View → Criteria or by clicking the Show/Hide Criteria toolbar button. The filter criteria are used to limit the number of rows returned from the external data source (which is akin to the Filter Data dialog box of the Query Wizard that was covered in Chapter 7). The criteria can be entered by simply clicking a blank cell in the Criteria section, selecting a field from the drop-down list, and specifying the filter information in the Value cell. Less-experienced users can choose Criteria → Add Criteria to launch a dialog box where the fields, field operators, and values can be selected using graphical tools. The criteria specified in the Query Wizard's Filter Data dialog box from Chapter 7 (refer back to Figures 7-7 and 7-8) are displayed in the Criteria Field section shown in Figure 8-7.

CROSS-REFERENCE Chapter 9 provides more information on using criteria fields.

Results Section

The field headings and results are displayed in the Results section of the Microsoft Query program. Unlike the Tables and Criteria sections, the results can always be displayed in this section, regardless of whether the query can be graphically displayed.

Fields can be added to the query by simply clicking a blank cell and then selecting a field from the drop-down list. You can also create a formula field by selecting a blank cell in the Results section and typing a formula.

The BicycleAnalysis example is shown in Figure 8-8. Notice that EnglishProductName is sorted in reverse alphanumeric order. This aligns with the instructions specified in the Sort dialog box, which can be accessed by choosing Records → Sort.

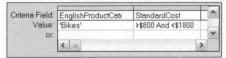

Figure 8-7: The filters in the Where or Having part of an SQL query are displayed in the Criteria section.

EnglishProductName	Size	Color	EnglishProductS	S
Touring-1000 Yellow, 60	60	Yellow	Touring Bikes	C
Touring-1000 Yellow, 54	54	Yellow	Touring Bikes	C
Touring-1000 Yellow, 50	50	Yellow	Touring Bikes	C
Touring-1000 Yellow, 46	46	Yellow	Touring Bikes	C
Touring-1000 Blue, 60	60	Blue	Touring Bikes	C
Touring-1000 Blue, 54	54	Blue	Touring Bikes	C
Touring-1000 Blue, 50	50	Blue	Touring Bikes	C
Touring-1000 Blue, 46	46	Blue	Touring Bikes	C
Road-450 Red, 60	60	Red	Road Bikes	
Road-450 Red, 58	58	Red	Road Bikes	
Road-450 Red, 52	52	Red	Road Bikes	

Figure 8-8: The Results section shows a preview of the data generated by the SQL query.

The Record Box and Status Bar Sections

The Record Box and Status Bar sections include the three components shown in Figure 8-9. The Record Box shows the record number currently selected. Pressing the F5 key routes your cursor to this area, where you can type the number of the record you want to have displayed in the Results section. You can use the arrows on either side of the Record Box to move to the previous or next record or the first or last record of the result set. The Status Bar at the bottom displays tooltips in the left section when you glide your mouse over a toolbar button. Keyboard settings such as Caps Lock, Num Lock, and Scroll Lock appear in the right section of the Status Bar. The Scroll Bar is simply used for scrolling left or right through the fields in the Results section when there are more fields in the result set than can be displayed in the Results section at one time.

Customizing the Environment

Now that you have a better grasp on the various sections of the Microsoft Query program, you're ready to start customizing the program to your own preference. This section describes how you can:

- Manage the display of columns
- Change row and column sizes in the Results section
- Modify the font style used in the Results section
- Work with multiple Microsoft Query windows

Before I delve into these topics, the next section provides a brief overview of how SQL queries are graphically displayed.

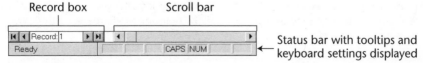

Figure 8-9: Tooltips, record selection, and keyboard settings are all displayed in the Record Box and Status Bar sections of the Microsoft Query program.

Displaying Queries Graphically

Queries generated by Microsoft Query can usually be graphically displayed, meaning that the tables and table joins, and the filter fields and filter criteria, are displayed in the Tables and the Criteria sections, respectively. However, queries pasted or typed into the SQL dialog box cannot always be graphically displayed. When this happens, Microsoft Query prompts you with the warning message SQL Query can't be displayed graphically. Continue Anyway? You must acknowledge this message by clicking OK. Although this message is often interpreted as an error, it isn't a problem. However, it does have a significant effect on what functions are enabled and what sections are displayed in the Microsoft Query environment. For example, the Tables and Criteria sections are not displayed because the program is unable to graphically represent the query. Several functions for adjusting the SQL query are also disabled in the program's menu, requiring you to perform them by editing the SQL query. Table 8-3 identifies many of these disabled functions and describes how to perform them under both circumstances.

> **TIP** If the SQL query cannot be graphically displayed, you're most likely using advanced SQL. If that's the case, you're probably savvy enough to adjust the query to perform many of the functions that are disabled in the Microsoft Query program.

Table 8-3: Performing Functions Based on Whether the Query Can Be Graphically Displayed

FUNCTION	GRAPHICALLY DISPLAYED	NOT GRAPHICALLY DISPLAYED
Hide Fields	Fields can be hidden or deleted using the program's graphical tools.	Fields can be hidden using the program's graphical tools, but only deleted by removing the fields in the Select part the SQL query.
Adding a Table	Add Tables feature enabled.	Tables can only be added by including them in the Join part of the SQL query.
Modify Sort Order	Columns can be sorted using the toolbar icons and menu items.	Columns can only be sorted by editing the Order By part of the SQL query.
Modify Field Order	Fields can be rearranged using drag-and-drop features.	Field order can only be adjusted by rearranging the order of the fields (left to right) in the Select part of the SQL query.

Table 8-3 *(continued)*

FUNCTION	GRAPHICALLY DISPLAYED	NOT GRAPHICALLY DISPLAYED
Modify Criteria	Criteria can be modified using the graphical tools.	Criteria can only be modified by editing the Where or Having part of the SQL query.
Modify Fields in Query	Fields can be added, removed, and renamed using graphical tools.	Fields can only be modified by editing the fields and formulas in the Select part of the SQL query.

Managing the Display of Columns

When using the Microsoft Query program, you may want to suppress the display of particular columns or fields to troubleshoot a query or to focus on some particular column. This can be accomplished by moving a field to a different position in the query, by temporarily hiding it, or even by permanently deleting it.

You can move a column in the query by simply selecting it in the Results section, dragging it left or right, and then dropping it in the desired location. You can also permanently remove a column from being displayed by selecting it and choosing Records → Remove Column or by pressing the Delete key.

WARNING If an SQL query cannot be displayed graphically, you will not be able to drag fields to a different position in the Results section. See Table 8-3 for a more complete list of functions that are disabled for queries that cannot be graphically displayed.

If you only want to temporarily hide a column, you can select the column or columns and then choose Format → Hide Columns. If you want to hide or show multiple columns, choose Format → Show Columns to launch the Show Columns dialog box shown in Figure 8-10. Here, you can select which columns to display or hide by selecting a field and clicking Hide or Show.

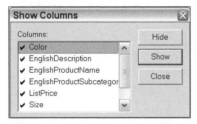

Figure 8-10: Temporarily show or hide columns in this dialog box.

NOTE Showing or hiding a column has no effect on the Excel report. If you want to permanently remove the column from the report, you have to delete it.

Changing Row and Column Sizes

By default, Microsoft Query displays the result set in a standard row height and column width. Depending on the type of data being extracted, you may want to adjust these settings. For example, if you include a field with a Text data type, such as the EnglishDescription field in the DimProduct table of the AdventureWorksDW database, the information in that field is not fully displayed. You can increase the row height and adjust the column width in order to see most of the information in that field. Of course, you could also use the Zoom feature (explained later in this chapter) to display all the data of a particular cell in a single dialog box.

WARNING Row and Column size settings are discarded when the Microsoft Query program is closed.

Row and Column sizes are adjusted in a manner similar to how the cells of an Excel spreadsheet are adjusted. In order to increase the row height, simply move the mouse pointer to the left of the cells, until it changes to a bar with arrows that point both up and down, as shown in Figure 8-11, and then click the mouse and move it up or down to adjust the row height.

Alternatively, you can adjust the row height by choosing Format → Row Height. This brings up the dialog box shown in Figure 8-12, where you can specify a particular row height or reset it to a Standard Height.

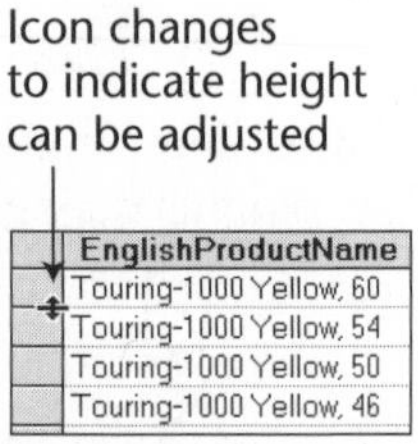

Icon changes
to indicate height
can be adjusted

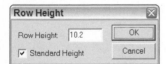

Figure 8-11: You can adjust row height by moving the mouse pointer to the row area and dragging the cell border down or up.

Figure 8-12: To reset the default height, check the Standard Height check box.

NOTE Unlike with a column cell, you cannot double-click a row cell to set the row height to a Best Fit in the Microsoft Query program.

You can adjust the width of a column by choosing Format → Column Width. When the dialog box shown in Figure 8-13 appears, you can reset the column width to the standard width or to a specific size by typing a number.

The Standard Width includes more space than the Best Fit. The default setting is to use the Standard Width. Notice that you can also apply the Best Fit option by double-clicking the right side of the cell border after the button changes, as shown in Figure 8-14.

NOTE The standard height and width vary with the type of font, the font style, and the font size being used.

Row height settings apply to all rows, whereas column width settings can be individually applied. If you want to apply the same column width to multiple cells, click each column and then choose Format → Columns to apply a specified width, Standard Width, or a Best Fit. Click the cell in the upper left of the Results section to select all columns.

NOTE Multiple columns can be selected only when they are next to one another.

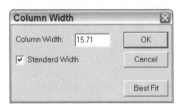

Figure 8-13: Unlike with the Row Height dialog box, you can set either a Standard Width or a Best Fit size for column cells.

Icon changes
to indicate width
can be adjusted

EnglishProductName	Size	Colo
Touring-1000 Yellow, 60	60	Yellow
Touring-1000 Yellow, 54	54	Yellow
Touring-1000 Yellow, 50	50	Yellow
Touring-1000 Yellow, 46	46	Yellow
Touring-1000 Blue, 60	60	Blue
Touring-1000 Blue, 54	54	Blue
Touring-1000 Blue, 50	50	Blue

Figure 8-14: You can adjust the column width by moving the mouse pointer to the column cell area and dragging the cell border right or left.

Modifying the Font Style

You can modify the font and font style by choosing Format → Font. Selecting this option brings up the Font dialog box shown in Figure 8-15. Here, you can choose to display the Results section in various types of available fonts, font styles, and font sizes. Note that the font style applied here does not impact the Excel report; it applies only to the data displayed in the Results section.

WARNING Font settings are discarded when you close the Microsoft Query program.

Working with Multiple Query Windows

Multiple query windows can be helpful for querying on data in another table or comparing the result sets between a test and a production database server. The various query windows can be vertically tiled (side by side) or cascaded (accessed in a full window view by choosing Window → *Query Name*).

Choose Window → Tile or Window → Cascade to work with only one query window at a time. Figure 8-16 shows how two query windows can be tiled to compare the results between two database servers.

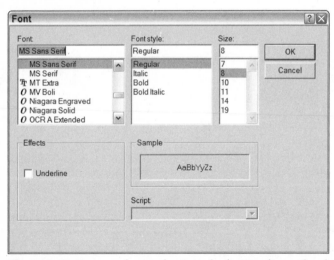

Figure 8-15: You can change the Fonts in the Results section from the Font dialog box.

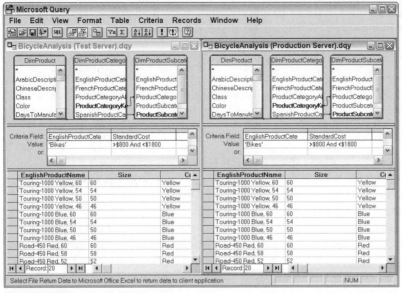

Figure 8-16: Tiling query windows can be useful for comparing the results between production and test databases.

Setting Program Options

Program options are maintained in the Options dialog box shown in Figure 8-17. These options, a potpourri of connection and query property settings, affect how Microsoft Query connects and interacts with external data sources. Connection properties, preview rows, and query edit features are all configured here. You can open this dialog box by choosing Edit → Options.

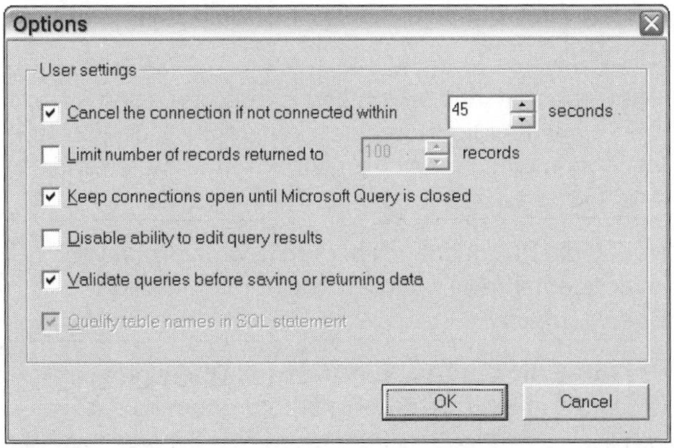

Figure 8-17: You can control query and connection properties from this dialog box.

WARNING Unlike font and column settings, options modified here are saved and affect future Query Wizard and Microsoft Query sessions.

The first option for connection time should need adjustment only when the initial connection to the database server or servers is taking longer than the time specified in that field. The next option for limiting rows applies only to the number of records read by the Microsoft Query program for previewing the result set. It does not control the number of records actually imported into the Excel report.

TIP If you want to control the number of records imported into the Excel report, use the SET ROWCOUNT n **function before the query (SQL Server) or use** Rownum = n **in the Where clause of the query (Oracle).**

The third option, for keeping the connection open, can be useful if it takes a long time to connect to the data source (use this option in conjunction with the first option). The fourth option enables the data from a single table query to be edited. It is used in conjunction with the Allow Editing item in the Records menu. Queries can optionally be validated before saving or returning data. Table 8-4 provides a more detailed explanation of each option.

Table 8-4: Explanation of Query Options

USER SETTING	EXPLANATION
Cancel the Connection if Not Connected within *n* Seconds	Use this option to control the query timeout period. If you have a slow network or you are accessing a couple of database servers in a single query, you might have to adjust this value upward.
Limit Number of Records Returned to *n* Records	Use this option to control the number of records returned and displayed in the Results section and in some preview functions. Note that this setting does not affect the number of records actually returned to the Excel report.
Keep Connections Open Until Microsoft Query Is Closed	When checked, this option keeps the connection open until the Microsoft Query program is closed. Use this option when making a connection to the external data source takes a long time.
Disable Ability to Edit Query Results	By default, this option is checked in order to prevent an accidental table update through the Microsoft Query program.
Validate Queries before Saving or Returning Data	Use this option to have the Microsoft Query program validate that the query works before returning data to Excel.

Working in the Environment

This section covers how you can use some of the basic navigation and operation functions of the Microsoft Query program environment. It shows you the primary features you're likely to use on a regular basis as you develop, manage, and save queries for Excel reports, including the following topics:

- Running a query
- Retrieving and saving queries
- Accessing the generated SQL
- Go to and zooming
- Editing data

Running a Query

A query can automatically be executed whenever it is opened or modified using the Automatic Query option. This option is toggled by clicking the Auto Query toolbar button or by choosing Records → Automatic Query.

TIP Enabling the Automatic Query option can be a nuisance when multiple changes to the SQL query are required because each change triggers a refresh.

If the Automatic Query option is disabled, the SQL query can be run using the following methods:

- Clicking the Query Now toolbar button
- Choosing Records → Query Now
- Pressing the F9 key

Retrieving and Saving Queries

Queries developed with the Query Wizard or with the Microsoft Query program can be saved for use in future Excel reports. Keep in mind that the SQL query is automatically embedded in the Excel report, so saving the query is only helpful if you plan to use it for creating *new* reports. The default location for retrieving or saving a query is (replace *user* with your Windows login):

```
c:\documents and settings\user\application data\microsoft\queries
```

You can retrieve queries from the Microsoft Query program by choosing File → Open to open a dialog box or by clicking the Open toolbar button.

> **WARNING** Microsoft Query can only retrieve query files that have a file extension of .dqy (database query), .qry (query), or .oqy (OLAP cubes).

Queries created in SQL development programs such as Query Analyzer (SQL Server 7.0/2000), Microsoft SQL Server Studio (SQL Server 2005), or Toad (Oracle) are best loaded into the Microsoft Query program using a cut-and-paste operation. Simply copy the query to your clipboard from the development program, press Alt+Tab to move to an open Microsoft Query session, click the View SQL button, and then paste the query into the SQL dialog box.

Accessing the Generated SQL

If you choose to build an SQL query using the program's graphical tools, an SQL query is still generated in the background. Adding or removing fields, modifying a filter condition, or changing a sort order using the program's graphical tools produces a corresponding change to the background SQL query. You can access this query at any time by clicking the View SQL button. Advanced users typically ignore the program's graphical tools and click the View SQL button to paste in queries developed from external SQL development programs.

Go To and Zooming

Although there is not a Find Text function, you can route to a specific record by choosing Records → Go To or by pressing the F5 key. The F5 key brings the cursor to the Record Box where you can type a record number to go to, use the buttons to move back or forward one record, or scroll to the first or last record in the Results section.

> **TIP** There is no Find function for locating specific text in the Results section. I recommend that you perform this type of operation from a true SQL development program (such as the Query Analyzer or the Microsoft SQL Server Management Studio) or from an Excel Spreadsheet report.

The Zoom function is useful for inquiring on data in fields where there is a lot of information and it cannot be fully displayed in the Results section. For example, clicking the EnglishDescription field in the DimProduct table of the AdventureWorksDW database provides a dedicated dialog box for examining the full contents of that particular cell, as shown in Figure 8-18.

You can zoom on a field by either right-clicking it twice or by choosing View → Zoom.

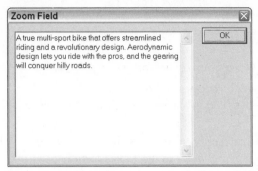

Figure 8-18: The Zoom feature is ideal for adding, editing, or viewing long strings of data in a single dialog box.

Editing Data

You can use Microsoft Query to add or modify the data in a database table. This feature can be useful when you are running a test or just need to modify or insert a few records into a table. In order for this function to work, the following conditions must be met:

- The Disabled Editing option must be unchecked.
- The query must utilize only a single table.
- The query must include all the required fields.
- The query cannot contain any Identity columns.
- The Allow Editing option must be enabled. (Choose Records → Allow Editing to toggle the setting of this option.)

Trying It Out in the Real World

Wendy Kahn, the Finance Manager at AdventureWorks, has been doing some research on the benefits of just-in-time inventory. She's interested in knowing more about how much it's costing AdventureWorks to maintain a safety level of stock for items that can be manufactured in less than three days. Wendy requested that you provide her with a PivotTable report that summarizes the safety stock level and the standard cost by product. As part of this request, Wendy would also like the ability to group the products by the number of days it takes to manufacture them and by subcategories.

Getting Down to Business

Follow these steps to complete this exercise:

1. From Excel, choose Data → From Other Sources → From Microsoft Query.

2. When the Choose Data Source dialog box appears, verify that the Use the Query Wizard to Create/Edit Queries field is unchecked, select the Adventure-WorksDW data source, and click OK.

3. When the Microsoft Query program is launched, you are presented with the Add Tables dialog box. Add the following tables to the Tables section:

   ▪ DimProduct

   ▪ DimProductCategory

   ▪ DimProductSubcategory

4. Click Close to close the Add Tables dialog box.

5. Double-click EnglishProductName, DaysToManufacture, SafetyStockLevel, StandardCost, and Status in the DimProduct table to add these fields to the Results section.

6. Double-click EnglishProductSubcategoryName in the DimProductSubcategory table to add this field to the Results section.

7. Double-click EnglishProductCategoryName in the DimProductCategory table to add this field to the Results section.

8. Choose View → Criteria if the Criteria section is not displayed.

9. Select DimProduct.DaysToManufacture or just type **DaysToManufacture** in the Criteria field of the Criteria section, and then type **<3** in Value, under DaysToManufacture.

10. Select DimProduct.StandardCost or type **StandardCost** in the Criteria field (directly to the right of DaysToManufacture); then type **> $0** in Value, under StandardCost.

11. Choose Records → Query Now if Automatic Query is not enabled.

12. Verify that your Microsoft Query window looks like Figure 8-19.

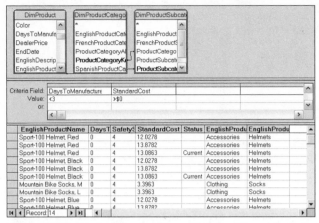

Figure 8-19: If you did everything right, the Microsoft Query window should look like this.

13. Type **StandardCost*SafetyStockLevel** in the first blank field in the Results section (next to the EnglishProductSubcategory field), as shown in Figure 8-20 to create a new field that calculates the total cost of the safety level for the selected item.

14. Click the Return Data button to exit the Microsoft Query program and bring up the Import Data dialog box.

15. Click the PivotTable Report and then OK in the Import Data dialog box to create a PivotTable report.

16. Drag EnglishProductCategoryName to the Report Filter area, EnglishProductName to the Row Labels area, and Expr (this is the new formula field that added in step 13) to the Values area of the PivotTable report.

17. Verify that your PivotTable report looks like Figure 8-21.

EnglishProductSubcategoryName	StandardCost*SafetyStockLevel
Helmets	48.1112
Helmets	55.5128
Helmets	52.3452
Helmets	48.1112
Helmets	55.5128
Helmets	52.3452
Socks	13.5852
Socks	13.5852

Figure 8-20: New fields that utilize formulas can be added to the query by simply typing them into the Results section.

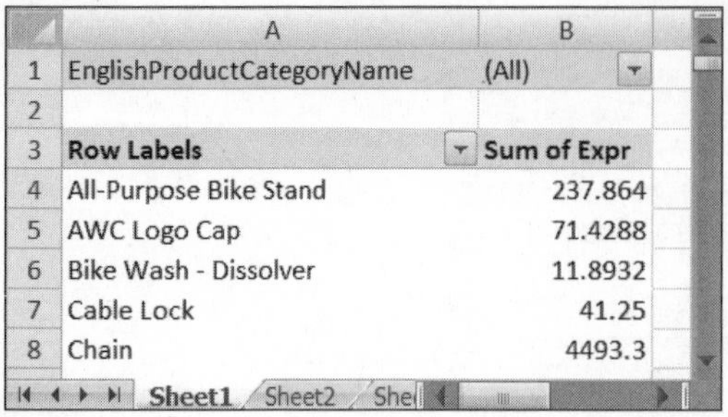

	A	B
1	EnglishProductCategoryName	(All) ▾
2		
3	**Row Labels** ▾	**Sum of Expr**
4	All-Purpose Bike Stand	237.864
5	AWC Logo Cap	71.4288
6	Bike Wash - Dissolver	11.8932
7	Cable Lock	41.25
8	Chain	4493.3

Sheet1 / Sheet2 / She

Figure 8-21: The PivotTable report for Laura appears as shown here.

WATCH THE VIDEO To see how this PivotTable report is created using the Microsoft Query program, click the file ch0801_video.avi at www.wiley.com/ go/excelreporting/2007 to watch the video.

Reviewing What You Did

This example gave you some practice building a basic SQL query using the graphical tools of the Microsoft Query program. I recommend that you review the functions and tools covered in this chapter to get more familiar with the environment and how queries are executed. Chapter 9 continues the discussion of the Microsoft Query program with more advanced SQL topics.

Chapter Review

This chapter reviewed the graphical tools of the Microsoft Query program and described how you can use them to customize and work in the environment. You learned how to access the Microsoft Query program for different types of Excel reports. In addition, the chapter discussed the purpose of each section of the Microsoft Query environment, how to toggle the display of different sections, how to configure program options, customize the environment, and perform basic functions.

CHAPTER 9

Working with SQL
in Microsoft Query

This chapter continues with the examination of the Microsoft Query program from the previous chapter, which covered the program environment, tabs, and menu items. In this chapter, you will see how the Microsoft Query program can be used to build SQL queries. All the components of a sophisticated query are reviewed, along with information on the nuances and limitations of the Microsoft Query program. The chapter also reviews the program's SQL utilities and how to use stored procedures and query multiple databases.

This chapter starts with a review of Microsoft Query's graphical tools and how they are mapped to each part of an SQL query. Next, it covers the various types of table joins that are available using the program's graphical tools. Following that, you examine the program's SQL utilities, including examples on how database objects can be created, indexed, and populated. Next, you explore detailed information and examples on stored procedures and parameter queries. Before concluding with a real-world example, you will see how to query multiple databases on one or more database servers.

Managing the SQL Query

This section shows you how to use Microsoft Query's graphical tools to build and adjust an SQL query. In Table 9-1, these tools are organized into the various parts of an SQL query to which they apply.

Table 9-1: Graphical Tools to SQL Statement

SQL PART	GRAPHICALLY SUPPORTED FUNCTIONS
Select	Adding and removing fields Creating formula fields Renaming fields Arranging the order of fields (left to right) in a query Aggregating fields Using Distinct
From	Adding tables
Where	Using criteria
Group By	Grouping records
Having	Using criteria with aggregated data

I intentionally left out the join part of the SQL query and moved it to the next section of this chapter. I did this because I've included a lot of information on table joins, and I thought it deserved its own section. There is also a lot of helpful information in the "Managing Table Joins" section for users who need a primer on the material, or for users who are unfamiliar with how the Microsoft Query program handles the various table joins and want to learn more.

Before You Begin

To set things up so that you can follow along with the examples in this section, complete these steps:

1. From Excel, choose Data → From Other Sources → From Microsoft Query.

2. When the Choose Data Source dialog box appears, verify that Use the Query Wizard to Create/Edit Queries is unchecked.

3. Select the AdventureWorksDW Database data source and click OK.

4. When the Microsoft Query program is launched, you are presented with the Add Tables dialog box. Select the DimProduct table, click Add to put this table in the Tables pane, and click Close to close the Add Tables dialog box.

5. Choose View → Criteria to show the Criteria pane if it is not already displayed.

6. Verify that your Microsoft Query window looks like Figure 9-1.

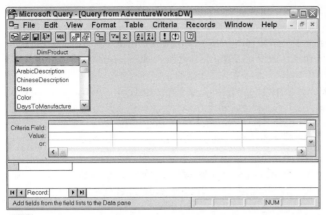

Figure 9-1: Add the DimProduct table to follow along with the examples in this section.

After you have completed these steps, you're ready to follow along with the examples in the rest of this section.

Working in the Select Part of an SQL Query

The Select part of an SQL query includes the fields, field headings (or field labels), and the order of the fields (left to right) in the query. Formula fields, aggregate functions, and keywords, such as Distinct, are also included here. This section reviews how you can use the Microsoft Query program to include these components in the Select part of your SQL query.

> **NOTE** All the functions in this section assume that the query can be displayed graphically. If the query cannot be displayed graphically, you need to perform these functions by editing the SQL query.

Adding and Removing Fields

In the Tables section, the fields in each table are listed in alphanumeric order. Looking at the DimProduct table in Figure 9-1, notice that an asterisk is displayed at the top of the table, followed by all the table's field names (in alphanumeric order). You can either choose to add individual fields to the query or add all the fields. The easiest way to add a single field to the query is usually to just double-click it. If you want to add all the fields to the query, just double-click the asterisk.

> **TIP** Double-clicking the asterisk performs a SELECT * FROM *TableName*. Thus, the fields in the query appear in the order in which they are defined in the database table, not in alphanumeric order as they are in the Tables section.

Like most things in Excel, you can choose from several methods to accomplish common tasks. Adding a field to a query is no exception; there are several ways to complete this task, and each technique does something slightly different. Table 9-2 provides a list of methods for adding fields to a query along with a short description about when to use each one.

It's just as easy to delete fields from the query. Just select the column (or columns) in the Results section and press the Delete key or choose Records → Remove Column. If you want to quickly remove all fields from a particular table in the Results section, just click the table in the Tables section and press the Delete key.

WATCH THE VIDEO To see how fields are added, moved, and deleted in this example, watch the video by clicking the ch0901_video.avi file at www.wiley.com/go/excelreporting/2007.

Complete the following steps to add fields using these different methods:

1. Double-click ProductKey in the DimProduct table to add this field to the query.

2. Double-click ReorderPoint in the DimProduct table to add it to the end of the query.

3. Select ReorderPoint in the Results section (the column is highlighted), and then Choose Records → Insert Column to insert a new column between ProductKey and ReorderPoint.

4. When the Insert Column dialog box appears, select EnglishProductName from the Field drop-down list, click Insert to add this field to the query, and click Close to close the Insert Column dialog box.

5. Drag SafetyStockLevel from the DimProduct table and drop it on top of ReorderPoint in the Results section to add it between EnglishProductName and ReorderPoint.

TIP If you make a mistake, just select Edit → Undo to undo the previous step.

6. Select Status by clicking a drop-down arrow in a blank cell of the Results section.

7. Now, try removing that column from the query by selecting the Status column (the column is highlighted) and pressing the Delete key.

8. Select Records → Query Now if Automatic Query is not enabled.

9. Verify that your Results section looks like Figure 9-2.

Table 9-2: Methods for Adding a Field to the Query

METHOD	USE WHEN
Double-click a field in a table	Quickly adding a field to the end of the query.
Drag-and-drop	Adding a field to a specific place in the query.
Results	Adding expression or formula fields at the end of the query.
Records → Add Column*	Adding a field to a particular location, specifying a name, and/or applying an aggregate function.

*If a cell is selected in the Results section, Records → Add Column is replaced with Records → Insert Column.

ProductKey	EnglishProductName	SafetyStockLevel	ReorderPoint
1	Adjustable Race	1000	750
2	Bearing Ball	1000	750
3	BB Ball Bearing	800	600
4	Headset Ball Bearings	800	600
5	Blade	800	600
6	LL Crankarm	500	375
7	ML Crankarm	500	375

Figure 9-2: If you did everything right, your Results section should look like this.

Creating Formula Fields

Formula fields are useful when you need to add a field to the query that doesn't currently exist in the database. This might include concatenating two or more fields into a single field or performing some type of mathematical or string operation on a field. For example, you could subtract the ReorderPoint quantity from the SafetyStockLevel quantity to derive the BufferLevel quantity. This BufferLevel field is referred to as a *formula field* because it uses an expression, or formula.

Follow these steps to create the BufferLevel formula field:

1. Verify that no records are selected in the Results section, and then choose Records → Add Column.

2. When the Add Column dialog box appears, type **SafetyStockLevel-ReorderPoint** in the Field field and press the Tab key to move to Column Heading.

3. Type **BufferLevel** in the Column Heading field and verify that your dialog box looks like Figure 9-3.

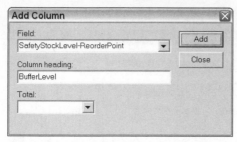

Figure 9-3: You can enter formulas, expressions, and operators into the Field box of this dialog box to create formula fields in your query.

4. Click the Add button to the insert the new formula field into the query and click Close to close the Add Column dialog box.

5. Select Records → Query Now if Automatic Query is not enabled.

6. Verify that the Results section looks like what is shown in Figure 9-4.

You can also create a formula field by selecting a blank cell in the Results section and then simply typing an expression or formula into the column heading cell. Table 9-3 includes some examples of formulas that you can use in your own SQL queries.

ProductKey	EnglishProductName	SafetyStockLevel	ReorderPoint	BufferLevel
1	Adjustable Race	1000	750	250
2	Bearing Ball	1000	750	250
3	BB Ball Bearing	800	600	200
4	Headset Ball Bearings	800	600	200
5	Blade	800	600	200
6	LL Crankarm	500	375	125
7	ML Crankarm	500	375	125
8	HL Crankarm	500	375	125
9	Chainring Bolts	1000	750	250

Figure 9-4: A formula field is useful when that particular field doesn't already exist in a database table and can be derived from other fields that do exist.

Table 9-3: Some Examples of Formula Fields

CALCULATION	EXPLANATION
GETDATE()	Produces the current date.
UPPER(EnglishProductName)	Uppercases EnglishProductName.
StandardCost*1.10	Adds 10 percent to the value of StandardCost.
1	Shows a 1 in the column.
'XYZ'	Shows XYZ in the column.
ProductKey + 'XYZ'	Adds the text XYZ to the end of the ProductKey.
LEFT(EnglishProductName,10)	Shows the first 10 positions of EnglishProductName.

You can also combine several operations into a single one. For example, instead of just using LEFT(EnglishProductName,10) to obtain the first 10 positions of the product name, you could use UPPER(LEFT(EnglishProductName,10)) to also obtain the results in uppercase, as shown in Figure 9-5.

CROSS-REFERENCE Read the SQL reference in Appendix A for a more complete list of available string functions and some examples of how you can use them to modify column text.

Changing a Column Name

The field names used in the AdventureWorksDW database tables are easy to understand. This is typically the case when you're working with OLAP databases (such as the AdventureWorksDW database). However, that's rarely the case when you're working with OLTP databases (such as the AdventureWorks database). There's usually some type of sensible technical naming convention in place, but the name is usually not entirely spelled out. If you're building reports that pull data from an OLTP database, you should consider changing the field heading to something more meaningful to the report user. For example, the field CUST_NUM could be labeled as Customer Number or Customer ID.

NOTE The AdventureWorks OLTP database uses full field names throughout its various database tables, but that's rarely the case when working with enterprise-level OLTP databases.

Besides changing a technical field heading to a layman-friendly heading, there are also several other reasons why you might want to change the column name. Perhaps the label isn't descriptive or suitable enough for the report. Renaming fields, such as from Discount to Sales Discount or from Amount to Amount Paid, may lead to a more understandable Excel report. If formula fields are being added to the report, an appropriate name should also be assigned to it. In Figure 9-3, this was accomplished in a single step. In Figure 9-5, however, the name of the field is the same as the formula.

Column names can be modified by double-clicking the field or by clicking the field in the Results pane, and choosing Records → Edit Column. Either method brings up the Edit Column dialog box shown in Figure 9-6.

UPPER(LEFT(EnglishProductName,10))
ADJUSTABLE
BEARING BA
BB BALL BE
HEADSET BA
BLADE
LL CRANKAR
ML CRANKAR
HL CRANKAR

Figure 9-5: You can combine multiple operations to create a formula field.

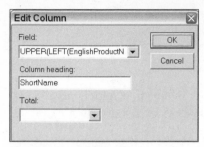

Figure 9-6: Field headings can be applied from this dialog box.

Follow these steps to practice changing the names of columns in the Results section:

1. Add the formula field shown in Figure 9-5 by selecting a blank cell in the Results section and typing in the formula **UPPER(LEFT(EnglishProduct-Name,10))**.

2. Select the new column and choose Records → Edit Column to launch the Edit Column dialog box.

3. Type **ShortName** in the Column Heading field, verify that your dialog box looks like Figure 9-6, and click OK to close the Edit Column dialog box.

4. Double-click the EnglishProductName column (second field from the left) to open the Edit Column dialog box.

5. Type **LongName** in the Column Heading field and click OK to close the Edit Column dialog box.

6. Select Records → Query Now if Automatic Query is not enabled.

7. Verify that the Results section looks like Figure 9-7.

ProductKey	LongName	SafetyStockLevel	ReorderPoint	BufferLevel	ShortName
1	Adjustable Race	1000	750	250	ADJUSTABLE
2	Bearing Ball	1000	750	250	BEARING BA
3	BB Ball Bearing	800	600	200	BB BALL BE
4	Headset Ball Bearings	800	600	200	HEADSET BA
5	Blade	800	600	200	BLADE
6	LL Crankarm	500	375	125	LL CRANKAR
7	ML Crankarm	500	375	125	ML CRANKAR
8	HL Crankarm	500	375	125	HL CRANKAR
9	Chainring Bolts	1000	750	250	CHAINRING
10	Chainring Nut	1000	750	250	CHAINRING
11	Chainring	1000	750	250	CHAINRING

Figure 9-7: EnglishProductName is renamed to LongName and the formula field is renamed to ShortName.

When the field heading is renamed, the background SQL statement is also modified by including an AS 'Field Heading' after the column name. You can click the View SQL button to review the SQL query shown here:

```
SELECT DimProduct.ProductKey,
       DimProduct.EnglishProductName AS 'LongName',
       DimProduct.SafetyStockLevel,
```

```
        DimProduct.ReorderPoint,
        SafetyStockLevel-ReorderPoint AS 'BufferLevel',
        UPPER(LEFT(EnglishProductName,10)) AS 'ShortName'
FROM AdventureWorksDW.dbo.DimProduct DimProduct
```

WARNING Although Microsoft Query puts the field heading in single quotes, this can be problematic when SQL queries are pasted into the SQL window. Try to use brackets ([ ]) instead of single quotes (' ') to ensure that Microsoft Query can properly interpret the field headings (explained later in the "Using SQL Functions" section).

Keep in mind that the Edit Column dialog box is only enabled when the query can be graphically displayed. If it cannot be graphically displayed, you need to specify the field names by modifying the underlying SQL query. In the PivotTable and Spreadsheet report chapters (Chapters 4 and 15, respectively), I show you how to rename fields from the Excel report, regardless of whether the query can be graphically displayed in the Microsoft Query program.

Arranging the Order of Fields in a Query

Arranging the order of the fields in a query (left to right) is just as easy as adding or removing a field. Just select the column and drag it to a new position in the query.

Complete these steps to follow along with the example in this chapter:

1. Click ShortName and verify that the column heading and its cell below are highlighted.

2. Drag ShortName between LongName and SafetyStockLevel.

3. Verify that the Results section looks like Figure 9-8.

ProductKey	LongName	ShortName	SafetyStockLevel	ReorderPoint	BufferLevel
1	Adjustable Race	ADJUSTABLE	1000	750	250
2	Bearing Ball	BEARING BA	1000	750	250
3	BB Ball Bearing	BB BALL BE	800	600	200
4	Headset Ball Bearings	HEADSET BA	800	600	200
5	Blade	BLADE	800	600	200
6	LL Crankarm	LL CRANKAR	500	375	125
7	ML Crankarm	ML CRANKAR	500	375	125
8	HL Crankarm	HL CRANKAR	500	375	125
9	Chainring Bolts	CHAINRING	1000	750	250
10	Chainring Nut	CHAINRING	1000	750	250
11	Chainring	CHAINRING	1000	750	250

Figure 9-8: You can change field order by using the drag-and-drop features of Microsoft Query.

As soon as you perform this step, the underlying SQL query is immediately modified. You can click the View SQL button to verify that the following query appears:

```
SELECT DimProduct.ProductKey,
       DimProduct.EnglishProductName AS 'LongName',
    UPPER(LEFT(EnglishProductName,10)) AS 'ShortName',
       DimProduct.SafetyStockLevel,
       DimProduct.ReorderPoint,
       SafetyStockLevel-ReorderPoint AS 'BufferLevel'
FROM AdventureWorksDW.dbo.DimProduct DimProduct
```

NOTE Adjusting the order of the fields in a query primarily applies to Spreadsheet reports. In a PivotTable, the fields are meant to be dynamically dragged to different locations in the report; so the order of fields in a query applies only to the PivotTable Field List dialog box. Of course, this can also be important because you should organize and group fields so that they can be easily located.

Using Aggregate Functions

Aggregate functions compute a single value result for a particular column or group of columns. So, rather than pulling all the records where a particular product was sold, you can return just a single product record with the sum of sales amount for all the records with that product. You also can calculate the average selling price for that product or find the minimum or maximum price across all the records. In short, aggregate functions scan through all the records for a particular column (or columns) while performing some type of function, such that only a single value is returned.

Microsoft Query provides graphical support for the following aggregate functions:

- **AVG:** Computes an average
- **COUNT:** Counts the number of records
- **MAX:** Finds the maximum value
- **MIN:** Finds the minimum value
- **SUM:** Computes a sum

NOTE Review the online help included in your database software for a complete list and description of aggregate functions.

You can create an aggregate function by double-clicking a column name or by choosing Records → Edit Column.

To see how this works, try this example:

1. Choose File → New from the Microsoft Query program to start a new query.

2. When the Choose Data Source dialog box appears, select the Adventure-WorksDW data source and click OK.

3. Double-click FactInternetSales in the Add Tables dialog box to add it to the Tables pane of the Microsoft Query program, and then click the Close button to close the Add Tables dialog box.

4. Add ProductKey and then OrderQuantity to the Results pane by double-clicking these fields in the FactInternetSales table.

5. Click OrderQuantity in the Results pane (the field heading and the cells below are highlighted), and then click the Cycle Through Totals button once to cycle the aggregation type to SUM.

6. Select Records → Query Now if Automatic Query is not enabled.

7. Verify that the Results section looks like Figure 9-9.

In the example shown in Figure 9-9, you might want to rename the field to something like TotalUnitsOnOrder. In practice, you may find it preferable to add an aggregated column through the Add Column dialog box by choosing Records → Add Column because you can define the field, the field heading, and the aggregation method all at the same time.

Here's the SQL generated by the Microsoft Query program. Notice that the Group By statement is automatically added:

```
SELECT FactInternetSales.ProductKey,
       Sum(FactInternetSales.OrderQuantity) AS 'Sum of OrderQuantity'
FROM AdventureWorksDW.dbo.FactInternetSales FactInternetSales
GROUP BY FactInternetSales.ProductKey
```

NOTE A Group By **statement is required for all the non-aggregated fields in an SQL query when an aggregate function is used.**

ProductKey	Sum of OrderQuantity
384	199
361	427
576	147
564	140
487	733

Figure 9-9: The Cycle Through Totals button cycles through each aggregate function for a selected column, each time it is clicked.

Using Distinct

You can use the Distinct function when you want to obtain only the unique rows of a result set. For example, you can use Distinct to create a unique list of promotion keys in the FactInternetSales table. Starting with a blank Results pane and the FactInternet-Sales table in the Tables pane, add PromotionKey to the Results pane, as shown in Figure 9-10. Notice the repeating "1"s under the PromotionKey column heading. This happens because the promotion key is pulled once for each record in the FactInternet-Sales table.

The SQL query produced for this query is as follows:

```
SELECT FactInternetSales.PromotionKey
FROM AdventureWorksDW.dbo.FactInternetSales FactInternetSales
```

In order to obtain only the unique values by adding the Distinct keyword to the SQL query, follow these steps:

1. Choose View → Query Properties.

2. When the Query Properties dialog box shown in Figure 9-11 appears, check Unique Values Only and click OK.

3. Select Records → Query Now if Automatic Query is not enabled.

4. Verify that the Results section looks like Figure 9-12.

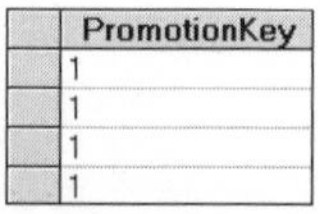

Figure 9-10: The promotion key is shown for each record in the FactInternetSales table.

Figure 9-11: Check Unique Values Only to add the Distinct keyword to the fields in the Select part of an SQL query.

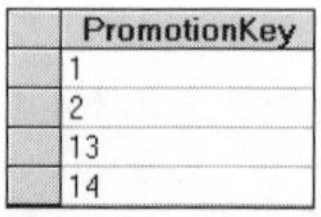

Figure 9-12: Only the unique values of PromotionKey are returned when the Unique Values Only option is checked.

As soon as you perform this step, the underlying SQL query is modified. You can click the View SQL button to verify that the query looks like this:

```
SELECT DISTINCT FactInternetSales.PromotionKey
FROM AdventureWorksDW.dbo.FactInternetSales FactInternetSales
```

Working in the Where and Having Parts

You can add filter conditions to either the Where or the Having clause of an SQL query to restrict the type of data returned. The principal difference between these two clauses is that the Where clause is used for filtering non-aggregated data, whereas the Having clause is used for filtering aggregated data. So if you want to select only the products having a certain average quantity sold, you would put the filter criteria in the Having clause because AVG is an aggregate function. If you are not familiar with SQL programming, this might sound a little confusing. Don't worry, a couple of examples are included later in this section to help contextualize how this works.

WARNING The Microsoft Query program usually builds either a Having clause or a Where clause, not both. If not properly corrected, this can lead to substantially reduced performance. See the "Distinguishing between Where and Having" section of this chapter for more information about this topic.

Introducing Some More Operators

Chapter 7 provided a list of the valid mathematical operators (Table 7-3) and string operators (Table 7-4) that could be used in a filter. All of these operators are available in the Microsoft Query program, along with the four more string operators listed in Table 9-4.

Table 9-4: Additional Operators in Microsoft Query

OPERATOR	EXPLANATION	SQL EQUIVALENT
Is Between	Between *x* and *y*	BETWEEN x AND y
Is Not Between	Not between *x* and *y*	NOT BETWEEN x AND y
Is One Of	Contains the specified values *A, B, C, n...* (Use when selecting multiple values.)	IN ('A','B','C')
Is Not One Of	Does not contain the specified values *A, B, C, n...* (Use when excluding multiple values.)	NOT IN ('A','B','C')

> **CROSS-REFERENCE** Read the SQL reference in Appendix A for a more complete list of the operators available with SQL programming.

Adding Criteria to a Query

Microsoft Query includes a few different graphical tools for creating filter conditions. You can choose to create them using the following methods:

- Choose Criteria → Add Criteria to open the Add Criteria dialog box where you can pick from a list of valid operators.
- Select a field from a blank Criteria Field cell in the Criteria section, and then specify an operator and value in the Value field.
- Select a value in the Results section, and then click the Criteria Equals tab button to apply a filter that pulls only those records with the selected value in that column.

Using the Add Criteria Dialog Box

Using the Add Criteria dialog box, you can choose from a list of predefined mathematical and string operators. This is similar to the Filter Data dialog box of the Query Wizard that you saw in Chapter 7, except that you have a few more operators and some additional features and functions.

Follow these steps to see how this method works:

1. Start with a new query that uses only the DimEmployee table in the AdventureWorksDW database.

2. Double-click the fields DepartmentName, Gender, LastName, and Vacation-Hours (in this order) to add these fields to the query.

3. Choose Criteria → Add Criteria to launch the Add Criteria dialog box.

4. Select DepartmentName in the Field drop-down box, and then select Is One Of in the Operator drop-down box, as shown in Figure 9-13.

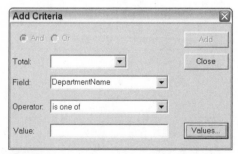

Figure 9-13: You select fields and operators from a drop-down list in the Add Criteria dialog box.

5. Click the Values button to open the Select Value(s) dialog box where you can specify the values to include in the query.

6. Notice that the unique values in DepartmentName appear in the Values dialog box. Select the values Executive and Finance.

7. Verify that the Select Value(s) dialog box looks like Figure 9-14 and click OK to close this dialog box and return to the Add Criteria dialog box.

8. Notice that in Figure 9-15, Executive, Finance is added to the Value field of the Add Criteria dialog box. Click the Add button to apply this filter and click Close to close the dialog box.

9. Select Records → Query Now if Automatic Query is not enabled.

10. Verify that your Microsoft Query window looks like Figure 9-15.

As soon as you perform this step, the underlying SQL query is modified. You can click the View SQL button to verify that the query looks like this:

```
SELECT DimEmployee.DepartmentName,
       DimEmployee.Gender,
       DimEmployee.LastName,
       DimEmployee.VacationHours
FROM AdventureWorksDW.dbo.DimEmployee DimEmployee
WHERE (DimEmployee.DepartmentName In ('Executive','Finance'))
```

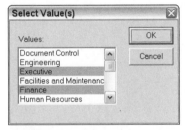

Figure 9-14: Select the unique values to include in the filter condition from the Select Value(s) dialog box.

Criteria Field:	DepartmentName			
Value:	In ('Executive','Finance')			
or:				

DepartmentName	Gender	LastName	VacationHours
Finance	F	Poe	60
Finance	F	Kahn	55
Finance	F	Spoon	61
Finance	M	Barber	56
Executive	M	Sánchez	99
Finance	M	Walton	62

Record: 9

Figure 9-15: The filter criteria are automatically added in the Criteria section of the Microsoft Query program.

Using the Criteria Section

You can also specify filter conditions in the Criteria section of the Microsoft Query program. This method provides some additional flexibility because you are not constrained to the list of valid operators in the Operator drop-down box. For example, the SQL function `Soundex` is not listed as a valid operator, but it is a supported SQL function that enables you to search for strings that *sound like* specified text: `Soundex(Smith)`, for example, returns Smith, Smithe, Smyth, and Smythe.

Looking at Figure 9-15, you can see that the Microsoft Query program simply added the filter criteria into the Criteria section from the Add Criteria dialog box. This time, bypass the Add Criteria dialog box and enter the filter conditions directly into the Criteria section.

To see how this works, follow these steps:

1. Click the Criteria Field cell to the right of DepartmentName in the Criteria section, type **Soundex(LastName)**, and press the down arrow to move to the Value field.

2. Type **Soundex('Lew')** in the Value field.

3. Choose Records → Query Now if Automatic Query is not enabled.

4. Verify that your Microsoft Query window looks like Figure 9-16.

You have now selected only the records that have a DepartmentName of Executive or Finance and a LastName that sounds like the word *Lew*. The SQL query has automatically been adjusted to include the new criteria shown here:

```
SELECT DimEmployee.DepartmentName,
       DimEmployee.Gender,
       DimEmployee.LastName,
       DimEmployee.VacationHours
FROM AdventureWorksDW.dbo.DimEmployee DimEmployee
WHERE (DimEmployee.DepartmentName In ('Executive','Finance'))
  AND (Soundex(LastName)=Soundex('Lew'))
```

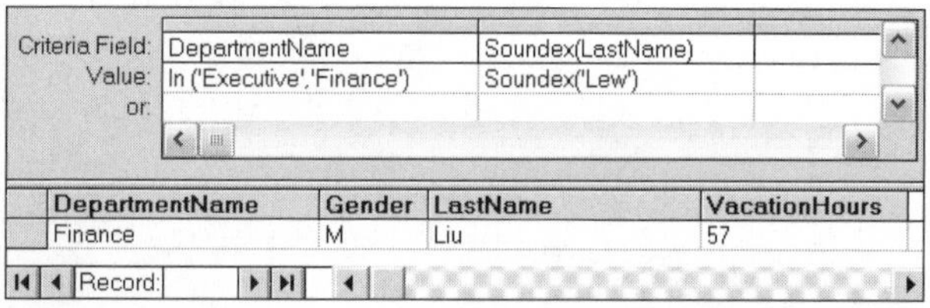

Figure 9-16: You can save time by entering filter conditions directly into the Criteria section of Microsoft Query.

TIP You can use other functions such as LEFT, SUBSTRING, and UPPER by simply including the criteria field inside that function, just like I did in the Criteria section of Figure 9-16.

Using the Criteria Equals Button

The Criteria Equals button provides a quick and easy method for applying a column filter based on a particular cell value that is selected in the Results section. In order to use this feature, simply select a cell in the Results section and click the Criteria Equals button. Keep in mind that this method permits only one value to be selected at a time, and the only operator that is used for the filter is Equals. If you are doing some preliminary analysis or troubleshooting, this tab button can be helpful for quickly honing in on particular records that have the specified value in the selected column.

Adding and Removing Criteria

Remove criteria displayed in the Criteria section by first selecting the column (or columns) in the Criteria section and then pressing the Delete key. Choose Criteria → Remove All Criteria to remove all the criteria shown in the Criteria section.

Distinguishing between Where and Having

The Where clause of an SQL query is used for filtering non-aggregated data, and the Having clause of an SQL query is used for filtering aggregated data. A Group By statement is also required for all the non-aggregated fields in an SQL query whenever the Having clause is used. Keep in mind that although all the filter conditions can be specified in the Having part of the SQL query, this can result in substantially reduced performance.

In order to illustrate the differences between the Where and Having clauses of an SQL query — and how the Microsoft Query program builds these parts of the query from its graphical tools — I've included an example.

Complete these steps to follow along:

1. Start with a new query that uses only the DimEmployee table in the AdventureWorksDW database.

2. Double-click the fields DepartmentName and VacationHours (in this order) to add these fields to the query.

3. Select Records → Query Now if Automatic Query is not enabled.

4. Verify that your Results section looks like Figure 9-17.

DepartmentName	VacationHours
Production	21
Marketing	42
Engineering	2
Tool Design	48
Tool Design	48
Tool Design	9
Marketing	40

Figure 9-17: The DepartmentName and VacationHours columns from the DimEmployee table.

Now, say that the AdventureWorks financial controller has requested a list of departments that have accumulated more than 500 vacation hours.

NOTE You may already know from reading Chapter 3 that the dataset could be put into a PivotTable to identify the departments that exceed the 500 total hours specified by the AdventureWorks financial controller. However, in the enterprise, you may encounter situations where this condition must be applied *prior* to the data being loaded into a PivotTable report; this is equivalent to applying a filter in the Criteria section (covered in the previous section of this chapter).

Now, aggregate VacationHours by DepartmentName and apply a filter in the Where clause to select only the records that have more than 500 vacation hours. Follow these steps to aggregate VacationHours by DepartmentName:

1. Double-click VacationHours in the Results section to bring up the Edit Column dialog box.

2. Type **Total Vacation Hours** in the Column Heading, and then select Sum from the Total drop-down box.

3. Verify that the Edit Column dialog box looks like Figure 9-18 and click OK to aggregate VacationHours by DepartmentName and to close the dialog box.

4. Choose Records → Query Now if Automatic Query is not enabled. The Results section displays the total vacation hours by department.

5. Verify that the Results section looks like Figure 9-19.

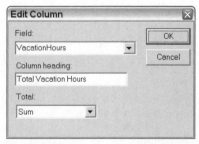

Figure 9-18: You can label and aggregate columns in a query from this dialog box.

DepartmentName	Total Vacation Hours
Document Control	385
Engineering	21
Executive	99
Facilities and Maintenance	623
Finance	595
Human Resources	309
Information Services	695
Marketing	436
Production	8787
Production Control	318

Figure 9-19: Vacation hours aggregated by Department.

Now that your Results section looks like Figure 9-19, take a look at the difference between applying a filter in the Where clause and the Having clause of an SQL query.

Deciding between the Where and Having Clause

Filters in the Having clause are applied *after* the records are aggregated. This is much different than filters in the Where clause, which are applied *before* records are aggregated. For example, if a filter is specified in the Where clause of this SQL query, only the records meeting that condition are pulled. After that, the *selected* records are aggregated. In contrast, if the filter is specified in the Having clause, then *all* the records are pulled and aggregated. After *all* the records are aggregated, the filter on the specified departments is applied. Do you see the difference here? Criteria specified in the Having clause results in all the records being selected and aggregated *before* the filter is applied. When you're working with large datasets, it can take much longer to select and aggregate all the records using the Having clause than to select and aggregate only a subset of them using the Where clause.

You might be asking yourself why you should ever use filters in the Having clause if the Where clause is so much faster. Even though filters are much faster in the Where clause, they are applied at the *individual* record level. Thus, filters in the Where clause of this section's example would be evaluated for each employee. If you want to select only the departments with 500 or more total vacation hours, you must filter the records on an *aggregated* total by specifying the filter in the Having clause.

> **WARNING** If you are using the graphical tools of Microsoft Query (rather than just pasting in an SQL query from an external query development program), you don't have a choice of whether the filter criteria is put into the Where or Having part of an SQL query. The Microsoft Query program does it automatically, combining all the filter criteria into the Having part of an SQL query whenever a field in the query is aggregated and there is more than one filter condition specified.

Applying a Filter in the Where Clause

Filters can be applied to the Where clause of an SQL query by choosing Criteria → Add Criteria. This brings up the Add Criteria dialog box (shown earlier in Figure 9-13).

Follow these steps to add a filter in the Where clause of your SQL query to select only the records that have more than 500 vacation hours:

1. Start with a new query that uses only the DimEmployee table in the Adven-tureWorksDW database.

2. Double-click the fields DepartmentName and VacationHours (in this order) to add these fields to the query.

3. Choose Criteria → Add Criteria to bring up the Add Criteria dialog box.

4. Select VacationHours in the Add Criteria dialog box, Is Greater Than in the Operator drop-down box, and type **500** in the Value field.

5. Click the Add button and then the Close button to apply the filter and to close the Add Criteria dialog box.

6. Select Records → Query Now if Automatic Query is not enabled.

The Results section should be empty. This is because the filter is being applied *before* the records are aggregated. And, because there aren't any employees with more than 500 hours, no records are selected.

Clicking the View SQL button displays the following query:

```
SELECT DimEmployee.DepartmentName,
       Sum(DimEmployee.VacationHours) AS 'Total Vacation Hours'
FROM AdventureWorksDW.dbo.DimEmployee DimEmployee
WHERE (DimEmployee.VacationHours>500)
GROUP BY DimEmployee.DepartmentName
```

Notice that VacationHours was used instead of SUM(VacationHours) in the Criteria section. The query eliminated all the records because the maximum Vacation-Hours for any *individual* employee is 99. Now, try this query again with 80 hours instead of 500 hours. Notice that only the individual records that have more than 80 hours are returned. Once you're done, set the hours back to 500.

Applying a Filter in the Having Clause

Filters can be applied to the Having clause of an SQL query by using an aggregated field in the Criteria section. In this section's example, the controller requested a list of departments that have a *total* of more than 500 vacation hours. In SQL terminology, that's HAVING SUM(VacationHours) > 500.

Follow these steps to select only the departments that have more than 500 vacation hours:

1. Start with a new query that uses only the DimEmployee table in the Adven-tureWorksDW database.

2. Double-click the fields DepartmentName and VacationHours (in this order) to add these fields to the query.

3. Double-click VacationHours in the Results section to bring up the Edit Column dialog box with VacationHours in Field. Choose Sum from the Total field, and click OK to close the Edit Column dialog box and to sum VacationHours by DepartmentName.

4. Choose Criteria → Add Criteria to bring up the Add Criteria dialog box. Select Sum from Total, VacationHours from Field, Is Greater Than from Operator, and type **500** in Value.

5. Verify that the Add Criteria dialog box looks like Figure 9-20 and then click Add to add the criteria field, and Close to close the dialog box.

6. Choose Records → Query Now if Automatic Query is not enabled.

Notice that six records are selected in the Results pane. This is because the filter criteria is included in the `Having` clause of the SQL query and is therefore not applied until after the rows are aggregated. If you click the View SQL button, the query is displayed as follows:

```
SELECT DimEmployee.DepartmentName,
       Sum(DimEmployee.VacationHours) AS 'Total Vacation Hours'
FROM AdventureWorksDW.dbo.DimEmployee DimEmployee
GROUP BY DimEmployee.DepartmentName
HAVING (Sum(DimEmployee.VacationHours)>500)
```

Figure 9-20: You can apply an aggregate function to the criteria field in this dialog box.

Working in the Order By Part

The `Order By` part of an SQL query is used to sort the result set of an SQL query. Keep in mind that a sort order should only be specified for a Spreadsheet report and not for a PivotTable report (explained in Chapter 7). There are two methods for applying a sort order:

■ Choose Records → Sort to view and modify the sort order information.

■ Select a column (or columns), click the Ascending or Descending button to first remove all the existing sort order information, and then add a sort for the selected column (or columns).

Continuing with the example from the previous section, choosing Records → Sort brings up the Sort dialog box shown in Figure 9-21.

You can add or remove column sorts in this dialog box. Notice that only the fields listed in the Results pane of Microsoft Query are displayed in the Column drop-down box. However, unlike the Query Wizard program (covered in Chapter 7), you can type in any field that is listed in the table.

WARNING You can only select available fields in the Column field of the Sort dialog box when a column in the query is being aggregated (as is the case in this example if you are following along). This is because the Microsoft Query program is not able to automatically adjust the Group By statement to ensure that the SQL query remains valid.

Looking at Figure 9-21, you can see that there are no up or down arrows for changing the sort order priority. If you want to change the sort order priority, follow these steps:

1. In the Sorts in Query pane, select the field you want to delete from the sort order and click Remove.

2. In the Sorts in Query pane, select the field that you want to insert the new field in front of.

3. From the Column drop-down box, select the field that you want to insert and click the Ascending or Descending button; and then click the Add button to insert this new field above the field you selected in step 2.

You can also apply a single sort order by selecting a column (or columns) and clicking the ascending or descending sort buttons. If you use this shortcut, keep in mind that it removes any existing sort order instructions defined in the query.

NOTE You should use a sort order only for Spreadsheet reports. A sort order doesn't provide any useful utility in PivotTable reports; it serves only to increase the amount of time it takes to execute the query.

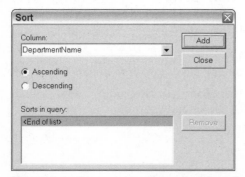

Figure 9-21: You manage the sort order information for a query by using the Sort dialog box.

Managing Table Joins

Table joins can be a confusing topic, especially for users who are not familiar with SQL programming. This section shows you how to use the graphical tools in Microsoft Query to create several types of table joins. It also describes each type of table join, demonstrates how different join types affect the result set produced from the query, and reviews the underlying SQL query that is produced. The joins described in this section include the following:

- Inner join
- Left join
- Right join
- Cross join
- Self join
- Full join

All of the joins, except the Full join, are supported by the graphical tools in the Microsoft Query program. The Right join is supported insofar as the tables are reversed in the SQL query to create a Left join. The Cross join is created by removing any link between the two tables, whereas the Self join is created by adding the table to the Tables section twice.

If you are using the Microsoft Query program to create table joins, keep in mind that some restrictions are imposed that wouldn't normally apply if you were using an SQL development program to create the query. However, because the Microsoft Query program can handle only so much complexity through its graphical tools, you are limited in what you can do. These limitations are explained in the appropriate sections.

Before You Begin

In order to follow along with this section, you need to create the DimCategoryForecast table in the AdventureWorksDW database, along with inserting some records into the new table.

To create the DimCategoryForecast table in the AdventureWorksDW database, follow these steps:

1. Open a Microsoft Query dialog box using the AdventureWorksDW Database data source.

2. Choose File → Execute SQL to bring up an Execute SQL dialog box. Verify that the AdventureWorksDW database is selected in the bottom part of the dialog box.

3. Paste the following SQL query into the Execute SQL dialog box to create the DimCategoryForecast table and click Execute:

```
CREATE TABLE [dbo].[DimCategoryForecast]
            ([ProductCategoryKey] [int] NOT NULL,
             [ForecastAmount] [int] NOT NULL,
             [Active] [char](1) NOT NULL,
CONSTRAINT   [PK_CategoryForecast]
PRIMARY KEY CLUSTERED ([ProductCategoryKey]) ON [PRIMARY])ON [PRIMARY]
```

ON THE WEB You can download the DimCategoryForecastTbl.txt file to your computer from this book's companion web site at www.wiley.com/go/excelreporting/2007. **Look in the Chap09.zip file or the Chap09 directory, depending on which file you download.**

4. Click OK to acknowledge that the SQL command ran successfully, and then clear the contents of the Execute SQL dialog box.

TIP The Execute button becomes disabled when the Execute SQL window is completely cleared.

5. Paste the following SQL query into the Execute SQL dialog box to insert records into the DimCategoryForecast table, and then click Execute:

```
INSERT INTO DimCategoryForecast
SELECT '0', 4000,'N'
UNION ALL
SELECT '2', 9000,'Y'
UNION ALL
SELECT '3',12000,'Y'
UNION ALL
SELECT '5', 10000,'Y'
UNION ALL
SELECT '7', 3000,'Y'
```

ON THE WEB You can download the DimCategoryForecastVal.txt file to your computer from this book's companion web site at www.wiley.com/go/excelreporting/2007. **Look in the Chap09.zip file or the Chap09 directory.**

6. Click OK to acknowledge that the SQL command ran successfully; then click Cancel to close the Execute SQL dialog box.

After you have created the DimCategoryForecast table, complete these steps to follow along with the examples in this section:

1. From Excel, choose Data → From Other Sources → From Microsoft Query.

2. When the Choose Data Source dialog box appears, verify that Use the Query Wizard to Create/Edit Queries is unchecked, select the AdventureWorksDW Database data source, and click OK.

3. When the Microsoft Query program is launched, you are presented with the Add Tables dialog box.

   a. First, add the DimCategoryForecast table.

   b. Then add the DimProductCategory table to the Tables section.

   c. Once the tables have been added, you'll notice that the tables are joined on ProductCategoryKey (the field name that is common to both tables). Click Close to close the Add Tables dialog box.

4. Add ProductCategoryKey from the DimCategoryForecast table to the query and rename it to **Forecast-CategoryKey**.

5. Add ProductCategoryKey from the DimProductCategory table to the query and rename it to **Category-CategoryKey**.

6. Choose Records → Query Now if Automatic Query is not enabled.

7. Verify that your Microsoft Query window looks like Figure 9-22.

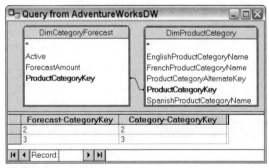

Figure 9-22: Microsoft Query automatically joins the tables on field names that are common to each table.

Before you start this section, carefully review the values in the DimCategoryForecast table (see Table 9-5) and the DimProductCategory table (see Table 9-6) to be sure that you understand the contents of each table and the differences.

The bolded ProductCategoryKey values are also in the DimProductCategory table. The records for the DimProductCategory table are shown in Table 9-6. For simplicity, I've included only two columns of the table. (There is no need to include the others because they aren't referenced in this section's examples.)

The bolded ProductCategoryKey values are also in the DimCategoryForecast table.

After you have created the new DimCategoryForecast table in the Adventure-WorksDW database and reviewed the contents of the DimProductCategory and the DimCategoryForecast table, you're ready to begin learning about each table join.

Understanding Joins and Join Types

The tables and the table joins of an SQL query are displayed in the Tables section of the Microsoft Query program. The primary key fields are shown in bold, and table joins are represented by connection lines. An Inner join is represented by a line with a ball on either side, whereas a Left or Right join is represented by a ball on one side and an arrow on the other side. Cross joins are marked by the lack of any connection line in the Tables section.

Table 9-5: Records in the DimCategoryForecast Table

PRODUCTCATEGORYKEY	FORECASTAMOUNT	ACTIVE
0	4000	N
2	**9000**	**Y**
3	**12000**	**Y**
5	10000	Y
7	3000	Y

Table 9-6: Records in the DimProductCategory Table

PRODUCTCATEGORYKEY	DESCRIPTION
1	Bikes
2	**Components**
3	**Clothing**
4	Accessories

NOTE Keep in mind that a table can be joined by more than one condition, and a join can be performed on fields with different names.

You can create table joins by choosing Table → Joins or by selecting a field from one table and dragging it on top of a field in another table. Figure 9-23 demonstrates how the ParentEmployeeKey field can be joined to EmployeeKey.

After you create a join, you can remove it by clicking the line and pressing the Delete key. Alternatively, you can choose Tables → Joins and delete the join in the dialog box by selecting it and clicking Remove.

Inner Joins

An Inner join links the table together using a value (or values) in one or more fields that is common to both tables. This type of join selects only the rows where the joined fields have matching values. An Inner join on ProductCategoryKey between the DimCategoryForecast and DimProductCategory table is graphically represented in the Tables section in Figure 9-24. Notice that the connection line has a ball on each end. Looking back at Tables 9-5 and 9-6, you can derive that only values 2–3 are selected because they are the only ones common to both tables. Although the DimProductCategory table has values 1 and 4 and DimCategoryForecast has values 0, 5, and 7, they are not common to both tables; therefore, they are not returned when an Inner join is used.

Keep in mind that Microsoft Query creates Inner joins only when tables are added to the Tables section. These Inner joins are created on fields that have the same name with one or both of them being defined as a primary key field. If both of these conditions cannot be satisfied, then Microsoft Query settles for just the field name being the same. If this second condition cannot be satisfied, then a join is not created.

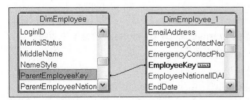

Figure 9-23: You can create a join by selecting a field and dragging it to another table.

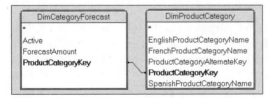

Figure 9-24: An Inner join is represented by a line with a ball on either side.

WARNING If a join line is not shown in the Tables section, a Cross join is created. This type of join is rarely needed and produces a Cartesian product. Read the "Cross Joins" section a little later in this chapter for more information about this type of join.

Here is the SQL query generated for the DimProductCategory and DimCategory-Forecast tables that were linked using an Inner join:

```
SELECT DimCategoryForecast.ProductCategoryKey AS 'Forecast-CategoryKey',
       DimProductCategory.ProductCategoryKey AS 'Category-CategoryKey'
FROM AdventureWorksDW.dbo.DimCategoryForecast DimCategoryForecast,
     AdventureWorksDW.dbo.DimProductCategory DimProductCategory
WHERE DimProductCategory.ProductCategoryKey =
      DimCategoryForecast.ProductCategoryKey
```

Left and Right Joins

Left and Right joins pull all the data from one table and then only the data in the other table with a matching record on the joined field. Using Tables 9-5 and 9-6 from earlier and assuming that DimCategoryForecast is on the left and DimProductCategory is on the right, a Left join on CategoryKey yields the values 0, 2, 3, 5, and 7. A Right join yields the values 2 and 3, and Null for values 1 and 4. The Null is used because there isn't a 1 or a 4 to pull in the DimCategoryForecast table, and because something must be pulled, a Null value is used.

NOTE A Null means that the field value is missing or unknown. It is not the same as a <blank> value and must be treated differently.

In order to change the Inner join to a Left join, follow these steps:

1. Verify that your Microsoft Query window looks like Figure 9-22.

2. Select Tables → Joins or double-click the line that links the two database tables to bring up the Joins dialog box (see Figure 9-25).

3. Click the existing join in the Joins in Query pane of the Joins dialog box to select it (if it is not already selected) and then click the Remove button to delete the existing Inner join between the DimCategoryForecast and DimProductCategory tables.

4. Click the button in the Join Includes section of the dialog box that reads "ALL Values from 'DimCategoryForecast' and ONLY Records from 'DimProductCategory' Where …", and then click the Add button to left join the DimProductCategory table with the DimCategoryForecast table. Click Close to close the dialog box.

5. Choose Records → Query Now if Automatic Query is not enabled.

6. Verify that the join line from DimCategoryForecast points to the DimProduct-Category table, as shown in Figure 9-26.

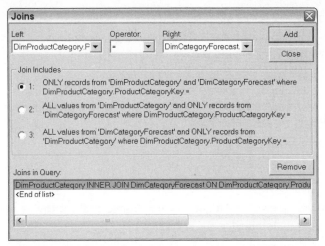

Figure 9-25: The first Inner join option is the default. You can change it to a Left join (Option 2) or a Right join (Option 3) in this dialog box.

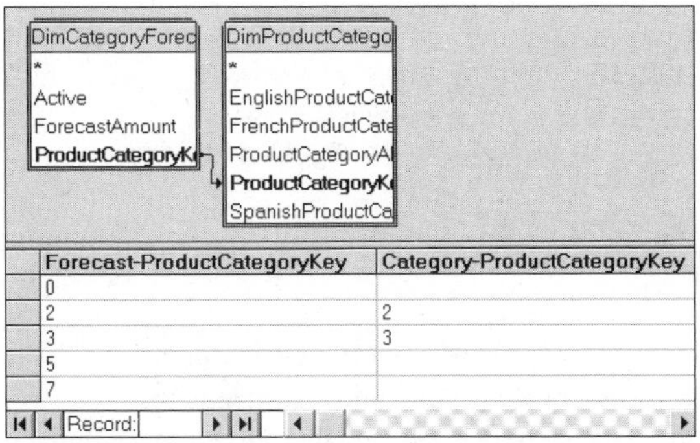

Figure 9-26: A right arrow indicates that the DimProductCategory table is left-joined to the DimCategoryForecast table.

Here is the query generated by Microsoft Query:

```
SELECT DimCategoryForecast.ProductCategoryKey AS 'Forecast-ProductKey',
       DimProductCategory.ProductCategoryKey AS 'Product-ProductKey'
FROM {oj AdventureWorksDW.dbo.DimCategoryForecast DimCategoryForecast
LEFT OUTER JOIN AdventureWorksDW.dbo.DimProductCategory DimProductCategory
        ON DimCategoryForecast.ProductCategoryKey =
            DimProductCategory.ProductCategoryKey}
```

Changing the join type to a Right join just switches the table in the SQL query to maintain a Left join. Essentially, the DimProductCategory table is moved to the FROM clause and the DimCategoryForecast table is moved to the JOIN clause to reflect how they appear in the query.

To modify the Left join to a Right join, follow these steps:

1. Choose Tables → Joins or double-click the line that links the two database tables together to bring up the Joins dialog box.

2. Click the button that reads "ALL Values from 'DimProductCategory' and ONLY Records from 'DimCategoryForecast' Where ..." in the Join Includes section of the dialog box, and then click the Add button to modify the Left join to a Right join. Click Close to close the dialog box.

3. Choose Records → Query Now if Automatic Query is not enabled.

4. Verify that the Microsoft Query window looks like Figure 9-27.

NOTE Microsoft Query never generates a Right join. Regardless of the arrow direction, a Left join is always maintained.

Although you may be expecting the join to be a Right join, the Microsoft Query program simply switched the tables in the query to maintain a Left join. You can verify this in the SQL query by clicking the View SQL button to see the following query displayed:

```
SELECT DimCategoryForecast.ProductCategoryKey AS 'Forecast-ProductKey',
       DimProductCategory.ProductCategoryKey AS 'Product-ProductKey'
FROM {oj AdventureWorksDW.dbo.DimProductCategory DimProductCategory
LEFT OUTER JOIN AdventureWorksDW.dbo.DimCategoryForecast DimCategoryForecast
ON DimProductCategory.ProductCategoryKey =
   DimCategoryForecast.ProductCategoryKey}
```

NOTE A query created using the graphical tools of the Microsoft Query program allows only one Outer join to be created. You can circumvent this limitation only by editing the SQL statement, which also results in the Microsoft Query program being unable to display the query graphically.

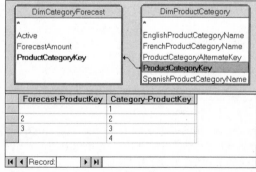

Figure 9-27: An arrow pointing to the left shows that the DimCategoryForecast table is left-joined to the DimProductCategory table.

Cross Joins

Cross joins produce a Cartesian product of the two tables, meaning that for each of the records in the first table, all the records in the second table are joined. This type of join is created by simply deleting the graphical join (selecting it and clicking Delete). Alternatively, the Cross join can be included in the SQL statement. Figure 9-28 shows how a Cross join is performed.

All the possible combinations of ProductCategoryKey in DimCategoryForecast and DimProductCategory are produced when tables are cross-joined. So, you have the pairs 0-1, 2-1, 3-1, 5-1, 7-1, and then 0-2, 3-2, and so forth until all 20 unique combinations are exhausted. (There are five rows in the DimCategoryForecast table and four rows in the DimProductCategory table, so 5 * 4 = 20.) Notice that the Cross join clause is not inserted into the SQL query, because it isn't required:

```
SELECT DimCategoryForecast.ProductCategoryKey AS 'Forecast-ProductKey',
       DimProductCategory.ProductCategoryKey AS 'Product-ProductKey'
FROM AdventureWorksDW.dbo.DimCategoryForecast DimCategoryForecast,
     AdventureWorksDW.dbo.DimProductCategory DimProductCategory
```

Self Joins

Self joins are required when you need to access information that is included in the same table. For example, in the DimEmployee table of the AdventureWorksDW database, there is a field for determining the employee manager (labeled as ParentEmployeeKey). All the employees are included in the table; but if you want to provide a list of the employees with the employee manager name next to it, you need to create a Self join.

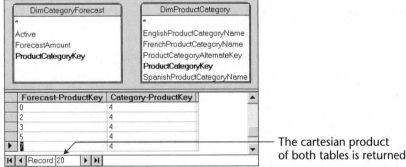

Figure 9-28: When there are no lines or arrows that join the tables, a Cross join is produced.

To create a Self join on the Employees table, follow these steps:

1. Start a new query or remove all current tables in the Tables section.

2. Click the Add Tables button to bring up the Add Tables dialog box.

3. Add the DimEmployee table to the Tables section by selecting the table and clicking Add.

4. Add the DimEmployee table to the Tables section again by selecting the table and clicking Add.

5. When you are prompted with the warning message that the table already exists, just click OK to acknowledge the warning and add the table.

6. Click Close to close the Add Tables dialog box.

7. Add the following fields to the query (in this order):

    a. EmployeeKey from the DimEmployee table

    b. LastName from the DimEmployee table

    c. ParentEmployeeKey from the DimEmployee table

    d. LastName from the DimEmployee_1 table

8. Choose Tables → Joins to bring up the Joins dialog box.

9. Delete the current join by selecting it in the bottom pane of the Joins dialog box and clicking Remove.

10. Select DimEmployee.ParentEmployeeKey in the Left field, = in the Operator field, and DimEmployee_1.EmployeeKey in the Right field.

11. Click the second button in the Join Includes pane to select all the records from DimEmployee and only the records from DimEmployee_1 where Dim Employee.ParentEmployeeKey = DimEmployee_1.EmployeeKey.

12. Click Add to create the Self join, verify that the Joins dialog box looks like Figure 9-29, and click Close to close the Joins dialog box.

13. Choose Records → Query Now if Automatic Query is not enabled.

14. Verify that your Microsoft Query window looks like Figure 9-30.

Looking at Figure 9-30, you can see that Sanchez appears in the DimEmployee (employee) columns, but not in the DimEmployee_1 (employee manager). This is because Sanchez is a manager and does not report to anyone at AdventureWorks. Adding ParentEmployeeKey <> ' ' in the Criteria pane prevents Sanchez (and other employees with no manager) from appearing in the Results pane. Keep in mind that other database systems may handle this type of situation differently. For example, the ParentEmployeeKey could be set to the EmployeeKey when the employee has no manager. In that case, you'd simply use EmployeeKey <> ParentEmployeeKey in the Criteria pane to account for this type of data condition.

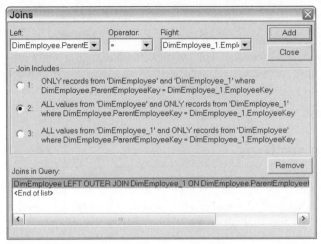

Figure 9-29: A Self join is created by joining the DimEmployee table to itself using ParentEmployeeKey = EmployeeKey.

EmployeeKey	LastName	ParentEmployeeKey	LastName
112 .	Sánchez		
4	Walters	3	Tamburello
5	Walters	3	Tamburello
11	Erickson	3	Tamburello
13	Goldberg	3	Tamburello
162	Miller	3	Tamburello
267	Cracium	3	Tamburello
271	Sullivan	3	Tamburello
274	Salavaria	3	Tamburello
275	Wood	7	Bradley

Figure 9-30: This Self join on ParentEmployeeKey on EmployeeKey shows employee names and their manager's last name.

The following SQL query is generated by the Microsoft Query program for this Self join example:

```
SELECT DimEmployee.EmployeeKey, DimEmployee.LastName,
       DimEmployee_1.ParentEmployeeKey, DimEmployee_1.LastName
FROM {oj AdventureWorksDW.dbo.DimEmployee DimEmployee
LEFT OUTER JOIN AdventureWorksDW.dbo.DimEmployee DimEmployee_1
  ON DimEmployee.ParentEmployeeKey = DimEmployee_1.EmployeeKey}
WHERE (DimEmployee_1.ParentEmployeeKey<>' ')
```

Full Joins

Full joins result in all rows being returned from either table, regardless of whether there is a record that matches in the other table. This can result in null values being produced. This join is not available through the graphical tools of the Microsoft Query program, but you can insert it by simply typing or pasting the query into the SQL dialog box.

Executing SQL Commands

Microsoft Query includes the Execute SQL dialog box for executing SQL commands and queries. This tool includes functionality for viewing, updating, and removing data and database objects. You can use this dialog box to:

- Create database tables and views
- Delete, update, or select data in a table
- Insert records into a table
- Execute or view a stored procedure

I recommend you use this tool only when you do not have access to the native database development programs such as the Query Analyzer or the SQL Server Management Studio, because these programs are much better suited for SQL programming and program development. However, if you find yourself without access to these programs, you can access the Execute SQL dialog box shown in Figure 9-31 by choosing File → Execute SQL.

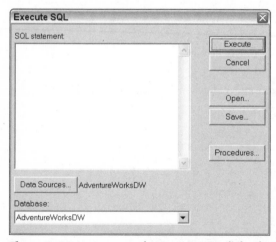

Figure 9-31: You can use the Execute SQL dialog box to run SQL commands from Microsoft Query.

The permissions to the data source for executing SQL commands are determined by the SQL or Windows login account that is used to access the data source. If you need to log in using another SQL login account, click the Data Sources button to create or access the data source using the appropriate credentials. The database currently selected to run the SQL commands is shown in the Database drop-down box at the bottom part of the Execute SQL dialog box. In Figure 9-31, the AdventureWorksDW database is selected in this box.

You can open and save queries in this dialog box by clicking the Open and Save buttons, respectively. Files can be saved and opened using a file extension type of .QRT (Query Template) only.

Clicking the Procedures button brings up the Select Procedure dialog box, shown in Figure 9-32, which lets you automatically paste a stored procedure into the Execute SQL dialog box.

Executing an SQL query that results in data being returned automatically creates a new query window and displays the data in the Results pane. Other SQL statements for creating or deleting database objects or modifying or inserting data just brings up a confirmation statement that prompts you with the message Executed SQL Statement Successfully, requiring you to acknowledge it by clicking OK.

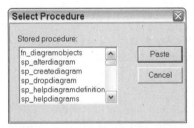

Figure 9-32: You can automatically paste a procedure into the Execute SQL dialog box from here.

Managing Tables

Microsoft Query includes the Select Tables dialog box for creating, viewing, updating, removing, and indexing database tables. You can also use it to view other types of files such as Excel workbooks and comma-delimited and fixed-width files. As with the Execute SQL dialog box, I recommend that you use the Select Tables dialog box tool only when you do not have access to the native database development programs. You can access this dialog box by following these steps:

1. Open a Microsoft Query dialog box and choose File → Table Definition to bring up the Choose Data Source dialog box.

2. Select the AdventureWorksDW Database data source and click OK to bring up the Select Table dialog box shown in Figure 9-33.

Clicking the View button in the Select Table dialog box brings up the View Definition Table dialog box. Here, you can view all the fields and field data types for each database table. Even though this dialog box is intended for viewing the table design, you can also add or remove fields.

Clicking the New button brings up a dialog box that is just like the View Definition Table dialog box except that all the fields are empty.

NOTE You can copy an existing table by first selecting it in the View Definition Table dialog box, changing its name in the Table Name field, and then clicking Create.

Clicking the Remove button deletes the selected table. Clicking the Index button brings up the Create Index dialog box, where you can select a field to create a unique or non-unique index. Clicking the Close button closes the Select Table dialog box. Clicking the Options button brings up the Table Options dialog box, where you can determine which objects are displayed in the Table pane (see Figure 9-33).

Figure 9-33: From this dialog box, you can create, modify, remove, and index tables.

Understanding How Microsoft Query Uses SQL

The Microsoft Query program has some interesting quirks that I've noticed over the years. I include a few of them here because I've found them to sometimes be problematic in report development. Once you understand them, however, you can easily circumvent them. Here's a list of the quirks I review in this section:

- A pasted query is automatically modified to conform to Microsoft Query's standard of SQL when the query can be displayed graphically.

- Field names should be put in brackets instead of single quotes.

- Criteria is incorrectly put into the Having clause instead of the Where clause.

- Stored procedures with input parameters work only with Spreadsheet reports and require the use of a very particular format.

I review these quirks here and show you a couple of examples that can help you better understand the nuances of the Microsoft Query program.

Automatic Query Modification

When you paste a query into the SQL dialog box (accessed by clicking the View SQL button on the program's toolbar), Microsoft Query first parses the query to ensure that there are no syntax errors. After this step is completed, the program attempts to produce a graphical representation of the query by reading and trying to figure out the query instructions. If the program is successful, the query is modified to Microsoft Query's style and a graphical representation of the query is produced. By that, I mean the tables and the table joins are shown in the Table section, and the filter fields and filter criteria are shown in the Criteria section. The sort instructions are also available in the Sort dialog box (accessed by choosing Records → Sort).

Try this example to see for yourself how this works:

1. Paste the following query into the SQL dialog box by clicking the View SQL button:

```
SELECT * FROM DimProductCategory
```

2. Click OK to close the SQL dialog box and execute the query.

3. Click the View SQL button to confirm that the query has been modified as shown in the following:

```
SELECT DimProductCategory.ProductCategoryKey,
       DimProductCategory.ProductCategoryAlternateKey,
       DimProductCategory.EnglishProductCategoryName,
       DimProductCategory.SpanishProductCategoryName,
       DimProductCategory.FrenchProductCategoryName
FROM AdventureWorksDW.dbo.DimProductCategory DimProductCategory
```

Numerous features are available when the query can be graphically displayed. However, for SQL experts, this might be an annoying feature because editing the modified queries can take a longer than you might prefer.

You can work around this feature by inserting a comment into the SQL query. The comments can be either single line (--) or block comment (/* */). After you add a comment line and leave the Microsoft Query program, the query will no longer be graphically displayed or modified by the Microsoft Query program.

Use Brackets Instead of Single Quotes

If you are pasting an SQL query into the SQL dialog box, always put field headings in brackets ([ ]) instead of single quotes (' '). Microsoft Query can get confused when trying to decipher date, string, and mathematical operators.

Follow these steps to see how the Microsoft Query becomes confused when single quotes are used with a string operator:

1. Paste the following query into the SQL dialog box by clicking the View SQL button:

```
SELECT ctgy.ProductCategoryKey                         AS 'ID',
       UPPER(LEFT(EnglishProductCategoryName,10))  AS 'Short Name',
       ForecastAmount                              AS 'Amount'
FROM   DimCategoryForecast fcst
INNER JOIN DimProductCategory ctgy
       ON fcst.ProductCategoryKey = ctgy.ProductCategoryKey
```

2. Click OK to close the SQL dialog box and execute the query.

3. Click OK when you are prompted with a message stating that the query cannot be graphically displayed.

4. Verify that the Results pane looks like Figure 9-34.

All the fields that follow an unreadable field become corrupt. Although you can modify the field names from Excel, they are permanently lost once the query is edited in the Microsoft Query program. You can avoid this problem by using brackets for field headings instead of apostrophes.

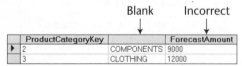

Figure 9-34: The field heading is missing for ShortName, and ForecastAmount is used instead of Amount.

Try the following simple queries, and you'll see the difference:

1. Clear out the existing query, and then paste the updated query with brackets instead of apostrophes into the SQL dialog box:

```
SELECT ctgy.ProductCategoryKey                        AS [ID],
       UPPER(LEFT(EnglishProductCategoryName,10))     AS [Short Name],
       ForecastAmount                                 AS [Amount]
FROM   DimCategoryForecast fcst
INNER JOIN DimProductCategory ctgy
        ON fcst.ProductCategoryKey = ctgy.ProductCategoryKey
```

2. Click OK to close the dialog box and execute the query.

3. Click OK when you are prompted with a message stating that the query cannot be graphically displayed.

4. Verify that the Results pane looks like Figure 9-35.

TIP Adding a Case statement anywhere in the SQL query often resolves the formatting problems. Although this method also works, I recommend sticking with the brackets (in lieu of single quotes) because it's an easier and more reliable method for ensuring that column headings are not corrupted.

Criteria Incorrectly Put into the Having Clause

The problem of Microsoft Query putting criteria into the Having clause instead of the Where clause was observed in the "Distinguishing between Where and Having" section of this chapter. Recall that the Having clause is used when an aggregate function is used in the Criteria pane. There is no magical workaround for this situation except to manually edit the SQL query. If report developers are relying on the Microsoft Query program to develop their queries, SQL experts should watch out for this problem within their organizations.

ID	Short Name	Amount
2	COMPONENTS	9000
3	CLOTHING	12000

Figure 9-35: The field headings work properly when included in brackets instead of single quotes.

Stored Procedures with Input Parameters

Stored procedures can accept input parameters that can be used to pull a range of data. In its most basic form, a stored procedure is essentially an SQL query with a *wrapper*. This wrapper is simply a few lines of program code before (and after) the query where the procedure name and input parameters are defined. Looking at the stored procedure here, you can see that an integer parameter is accepted for pay frequency and a one-character parameter is accepted for gender. At the end of the query, you can see that the `Where` statement restricts the dataset to only the pay frequency and gender input variables. The remaining part of the code is just an SQL query.

```
CREATE PROCEDURE "AW Vacation Hours"
(@Payf INT,
 @Gndr CHAR(1))
AS
SELECT EmployeeKey,
       LastName,
       DepartmentName,
       VacationHours
FROM DimEmployee
WHERE PayFrequency = @Payf
  AND Gender = @Gndr
```

Stored procedures do not require parameters. However, one or more parameters can be useful for returning a more focused result set. In this stored procedure example, the employee number, last name, department, and vacation hours are returned for a specified employee gender and payment frequency.

If you do not want to prompt the user to input the parameters into the report, the stored procedure can work in both PivotTable and Spreadsheet reports. However, if you want to prompt the user to enter a value (or values) for the stored procedure, you can use only a Spreadsheet report or a PivotTable list with the stored procedure (note that a PivotTable list is essentially a web-enabled PivotTable report and is covered in Chapter 15). When specifying input variables, you must input the stored procedure in exactly this format:

```
{Call "Stored Procedure Name" (?,?)}
```

This format assumes that the stored procedure has two parameter variables, which is why there are two question marks in the parentheses. If you want to execute the AW Vacation Hours stored procedure for a pay frequency of 1 and a gender of female, you can write the query as follows:

```
{Call "AW Vacation Hours" (1,"F")}
```

TIP Note that alphanumeric input variables must be specified inside single quotes.

Inserting a Stored Procedure

Instead of pasting a query into the SQL dialog box, you can simply enter in a stored procedure. Stored procedures typically run much faster than regular SQL queries because the *query plan* (that is, the instructions for how the database server calculates the most efficient path for obtaining the data) has already been created by the SQL query optimizer. Additionally, the stored procedure can simply be modified if fields are added or removed or the query logic is changed. A simple refresh of the report with the stored procedure automatically makes the corresponding changes to the Excel report.

> **WARNING** Stored procedures are stored with the database on the database server. If you plan to use stored procedures in your reports, ensure that you properly evaluate the organizational implications. This may include developing a sensible naming convention, implementing sound change control procedures, and creating a stored procedure library in the event that the database becomes corrupted.

In order to use an SQL query with the report, just select the data source and enter the stored procedure name. If there are spaces in the stored procedure name, put the stored procedure in double quotes. If there are no spaces, just type the stored procedure name. For example, if you want to execute the built-in SQL stored procedure that returns all the users with open connections to a Microsoft SQL Server, simply enter the following text into the SQL dialog box:

```
sp_who
```

If the stored procedure has input variables, specify them after the stored procedure name. To execute the AW Vacation Hours stored procedure, for example, a pay frequency and gender are required. So you would enter the following text into the SQL dialog box to pull records for a payment frequency of 2 for males:

```
"AW Vacation Hours" 2,'M'
```

If you want to prompt the user to specify the beginning and ending date each time the report is requested, you must use the following format:

```
{Call "AW Vacation Hours" (?,?)}
```

These prompts for the Payment Frequency and Gender are referred to as *parameter values*, and there are some restrictions and program options tied to it. The next section covers these options.

Using Parameters

A parameter allows the user to specify a value each time the report is refreshed. You can use parameters only with Spreadsheet reports and PivotTable lists, not with Pivot-Table reports. Additionally, parameters only work with stored procedures or with queries that can be graphically displayed. Chapter 14 provides some detailed examples on how to use parameter queries. This section includes a brief example of how they are used only in the context of the Microsoft Query program with the AW Vacation Hours stored procedure. There are numerous related topics included as part of parameter queries, so be sure to read Chapter 14 if you plan to implement this technology with your Excel reports.

In order to create a Spreadsheet report with parameters for the AW Vacation Hours stored procedure, follow these steps:

1. Verify that the AW Vacation Hours stored procedure has been created.

2. Starting with a new Excel spreadsheet, choose Data → From Other Sources → From Microsoft Query.

3. When the Choose Data Source dialog box appears, select the Adventure-WorksDW data source and click OK to open the Microsoft Query program.

4. Close the Add Tables dialog box and click the View SQL button to open the SQL dialog box.

5. Type the following text into the SQL dialog box and click OK:

   ```
   {Call "AW Vacation Hours" (?,?)}
   ```

6. Click OK to acknowledge that the query cannot be displayed graphically.

7. When the Enter Parameter Value dialog box appears (see Figure 9-36), type **2** and click OK.

8. When the second Enter Parameter Value dialog box appears, type **F** and click OK.

9. Verify that your Microsoft Query window looks like Figure 9-37.

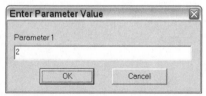

Figure 9-36: Enter a parameter value in this dialog box to limit the number of rows returned from a stored procedure or SQL query.

	EmployeeKey	LastName	DepartmentName	VacationHours
▶	9	Dobney	Production	82
	11	Erickson	Engineering	5
	14	Duffy	Engineering	1
	18	Brown	Production	80
	32	Barreto de Mattos	Human Resources	54
	44	Trenary	Information Services	65
	61	Poe	Finance	60
	68	Bueno	Information Services	71

Figure 9-37: All female employees with a pay frequency of 2 are returned.

You can change the parameter names by choosing View → Parameters to bring up the Parameters dialog box. Just select a parameter and click the Edit button. In Figure 9-38, I changed the name for Parameter 1 to Pay Frequency and Parameter 2 to Gender.

TIP Try to use a consistent naming structure with parameters. For example, if you use Begin Date, don't switch some reports to Start Date, Beginning Date, From, and so forth. Implementing a uniform naming structure is easier for you, for the report user, and for an organization to understand and maintain.

With the parameter names changed, the dialog box prompts you for Pay Frequency (see Figure 9-39) instead of just Parameter 1 when the query is next run.

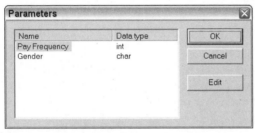

Figure 9-38: You can change the parameter name in the Parameters dialog box.

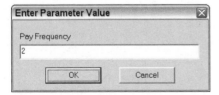

Figure 9-39: The parameter name has been renamed from Parameter 1 to Pay Frequency.

Accessing Multiple Databases in a Single Session

The Microsoft Query program includes graphical tools that enable you to create a query that accesses multiple databases on a single server. However, it does not include graphical tools for accessing multiple databases on different servers. If you want to do that, you have to make adjustments in the SQL query. This section demonstrates how you can create a query for both circumstances.

Multiple Databases on a Single Server

In order to follow along with this example, you must have created the DimCategory-Forecast table in the "Executing SQL Commands" section of this chapter. In addition, you must also have access to the AdventureWorks database that is included as part of a default installation of Microsoft SQL Server 2005. This database is different from the AdventureWorksDW database referenced throughout most of this chapter. You must have each database installed because the SQL query in this exercise references both of them.

To create a query that accesses multiple databases on a single server, follow these steps:

1. Start a new query session in Microsoft Query that uses the Adventure-WorksDW data source.

2. Click the Add Tables button and add the DimCategoryForecast table to the Tables pane.

3. Change the database from AdventureWorksDW to AdventureWorks in the Database drop-down list of the Add Tables dialog box. This action refreshes the tables shown in the Tables pane of the dialog box.

4. Add the ProductCategory table to the query as shown in Figure 9-40, and then click Close to close the Add Tables dialog box.

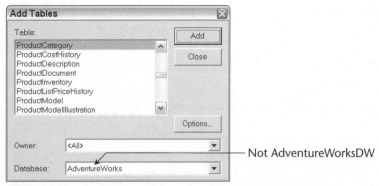

Figure 9-40: Change the database from AdventureWorksDW to AdventureWorks in the Database drop-down list.

5. Drag ProductCategoryKey from the DimCategoryForecast table and drop it on top of the ProductCategoryID field of the ProductCategory table. This results in an inner join being created between the two tables on DimCategoryForecast .ProductCategoryKey = ProductCategory.ProductCategoryKey.

6. Add the ProductCategoryKey field from the DimCategoryForecast table, the Name field from the ProductCategory table, and then ForecastAmount from the DimCategoryForecast table (in this order) to the query.

7. Choose Records → Query Now if Automatic Query is not enabled.

8. Verify that your Microsoft Query window looks like Figure 9-41.

Congratulations! You have now successfully created a multiple database query that accesses tables in the AdventureWorks and AdventureWorksDW databases. Clicking the SQL button shows the SQL query generated by the Microsoft Query program:

```
SELECT DimCategoryForecast.ProductCategoryKey,
       ProductCategory.Name,
       DimCategoryForecast.ForecastAmount
FROM AdventureWorksDW.dbo.DimCategoryForecast DimCategoryForecast,
     AdventureWorks.Production.ProductCategory ProductCategory
WHERE DimCategoryForecast.ProductCategoryKey =
       ProductCategory.ProductCategoryID
```

Multiple Databases on Different Servers

Microsoft Query does not include graphical tools for accessing databases on different servers, but it's easy to do if you are familiar with SQL query programming. This is a useful function if you are trying to compare the differences between two database servers. For example, if you have one enterprise application used for order entry and another enterprise application used for warehouse management, you could query both databases to see which orders have been sent, but not shipped. You could even do this when one of the database servers is connected over a Virtual Private Network (VPN). I use a much simpler example in this section because the topic is already complex enough on its own.

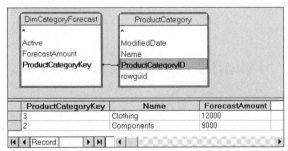

Figure 9-41: A query that accesses fields from two different databases in a single Microsoft Query session.

Before you try to create a query that accesses multiple database servers, keep in mind that you'll need to ensure that the following conditions are met:

- You have already created a linked server on both SQL servers and verified that access works both ways.

- The database servers are installed with the same collation type. If this isn't the case and can't be done, you may run into problems when trying to execute the multiple server queries.

- You have tested that the multiple server query works in the Query Analyzer or Microsoft Server Management Studio. If you can't get it to work there, it's probably not going to work in the Microsoft Query program.

- You understand which server is the source server and which server is the destination server in the context of your selected data source, because the linked server acts in only one direction.

Here's an example of a query that pulls all the records in the DimProductCategory table of the AdventureWorksDW database on one database server that are not in the DimCategoryForecast table of the second database server:

```
SELECT *
FROM    DatabaseServer1.AdventureWorksDW.dbo.DimProductCategory
WHERE   ProductCategoryKey NOT IN
        (SELECT ProductCategoryKey
         FROM DatabaseServer2.AdventureWorksDW.dbo.DimCategoryForecast)
```

NOTE Notice that the objects are fully qualified in the `From` part of the SQL query: `ServerName.DatabaseName.ObjectOwner.TableName`. If the database server name was Jupiter, the fully qualified name in the subquery would be `Jupiter.AdventureWorksDW.dbo.DimCategoryForecast`.

This is a very advanced topic and requires you to be knowledgeable about SQL administration and SQL programming. To learn more about these topics, I suggest that you read the SQL books online or these Wiley books: *Professional SQL Server 2000 Programming* by Robert Vieira, *SQL Server Developer's Guide* by Joseph J. Bambara and Paul R. Allen, and *MCSE SQL Server 2000 Administration For Dummies* by Rozanne Whalen and Dan Whalen.

Trying It Out in the Real World

Garrett Vargas, a sales representative at AdventureWorks, has requested that you provide him with a report that shows the average markup (defined as list price minus standard cost) and the total expected profit (defined as quantity on hand multiplied by markup) by product subcategory. This report analysis should only include current products. After discussing the report requirements with the AdventureWorks database administrator, you learn that the fields are best pulled from both the AdventureWorks (OLTP database) and the AdventureWorksDW (OLAP database).

Getting Down to Business

Follow these steps to complete this exercise:

1. From Excel, choose Data → From Other Sources → From Microsoft Query.

2. When the Choose Data Source dialog box appears, verify that Use the Query Wizard to Create/Edit Queries is unchecked, select the AdventureWorksDW Database data source, and click OK.

3. When the Microsoft Query program is launched, you are presented with the Add Tables dialog box. Add the following tables to the Tables section:

   ■ DimProduct from the AdventureWorksDW database

   ■ DimProductSubcategory from the AdventureWorksDW database

   ■ ProductInventory from the AdventureWorks database

4. Drag ProductKey from the DimProduct table on top of ProductID in the Product-Inventory table to inner-join DimProduct and ProductInventory.

5. Double-click EnglishProductSubcategoryName in the DimProductSubcategory table to add this field to the Results section.

6. Click a blank cell in the Results pane and type **(ListPrice-StandardCost)**. Press the Tab key to add this new field to the query.

7. Click again on a blank cell in the Results pane and choose Records → Add Column to bring up the Add Column dialog box. Type **(ListPrice-StandardCost)*Quantity** in the Field section, click Add to insert this new field into the Results pane, and then click Close to close the Add Column dialog box.

8. Choose View → Criteria to display the Criteria pane.

9. Click a blank cell in the Criteria pane and type **Status** in Criteria Field and = **'Current'** in the Value field below it.

10. Double-click the second column in the Results pane to bring up the Edit Column dialog box. Type **Average Markup** in the Column Heading field and choose Avg from the Total drop-down field. Click OK to apply the changes and to close the dialog box.

11. Double-click the third column in the Results pane to bring up the Edit Column dialog box. Type **Total Expected Profit** in the Column Heading field, and choose Sum from the Total drop-down field. Click OK to apply the changes and to close the dialog box.

12. Choose Records → Query Now if Automatic Query is not enabled.

13. Verify that your Microsoft Query window looks like Figure 9-42.

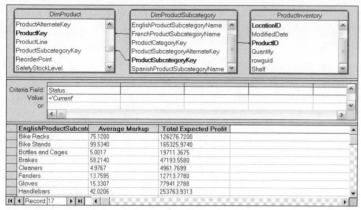

Figure 9-42: If you did everything right, the Microsoft Query window should look like this.

WATCH THE VIDEO **To see how to build this SQL query in the Microsoft Query program, click the ch0902_video.avi file at** `www.wiley.com/` `go/excelreporting/2007` **and watch the video.**

Reviewing What You Did

This example provided you with a way to practice much of what you learned in this chapter. Although the Microsoft Query program includes many useful and powerful tools for building SQL queries that can be integrated into your reports, there are also several limitations. For example, using the graphical tools, I'm unable to create a formula field that groups the markups into different levels. As a report user with high expectations, I want a Markup Level field that groups markups under $100 as Silver, markups between $100 and $999 as Gold, and markups over $1,000 as Platinum. However, the only way to add this field to the report is by using Case logic in the SQL query because that functionality is not included as a graphical tool in the Microsoft Query program. (See Appendix A for more information about Case logic and how it is used.)

Chapter Review

This chapter organized the various query tools into each part of an SQL query and identified which functions were disabled when a query could not be graphically displayed. It also described the various types of table joins and provided examples of how each one works using a new database table that was created in the Adventure-WorksDW database. After reviewing the basics, the chapter provided a quick introduction to some of the more advanced features, such as parameter queries and queries that reference multiple databases.

PivotTable Reporting

Designing PivotTable Reports

In this chapter, I show you how to design PivotTable reports using the robust suite of tools, functions, and features included with Excel 2007. Here, I cover an extensive array of PivotTable topics, including how to build and apply advanced filters, customize inner and outer fields, sort data, group items, and create Calculated Fields, Calculated Items, and custom formulas.

I start this chapter with a review of Excel's filters, where I cover several types of basic and advanced filtering tools, including Label and Value filters. After that, I review the intricacies of using inner and outer fields, demonstrating how you can manage subtotals and collapse and expand data. Next, I cover how you can use the numerous sorting functions to sort report items in a variety of different ways. Following that, I cover how you can group items into new fields, rename fields, and create Calculated Items, Calculated Fields, and custom formulas. I conclude with a real-world example that ties together much of the material in this chapter into an example that you might encounter in the real world.

Before You Begin

All the examples in this chapter, including the "Trying It Out in the Real World" exercise, utilize the SQL query and PivotTable report outlined in this section. If you plan to follow along with the material and examples throughout this chapter, I recommend that you start by creating this PivotTable report that accesses the AdventureWorksDW database.

Complete these steps to create the PivotTable report and follow along with the examples used throughout this chapter:

1. From Excel, choose Data → From Other Sources → From Microsoft Query to bring up the Choose Data Source dialog box.

2. When the Choose Data Source dialog box appears, verify that Use the Query Wizard to Create/Edit Queries is unchecked, select the AdventureWorks Data Warehouse data source, and click OK.

3. When the Microsoft Query program is launched, you are presented with the Add Tables dialog box. Close this dialog box and click the SQL button.

4. Paste or type the following query into the SQL dialog box and click OK:

```
SELECT prod.EnglishProductName              AS [ProductName],
       subc.EnglishProductSubcategoryName   AS [ProductSubCategory],
       catg.EnglishProductCategoryName      AS [ProductCategory],
       (CAST(catg.ProductCategoryKey
          AS CHAR(1))
        + ' - '
        + catg.EnglishProductCategoryName)  AS [ProductCategoryDesc],
       (empl.FirstName
        + ' '
        + empl.LastName)                     AS [SalesPerson],
       rsel.ResellerName                     AS [ResellerName],
       rsel.BusinessType                     AS [ResellerType],
       trty.SalesTerritoryGroup              AS [SalesGroup],
       trty.SalesTerritoryCountry            AS [SalesCountry],
       trty.SalesTerritoryRegion             AS [SalesRegion],
       otme.FullDateAlternateKey             AS [OrderDate],
       stme.FullDateAlternateKey             AS [ShipDate],
       crcy.CurrencyAlternateKey             AS [CurrencyCode],
       crcy.CurrencyName                     AS [CurrencyName],
       fact.UnitPrice                        AS [UnitPrice],
       fact.ExtendedAmount                   AS [ExtendedAmount],
       fact.OrderQuantity                    AS [Quantity],
       fact.SalesAmount                      AS [SalesAmount],
       fact.TaxAmt                           AS [TaxAmount],
       fact.Freight                          AS [Freight]
FROM FactResellerSales fact
INNER JOIN DimProduct prod
  ON prod.ProductKey = fact.ProductKey
INNER JOIN DimProductSubcategory subc
  ON subc.ProductSubcategoryKey = prod.ProductSubcategoryKey
INNER JOIN DimProductCategory catg
  ON subc.ProductCategoryKey = catg.ProductCategoryKey
INNER JOIN DimReseller rsel
  ON rsel.ResellerKey = fact.ResellerKey
```

```
INNER JOIN DimEmployee empl
  ON empl.EmployeeKey = fact.EmployeeKey
INNER JOIN DimSalesTerritory trty
  ON trty.SalesTerritoryKey = fact.SalesTerritoryKey
INNER JOIN DimTime otme
  ON otme.TimeKey = fact.OrderDateKey
INNER JOIN DimTime stme
  ON stme.TimeKey = fact.ShipDateKey
INNER JOIN DimCurrency crcy
  ON crcy.CurrencyKey = fact.CurrencyKey
```

ON THE WEB You can download the ch10_example.txt query file to your computer from the companion web site at www.wiley.com/go/ excelreporting/2007. **Look for this document in either the Chap10.zip file or Chap10 directory, depending on which .zip file you download.**

5. Click OK to acknowledge that the query cannot be displayed graphically.

6. Click the Return Data to Microsoft Excel button to return the data to Excel and continue.

7. When the Import Data dialog box appears (see Figure 10-1) choose PivotTable Report, and click OK to create the PivotTable and the PivotChart.

8. Drag SalesRegion to the Row Labels area, SalesGroup to the Column Labels area, and Quantity to the Values area.

9. Verify that your PivotTable report looks like Figure 10-2.

Figure 10-1: Select the PivotTable Report option to create a PivotTable.

	A	B	C	D	E
1	Sum of Quantity	Column Labels ▾			
2	Row Labels ▾	Europe	North America	Pacific	Grand Total
3	Australia			4948	4948
4	Canada		41761		41761
5	Central		19473		19473
6	France	14348			14348
7	Germany	7380			7380
8	Northeast		19816		19816
9	Northwest		27783		27783
10	Southeast		18836		18836
11	Southwest		46840		46840
12	United Kingdom	13193			13193
13	Grand Total	34921	174509	4948	214378

H ◂ ▸ H Sheet1 Sheet2 Sheet3

Figure 10-2: To follow along with the examples in this chapter, format your PivotTable report to look like this.

Filtering Data

Have you ever had to apply a filter to a PivotTable field with hundreds or even thousands of unique items? No report user wants to manually check or uncheck items scattered liberally throughout a lengthy drop-down field list; it simply takes too long and it's too easy to miss selecting or deselecting an item in the list. The traditional workaround to this problem has been to add a field in the SQL query or OLAP cube that ties all the field items together that are required for the filter. This new field, with only a few items, can then be used to toggle whether certain fields are displayed. Although this workaround generally works well, it makes the report design job more difficult and the report user more reliant on some technical resource to program and maintain the field logic.

Now, with Excel 2007, you can program your own filters by specifying criteria and choosing from an extensive list of operators. You can also configure filters to be applied in an additive manner; that is, each new filter further reduces the list of items from the previous filter. You even have the added capability of filtering by selection if you prefer to rapidly hide or only show selected items from the Report Layout area. Of course, you still have access to the manual drop-down filters that enable you to simply check or uncheck items in the drop-down field list. Regardless of whatever filters you choose to use, you can easily view and clear them using handy buttons and icons.

Choosing When a Filter Is Applied

Filters can be applied before or after the data is loaded into the Excel report. If a filter is applied before the data is loaded into the report, the filter criteria could be specified in the Query Wizard (covered in Chapter 7), the Microsoft Query program (covered in Chapters 8 and 9), or in the SQL query (covered in Appendix A). Though it's possible to apply a number of filters before the data is loaded into a PivotTable report, it's usually not possible to apply all of them. This is because PivotTable reports are intrinsically designed to support the interactive needs and whims of report users. As the data is summarized and turned round-and-round, report users may elect to show only certain items — and then a minute later, decide to show a different set of items — or even remove a filter altogether. Its not practical — and often not even realistic — to modify an SQL query or edit the external data source each time the user decides to restrict the dataset. That's where report filters can be helpful.

CROSS-REFERENCE Removing unnecessary data before it is imported into an Excel report improves performance, because Excel does not have to process and summarize as many records. Read the section "Filtering Data" in Chapter 7 for more information about filtering data in the SQL query.

Selecting a Filter Type

Three types of filters are available for selecting only specified data in your Excel PivotTable report:

- **Manual filters:** This type of filter is applied by manually checking or unchecking items in the selected field's drop-down list.
- **Label filters:** This type of filter is applied by selecting an operator and specifying criteria for items in the Row Labels or Column Labels area.
- **Value filters:** This type of filter is applied by selecting an operator and specifying criteria for Row Labels or Column Labels item grand totals.

Manual filters can be applied to fields in any area of the PivotTable report except the Values area. You can simply click the drop-down arrow of any field and check or uncheck which items you want to use for the PivotTable report. I covered this type of filter in the "Working in the Report Layout Area" section of Chapter 3. The more advanced Label and Value filters are new in Excel 2007 and provide more sophisticated filtering capability. Using these types of filters, you can choose to select items based on some type of string or numeric component. For example with Label filters, you can select only those items that end with, begin with, or contain a certain character or sequence of characters. Value filters, which work on the grand totals for items in the Row Labels or Column Labels area, enable you to select only those items that meet specific numeric criteria that you specify (for example, greater than or less than some particular number that you input). Figure 10-3 illustrates how Label and Value filters operate in a PivotTable report.

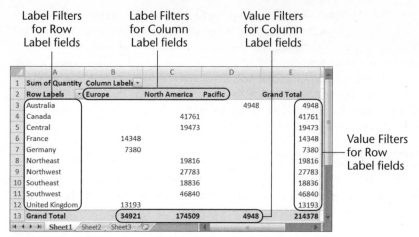

Figure 10-3: The sections where Label and Value filters work for Row Label and Column Label fields.

Creating Label Filters

Label filters are used to restrict items for fields in the Row Labels or Column Labels areas. This type of filter is more sophisticated than a manual filter, which only enables items in the drop-down list to be manually selected or deselected. Imagine how long that could take if you had several thousand unique items and you only wanted to display a few hundred items that were scattered liberally throughout the item list. It could take you hours to apply the filter. In contrast, Label filters provide a more robust filtering capability that is delivered through an easy-to-use dialog box. Using this type of filter, you can select from an extensive list of operators (see Table 10-1) for choosing which items should be selected.

There are three methods that you can use to create a filter to a Label filter:

- Left-click the Row Labels or Column Labels field in the Report Layout area and choose Label Filters from the pop-up menu. This brings up another submenu where you can choose from a list of available operators (see Table 10-1).

- Right-click an item in the Row Labels or Column Labels area and choose Filter → Label Filters from the pop-up menu.

- Left-click a field in the Fields section of the PivotTable Field List dialog box and choose Label Filters from the pop-up menu. This brings up another submenu where you can choose from a list of available operators (see Table 10-1).

All three methods bring up the Label Filter dialog box shown in Figure 10-4, although each method works a little differently. For example, if you left-click a field in the Report Layout area to create the filter, you must select the filter operator before you can bring up the Label Filter dialog box. In contrast, you do not have to select a filter operator first when you choose to use the second option, right-clicking an item in the

Row Labels or Column Labels areas. Lastly, the first two options automatically apply the Label filter to a selected field already in the Row Labels or Column Labels area, whereas the third option (left-clicking a field in the Fields section of the PivotTable Field List dialog box) only creates the filter but does not apply it. The filter is only applied when it is dragged into one of the PivotTable report areas. Of course, if the field is already in the report, the filter is immediately applied because it would be using the first two options.

To apply a Label filter to the PivotTable report in Figure 10-3, follow these steps:

1. Left-click the Row Labels drop-down arrow in cell A2 and choose Label Filters → Does Not Contain to bring up the Label Filter dialog box with the Does Not Contain operator defaulted.

2. Type **east** in the criteria field (see Figure 10-4) and click OK.

3. Verify that your PivotTable report no longer shows North*east* and South*east* in the Row Labels area for Sales Region.

As you can see from this last example, it's easy to apply a Label filter. And, there are numerous operators that you can choose from for this type of filter. The operators and their associated descriptions are listed in Table 10-1.

Figure 10-4: You can use this dialog box to filter items in a selected Row Label or Column Label filter using the operators listed in Table 10-1.

Table 10-1: Label Filter Operators

OPERATOR	DESCRIPTION
Equals	Shows items that are equal to the number or text specified in the Filter Value field.
Does Not Equal	Shows items that are not equal to the number or text specified in the Filer Value field.
Begins With	Shows items that begin with the text specified in the Filter Value field.
Does Not Begin With	Shows items that do not begin with the text specified in the Filter Value field.

(continued)

Table 10-1 *(continued)*

OPERATOR	DESCRIPTION
Ends With	Shows items that end with the text specified in the Filter Value field.
Does Not End With	Shows items that do not end with the text specified in the Filter Value field.
Contains	Shows items that contain the text specified in the Filter Value field.
Does Not Contain	Shows items that do not contain the text specified in the Filter Value field.
Is Greater Than	Shows items that are greater than the number or text specified in the Filter Value field.
Is Greater Than Or Equal To	Shows items that are greater than or equal to the number or text specified in the Filter Value field.
Is Less Than	Shows items that are less than the number or text specified in the Filter Value field.
Is Less Than Or Equal To	Shows items that are less than or equal to the number or text specified in the Filter Value field.
Is Between	Shows items that are between the text or numbers specified in the first and last Filter Value fields.
Is Not Between	Shows only items that are not between the text or numbers specified in the first and last Filter Value fields.

Using Wildcards

Wildcards can be used with Label filters to represent a single character or a series of characters. A question mark (?) is used to represent a single character and an asterisk (*) is used to represent a series of characters. So, for the PivotTable report example in Figure 10-3, selecting the Begins With operator and typing **C*** in the Filter Value field shows all the sales regions that begin with the letter *C*, which are Canada and Central. Typing ***west** instead of C* in the Filter Value field shows all the sales regions that end with the string *west*, which are Northwest and Southwest. Typing **?o** in the Filter Value field shows all the sales regions that have the letter *o* in the second position of the sales region name, which are Northeast, Northwest, Southeast, and Southwest.

Working with Date Fields

If you're working with a field that is date-formatted (such as 1/1/07, 01-01-2007, Jan 1, 2007, and so on), you'll see Date Filter in place of Label Filter in the pop-up menus. One powerful feature of Date Filters is that you can create dynamic filters that pull only the items that have a date that is in the previous, current, or next day, week, month, quarter, or year. This dynamic filtering can be a much more attractive option than a static filter, where the range must be regularly updated. For example, a static filter on today's date would need to be updated for each new day. In contrast, a dynamic filter that specified *Today* would continue to remain current as each new day passes.

Creating Value Filters

You can use Value filters to select items that have only a specified grand total amount. Using this type of filter, you can cull out items for fields in the Row Labels or Column Labels areas that have aggregated data in the Values area that do not meet a specified minimum or maximum number, or fall within a specified range.

There are three methods that you can use to apply a filter to a Value field:

- Left-click the Row Label or Column Label field in the Report Layout area and choose Value Filters from the pop-up menu. This brings up another submenu where you can choose from a list of available operators (see Table 10-2).

- Right-click an item in the Column Labels or Row Labels area and choose Filter → Value Filters from the pop-up menu.

- Left-click a field in Fields section of the PivotTable Field List dialog box and choose Value Filters from the pop-up menu. This brings up another submenu where you can choose from a list of available operators (see Table 10-2).

Like Label filters, the Value Filter dialog box in Figure 10-5 appears regardless of which method you choose to bring up this dialog box. Likewise, each method works slightly differently. For example, you must first select a filter operator before you can bring up the Value Filter dialog box when you left-click a field in the Report Layout area to create a filter. In contrast, you do not have to select a filter operator when you choose to use the second option, right-clicking an item in the Row Labels or Column Labels area.

The first two options (left-clicking or right-clicking fields in the Row Labels or Column Labels areas) automatically apply the Value filter to a selected field in the Row Labels or Column Labels area, whereas the third option (left-clicking a field in the Fields section of the PivotTable Field List dialog box), only creates the filter; it isn't applied to the field is dragged into a PivotTable area. If, however, the field is already in a PivotTable report area, the filter is immediately applied.

To apply a Value filter to the PivotTable report, follow these steps:

1. Left-click the Row Labels drop-down arrow in cell A2 and choose Value Filters → Between to bring up the Value Filter dialog box with Sum of Quantity defaulted in the Values field and Is Between defaulted in the Operator field.

2. Type **10000** in the first criteria field and **20000** in the second criteria field (see Figure 10-5) and click OK.

3. Verify that your PivotTable report only shows items with row grand totals between 10,000 and 20,000.

As you can see from this last exercise, it's easy to apply a Value filter. And there are numerous operators that you can choose from for this type of filter. The operators and their associated descriptions are listed in Table 10-2.

Figure 10-5: Value filters enable you to filter items using their grand total amounts in the Row Labels or Column Labels area.

Table 10-2: Value Filter Operators

OPERATOR	DESCRIPTION
Equals	Shows only items with grand totals that are equal to the number specified in the Filter Value field.
Does Not Equal	Shows only items with grand totals that are not equal to the number specified in the Filter Value field.
Is Greater Than	Shows only items with grand totals that are greater than the number specified in the Filter Value field.
Is Greater Than Or Equal To	Shows only items with grand totals that are greater than or equal to the number specified in the Filter Value field.
Is Less Than	Shows only items with grand totals that are less than the number specified in the Filter Value field.
Is Less Than Or Equal To	Shows only items with grand totals that are less than or equal to the number specified in the Filter Value field.
Is Between	Shows only items with grand totals that are between the numbers specified in the first and last Filter Value fields.
Is Not Between	Shows only items with grand totals that are not between the numbers specified in the first and last Filter Value fields.
Top 10	Shows only the items with the 10 highest grand totals.

Applying Multiple Filters

Filters can be applied additively or non-additively. If you choose to enable additive filtering, each new filter further reduces the list of items that have already been culled from the previous filter. In contrast, non-additive filtering (the default setting) removes whatever filter was previously in place before the new filter is applied to the report.

There are some important points that you should keep in mind when using additive filters:

- Additive filtering must be enabled through the PivotTable Options dialog box.

- Each new additive filter must be of a different type (for example, only one manual filter, one Label filter, and one Value filter can be used additively).

- Additive filters are evaluated as follows: Manual → Label → Value.

You can toggle whether filters are additive or non-additive from the Totals & Filters tab of the PivotTable Options dialog box.

To make PivotTable filters additive, follow these steps:

1. Right-click the PivotTable report and choose PivotTable Options from the pop-up menu.

2. Click the Totals & Filters tab of the PivotTable Options dialog box and check the Allow Multiple Filters per Field option, as shown in Figure 10-6.

Check this box to enable additive filters for the PivotTable.

Figure 10-6: Check the Allow Multiple Filters per Field option to enable additive filtering of fields in the PivotTable report.

Filtering by Selection

All the filters that I have shown so far in this section require that you open a dialog box or navigate through a drop-down field list. These additional steps can make the process of filtering data more difficult when you're rapidly trying to select or deselect items in the PivotTable report. Routing back and forth from the Report Layout area to the drop-down field list to select or deselect items can break your concentration and cause you to spend more time than you'd like. Here's where Filtering By Selection can come in handy.

Filtering By Selection enables you to either keep or suppress selected items for a field in the Row Labels or Column Labels area of a PivotTable report. This filtering method provides a more rapid means for restricting data than navigating through drop-down lists, dialog boxes, and pop-up menus.

To see how Filtering By Selection works, follow these steps:

1. Select one or more items from a field in a Row Labels or Column Labels area. (Hold down the Control key if you want to select multiple items that are not consecutively ordered.)

2. Right-click one of the selected items and choose Filter → Keep Only Selected Items to hide all the items in the field except the highlighted selection or Filter → Hide Selected Items to hide only the items in the field that are selected.

Viewing Applied Filters

Besides just seeing the filter icon next to fields in the PivotTable Field List dialog box and the Report Layout area, you can also view the filter details that have been applied to a field in the PivotTable report by moving your mouse pointer over the filter icon field. In Figure 10-7, you can see that three filters have been applied to the SalesRegion field.

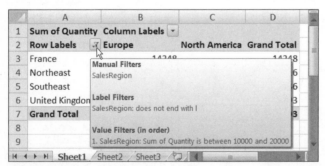

Figure 10-7: Drag your mouse on top of a filter icon to see what filters are being applied to the report field.

Filtering for Top *n* and Bottom *n*

You can apply a Top *n* or Bottom *n* filter by right-clicking an item in a Row Labels or Column Labels field and choosing Filter → Top 10 from the pop-up menu. This brings up the Top 10 Filter dialog box where you can choose to display only the Top *n* or Bottom *n* items, percent, or sum of items (note that *n* denotes a number that you specify).

NOTE Keep in mind that even though the menu item says "Top 10 Filter," this filter setting can be applied to any number of items that you input into the filter criteria box. Additionally, the filter can be set up to look for the Bottom or the Top values of the selected field.

Clearing Filters

You can clear a single filter on a single field, all the filters on a single field, or all the filters on all the fields in the PivotTable report. If you only want to clear a single filter on a field, simply back out the filter by repeating the same steps that were used to define the filter, except blank out the criteria. In the case of manual filters, this might mean rechecking items that were previously unchecked. If you want to clear all the filters on a field, click the filter icon next to the field in either the Report Layout area or in the Fields section of the PivotTable Field List dialog box and then choose Clear Filter From <Field Name> from the drop-down menu. To remove the filters on all the fields in the PivotTable report, choose PivotTable Tools → Clear → Clear Filters.

Working with Inner and Outer Fields

When multiple fields are dragged to either the Row Labels or the Column Labels areas, the fields on the left of the Report Layout area are considered outer fields and the fields on the right are considered inner fields. It's also possible that a field can act as both an inner field as well as an outer field. For example, if you drag three fields into the Row Labels area, the field in the middle is an outer field to the right-most field, while at the same time it is an inner field to the left-most field.

Inner and outer fields act much differently from one another. For example, the items in an inner field are displayed multiple times for each unique outer field item. Inner field items are also subtotaled for each unique outer field item. Additionally, outer fields appear in a bolded font. To see how inner and outer fields work with one another and to follow along with the examples in this section, complete these steps:

1. Starting with the PivotTable report in Figure 10-2, drag SalesRegion in the Row Labels area off the PivotTable report.

2. Drag ProductSubcategory to the Row Labels area.

3. Drag SalesGroup under ProductSubcategory in the Row Labels area, making SalesRegion an inner field and ProductSubcategory an outer field.

4. Verify that your PivotTable report looks like Figure 10-8.

Buttons for expanding
and collapsing detail

Subtotals of inner items
for each unique outer item

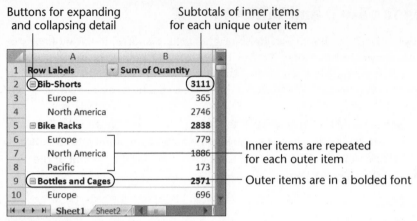

Inner items are repeated
for each outer item

Outer items are in a bolded font

Figure 10-8: A PivotTable report that shows SalesGroup as an inner field of Product-Subcategory. Notice that both fields in the Row Labels area are displayed in a single column of the PivotTable report.

NOTE Inner and outer fields are only relevant in the Row Labels and Column Labels areas; there is no such type of relationship in the Report Filter area or the Values area of a PivotTable report.

Looking at Figure 10-8, you can see that:

- Expansion buttons are added to the left of each outer item.
- Outer items are formatted in a bolded font.
- Inner items are repeated and subtotaled for each outer item.

Looking at Figure 10-8, notice how the items in ProductSubcategory (the outer field) are only displayed one time in a bolded font, whereas the items in SalesGroup (the inner field) are repeated and subtotaled for each new ProductSubcategory item. The expansion buttons to the left of each outer item can be used to toggle whether inner items are displayed.

TIP Notice in Figure 10-8 that the number of inner items for SalesGroup can be different for each outer ProductSubcategory item. For example, Europe and North America only appear for Bib-Shorts, but Europe, North America, and Pacific all appear for Bike Racks. This is because, by default, the PivotTable report only displays the data for which there are records with a valid combination of inner and outer field items. You can, however, change the setting to show all the possible combinations of inner field for each outer item field by checking the Show Items with No Data option.

Expanding and Collapsing Detail

Toggling the display of inner items is referred to as expanding detail (showing the inner items) or collapsing detail (hiding the inner items). You can expand or collapse the detail for an outer field by using the expansion buttons that are displayed to the left of each outer field item. If you prefer using the right-click pop-up menu to toggle whether the detail is shown, you can right-click an outer item and choose Expand/Collapse → Expand from the pop-up menu to expand the detail for a selected item(s) or Expand/Collapse → Collapse from the pop-up menu to collapse the detail for a selected item(s).

Expanding and collapsing detail can be performed for a single item in an outer field, for multiple items of an outer field, or for all the items of an outer field. To select multiple items, simply hold down the Control key to highlight the items that you want to select in the field.

Single Items

The detail for a single outer item can be collapsed or expanded by using one of the following methods:

- Click the expansion button to the left of the outer item to expand (+) or collapse (-) the detail.

- Right-click the outer item and choose Expand/Collapse → Expand or Expand/Collapse → Collapse from the pop-up menu to expand or collapse the detail.

- Double-click the outer field item in the Report Layout area to toggle whether the inner items are displayed.

Multiple Items

You can collapse or expand the detail for multiple items by holding down the Control key to individually select each outer item. After the items are selected, you can use the right-click menu to expand or collapse the detail. To see how this works, follow these steps:

1. Move your mouse pointer over the expansion button that is located to the left of an outer item on the Report Layout area until the pointer turns to a right-facing arrow and then left-click the outer field to select it.

2. Hold down the Control key and left-click each outer item that you want to expand or collapse.

3. Right-click one of the highlighted outer items and choose Collapse/Expand → Collapse or Collapse/Expand → Expand to collapse or expand the detail.

All Items

You can collapse or expand the detail for all outer items by selecting an item in an outer field and clicking the Expand Entire Field or the Collapse Entire Field button in the Active Field toolbar, located under the PivotTable Tools tab, to expand or collapse the detail. Note that you can also use the right-click pop-up menu to accomplish this task. You use Expand/Collapse → Expand Entire Field to show all the inner items of a selected outer field or Expand/Collapse → Collapse Entire Field to hide all the inner items of a selected outer field.

Managing Subtotals

The default handling for PivotTable reports is to subtotal all the inner items for each unique item in an outer field. This subtotaling can be customized from the Field Settings dialog box. You can bring up this dialog box (see Figure 10-9) by right-clicking an outer field and choosing Field Settings from the pop-up menu.

From the Field Settings dialog box you can set subtotals in one of three ways:

- **Automatic:** Default subtotal (Count or Sum)
- **Custom:** More than one subtotal or a different subtotal than the default
- **None:** No subtotals displayed

In Figure 10-9, I have selected Sum, Count, and Average in the Field Settings dialog box for ProductSubCategory. After these subtotals settings have been applied, the Pivot-Table report looks like Figure 10-10.

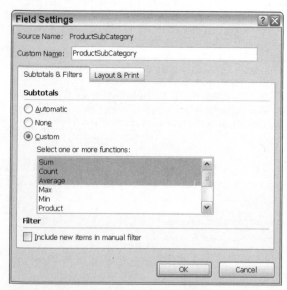

Figure 10-9: Subtotaling of inner fields can be customized by accessing the outer field's Field Settings dialog box.

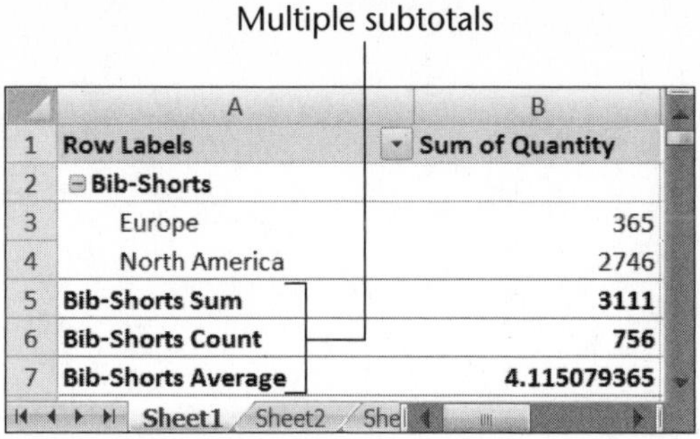

Multiple subtotals

Figure 10-10: Multiple subtotals calculated for an inner row field.

Handling Items with No Data

You can opt to show all items in an inner field, even if there is not a valid combination with an outer item. For example, looking back at Figure 10-8, you can see that the sales region *Pacific* does not appear for the product subcategory *Bib-Shorts*. This is because there are no records in the dataset that have a product subcategory of Bib-Shorts for the Pacific sales region.

You may find that a report user wants to show all the possible items of an inner field for every item in an outer field of the PivotTable report, regardless of whether a valid combination exists. This request is often made when the report user wants a fixed report layout and the current combinations don't already exist, but are expected to take place (for example, a direct mail promotion where the second group of offers was sent out a couple of weeks after the first group).

The default setting is to display only the inner items with data. You can change this setting by checking the Show Items with No Data option, located under the Layout & Print tab of the Field Settings dialog box. Keep in mind that this option is controlled from the inner field item (not the outer field as is the case for subtotaling).

> **TIP** Checking the Show Items with No Data option results in all the items of the inner field being shown, regardless of whether a valid combination with an outer field exists. You can also use this option when filters are applied to the PivotTable report. However, keep in mind that the item must exist in the dataset for it to be displayed in the report.

To show items with no data and to follow along with the example in this section, follow these steps:

1. Verify that your PivotTable report looks like Figure 10-8, right-click any Sales-Group item in the PivotTable, and choose Field Settings from the pop-up menu.

2. Click the Layout & Print tab in the Field Settings dialog box, check the Show Items with No Data box (see Figure 10-11), and click OK to close the Field Settings dialog box.

3. Verify that your PivotTable report looks like Figure 10-12.

Check this box to show items with no data.

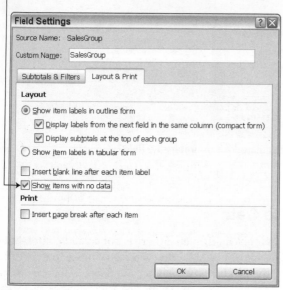

Figure 10-11: Check Show Items with No Data to display all SalesGroup items for each ProductSubcategory, regardless of whether a valid combination exists.

No data exists for Pacific, but it now appears.

	A	B
1	**Row Labels** ▼	**Sum of Quantity**
2	⊟ **Bib-Shorts**	**3111**
3	Europe	365
4	North America	2746
5	→ Pacific	
6	⊟ **Bike Racks**	**2838**
7	Europe	779
8	North America	1886
9	Pacific	173
10	⊟ **Bottles and Cages**	**2571**

Figure 10-12: Pacific has no data, but it still appears under Bib-Shorts.

After this option is checked, all the SalesGroup items appear for each ProductSubcategory item, even if there is not a valid combination between the inner and outer field items. You can also use the For Empty Cells Show option in the PivotTable Options dialog box in conjunction with the Show Items with No Data option in the Field Settings dialog box to format the report. I checked the option Show Items with No Data for the SalesGroup field (refer to Figure 10-11) and also set the For Empty Cells Show option to "*" in the PivotTable Options dialog box. (You can bring up this dialog box by right-clicking the PivotTable and choosing PivotTable Options from the pop-up menu.) The result is shown in Figure 10-13.

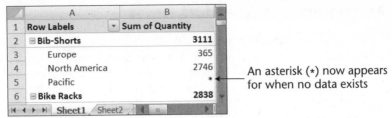

An asterisk (*) now appears for when no data exists

Figure 10-13: An asterisk in the Values area now indicates that the inner item has no data.

> **TIP** Report users might be confused when they see a 0 in the Values area for a Column Labels or Row Labels item. They may not understand why a 0 appears if blank values are not normally displayed. Until they drill down on the data, they might not realize that there are one or more records behind that 0. If you decide to display some text for blank values, I don't recommend using a 0 because you lose the capability to readily distinguish a blank value from a 0.

Sorting Data

The items in a field are automatically sorted in an ascending alphanumeric order as fields are dropped into the PivotTable report. Though this sort order is the default setting, you can choose to sort fields in any of the following ways:

- Ascending alphanumeric (default setting)
- Descending alphanumeric
- Based on a value in the Values area
- Custom

Sorting can be performed in every area of the PivotTable report except the Report Filter area. If you want to sort the items for a Report Filter area field, you first drag it to either the Row Labels or Column Labels area, perform the required sort, and then drag it back to the Report Filter area.

> **TIP** In a PivotTable, the unique items of a Column Labels or Row Labels field are sorted alphanumerically when the field is dropped into the report. As a result, you should never use an Order By statement in the SQL query for a PivotTable. This statement works on the entire dataset and only serves to increase the amount of time it takes to execute the query and refresh the report.

Sorting in Ascending or Descending Order

You can apply an ascending or descending sort to fields in the Row Labels or Column Labels area by first clicking a field item in the Report Layout area and then clicking the A → Z button or the Z → A button in the Sort toolbar, located under the PivotTable Tools tab. You can also sort data based on values in the Values area, the Grand Total Row area, or the Grand Total Column area. Just highlight the desired area and click the applicable sort button to sort the data.

If you're working with date fields, you should click the Sort button that is next to the A → Z and Z → A buttons in the Sort toolbar. Clicking the Sort button brings up the Sort dialog box, where you can choose to perform a manual, an ascending alphanumeric, or a descending alphanumeric sort. Clicking the More Options button brings up the More Sort Options dialog box where you can automatically sort items that are days of the week or months of the year.

TIP Report Filter area fields are often not sorted in alphanumeric order, and you cannot sort a field that is dropped in this location. However, you can drag it to the Row Labels or Column Labels area, sort it there, and then drag it back to the Report Filter area where the sort will be maintained. You can even apply a custom sort before moving it back to the Report Filter area.

Sorting on a Values Area Field

You can sort items by their summarized values in Values area of the PivotTable report by clicking the value in the Values area and then clicking the A → Z button (sort ascending) or the Z → A button (sort descending) in the Sort toolbar, located under the PivotTable Tools tab. You can also perform this type of sort by clicking the Sort button next to the A → Z and Z → A buttons in the Sort toolbar. When you click the Sort button, the Sort dialog box appears. In Figure 10-14, the sort is based on Sum of Quantity in descending order.

Figure 10-14: In this dialog box, you can sort PivotTable fields in the Row Labels or the Column Labels area based on a value in the Values area.

In the Sort Options section of this dialog box, you can choose to sort the field values in an Ascending, Descending, or Manual (custom) order. Clicking the More Options button brings up the More Sort Options dialog box where you can toggle whether the items for the selected field are automatically sorted every time the report is updated. You can also access the custom sort lists from this dialog box.

Custom Sort Order

You can also perform a custom sort by simply selecting a field and dragging it to the preferred location in the Column Labels or Row Labels area. The field is ready to be moved when the button changes from a plus sign to the mouse pointer combined with an arrow that points in four directions. Try organizing the fields as shown in Figure 10-15.

WARNING If the button does not change shape, the sort order is not set to manual. Right-click an item in the field and choose Sort → More Sort Options to bring up the Sort dialog box. Once the Sort dialog box is open, click the Manual button under Sort Options and then OK to change the sort method and to close the Sort dialog box.

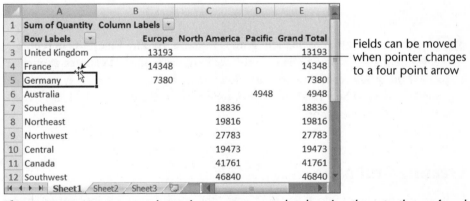

Fields can be moved when pointer changes to a four point arrow

Figure 10-15: You can sort items in a custom way by dragging them to the preferred location in the Row Labels or Column Labels hierarchy.

Grouping Items

Earlier in this chapter, I discussed how filtering can be done before or after the dataset is loaded into the Excel PivotTable report. This same principle also applied to grouping items; groups can easily be created by adding some conditional logic to the SQL query (OLTP data) or the OLAP cube (OLAP data). However, just like filters, grouping items before the data is loaded into the PivotTable report may not be optimal for the following reasons:

- The report user may not have access or authorization to create the conditional logic necessary for grouping the items into a new field.

- The report user may not have the technical skills to modify the SQL query or the OLAP cube to create the group field.

- The groups are being defined interactively, as the report is being shaped. Redefining the SQL query or the OLAP cube isn't practical.

Because the grouping functions are so easy to use, report users do not need to access or be trained on how to modify an SQL query or OLAP cube for creating a new group. Instead, they can rely on the straightforward grouping functions that are included with Excel to group and ungroup items into new fields however they see fit. They can perform all sorts of grouping functions such as grouping particular months into a specific fiscal quarter, sales representatives into a designated territory, or geographic locations into a region.

TIP Keep in mind that permanent groups that are used by a majority of report users should generally be defined in the data source or the data source extract query. If the group is continually redefined in a non-programmable way or the group is only used by a small number of report users, the group is typically better defined in the report.

Creating Groups

In order to group items into a new field, select the items that you want to group in the Row Labels or the Column Labels area, right-click one of the selected items, and then choose Group from the pop-up menu. If you prefer using the PivotTable tab, you can click the Group Selection button in the Group group, once the items are selected.

To follow along with the example in this section and to group the sales regions into a new field called Territory, follow these steps:

1. Verify that your PivotTable report looks like Figure 10-2, highlight cells A3–A6, right-click the highlighted section, and then choose PivotTable Tools → Group from the pop-up menu.

2. Notice that Excel creates a new field in the PivotTable report called SalesRegion2 and a new group called Group 1.

3. Click Group 1 in cell A3, type **Territory A**, and press Enter to change the item name from Group1 to Territory A.

4. Verify that your PivotTable report looks like Figure 10-16.

5. Highlight cells A9–A13, right-click the highlighted cells, and choose Group from the pop-up menu to group Germany, Northeast, and Northwest into Group2.

6. Select cell A8, type **Territory B**, and press Enter to change the group name from Group2 to Territory B.

7. Highlight cells A13–A17, right-click the highlighted cells, and choose Group from the pop-up menu to group Southeast, Southwest, and United Kingdom into Group3.

8. Select cell A12, type **Territory C**, and press Enter to change the group name from Group3 to Territory C.

9. Right-click Territory A in cell A3 and choose Field Settings from the pop-up menu to bring up the Field Settings dialog box. Type **TerritoryName** in the Custom Name field and click OK to change the group field name from SalesRegion2 to TerritoryName.

10. Verify that your PivotTable report looks like Figure 10-17.

WATCH THE VIDEO To see how the categories are grouped into territories, click the **ch1001_video.avi file at** www.wiley.com/go/excelreporting/2007 **to watch the video.**

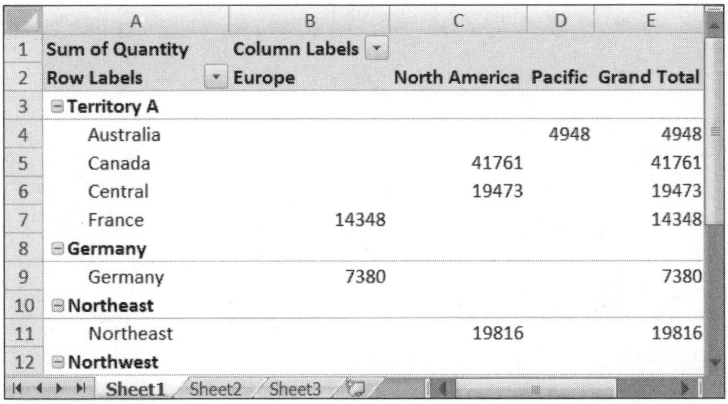

	A	B	C	D	E
1	Sum of Quantity	Column Labels			
2	Row Labels	Europe	North America	Pacific	Grand Total
3	⊟Territory A				
4	Australia			4948	4948
5	Canada		41761		41761
6	Central		19473		19473
7	France	14348			14348
8	⊟Germany				
9	Germany	7380			7380
10	⊟Northeast				
11	Northeast		19816		19816
12	⊟Northwest				

Sheet1 / Sheet2 / Sheet3

Figure 10-16: It's easy to group items into new fields and customize the name of the items in the group.

	A	B	C	D	E
1	Sum of Quantity	Column Labels			
2	Row Labels	Europe	North America	Pacific	Grand Total
3	⊟ Territory A				
4	Australia			4948	4948
5	Canada		41761		41761
6	Central		19473		19473
7	France	14348			14348
8	⊟ Territory B				
9	Germany	7380			7380
10	Northeast		19816		19816
11	Northwest		27783		27783
12	⊟ Territory C				
13	Southeast		18836		18836
14	Southwest		46840		46840
15	United Kingdom	13193			13193
16	Grand Total	34921	174509	4948	214378

Sheet1 / Sheet2 / Sheet3

Figure 10-17: You can group fields in the Row Labels or Column Labels area into new fields by using the Group function in the PivotTable Tools tab or the pop-up menu.

If you accidentally grouped an item in the wrong category, you must ungroup the category the item is currently in and the category that the item should be in. After that, you can rearrange the items to the correct location and re-create the group.

Ungrouping Items

After the group field is created, it exists as its own field name in the PivotTable report. Dragging the Category Name field off the PivotTable report doesn't remove the field from the PivotTable Field List. The only way to remove the new item is to ungroup all the items in the group.

Renaming Fields

You may find it necessary to rename fields in the PivotTable report. This could be due to a variety of reasons. Perhaps the field should utilize a layman title instead of a technical database field name; technical names appear when database fields are selected without being renamed (see Appendix A to learn more about renaming fields in an SQL query). Another possibility is that the field name is too long and must be abbreviated to fit well in the overall report format. I often rename fields that I drag into the Values area of the report, because I don't like the convention *Sum of <Field>* or *Count of <Field>* to be used as the field name. (For example, dragging the field Quantity into the Values area of the report results in the field being named as Sum of Quantity; I would typically rename the field as Total Quantity.)

Techniques to rename fields can vary, depending on where the field is located (or not located) in the PivotTable report. Despite the wide array of methods, you can always rely on one uniform technique for renaming fields, which simply involves bringing up the Field Settings dialog box. Recall from Chapters 2 and 3 that the Field Settings dialog box can be brought up using a variety of methods, including:

- Left-clicking the field in the Areas section of the PivotTable Field List dialog box and choosing Field Settings from the pop-up menu.

- Right-clicking a field item in the Report Layout area and choosing Field Settings from the pop-up menu.

- Clicking a field item in the Report Layout area and choosing PivotTable Tools → Active Field → Field Settings.

Once the Field Settings dialog box is open, you can rename the field to any string that is less than 32kb in length. (The limit used to be 255 positions in earlier versions of Excel.) In Figure 10-18, I renamed ProductSubcategory to the shorter label, SubCategory.

The other methods for changing the name of fields are a bit quicker. If the field is in the Values area, you can just type the new name over the old name. Note that if the field name in the Values area appears multiple times (usually due to having two or more fields in the Values area with fields in both the Row Labels area and the Column Labels area), typing over one of the labels changes the name of all the labels for the selected field. If the field is in the Report Filter area, you can simply type the new name over the old one. If the field is in the Row Labels or Column Labels area, just select one of the items in the field, click the PivotTable Tools tab, and then type the new name in the Active Field box, which is located in the Active Field group.

Figure 10-18: Although there are several ways to rename fields, they can always be renamed from the Field Settings dialog box.

Creating Calculated Items and Calculated Fields

Excel provides support for creating Calculated Items and Calculated Fields for your PivotTable report. A Calculated Item is essentially a new item that appears in the drop-down list of a field in either the Row Labels or the Column Labels area of the Pivot-Table. A Calculated Field, on the other hand, appears as a new field in the Values area. This type of field can only be displayed in the Values area of the PivotTable report.

Calculated Fields and Calculated Items are useful in the following situations:

- The report user does not have the technical skills to modify the SQL query to add the additional fields.

- The report user does not have security or access to modify the SQL query to add the additional fields.

- The Calculated Field and Calculated Item reference other Total fields that have been derived from complex, high-cost (that is, requiring extensive CPU pro-cessing time) fields in the SQL query.

I typically use Calculated Fields and Calculated Items when the formulas are based on multiple fields that are derived from complex subqueries. Instead of trying to pro-gram these fields into the SQL query by writing a convoluted query with multiple sub-queries, I can simply reference them in the PivotTable report. This can save a lot of processing time because the fields are simply numerical values in the PivotTable report and I do not have to run numerous subqueries to calculate the value or item. I've also seen many non-technical report users add Calculated Fields and Calculated Items to their reports to avoid having to go back and forth with an SQL programmer to get the fields or items that they need in their report.

WARNING Using Calculated Fields and Calculated Items spreads the report logic into more locations than just the SQL query, stored procedure, or OLAP cube. This adds an additional burden for managing change and configuration.

In this section, I provide more information about these special fields and demon-strate how you can use them in a PivotTable report.

Before You Begin

In order to follow along with the examples in this section, you must customize the Pivot-Table report. Before you begin, complete these steps:

1. Starting with the PivotTable report in Figure 10-2, drag the SalesRegion and the SalesGroup fields off the report.

2. Drag ResellerType to the Report Filter area, ProductCategory to the Row Labels area, and Quantity to the Values area.

3. Right-click the PivotTable and choose PivotTable Options from the pop-up menu to bring up the PivotTable Options dialog box. Click the Totals & Filters tab, uncheck the option Show Grand Totals for Rows, and then click OK to close the dialog box and suppress the grand total calculation for rows in the PivotTable report.

4. Verify that your PivotTable report looks like Figure 10-19.

Creating a Calculated Item

A Calculated Item appears as an item for a field in the Row Labels or Column Labels areas. You can use Calculated Items to create new items in the list by referencing existing items in that field or other fields of the report. For this example, I'm going to add a new item called Energy Drinks to the ProductCategory field. In the real world, this example might be applied to demonstrate how a new product category could impact sales. In order to keep things simple, I forego complex formulas by simply estimating that the Energy Drink sales units are 65 percent of Accessories sales units.

To create a Calculated Item field for Energy Drinks that estimates the sales units at 65 percent of Accessories, follow these steps:

1. Click Accessories in cell A4 of the PivotTable report and choose PivotTable Tools → Formulas → Calculated Item to bring up the Insert Calculated Item In dialog box (note that you must click the Formulas button and not the Formulas tab).

2. Type **Energy Drinks** in the Name field and press Tab to move to the Formula field.

3. Type **= Accessories * .65** in the Formula field.

4. Verify that the Insert Calculated Item In dialog box looks like Figure 10-20, and then click the Add button to add Energy Drinks as a new item in ProductCategory.

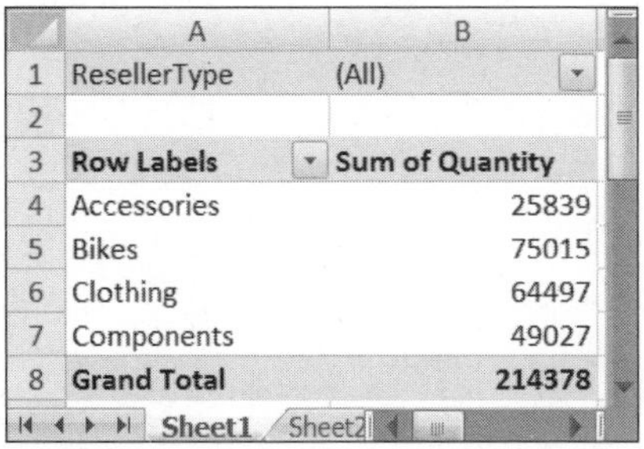

	A	B
1	ResellerType	(All)
2		
3	**Row Labels**	**Sum of Quantity**
4	Accessories	25839
5	Bikes	75015
6	Clothing	64497
7	Components	49027
8	**Grand Total**	**214378**

Sheet1 Sheet2

Figure 10-19: Start with this PivotTable to follow the examples in this section.

New item in ProductCategory

Figure 10-20: You can add Calculated Items as new items to fields in the Row Labels or Column Labels areas.

5. Click OK to close the dialog box and add the Calculated Item to the PivotTable report.

6. Verify that your PivotTable report looks like Figure 10-21.

You have now created a new Calculated Item field that estimates the units sold for Energy Drinks equal to 65 percent of the units sold in the Accessories product category.

WARNING Fields with Calculated Items cannot be moved to the Report Filter area until the Calculated Items have been removed from the field.

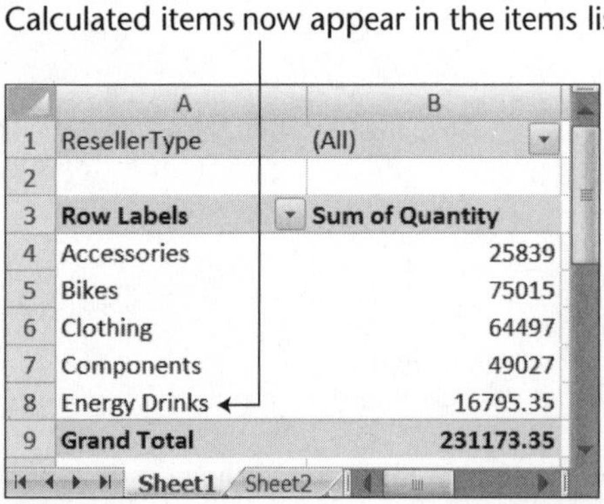

Calculated items now appear in the items list.

Figure 10-21: The Calculated Item, Energy Drinks, is added as a new item under ProductCategory with estimated units sold equal to 65 percent of Accessories.

You can remove Calculated Items by opening the Insert Calculated Item In dialog box, selecting the Calculated Item field from the Field drop-down box, and clicking Delete.

Creating a Calculated Field

Unlike a Calculated Item that appears as an item in a Column Labels or Row Labels area field, a Calculated Field is a new field that is added to the Values area of the Pivot-Table report. The following example demonstrates how the estimated returns can be added as a new field in the Values area of the PivotTable report. In order to keep things simple, I forego complex formulas by simply calculating returned units as 12 percent of sales units.

To create a new Calculated Field called Returned Units that shows returns as 12 percent of sales units, follow these steps:

1. Starting with the PivotTable report in Figure 10-19, click any cell in the Pivot-Table and choose PivotTable Tools → Formulas → Calculated Field to bring up the Insert Calculated Field dialog box (note that you must click the Formulas button and not the Formulas tab).

2. Type **Returned Units** in the Name field and press Tab to move to the Formula field.

3. Type **= Quantity * -.12** in the Formula field.

4. Verify that the Insert Calculated Field dialog box looks like Figure 10-22 and then click the OK button to add Returned Units as a new Calculated Field in the PivotTable report and close the Insert Calculated Field dialog box.

5. Type **Gross Sales Units** over Sum of Quantity in cell B4 and **Est. Return Units** over Sum of Returned Units in cell C4 to change the name of the Values area field labels.

6. Verify that the PivotTable report looks like Figure 10-23.

Figure 10-22: Calculated Fields are added from this dialog box.

Calculated Field appears as a new field in the Values area

	A	B	C
1	ResellerType	(All)	
2			
3		**Values**	
4	**Row Labels**	**Gross Sales Units**	**Est. Return Units**
5	Accessories	25839	-3100.68
6	Bikes	75015	-9001.8
7	Clothing	64497	-7739.64
8	Components	49027	-5883.24
9	Energy Drinks	16795.35	-2015.442
10	**Grand Total**	**231173.35**	**-27740.802**

Figure 10-23: The Calculated Field has been added to the PivotTable report as a new field in the Values area.

NOTE The only aggregate function that can be performed on a Calculated Field is Sum.

After the Calculated Field is created, you can delete it by opening the Insert Calculated Field dialog box, selecting Calculated Field from the drop-down box, and clicking Delete. You can also change the formula of these fields by selecting the field from the drop-down list, entering the new formula, and clicking Modify.

Displaying Formulas

You can display all the formulas for Calculated Items and Calculated Fields by choosing PivotTable Tools → Formulas → List Formulas. Selecting this function creates a new worksheet that lists all the formulas for Calculated Fields and Calculated Items in the selected PivotTable report, as shown in Figure 10-24.

	A	B	C	D
1	*Calculated Field*			
2	**Solve Order**	**Field**	**Formula**	
3		1	Returned Units	=Quantity * -0.12
4				
5	*Calculated Item*			
6	**Solve Order**	**Item**	**Formula**	
7		1	'Energy Drinks'	=Accessories * 0.65
8				
9				
10	*Note:*		When a cell is updated by more than one formula,	
11			the value is set by the formula with the last solve o	

Figure 10-24: You can display the formulas for Calculated Fields and Calculated Items by choosing the List Formulas function.

Handling Error Conditions

Error conditions in a PivotTable report usually result from division-by-zero errors. Although the message doesn't cause any problems with the PivotTable, it can certainly ruin the presentation effect, as demonstrated in Figure 10-25.

You can fix division-by-zero problems from the PivotTable Options dialog box by right-clicking the PivotTable and choosing Table Options from the pop-up menu. Check the option For Error Values, Show, and then enter the text string you want to display in place of the error message. The text string can be up to 255 characters, although I recommend leaving the box blank, using a 0, or using an asterisk to indicate the formula error. In Figure 10-26, I used an asterisk to indicate the formula error.

	A	B	C
1	ResellerType	(All)	
2			
3		**Values**	
4	**Row Labels**	**Quantity Sold**	**Damaged Units**
5	Accessories	25839	#DIV/0!
6	Bikes	75015	#DIV/0!
7	Clothing	64497	#DIV/0!
8	Components	49027	#DIV/0!
9	Energy Drinks	16795.35	#DIV/0!
10	**Grand Total**	**231173.35**	**#DIV/0!**

Sheet4　**Sheet1**　Shee

Figure 10-25: Unless fixed, division-by-zero errors can ruin the appearance of your report.

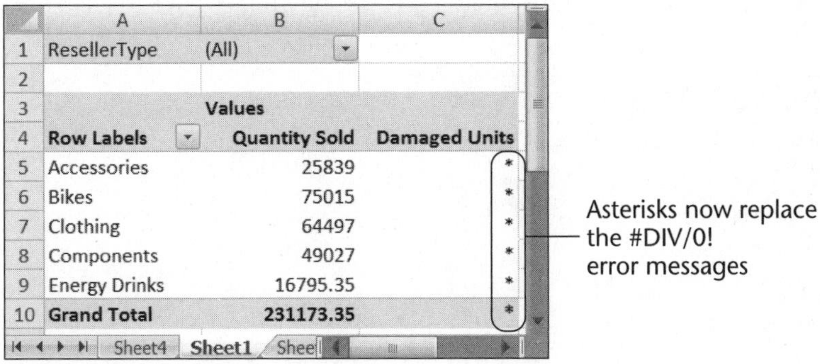

	A	B	C
1	ResellerType	(All)	
2			
3		**Values**	
4	**Row Labels**	**Quantity Sold**	**Damaged Units**
5	Accessories	25839	*
6	Bikes	75015	*
7	Clothing	64497	*
8	Components	49027	*
9	Energy Drinks	16795.35	*
10	**Grand Total**	**231173.35**	*

Sheet4　**Sheet1**　Shee

Asterisks now replace the #DIV/0! error messages

Figure 10-26: You can configure the PivotTable report to overwrite the division-by-zero error messages with a text string of your choosing.

Creating Custom Formulas

As you probably already know from practicing with the PivotTable reports and reading earlier sections of this book, PivotTables essentially perform some type of aggregate function on the field in the Values area. This might be a Count, a Sum, an Average, or a Min or Max. In addition to these well-known functions, you can also configure fields in the Values area to perform several other types of custom calculations, including:

- Running totals
- Percentage of a specified cell, row, column, or grand total value
- Difference or percentage-difference from a base item, row, or column value

This section covers the basics of managing Values area fields and shows you how to change the type of aggregate function, calculate running totals, and display data as a percentage of a particular base item (that is a row total, a column total, or a grand total).

Aggregate Function and Custom Calculations

Fields dropped into the Values area of a PivotTable are automatically aggregated. If the field is an alphanumeric field, it is counted. If the field is a numeric field, it is summed. You can change this aggregate function — or summary type — from the Value Field Settings dialog box (see Figure 10-27).

The various types of aggregate functions are displayed in the Summarize By tab of the dialog box. Clicking the Number Format button brings up the Format Cells dialog box, where you can format the display of this Values area field. Clicking the Show Values As tab reveals the second view of this dialog box, as shown in Figure 10-28.

Figure 10-27: The aggregate function of a Values area field is modified from this dialog box view.

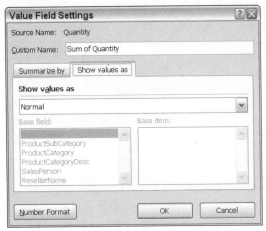

Figure 10-28: The second view of the Value Field Settings dialog box.

From the Show Values As drop-down field, you can select from the options listed in Table 10-3. Keep in mind that the aggregate function you select in the Summarize By tab is closely related to the option you select in this Show Values As drop-down box. For example, a Count function used with a Running Total produces very different results than a Sum function used with a Running Total.

Table 10-3: Custom Calculations

OPTION	DESCRIPTION
Normal	The Values area field is summarized in its normal way without any special function.
Difference From	The Data area field is summarized as a difference from a base field item. The next or previous item can also be selected.
% Of	The Data area field is shown as a percentage of a base field item.
% Difference From	The Data area field is shown as a percentage-difference from a base field item.
Running Total In	The Data area field is shown as a running total in a base field.
% Of Row	The Data area field is shown as a percentage of the total row value.
% Of Column	The Data area field is shown as a percentage of the total column value.
% Of Total	The Data area field is shown as a percentage of the total value displayed in the report.
Index	Calculates values as: ((Cell Value) * (Grand Total of Grand Totals)) / ((Grand Row Total) * (Grand Column Total)).

These options add a new dimension to how the data can be displayed in the Pivot-Table. Rather than just looking at numerical values, you can also examine how they are allocated as a percentage of some base field item, column, row, or report total. You can even examine product revenue or cost as a percentage of a particular product category or compared to another product category. There are almost endless possibilities for how you can choose to display the data in your PivotTable report.

Calculating Running Totals

Running totals can be calculated in a PivotTable report from the Show Values As tab of the Value Field Settings dialog box. Using this feature, you can display a running total of a Values area field, instead of just show the field value for a particular combination of items in the Row Labels and Columns Labels area. To see how this works, try calculating a running total of Quantity in SalesRegion, by following these steps:

1. Starting with the PivotTable report in Figure 10-2 that has SalesRegion in the Row Labels area and Quantity in the Values area, right-click Sum of Quantity in cell A1 of the PivotTable report, and choose Value Field Settings from the pop-up menu to bring up the Value Field Settings dialog box.

2. Click the Show Values As tab, type **Total Quantity** in the Custom Name field, select Running Total In from the Show Values As drop-down box, and then click SalesRegion in the Base Field pane. Verify that the Value Field Settings dialog box looks like Figure 10-29 and click OK.

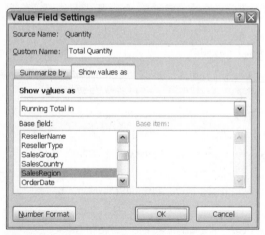

Figure 10-29: Running Totals requires a base field that is already in the Row Labels or Column Labels area of the PivotTable report.

3. Right-click the PivotTable and choose PivotTable Options from the pop-up menu to bring up the PivotTable Options dialog box. Click the Totals & Filters tab, uncheck the option Show Grand Totals for Rows, and then click OK to close the dialog box and suppress the grand total calculation for rows in the PivotTable report.

4. Verify that your PivotTable report looks like Figure 10-30.

Showing Data as a Percentage of a Base Value

You can show data in the Values area as a percentage or percentage-difference of

- A row
- A column
- An item in a field (specific item, next item, or previous item)
- The total value displayed in the report

	A	B	C	D
1	Total Quantity	Column Labels ▾		
2	Row Labels ▾	Europe	North America	Pacific
3	Australia	0	0	4948
4	Canada	0	41761	4948
5	Central	0	61234	4948
6	France	14348	61234	4948
7	Germany	21728	61234	4948
8	Northeast	21728	81050	4948
9	Northwest	21728	108833	4948
10	Southeast	21728	127669	4948
11	Southwest	21728	174509	4948
12	United Kingdom	34921	174509	4948
13	Grand Total			

H ◀ ▶ H   Sheet1 Sheet2 Sheet3

Figure 10-30: Compare this PivotTable report to Figure 10-2 and notice how a running total of quantity is calculated for SalesRegion.

Starting with the PivotTable report in Figure 10-2, complete these steps to create a custom calculation that shows the percentage of quantity sold as a percentage of the report total:

1. Right-click Sum of Quantity in cell A1 of the PivotTable report and choose Value Field Settings from the pop-up menu to bring up the Value Field Settings dialog box.

2. Click the Show Values As tab, type **% Of SalesGroup** in the Custom Name field, and select % of Column from the Show Values As drop-down box. Verify that the Value Field Settings dialog box looks like Figure 10-31 and click OK.

3. Right-click the PivotTable and choose PivotTable Options from the pop-up menu to bring up the PivotTable Options dialog box. Click the Totals & Filters tab, uncheck the option Show Grand Totals for Rows, and then click OK to close the dialog box and suppress the grand total calculation for rows in the PivotTable report.

4. Verify that your PivotTable report looks like Figure 10-32.

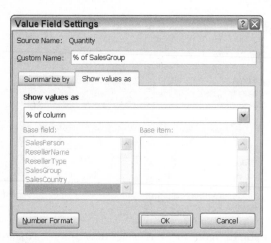

Figure 10-31: You can show values as a percentage of a row total, a column total, a report total, or a base item.

	A	B	C	D
1	% of SalesGroup	Column Labels ▾		
2	Row Labels ▾	Europe	North America	Pacific
3	Australia	0.00%	0.00%	100.00%
4	Canada	0.00%	23.93%	0.00%
5	Central	0.00%	11.16%	0.00%
6	France	41.09%	0.00%	0.00%
7	Germany	21.13%	0.00%	0.00%
8	Northeast	0.00%	11.36%	0.00%
9	Northwest	0.00%	15.92%	0.00%
10	Southeast	0.00%	10.79%	0.00%
11	Southwest	0.00%	26.84%	0.00%
12	United Kingdom	37.78%	0.00%	0.00%
13	Grand Total	100.00%	100.00%	100.00%

I◀ ◀ ▶ ▶I Sheet1 / Sheet2 / Sheet3

Figure 10-32: Notice how the cells in each column add up to 100% of the column total when you choose to show values as a percentage of the column total.

Trying It Out in the Real World

Syed Abbas, the Pacific Sales Manager for AdventureWorks, is preparing a sales report that summarizes the total unit price by product category and reseller type for the country of Australia. Syed needs your help to show the unit price in both Australian and United States dollars. He also would like to sort the results from highest amount to the lowest amount, grouping the top two product categories into revenue leaders and the bottom two product categories into revenue losers. This report should only show the sales for Australia and the figures must be formatted in an accounting format. Lastly, due to some internal politics, it's important that Syed summarize the amounts for reseller type in the following order: Specialty Bike Shop, Warehouse, and then Value Added Reseller.

Getting Down to Business

Starting with the PivotTable report in Figure 10-2 of this chapter, follow these steps to complete the real-world example:

WATCH THE VIDEO To see how this example is completed, click the **ch1002_video.avi file at** www.wiley.com/go/excelreporting/2007 **and watch the video.**

1. Drag SalesRegion, SalesGroup, and Sum of Quantity off the PivotTable report.

2. Drag SalesCountry to the Report Filter area, ResellerType to the Column Labels area, ProductCategory to the Row Labels area, and Unit Price to the Values area.

3. Drag CurrencyCode under ProductCategory in the Row Labels area, making CurrencyCode an inner field of ProductCategory.

4. Click the SalesCountry drop-down arrow in cell B1, choose Australia from the drop-down list, and click OK.

5. Click AUD in cell A6 and then choose PivotTable Tools → Formulas → Calculated Item to bring up the Calculated Item dialog box.

6. Type **USD Equiv** in the Name field and **= AUD/1.35** in the Formula field. Click OK to create the new Calculated Item and to close the dialog box.

7. Click Warehouse in cell D4 to select it, move the mouse pointer toward the bottom of the field until the pointer changes to four cross-arrows, and then drag Warehouse between Specialty Bike Shop and Value Added Reseller.

8. Right-click Sum of Unit Price in cell A3 and choose Value Field Settings from the pop-up menu to bring up the Field Settings dialog box. Type **Gross Revenue** in the Custom Name field and click the Number Format button.

9. Select Accounting from the Category pane and then None from the Symbol drop-down field. Click OK to close the Format Cells dialog box and then OK again to close the Value Field Settings dialog box.

10. Right-click Accessories in cell A5 and choose Sort → More Sort Options from the pop-up menu to bring up the Sort dialog box. Click Descending and then select Gross Revenue for the field on which to base the sort. Click OK to apply the sort and to close the Sort dialog box.

11. Highlight cells A11 to A16 and then right-click the highlighted cells and choose Group from the pop-up menu to group the bottom two items into a new field called Group1.

12. Highlight cells A12 to A19 and then right-click the highlighted cells and choose Group from the pop-up menu to group the top two items into a new field called Group2.

13. Click cell A5 and type **Revenue Losers** over Group 1, and then click cell A12 and type **Revenue Leaders** over Group 2.

14. Click cell A5 and then click the A → Z button in the Sort group of the Pivot-Table Tools tab.

15. Right-click Bikes in cell A6 and choose Field Settings from the pop-up menu. Click None under the Subtotals section and then OK to suppress subtotaling of the two currency codes.

16. Verify that your report looks like Figure 10-33.

	A	B	C	D	E
1	SalesCountry	Australia			
2					
3	Gross Revenue	Column Labels			
4	Row Labels	Specialty Bike Shop	Warehouse	Value Added Reseller	Grand Total
5	⊟ Revenue Leaders				
6	⊟ Bikes				
7	AUD	177,563.90	113,646.87	363,428.40	654,639.17
8	USD Equiv	131,528.82	84,182.86	269,206.22	484,917.90
9	⊟ Components				
10	AUD	6,665.33	49,852.44	43,829.92	100,347.69
11	USD Equiv	4,937.28	36,927.74	32,466.60	74,331.62
12	⊟ Revenue Losers				
13	⊟ Clothing				
14	AUD	2,945.44	636.50	4,643.66	8,225.60
15	USD Equiv	2,181.81	471.48	3,439.75	6,093.04
16	⊟ Accessories				
17	AUD	1,306.46	58.36	3,152.37	4,517.19
18	USD Equiv	967.75	43.23	2,335.09	3,346.07
19	Grand Total	328,096.78	285,819.47	722,502.01	1,336,418.26

Figure 10-33: If you did everything right, your report should look like this.

Reviewing What You Did

This example provides you with some more practice with some of the material covered in this chapter, including how to create a Calculated Item, apply an advanced sort based on the aggregated data in the Values area, group items into a new field, and format fields in the Values area. There's a tremendous amount of material in this section, and I recommend that you experiment with numerous options, functions, and tools to get a better handle on how they affect the report.

Chapter Review

This chapter showed you how to design and format PivotTable reports using the powerful filtering, sorting, grouping, and summarizing tools and functions available in Excel. It assumed that you had already read Chapters 2 and 3 or were at least familiar with the basic features and functions of PivotTable reports. I started with a review of the filtering tools, where I covered the numerous types of filters that are available. After that, I reviewed how inner and outer fields are used in a PivotTable report. Next, I covered how to sort and group items. Following that, I covered Calculated Fields, Calculated Items, and custom calculations.

CHAPTER 11

PivotTable Report Formatting

There are powerful formatting tools that you can use to customize the display of your PivotTable report data — both on the screen and on printed paper. A robust suite of tools provides quick access for conditionally adding icons, data bars, and color scales to your PivotTable report, which can greatly enhance the data presentation and automatically update as report figures are changed. There are also excellent tools for setting up your own PivotTable report styles, an especially useful utility if you develop numerous Excel reports that require specific types of formatting.

I start this chapter with a review of the PivotTable styles toolkit. Here, I review how you can add new styles and select predefined styles for your PivotTable report. Next, I cover the general formatting options and tools that are included with PivotTable reports. This includes report update options and field formatting functions. After that, I show you how to use all the new conditional formatting tools, including icon sets, data bars, and color scales. I also demonstrate how conditional formatting rules can be added, edited, and removed. Before concluding with a real-world example, I cover the report printing features that are available for best laying out your PivotTable report on paper. I wrap up this chapter with a real-world example that ties much of the material presented in this chapter into an example that you might encounter in the real world.

Before You Begin

All the examples in this chapter, including the "Trying It Out in the Real World" exercise, utilize the SQL query and PivotTable report outlined in this section. If you plan to follow along with the material and examples throughout this chapter, I recommend that you start by creating this PivotTable report that accesses the AdventureWorksDW database.

Complete these steps to create the PivotTable report and follow along with the examples used throughout this chapter:

1. From Excel, choose Data → From Other Sources → From Microsoft Query to bring up the Choose Data Source dialog box.

2. When the Choose Data Source dialog box appears, verify that Use the Query Wizard to Create/Edit Queries is unchecked, select the AdventureWorks Data Warehouse data source, and click OK.

3. When the Microsoft Query program is launched, you are presented with the Add Tables dialog box. Close this dialog box and click the SQL button.

4. Paste or type the following query into the SQL dialog box and click OK:

```
SELECT catg.EnglishProductCategoryName      AS [ProductCategory],
       (CAST(catg.ProductCategoryKey
          AS CHAR(1))
       + ' - '
       + catg.EnglishProductCategoryName) AS [ProductCategoryDesc],
       rsel.BusinessType                    AS [ResellerType],
       trty.SalesTerritoryGroup             AS [SalesGroup],
       trty.SalesTerritoryCountry           AS [SalesCountry],
       trty.SalesTerritoryRegion            AS [SalesRegion],
       fact.UnitPrice                       AS [UnitPrice],
       fact.OrderQuantity                   AS [Quantity]
FROM FactResellerSales fact
INNER JOIN DimProduct prod
  ON prod.ProductKey = fact.ProductKey
INNER JOIN DimProductSubcategory subc
  ON subc.ProductSubcategoryKey = prod.ProductSubcategoryKey
INNER JOIN DimProductCategory catg
  ON subc.ProductCategoryKey = catg.ProductCategoryKey
INNER JOIN DimReseller rsel
  ON rsel.ResellerKey = fact.ResellerKey
INNER JOIN DimSalesTerritory trty
  ON trty.SalesTerritoryKey = fact.SalesTerritoryKey
```

ON THE WEB You can download the ch11_example.sql query to your computer from the companion web site at www.wiley.com/go/ excelreporting/2007. **Look for this document in either the Chap11.zip file or Chap11 directory, depending on which .zip file you download.**

5. Click OK to acknowledge that the query cannot be displayed graphically.

6. Click the Return Data to Microsoft Excel button to return the data to Excel and continue.

7. When the Import Data Dialog box appears (see Figure 11-1) choose PivotTable Report, and then click OK to create the PivotTable and the PivotChart.

8. Drag ProductCategoryDesc to the Report Filter area.

9. Drag SalesGroup, SalesCountry, and SalesRegion to the Row Labels area, organizing these three fields in the hierarchy SalesGroup → SalesCountry → SalesRegion.

10. Drag Quantity and then Unit Price under Quantity in the Values area.

11. Verify that your PivotTable report looks like Figure 11-2.

Figure 11-1: Select the PivotTable Report option to create a PivotTable.

	A	B	C
1	ProductCategoryDesc	(All)	
2			
3		**Values**	
4	**Row Labels**	**Sum of Quantity**	**Sum of UnitPrice**
5	⊟ **Europe**	34921	3375865.458
6	⊟ **France**	14348	1315908.847
7	France	14348	1315908.847
8	⊟ **Germany**	7380	682744.6497
9	Germany	7380	682744.6497
10	⊟ **United Kingdom**	13193	1377211.962
11	United Kingdom	13193	1377211.962
12	⊟ **North America**	174509	22902260.65
13	⊟ **Canada**	41761	4869006.061
14	Canada	41761	4869006.061

Sheet1 / Sheet2 / Sheet3

Figure 11-2: Format your PivotTable report to look like this in order to follow along with the examples in this chapter.

ON THE WEB If you prefer to start this chapter with the PivotTable report, in lieu of creating the report from scratch, you can download the ch11_example.xls report shown in Figure 11-2 to your computer from the companion web site at www.wiley.com/go/excelreporting/2007. **Look for this document in either the Chap11.zip file or Chap11 directory, depending on which .zip file you download.**

PivotTable Styling

Instead of customizing each PivotTable report with specific font styles, borders, and background cell colors, you can instantly apply a saved style template to your Pivot-Table. This new PivotTable styles feature in Excel 2007 enables you to create and save custom formats for numerous elements of a PivotTable report. This is an especially helpful feature for report developers who customize their PivotTable reports with particular fonts, font colors, font styles, borders, and background fill colors.

Creating a New Style

You can create a new PivotTable style by choosing Home → Format As Table → New PivotTable Style or by choosing Design → PivotTable Styles → New PivotTable Style. Selecting either one of these methods brings up the New PivotTable Quick Style dialog box shown in Figure 11-3.

Figure 11-3: Use this dialog box to define a new PivotTable style with custom font styles, font colors, cell borders, and fill effects for each element of your PivotTable.

The name of the PivotTable style should be entered into the Name field of the New PivotTable Quick Style dialog box. This name is important for associating the style with a meaningful description, especially when there are multiple styles defined. For example, an accounting report might be formatted differently than a marketing report.

Customizing Table Elements

There are 25 elements that can be customized for a PivotTable report style. These elements are available in the Table Element pane of the New PivotTable Quick Style dialog box (see Figure 11-3). You do not have to define all the elements for a PivotTable style, because some elements cannot be used concurrently, and some element settings override other element settings. For example, setting the Whole Table element formats all the cells in the PivotTable report, but any other element setting overrides the Whole Table setting. So, for example, if the Whole Table element is defined to use a Regular font style and the Grand Total Row element is set to use a Bold font style, the cells in the Grand Total Row would be set to a bolded font, because the Grand Total Row setting overrides the Whole Table setting.

When you apply formatting options to an element by highlighting the element and clicking Format, the element becomes bolded in the Table Element pane. This feature is designed to help you readily identify which elements have formatting options applied to them. You can clear the format by highlighting an element in the Table Element pane and clicking the Clear button.

The Preview icon to the right of the Table Element pane (see Figure 11-4) provides a graphical depiction of how the PivotTable report will look once the style is applied. To use the new table style as the default table style for new PivotTable reports in the current workbook, check the Set as Default PivotTable Quick Style for This Document option.

NOTE Styles are saved to a specific workbook and not globally to the general Excel application. If you want to make them global, you'll need to create a workbook template or modify the default Excel template.

I provide a brief description for each of the 25 elements listed in the Table Element pane of the New PivotTable Quick Style dialog box (see Figure 11-4) in Table 11-1.

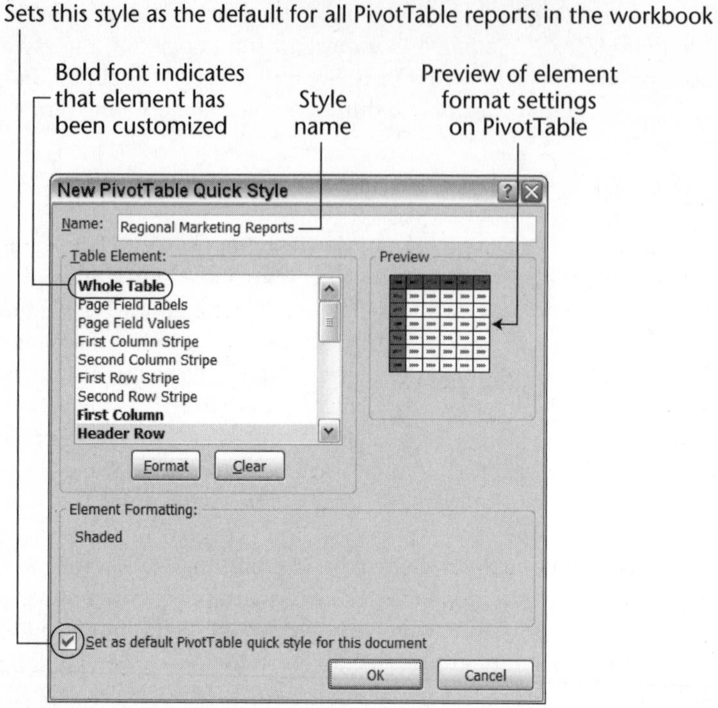

Sets this style as the default for all PivotTable reports in the workbook

Bold font indicates that element has been customized

Style name

Preview of element format settings on PivotTable

Figure 11-4: The New PivotTable Quick Style dialog box provides helpful information about what elements have been customized and how they affect the PivotTable report.

Table 11-1: PivotTable Style Element Descriptions

ELEMENT	DESCRIPTION
Whole Table	Sets a default format for all the elements in a selected PivotTable report. Note that other option settings, if defined, override the options set up for this element.
Page Field Labels	Formats fields in the Report Filter area.
Page Field Values	Formats items in the Report Filter area fields.
First Column Stripe	Formats the first column stripe of a PivotTable (note that the Banded Columns option must be enabled under the Design tab).
Second Column Stripe	Formats the second column stripe of a PivotTable (note that the Banded Columns option must be enabled under the Design tab).
First Row Stripe	Formats the first row stripe of a PivotTable (note that the Banded Rows option must be enabled from the Design tab).

Table 11-1 *(continued)*

ELEMENT	DESCRIPTION
Second Row Stripe	Formats the second row stripe of a PivotTable (note that the Banded Rows option must be enabled under the Design tab).
First Column	Formats the items in the Row Labels area.
Header Row	Formats the items in the Column Labels area.
First Header Cell	Formats the cell where the Row Labels and Column Labels headers intersect.
Subtotal Column 1	Formats the subtotals for the outermost items in the Column Labels area.
Subtotal Column 2	Formats the subtotals for the second outermost items in the Column Labels area.
Subtotal Column 3	Formats the subtotals for the third outermost items in the Column Labels area.
Subtotal Row 1	Formats the subtotals for the outermost items in the Row Labels area.
Subtotal Row 2	Formats the subtotals for the second outermost items in the Row Labels area.
Subtotal Row 3	Formats the subtotals for the third outermost items in the Row Labels area.
Blank Row	Formats the blank row (if added from the Layout & Print tab of the Field Settings dialog box).
Column Subheading 1	Formats the column subheadings for the outermost items in the Column Labels area.
Column Subheading 2	Formats the column subheadings for the outermost outer items in the Column Labels area.
Column Subheading 3	Formats the column subheadings for the outermost outer items in the Column Labels area.
Row Subheading 1	Formats the row subheadings for the outermost items in the Row Labels area.
Row Subheading 2	Formats the row subheadings for the outermost outer items in the Row Labels area.
Row Subheading 3	Formats the row subheadings for the outermost outer items in the Row Labels area.
Grand Total Column	Formats the grand total column.
Grand Total Row	Formats the grand total row.

Applying and Clearing Styles

You can apply a specific style to your PivotTable report by clicking the PivotTable report to select it and choosing a style from the PivotTable Styles group in the Design tab. You can also choose from a list of styles by clicking the Format As Table button in the Styles group, located under the Home tab.

You can clear the style from a PivotTable report by clicking it and choosing Design → PivotTable Styles → Clear. This function removes all the PivotTable report formatting.

There are two ways to apply a style. The first method is to Apply and Clear Formatting. The second method is to Apply and Maintain Formatting. If you choose to Apply and Clear Formatting, the formats are cleared prior to the new format being applied. In contrast, if you choose Apply and Maintain Formatting, the existing formats are maintained and only formats defined in the new style are applied to the report.

Managing Styles

Numerous styles are provided with Excel. These styles are grouped into Light, Medium, and Dark. You can also create and save new styles that can be accessed under a Custom tab that appears at the top of this drop-down box. As you peruse the template styles, you may find some of them to be helpful for your PivotTable report formatting.

Once a style is added to the PivotTable Styles box, you can duplicate, remove, modify, and set the style as a default. The next few sections demonstrate how this is done.

Duplicating Styles

Duplicating styles is useful when you want to keep most of the existing formats from a selected style and customize just a few of the elements. You can duplicate a style by right-clicking a style under the Format As Table button (located in the Styles group under the Home tab) and choosing Duplicate from the pop-up menu. Duplicating a style results in all the settings from the selected style being copied over to the new style. The style name also has a "2" added to the end of the name to distinguish it from the original style.

Once the style is duplicated, you can customize the name and make any adjustments to the table elements settings that are necessary. Note that the new style appears under the Custom group.

Removing Styles

You can remove a style by right-clicking it under the Format As Table button (located in the Styles group under the Home tab) and choosing Remove from the pop-up menu. Note that default styles in the Light, Medium, and Dark groups cannot be deleted. Only the styles under Custom can be deleted.

TIP If you accidentally remove a custom style, you can use the Undo button (available from the Quick Access toolbar ribbon) to add it back to the Styles group.

Modifying Styles

You can modify a style by right-clicking it and choosing Modify from the pop-up menu. Note that default styles in the Light, Medium, and Dark groups cannot be modified, although you can always create a custom version of an existing style by first duplicating it and then making the necessary changes in the New PivotTable Quick Style dialog box.

Setting the Style as a Default

New styles added to the PivotTable Styles drop-down box are placed under the Custom group, located at the top of the box. Right-clicking a Style and choosing Set as Default PivotTable Quick Style for This Document sets the style as the default style for all new PivotTable reports in the workbook. Note that the style is saved to the workbook or the template file that you created. It is not saved globally to Excel.

Choosing a Report Layout

Excel 2007 provides you three different types of PivotTable report layouts. These layouts each provide unique combinations for displaying the field labels, column headings, subtotals, expand/collapse buttons, and inner fields. You can choose from the following three layout options:

- **Compact:** This default report layout shows field labels instead of field headings, subtotals at the top of each group (no subtotal line), and merges all the fields in the Row Labels area into one column in the PivotTable report.

- **Outline:** This report layout shows field headings instead of field labels, subtotals at the top of each group (no subtotal line), and each field in the Row Labels area in its own column.

- **Tabular:** This report layout most closely mirrors the Classic PivotTable layout where field headings are shown in place of field labels, subtotals are displayed at the bottom of each group with a subtotal line, and each field in the Row Labels area in its own column. Additionally, a grid is displayed in the report background for all the cells in the PivotTable.

These report layouts are accessible from the Report Layout button, located in the Layout group in the Design tab (keep in mind that the PivotTable report must be selected for the Design tab to appear).

Using the Compact Report Layout Format

The Compact format (see Figure 11-5) is the default layout for a PivotTable report. When this format is selected:

- Field labels are used instead of column headings.
- Subtotals are displayed at the top of each group, next to the outer field item.
- Multiple fields in the Row Labels area are grouped into a single Row Label column.

To set the Compact report layout, click the PivotTable report to select it and then choose Design → Report Layout → Show in Compact Form. Because this is the default format, you do not have to select this layout unless you previously changed the report layout to Tabular or to Outline.

> **TIP** You can control the number of positions that inner items are indented from the Layout & Format tab of the PivotTable Options dialog box. Read the "Indenting Row Label Fields" section later in this chapter for more information about indenting fields in the Compact format.

Field labels in lieu of field headings

Multiple Row Label fields grouped into one column

Subtotals at top of group with no subtotal name

	A	B	C
1	ProductCategoryDesc (All)		
2			
3		Values	
4	Row Labels	Sum of Quantity	Sum of UnitPrice
12	North America	174509	22902260.65
13	Canada	41761	4869006.061
14	Canada	41761	4869006.061
15	United States	132748	18033254.59
16	Central	19473	2679790.109
17	Northeast	19816	2475750.305
18	Northwest	27783	3929388.861
19	Southeast	18836	2893853.571
20	Southwest	46840	6054471.746
21	Pacific	4948	767729.6402
22	Australia	4948	767729.6402
23	Australia	4948	767729.6402
24	Grand Total	214378	27045855.75

Sheet1 / Sheet2 / Sheet3

Figure 11-5: The Compact report layout form shows field labels, indents inner items, and displays subtotals at the top of each group.

Using the Outline Report Layout Format

The Outline format (see Figure 11-6) displays data in an outline form. When this format is selected:

- Column headings are used instead of field labels.
- Subtotals are displayed at the top of each group, next to the outer field item.
- Each field in the Row Labels area is displayed in its own column.

To set the Outline report layout shown in Figure 11-6, click the PivotTable report to select it and then choose Design → Report Layout → Show in Outline Form.

Using the Tabular Report Layout Format

The Tabular format (see Figure 11-7) displays data in a table layout. When this format is selected:

- Column headings are used instead of field labels.
- Subtotals are named and displayed at the bottom of each group.
- A grid is displayed in the PivotTable background.
- Each field in the Row Labels area is displayed in its own column.

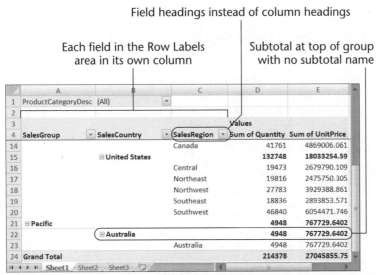

Figure 11-6: The Outline report layout form shows field labels, indents inner items, and displays subtotals at the top of each group.

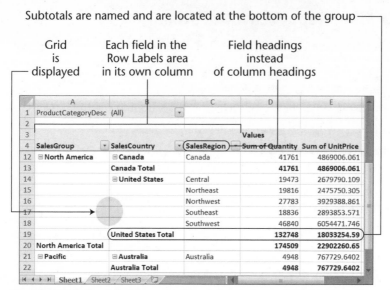

Figure 11-7: The Tabular report layout form shows field labels, indents inner items, and displays subtotals at the top of each group.

To set the Tabular report layout shown in Figure 11-7, click the PivotTable report to select it and then choose Design → Report Layout → Show in Tabular Form.

Formatting the PivotTable Report

Microsoft Excel offers several tools and functions that help you present your report in the best possible light. In this section, I cover numerous formatting options and tools that you can use to present your report onscreen. In this section, I cover the following topics:

- Formatting PivotTable reports fields
- Setting PivotTable format options
- Customizing layout and format options
- Setting totals and filters options
- Configuring display options

In the "Formatting PivotTable Report Fields" section, I review how fields in the Values area and the Report Filter area can be designed and formatted in the report. Next, I cover the numerous options that are available for managing report fields, layout settings, and formatting features in the "Customizing Layout and Format Options" section. The "Setting Totals and Filter Options" section includes information about grand total displays, filter settings, and custom sort lists. In the "Configuring Display Options" section, I cover the numerous types of display settings that can be customized for the PivotTable report.

Formatting PivotTable Report Fields

I provided some basic information about where to drop fields in a PivotTable report in Chapter 2 of this book. The general rule for the Row Labels and Column Labels areas is to drop fields into the Row Labels area where there are numerous items and the item descriptions are long. This is mainly because it's generally easier to view numerous items and items with long descriptions in rows than in columns. For fields in the Values area and the Report Filter area, I provide some additional information here that I thought you might find helpful.

Formatting Values Area Fields

Fields in the Values area of the PivotTable report should be formatted from the Pivot-Table Field dialog box. This is because formats applied from the worksheet columns or rows can be lost when the shape of the PivotTable is changed (by modifying a filter, dragging in a new field, or refreshing the report).

To set the format for a field in the Values area:

1. Left-click the field from the Areas section of the PivotTable Field List dialog box and choose Value Field Settings from the pop-up menu to bring up the Value Field Settings dialog box.

2. Click Number Format toward the bottom left of the Value Field Settings dialog box to bring up the Format Cells dialog box.

3. Choose the desired number format from the Category pane, customize the selected format if necessary, and click OK to close the Format Cells dialog box.

4. Click OK to close the Value Field Settings dialog box and apply the format changes to the Values area field.

After you have applied a format to a field in the Values area, it is maintained for all the items, regardless of what shape the PivotTable takes. You can remove the format by dragging it off and then back on to the PivotTable report, or by changing the field format using the steps that I just outlined in this section.

TIP Conditional formatting can be applied to fields in the Values area to selectively apply number formats, font colors, font styles, and background colors. Read the "Conditional Formatting" section of this chapter to learn more.

Designing Report Filter Area Fields

Report Filter area fields act much differently than fields in the Column Labels and Row Labels area of a PivotTable report. Selecting an item in the Report Filter area filters what is displayed in the main body of the report (defined as all the fields in the Column Labels, Row Labels, and Values areas of the PivotTable). Because these fields are so unique, I generally try to identify what fields are going to be in the Report Filter area when initially developing an SQL query so that I can customize how the values are displayed in the drop-down list.

In the SQL query used in the "Before You Begin" section of this chapter, the Report Filter area field, ProductCategoryDesc, was created by concatenating the field code with a dash and the product category name. In order for this to work properly, I changed the data type from Identity to Character for the ProductCategoryKey field. This was necessary, because fields with different data types cannot always be concatenated. Here's the SQL code that I used to make this new field:

```
(CAST(catg.ProductCategoryKey
    AS CHAR(1))
  + ' - '
  + catg.EnglishProductCategoryName) AS [ProductCategoryDesc],
```

Although the ProductCategoryKey for AdventureWorks might be more oriented to a database, this is not always the case for many organizations that use codes to track important business data. Common codes include promotion codes, sales analysis codes, and customer contact codes. Several pieces of logic might also be embedded into a particular code, such as date information, market segment, market channel, and product information. Although this kind of complexity is not built into the AdventureWorks database, I include this reference because it can be useful for your PivotTable report development. Basically, you can break apart the different positions of a single field code and display each component as if it were a real field. In my experience, I've found that this method of separating the various positions of a field code into multiple fields is often seen as innovative and valuable to key decision-makers in an organization.

Following the simpler example used in the SQL query, product category keys are assigned to each product category in the database. For example, the category Bikes has a category key of 1, Components a category key of 2, Clothing a category key of 3, and so on. I concatenated the category key with its descriptions in the SQL query, so report users could see both the code and its description as a single field in the report. Figure 11-8 shows the drop-down list for the ProductCategoryDesc field.

Figure 11-8: Concatenating codes with a dash and its description provides an innovative method for Report Filter area fields.

Customizing Layout and Format Options

Numerous options are available for customizing the layout and format settings of the PivotTable report. These options are accessed from the Layout & Format tab of the PivotTable Options dialog box (see Figure 11-9). You can bring up this dialog box by right-clicking the PivotTable report and choosing PivotTable Options from the pop-up menu.

Note that the Layout & Format tab in Figure 11-9 is organized into two sections: Layout and Format. In the Layout section, there are options for controlling label display and fields in the Report Filter area. In the Format section, there are options for handling error values, empty cells, and report formatting options that are associated with report refreshes.

Setting Layout Options

There are four options in the Layout section of the Layout & Format tab of the PivotTable Options dialog box. The first option, Merge and Center Cells with Labels, toggles whether the Row Labels and Column Labels headings are centered. The items in the both the Row Labels and Column Labels areas also merge and center the outer items over inner items, as shown in Figure 11-10.

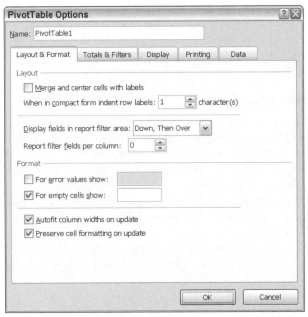

Figure 11-9: The layout and formatting options for a PivotTable report are controlled from this tab of the PivotTable Options dialog box.

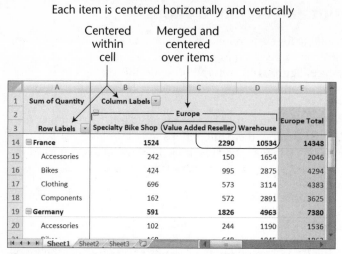

Figure 11-10: Checking the Merge and Center with Labels option centers items in the Column Labels area both vertically and horizontally.

Indenting Row Label Fields

The When in Compact Form Indent Row Labels *n* Character(s) option (where *n* is a number between 0 and 127) indents inner row label items when the PivotTable report is displayed in Compact form (recall that the PivotTable display can be in a Tabular, Compact, or Outline form, as described earlier in the "Choosing a Report Layout" section of this chapter).

Positioning Report Filter Area Fields

The Display Fields in Report Filter Area and Report Filter Fields per Column options control how Report Filter area fields are displayed. You can choose to first display them horizontally across the report and then vertically down, or vertically down and then horizontally across. Setting the Display Fields in Report Filter Area to *Down, Then Over* adds new fields in the Report Filter area down one column first and then across into a new row. If you prefer to add new fields to first move across the same row, before starting a new column, set this option to *Over, Then Down*. If you change this option, notice that the option Report Filter Fields per Column (located directly below the Display Fields in Report Filter Area option in Figure 11-9) is changed to Report Filters per Row. Looking at Figure 11-11, you can see how setting these two options varies the display of Report Filter fields.

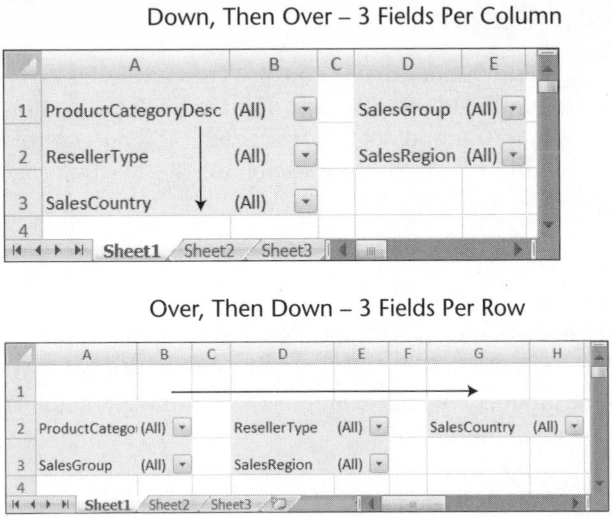

Down, Then Over – 3 Fields Per Column

Over, Then Down – 3 Fields Per Row

Figure 11-11: Fields in the Report Filter area can be moved *down, then over* (top) or *over, then down* (bottom).

TIP Set Report Filter areas to move *over, then across* when there are numerous columns in the PivotTable report, because this generally results in much better display optimization than numerous fields stacked in a single column.

Looking at Format Options

There are four options in the Format section of the Layout & Format tab of the Pivot-Table Options dialog box. The For Error Values Show option can be used to replace errors in the Values area of the PivotTable with a string that is up to 255 characters in length. Formula errors, such as Division by Zero, can ruin the presentation effect of your report. Setting this option to zero or to blank can remedy the problem of numerous errors appearing the Values area of the report.

When there are no values in the Values area of the PivotTable report, an empty cell is displayed. If you prefer seeing an asterisk, a zero (0), or some other string (up to 255 characters) instead of an empty cell, check the For Empty Cells Show box, and then type in the string that you prefer to see displayed for blank cells in the report.

Checking the Autofit Column Widths on Update option automatically sets the column width to the widest text or numeric value whenever the PivotTable report is updated. If you are relying on a specific column size for report printing, you might want to uncheck this option, because the column width is automatically resized each time the report is updated.

The Preserve Cell Formatting on Update option toggles whether the format and layout settings are maintained (checked) or cleared (unchecked) whenever the report is updated.

Setting Totals and Filter Options

The Totals & Filters tab of the PivotTable Options dialog box (see Figure 11-12) is organized into three sections: Grand Totals, Filters, and Sorting. The Grand Totals section toggles the display of column and row grand totals. The Filters section controls whether filters are additive or non-additive. The Sorting section toggles whether custom lists are used when sorting data.

Grand Totals

The Show Grand Totals for Rows and Show Grand Totals for Columns options toggle whether grand totals for the rows and columns of the PivotTable report are displayed. Note that the row grand totals are grouped into one column, and column grand totals are grouped into one row, as shown in Figure 11-13.

> **TIP** You can also use the Grand Totals button in the Layout group, located under the Design tab, to toggle the display of grand totals. If you're readily turning the grand totals on and off, the Grand Totals button is typically much quicker than accessing the Totals & Filters tab of the PivotTable Options dialog box.

Figure 11-12: The Totals & Filters tab of the PivotTable Options dialog box controls grand total, filter, and sorting options.

Grand Totals
for Columns

Grand Totals
for Rows

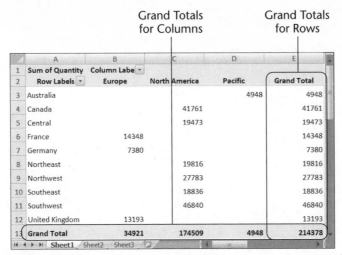

	A	B	C	D	E
1	Sum of Quantity	Column Labe ▾			
2	Row Labels ▾	Europe	North America	Pacific	Grand Total
3	Australia			4948	4948
4	Canada		41761		41761
5	Central		19473		19473
6	France	14348			14348
7	Germany	7380			7380
8	Northeast		19816		19816
9	Northwest		27783		27783
10	Southeast		18836		18836
11	Southwest		46840		46840
12	United Kingdom	13193			13193
13	Grand Total	34921	174509	4948	214378

Sheet1 / Sheet2 / Sheet3

Figure 11-13: Grand totals for PivotTable report columns and rows can be individually toggled on or off.

Filters Section

The Allow Multiple Filters per Field Option toggles whether PivotTable filters are additive or non-additive. An additive filter enables additional filters to continue working on the prior filter, and non-additive filters first remove the previous filter before applying the new filter.

CROSS-REFERENCE Read Chapter 10 for more information about additive and non-additive filters.

Sorting Section

The Use Custom Lists When Sorting option toggles whether custom lists (covered in Chapter 10) are used for sorting data. When this option is checked, the custom lists are used. Note that performance is not as quick when custom lists are being utilized, so consider unchecking this option if your workbook uses custom lists, but they are not required for sorting data in the selected PivotTable report.

Configuring Display Options

The Display tab of the PivotTable Options dialog box (see Figure 11-14) is organized into two sections: Display and Field List. The Display section controls many of the new PivotTable features in Excel 2007, such as the expand/collapse buttons, field captions, filter drop-downs, and contextual tooltips. Additionally, the PivotTable Classic setting is controlled from this section of the dialog box. The Field List section is used to toggle whether items in each field are sorted alphanumerically or in the data source order.

Figure 11-14: The Display tab of the PivotTable Options dialog box can be used to customize many of the new PivotTable display options.

Display Settings

The Show Expand/Collapse Buttons option toggles whether the +/− buttons are shown in the PivotTable report when there is more than one field in either the Row Labels or the Column Labels area. Clicking this button in the PivotTable report expands (+) or collapses (−) the items for the selected outer item, as shown in Figure 11-15.

Expand/collapse button

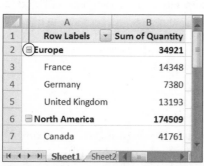

Figure 11-15: Click the "+" button to expand detail or the "−"button to hide detail.

Contextual Tooltips

Contextual tooltips are enabled by default for PivotTable reports. These tooltips show the items being selected for fields in the Row Labels, Column Labels, and Values area of the PivotTable. The value for this intersection is also displayed in this cell. This tooltip automatically appears as you hover your mouse pointer over a particular intersection and keep it there for a moment, as shown in Figure 11-16. If you prefer to turn this feature off, simply uncheck the Show Contextual Tooltips option.

Field Captions and Filter Drop Downs

The Display Field Captions and Filter Drop Downs option controls whether the labels and drop-down arrows for the Row Labels and the Column Labels areas are displayed (see Figure 11-17). The default setting is to display these labels and drop-down arrows, although you can turn this feature off by unchecking this option. Recall from Chapter 2 that the drop-down arrows provide a means of accessing the filter and sorting drop-down box. You can also customize these field labels, which can be especially helpful if you have multiple fields dropped into the Row Labels or Column Labels areas of the PivotTable. For example, if Country, State, and City were all dropped in the Row Labels area, you might change the Row Labels heading to Region.

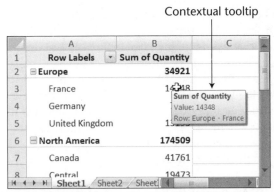

Figure 11-16: Contextual tooltips show the value and the item details for an intersection of field items in Row Labels, Column Labels, and Values areas of a PivotTable report.

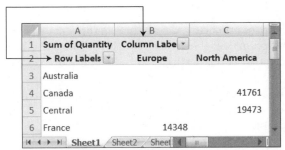

Figure 11-17: Column labels can be renamed and used to access filter and sort functions.

Classic PivotTable Setting

Excel 2007 does not allow fields to be dragged on or off the PivotTable from the Report Layout area. This change is mainly due to the new PivotTable design with row and column labels, instead of field headings (recall that numerous fields are grouped into a single column in the Row Labels area). If you prefer using the earlier method of dragging fields on and off the Report Layout area, you can check the Classic PivotTable Layout option. This option setting removes the labels from the Row Labels and Column Labels areas of the PivotTable report, replacing them instead with field headings.

> **TIP** If you're accustomed to the earlier method of dragging fields on and off the report, it may take some time for you to get used to the new method of using the PivotTable Field List dialog box to shape the PivotTable report. I suggest that you give it a try for a few weeks, because the updated method in Excel 2007 provides much better optimization than previous versions of Excel for displaying multiple fields in a single area of the PivotTable report.

Field List Settings

There are two options under the Field List section of the PivotTable Options dialog box: Sort A → Z and Sort in Data Source Order. The first option, Sort A → Z, sorts the fields returned from the SQL query in alphanumeric order in the PivotTable Field List dialog box. This is the default setting and may be problematic if the fields in the SQL query are arranged in some logical order. For example, the SQL query in the "Before You Begin" section of this chapter arranged the Value area fields (Unit Price and Quantity Sold) at the end of the query and the Sales Group, Country, and Region fields next to one another and in their natural hierarchy. In my experience, I've found that this arrangement makes it easier for the report user to locate numeric fields, understand hierarchies, and work more efficiently in the PivotTable report.

> **CROSS-REFERENCE** Read the OLAP chapter (online) for more information about the powerful OLAP tools in Excel 2007 that enable hierarchies to be viewed and managed in both the PivotTable report and the PivotTable Field List dialog box.

If you have arranged your fields in a particular order in the external data source, check the Sort in Data Source Order option to enable fields in the PivotTable Field List dialog box to be retuned in the order that they are specified in the query or external data source.

Figure 11-18 shows how the fields in the PivotTable Field List dialog box are arranged for each option setting. Compare this figure to the SQL query outlined in the "Before You Begin" section of this chapter.

Alphanumeric Order   Data Source Order

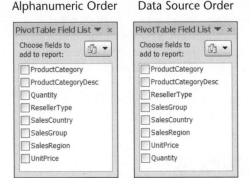

Figure 11-18: Fields in the PivotTable Field List dialog box are sorted in alphanumeric order (default) or in the external data source order.

Conditional Formatting

You can use the conditional formatting tools in Excel 2007 to highlight important business data with text formatting, cell designs, data bars, color scales, and icons. Some of these formatting options can either complement the numeric data in the Value area or replace it altogether. You can even configure the conditional formatting to run multiple times over the data, such that an icon, a data bar, and a color scale are all potentially applied to the data.

Conditional formatting is designed to be used on data in the Values area of the Pivot-Table report. This is because the Values area is the only area of the PivotTable that is programmed to account for changes in shape. Although it could be used on other areas of the PivotTable report, the formatting does not stay with the areas changing shape as fields are moved on or off the report, filter settings are changed, and so forth.

> **NOTE** I only cover conditional formatting as it applies to Values area fields, because this is the only area of the PivotTable report that maintains its conditional format logic as the PivotTable shape changes.

There are a few important items to keep in mind with conditional formatting for PivotTable reports. First, conditional formatting can be additive or non-additive. This is the same kind of principle that I covered in Chapter 10 with report filters. Basically, you can apply multiple formats to report cells, but only one unique type of formatting per cell. So, for example, you could combine icons with data bars, but you couldn't use two data bars or two icons in the same PivotTable cell.

> **NOTE** Excel 2003 limited conditional formatting to only three rules. Excel 2007 has no such restriction; you're limited only by your computer's available memory.

Second, because you can set up multiple conditional formatting rules for a selected field in the Values area of the PivotTable, rules can conflict with one another. For example, one rule might format cells that are greater than the average value, and another rule formats cells that are in the top 10 percent of values in the report. These rules can also be mutually exclusive or they can overlap. When they overlap and utilize the same format, conflicts can arise. In the next few sections, I review the various types of conditional formatting tools and discuss how you can build conditional rules, set up additive rules, and handle conditional formatting conflicts.

Adding Conditional Formatting Rules

Conditional formatting rules are added from the Conditional Formatting button, located in the Styles group under the Home tab. There are three ways to add a new conditional formatting rule for a PivotTable report:

- Choose New Rule from the Conditional Formatting button.
- Choose the Manage Rules item under a particular format option.
- Click New Rule from the Conditional Formatting Rules Manager dialog box.

The first method is to just choose Home → Conditional Formatting → New Rule to bring up the New Formatting Rule dialog box (see Figure 11-19). The second method involves first choosing the type of conditional format to be used, such that the New Formatting Rule dialog box appears with the chosen format already selected. The third method is to add the rules from the Conditional Formatting Rules Manager dialog box. This last method is best used when there are multiple rules in force, because it allows you to easily view the other rules and define their precedence.

The New Formatting Rule dialog box is where new rules are created. The same view of this dialog box appears if you add a rule and later modify it; the only difference is that the title is changed from New Formatting Rule to Edit Formatting Rule. As you can see from Figure 11-19, this dialog box is organized into three sections. In the first section, Rule Domain, you define the area where the rule is being applied. This could be a selected cell range in the worksheet or some component of a selected Values area field in the PivotTable report. The second section, Select a Rule Type, is where you select the type of rule being used. Here, you can choose from five different types of general rules for formatting the data. Once you choose a rule type, the Edit the Rule Description section (the bottom section of Figure 11-19) is customized to accept more specific details that are associated with the selected rule type. I provide more information about each section of the New Formatting Rule dialog box in the following sections.

Choose one of these options for a PivotTable   Select a formatting option

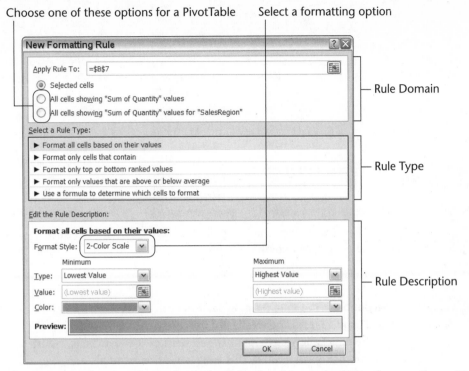

Figure 11-19: The New Formatting Rule dialog box is organized into three sections: (1) Rule Domain, (2) Rule Type, and (3) Rule Description.

Setting the Rule Domain

The first section of the New Formatting Rule dialog box is used to set the rule domain (the location where the conditional formatting rule is being applied). You can choose from three buttons in this dialog box (see Figure 11-19). The first button, Selected Cells, enables you to specify a specific range of cells for the rule. Because the PivotTable report is apt to change shape and size as fields are moved on and off the report, this is typically not a good option to choose. The second button, All Cells Showing "Sum of Quantity" Values, evaluates all the numeric data in the Values area field, including subtotals. The third option, All Cells Showing "Sum of Quantity" Values for "SalesRegion," evaluates the numeric data in the Values area field in the context of the subtotal(s) for the outermost Column Labels and Row Labels field item(s). In Figure 11-20, I identify the affected cells if the third button is selected. If the second button is selected, all the data in the Values area of the PivotTable is formatted.

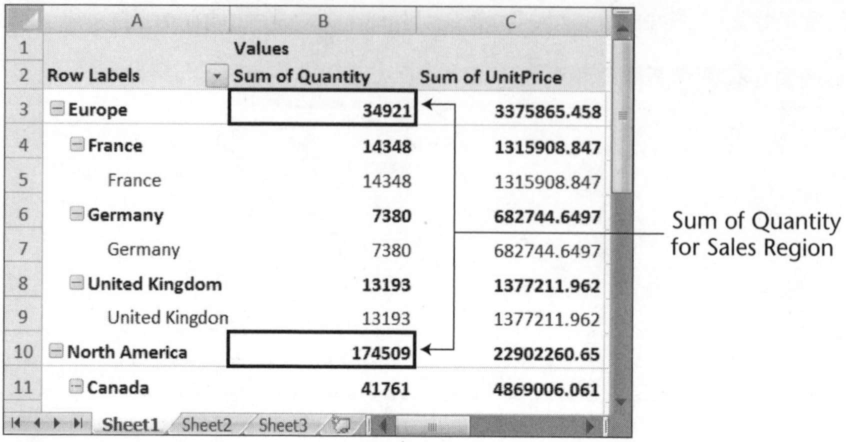

	A	B	C
1		Values	
2	Row Labels	Sum of Quantity	Sum of UnitPrice
3	⊟Europe	34921	3375865.458
4	⊟France	14348	1315908.847
5	France	14348	1315908.847
6	⊟Germany	7380	682744.6497
7	Germany	7380	682744.6497
8	⊟United Kingdom	13193	1377211.962
9	United Kingdon	13193	1377211.962
10	⊟North America	174509	22902260.65
11	⊟Canada	41761	4869006.061

Sum of Quantity
for Sales Region

Sheet1 Sheet2 Sheet3

Figure 11-20: Conditional formatting can be applied to all the cells in the Values area or only to the subtotaled cell for the outermost items.

TIP The third option in the Rule Domain section of the New Formatting Rule dialog box (see Figure 11-19) is generally not useful when there are multiple fields in either the Row Labels or Column Labels area of the PivotTable report and outer items are being subtotaled. This is because the subtotals are considered part of the dataset and are not handled differently than the non-subtotaled data.

Selecting a Rule Type

After setting the rule domain, the next step in adding a new rule is to select a type of rule from the Select a Rule Type section of the New Formatting Rule dialog box. The type of rule that you select determines the formatting options that can be used and how they are applied. Rule types enable you to format data based on:

- Only the cell value
- A specified value or range
- A top or bottom ranked value or percentile range
- Values above or below a specified average
- A custom formula that you can define

As you select different rule types, the rule description and formatting options in the New Formatting Rule dialog box change (bottom section of Figure 11-19). Each rule type provides different formatting options and criteria fields that can be used for specifying the details of the selected rule type.

Formatting Cells Based on Their Values with Graphical Items

The first rule type, Format All Cells Based on Their Values, is the only option that enables you to display data bars, color scales, and icon sets. And, because this option formats all the cells in the rule domain with this rule type, there are no fields needed for specifying more detailed criteria. If you choose this option, skip to the sections on data bars, color scales, and icon sets in the "Formatting the Data" section for more information about how these graphical features can be used in a PivotTable report.

Formatting Cells Based on a Value or Range

If you want to format cells based on a particular value or range of values, choose the Format Only Cells That Contain rule type from the Select a Rule Type section of the New Formatting Rule dialog box. This rule type enables you to format data that is:

- Between or Not Between a specified range.
- Equal To or Not Equal To a specified number or cell value.
- Greater Than or Less Than a specified number or cell value.
- Greater Than or Equal To or Less Than or Equal To a specified number or cell value.
- Is Blank or Not Blank.
- Has Errors or has No Errors.

When you select this rule type, the Edit the Rule Description section of the New Formatting Rule dialog box appears, as shown in Figure 11-21. If you want to format cells based on whether they have errors or blanks, click the Format Cell drop-down box and choose the desired option.

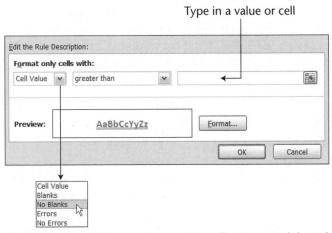

Figure 11-21: Cells can be conditionally formatted based on a particular value or characteristic (blank or error).

> **TIP** You can specify a cell reference instead of typing in a number into the Edit the Rule Description section. This feature might be helpful if the conditional value is dynamic and can be calculated in a spreadsheet cell.

Once the criteria for the rule description is set up, click the Format button to bring up the Format Cells dialog box, where you can customize the cell formatting (explained later in this chapter).

Formatting Top or Bottom Ranked Values

You can conditionally format cells that are in the top or the bottom n or n% (where n is a number between 0 and 100 that you specify) by choosing Format Only Top or Bottom Ranked Values from the Select a Rule Type section of the New Formatting Rule dialog box (refer back to Figure 11-19). If the rule domain is applied to an outer item subtotal, the conditional formatting can be applied to the inner items in the context of each outer item by choosing Each Row Group or Each Column Group for the % of the Selected Range For field.

> **TIP** Don't forget that the New Rule Formatting dialog box is organized into three sections: Rule Domain, Rule Type, and Rule Description. And, as you change from one Rule Type to another, the fields and options in the Rule Description are also changed.

Formatting Above or Below Average Values

You can conditionally format cells that are above or below the average value for the selected Values area field by choosing Format Only Values That Are Above or Below Average from the Select a Rule Type section of the New Formatting Rule dialog box. Note that if you click the third button in the Rule Domain section of the New Formatting Rule dialog box (refer back to Figure 11-19), the conditional formatting can be applied to the selected item's subtotals by choosing Each Row Group or Each Column Group for The Average for the Selected Range For field.

Formatting Data Using Custom Formulas

You can conditionally format cells that are true for a custom formula that you create by choosing Use a Formula to Determine Which Cells to Format from the Select a Rule Type section of the New Formatting Rule dialog box. When you select this option, keep in mind that the formula must begin with an equals sign ("=") and the formula must return a True or a False.

Highlighting Cells

The Highlight Cells conditional formatting option applies to all the rule types except Format All Cells Based on Their Values. This formatting feature uses some aspect of the data to determine which cells should be formatted. For example, you could use this rule type to format only the Values area cells that are greater than a number that you specify.

The formatting options that can be applied using this rule type include:

- Number formats
- Font styles, colors, and effects
- Border styles and colors
- Cell background colors, patterns, and fill effects

Once you have defined the rule domain, the rule type, and specified the rule criteria, just click the Format button in the New Formatting Rule dialog box to bring up the Format Cells dialog box. This enables you to specify the formatting options that you want to apply to the data for the selected Values area field.

Adding Data Bars

A data bar represents data using a bar that varies in length with the data value. You can either use data bars to replace the numeric text altogether or configure them to appear in the background, complementing the numeric data. By default, the lowest value appears as the shortest bar and the highest value appears as the longest bar. Of course, this display setting can easily be customized and even reversed.

You can bring up the Data Bar dialog box by clicking the PivotTable and choosing Conditional Formatting → Data Bars → More Rules. This brings up the New Formatting Rule dialog box with the Data Bar section displayed in the Edit the Rule Description section of the dialog box (see Figure 11-22).

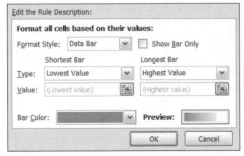

Figure 11-22: The New Formatting Rule dialog box is organized into three sections for setting the rule domain, choosing a rule type, and setting formatting options.

Check the Show Bar Only option to hide the numeric data and show just the data bar. The default setting for a data bar is to use Lowest Value for Shortest Bar and Highest Value for Longest Bar. However, you can change these settings by clicking the Type drop-down fields under Shortest Bar and Longest Bar. The other available types are:

- **Number:** Format the shortest or longest bar to be a specified number.
- **Percent:** Format the shortest or longest bar to be a specified percent.
- **Percentile:** Format the shortest or longest bar to be a specified percentile.
- **Formula:** Format the shortest or longest bar based on a formula.

These other options are useful when the smallest or highest value in the dataset should not represent the shortest or longest data bar, or when the data should not necessarily be represented in a completely discrete manner. For example, perhaps the longest data bar could represent salespersons that are in the top 90th percentile.

You can change the color of the data bar by clicking the Bar Color field. The Preview field, next to Bar Color, shows how the data bar will appear in the PivotTable report.

Applying Graded Color Scales

A graded color scale represents data using a color spectrum that changes in color with the value of the data. This is something like data bars, except that the cell color varies, instead of the length of the bar. Using this format option, you can choose from a two-color or three-color spectrum. If you choose to use two colors, then colors are specified for the minimum and for the maximum. If you choose three colors, then colors are specified for the minimum, the midpoint, and the maximum. You can also specify each one of these points to utilize a number, a percent, a percentile, or a formula.

NOTE Unlike data bars, color scales cannot be configured to replace the data; they simply highlight the data with a varying spectrum of color.

You can bring up the Color Scales dialog box by clicking the PivotTable and choosing Conditional Formatting → Color Scales → More Rules. This brings up the New Formatting Rule dialog box with the 2-Color Scale section displayed in the Edit the Rule Description section of the dialog box. You can change this to a three-color scale by clicking the Format Style field arrow and choosing 3-Color Scale from the drop-down list. Selecting this option displays Minimum, Midpoint, and Maximum fields in the Edit the Rule Description section of the dialog box, as shown in Figure 11-23.

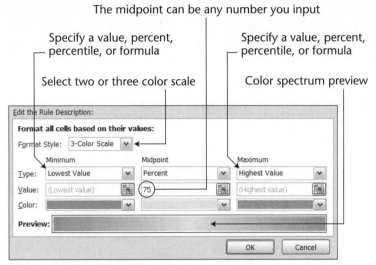

Figure 11-23: You can choose from a two- or three-color scale from the Color Scales view.

The Minimum, Midpoint, and Maximum fields are used to indicate what colors should be used to represent the data. The default setting for a three-color scale is to use a red accent for the Lowest Value under Minimum, a yellow accent for 50 percent under Midpoint, and a green accent for the Highest Value under Maximum. However, you can change these settings by clicking the Type drop-down fields under Minimum, Midpoint, and Maximum. The other available types are:

- **Number:** Format cell color based on a specified number.
- **Percent:** Format cell color based on a specified percent.
- **Percentile:** Format cell color based on a specified percentile.
- **Formula:** Format the shortest or longest bar based on a formula.

These other options are very useful when the lowest, middle, or highest values in the dataset are not represented evenly. For example, perhaps yellow should be represented as 75 percent, instead of 50 percent (see Figure 11-23).

You can change the color of the data bar by clicking the color fields under Minimum, Midpoint, and Maximum. The Preview field at the bottom shows how the color scale will appear in the PivotTable report.

Using Icon Sets

You can choose from a library of icon sets to represent your data. These icons can either replace the numeric text altogether, or appear to the right of the numeric data. The default icon set is three unrimmed traffic lights. However, you can choose from a list of several icon sets that range from three icons to five icons. The order of these icons can be configured to display in ascending or descending order.

You can bring up the Icon Set dialog box by clicking the PivotTable and choosing Conditional Formatting → Icon Sets → More Rules. This brings up the New Formatting Rule dialog box with the Icon Sets section displayed in the Edit the Rule Description section of the dialog box (see Figure 11-24).

For each icon in the selected icon set, you specify an operator, a value, and a type. You can choose from two operators: Greater Than (>) or Greater Than Or Equal To (>=). You can either input a value or a cell reference into the Value field. The available types include Number, Percent, Percentile, and Formula. Notice that the icon rules are displayed from highest to lowest. As you define each level in the icon hierarchy, the icon below it starts with either a Less Than (<) or a Less Than Or Equal To (<=) operator. As you experiment with the rules, you'll notice that changing an operator from Greater Than (>) to Greater Than Or Equal To (>=), or vice versa, changes the operator description directly below it. The same is also true for any number that you type into the Value column. These changes are made to ensure that the rules do not overlap and that all the possible values are evaluated by the rule. For example, in Figure 11-24, the green traffic light (the first light shown in grayscale under Icon) is >= 67 and the yellow traffic light description (the second light shown in grayscale under Icon) is <67. Changing the operator to > and the value to 50 for the green light (the first light), automatically changes the yellow light description from <67 to <=50. If this change hadn't been automatically applied, the rules could have overlapped. This feature eliminates most conflicts, although it's still possible to make a mistake. However, if any of the rules do overlap, you'll get a message box stating that one or more icon data ranges overlap, requiring the error to be fixed before the rule can be created.

Checking the Reverse Icon Order box reverses the order of the icons, although the values are still specified from highest to lowest. Checking the Show Icon Only option hides the numeric data and shows just the icon.

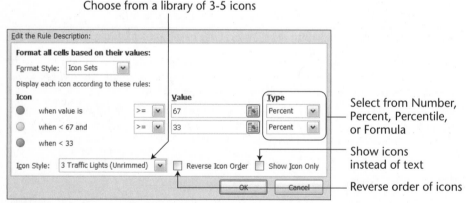

Figure 11-24: Choose from several types of icon sets to enhance or represent the display of numeric data.

Using the Conditional Formatting Rules Manager

The conditional formatting rules are managed from the Conditional Formatting Rules Manager dialog box (see Figure 11-25). Here, you can choose to apply a filter that shows only the rules for only a specified domain, such as a worksheet, a PivotTable report, a Spreadsheet report, or selected cells in the worksheet. From this dialog box, you can also:

▪ Add, delete, and edit conditional formatting rules

▪ Set rule precedence

▪ View rule formats for data bars, color scales, and icon sets

▪ View the area where a rule is applied

▪ Manage rule conflicts

All the rules in force for the workbook appear in the Conditional Formatting Rules Manager dialog box. You can use the Show Formatting Rules For drop-down field to filter the rules to a particular rule domain, such as the selected PivotTable.

The rules in force for the selected rule domain are shown in the Rule pane of the Conditional Formatting Rules Manager dialog box. The rules could be cell formats, data bars, graded color scales, or icon sets. The selected rule format also appears next to each rule in this dialog box. So, for example, if you choose to use a specific icon set or graded color scale, the selected configuration appears in this dialog box. The rule evaluation scope, that is, the area where the rule is being applied, appears next to the Format column.

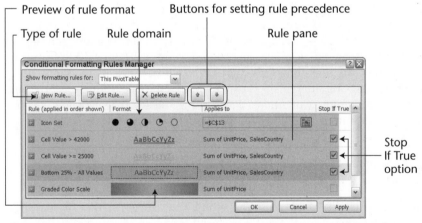

Figure 11-25: Conditional formatting rules are managed from this dialog box.

Setting Rule Precedence

The number of conditional formatting rules that can be added to your PivotTable report is limited only by your imagination and your computer's available memory. Keep in mind, however, that only one type of unique format rule can be applied. Additionally, the first rule that does the formatting is the rule that prevails when multiple rules are set up. For example, if Rule A formats cells with a green font for field values over 100 and Rule B formats cells with a yellow font for field values over 50, then a cell value of 175 would be formatted in a yellow font, if rule B was first applied. Thus, the ordering of the rules is very important whenever two types of formats are the same or overlapping.

You can set the rule precedence from the Conditional Formatting Rules Manager dialog box (see Figure 11-25). Choose Conditional Formatting → Manage Rules to bring up this dialog box. Once this dialog box is opened, highlight a rule and then click the up or down arrows to move the rule up or down in the rule hierarchy. Clicking the Stop If True box halts all formatting to the selected cell, should the cell meet the specified criteria defined for the rule.

NOTE The Stop If True option is not enabled when the rule type is set to Format All Cells Based on Their Values. This is because this rule type does not utilize any criteria to turn formatting on or off. It simply varies the formatting based on the cell value.

Changing and Deleting Rules

Rules can be added, changed, or deleted from the Conditional Formatting Rules Manager dialog box (refer back to Figure 11-25). You can bring up this dialog box by choosing Conditional Formatting → Manage Rules. To modify a rule, open the Conditional Formatting Rules Manager dialog box, select the rules, and click the Edit Rule button. This brings up the Edit Formatting Rule dialog box, which is exactly the same dialog box as the New Rule Formatting dialog box, except that the title is different. To delete a rule, select the rule in the Conditional Formatting Rules Manager dialog box and click the Delete Rule button.

Preparing the Report for Printing

If you plan to print the PivotTable report for offline analysis, you may want to configure the PivotTable format options and Excel's print options for the report to look best on paper. The items in your checklist should include the following:

- Printer orientation
- Field labels
- Headers and footers
- Layout options with Outer Row and Column fields

TIP If you have several worksheets that use the same PivotTable data, set all the print features in the first PivotTable worksheet before copying the worksheet. Thus, you may only have to make slight adjustments to the remaining worksheets instead of individually applying all the format settings to each worksheet.

Setting and Adjusting the Printer Orientation

The printer orientation can be set either to Portrait or Landscape from the Orientation button, located in the Page Setup group under the Layout tab. If the report is wider than it is long, set the orientation to Landscape by choosing Page Layout → Orientation → Landscape. If the report is longer than it is wide, set the orientation by choosing Page Layout → Orientation → Portrait.

The Page Break Preview feature is very useful for ensuring that your report is properly printed. You can switch to this view by choosing View → Page Break Preview. After you have finished adjusting the print layout options, choose View → Normal to return to the normal worksheet view.

WARNING Customizing the Page Break Preview automatically adjusts the scaling in the Page Setup dialog box. If you change the printer orientation of a report that already has customized Page Break settings, reset the scaling to 100 Percent of Normal Size from the Page Setup dialog box and reapply the Page Break Preview settings. If you don't follow this procedure, the report size may not be optimized in the new page orientation, making it smaller than it might otherwise appear.

Working with Field Labels

You can configure field labels to be repeated on each printed page either from the Sheet tab of the Page Setup dialog box or from the PivotTable Options dialog box. If you are using a report title and logo, you should use the Page Setup dialog box to repeat column headings because the Rows to Repeat at Top option allows you to also print the report title and related information on each page. If you aren't using a report title or logo, just check the Set Print Titles option under the Printing tab of the PivotTable Options dialog box.

If the report has Outer Row or Outer Column fields and does not fit on one page, check the Repeat Row Labels on Each Printed Page option to automatically print the field labels on the second page when it splits across a single page.

Using Headers and Footers

Many organizations already have guidelines in place for what information should be included in headers and footers. This might include some confidentiality warning, a corporate name or logo, or some particular font style. I generally try to include the following information in a report header or footer:

- ▪ **Report title:** The name of the report
- ▪ **Database area:** Production, Test, Staging, and so on
- ▪ **Print date:** The date that the report is printed
- ▪ **Report revision number:** Important in early parts of the development cycle
- ▪ **Page number:** Usually in the form of Page *n/n* (for example, Page 1/3)

I've found that questions or problems related to a report are often more easily diagnosed when you have a report title, print date, report revision number, and database area included with the report.

Setting General Print Options

The Printing tab of the PivotTable Options dialog box (see Figure 11-26) includes three options for configuring the report to be printed. The first option, Print Expand/Collapse Buttons When Displayed on PivotTable, toggles whether the +/− buttons (refer back to Figure 11-15) are printed when this display option is checked. The Repeat Row Labels on Each Printed Page option toggles whether the fields in the Row Labels area of the PivotTable report are automatically repeated when the printed report spans multiple pages in a horizontal direction. The Set Print Titles option toggles whether row and column field headings and labels are printed for each page of the PivotTable when the printed report spans multiple pages in a horizontal or vertical direction. This option is used in conjunction with the Rows to Repeat at Top and Columns to Repeat at Left under the Print Titles group.

TIP The Set Print Titles option can be very handy if report users are going to be printing the report, because this option automatically prints the column headings and labels on each page. Checking this option is usually more efficient than trying to set rows and columns to be repeated.

Setting Print Options for Outer Fields

If the PivotTable report has multiple Row Labels area fields or multiple Column Labels area fields, you can configure the report to automatically insert a blank line or a page break before each new outer Row Labels field or each new outer Column Labels field. You set this option from the Layout & Print tab (see Figure 11-27) of the Field Settings dialog box. You can access this dialog box by right-clicking an outer Row Labels or outer Column Labels item and choosing Field Settings from the pop-up menu.

Figure 11-26: Click the Printing tab of the PivotTable Options dialog box to access options for printing the PivotTable report to paper.

Figure 11-27: The Layout & Print tab of the Field Settings dialog box provides options for inserting blank lines or page breaks for each new outer item.

Check the Insert Blank Line After Each Item Label option to insert a blank line after each new outer item. Check the Insert Page Break After Each Item option to insert a page break after each new outer item.

Trying It Out in the Real World

Syed Abbas, the Pacific Sales Manager for AdventureWorks, was very pleased with your sales report that you created for him (in the previous chapter). Syed's presentation of the report to the executive team was so impressive (mainly due to the excellent reporting technology) that he received a big promotion, exclusive access to the company yacht, and an unlimited expense account. Syed feels indebted to you and has agreed to buy you lunch, while he discusses how his next sales report should look.

While at lunch, Mr. Abbas (he's asked you to not refer to him as Syed any longer now that's he on the executive team) requests that you brighten up this next sales report with some cool formatting technology. Specifically, Syed has asked that you create a report that shows the quantity of units sold by sales region within product category. Syed also wants to have the product category code and the product category description combined into one field in the Report Filter area, because some of the finance and marketing teams often refer to product category codes, instead of product category names. The reseller type should also appear in the report, although it does not have to be arranged in any particular order because Mr. Abbas no longer has to worry about internal politics given his new position in the company.

While eating your sandwich at lunch, Syed also asks that you provide the following types of formatting in the report:

- Format the PivotTable report in a compact, tabular format with a blank line and a page break for each new outer item

- Suppress subtotaling of Quantity by sales regions

- Sort the fields in the PivotTable Field List dialog box as specified in the SQL query outlined in the "Before You Begin" section of this chapter

- Format the Sum of Quantity field in accounting format with 0 decimal points

- Format the values for the top 3 sales regions for each product category group in a bolded, double-underline font in a green color

- Format the below average values for each product category group in a bolded, double-underline font in a red color

- Format the above average and below average values (except those in the top three sales regions) with a data bar that shows the smallest value with the shortest data bar and the highest value with the longest data bar. Configure the data bar to replace the numeric data.

As you hurriedly jot down all the information, Mr. Abbas unexpectedly excuses himself for an important teleconference that he must attend. He requests that you pick up the lunch tab and complete the report by the end of the day.

Getting Down to Business

Starting with the PivotTable report in Figure 11-2 of this chapter, follow these steps to complete the real-world example:

WATCH THE VIDEO To see how this example is completed, click the
ch1101_video.avi file at www.wiley.com/go/excelreporting/2007 **and
watch the video.**

1. Drag SalesGroup, SalesCountry, and Sum of UnitPrice off the PivotTable report.

2. Drag ResellerType to the Column Labels area, and then drag ProductCategory above SalesRegion in the Row Labels area.

3. Right-click Sum of Quantity in cell A3 and choose Value Field Settings from the pop-up menu to bring up the Value Field Settings dialog box. Type **UnitsSold** in the Custom Name field and click the Number Format button to open the Format Cells dialog box.

4. From the Format Cells dialog box, select Accounting from the Category pane, type **0** over the 2 in the Decimal Places field, and then select None from the Symbol drop-down field. Click OK to close the Format Cells dialog box and then OK again to close the Value Field Settings dialog box.

5. Choose Design → Report Layout → Show In Tabular Form to switch to the Tabular Form display.

6. Right-click the outer item, Australia, in cell A5 of the PivotTable report and choose Field Settings from the pop-up menu to bring up the Field Settings dialog box.

7. From the Field Settings dialog box, click None under the Subtotals section, and then click the Layout & Print tab to switch dialog box views.

8. From the Layout & Print tab of the Field Settings dialog box, click Show Items in Tabular Form, and then check the options Insert Blank Line After Each Item in the Layout section and Insert Page Break After Each Item Label in the Print section.

9. Click OK to close the Field Settings dialog box and apply the changes.

10. Right-click the PivotTable report and choose PivotTable Options from the pop-up menu to bring up the PivotTable Options dialog box. Click the Display tab and then click the Sort in Data Source Order button to sort the fields in the PivotTable list in the order specified in the SQL query. Click OK to apply the change and close the dialog box.

11. Click any numeric figure in the Values area of the PivotTable report (I selected cell C5) and then choose Home → Conditional Formatting → Manage Rules to bring up the Conditional Formatting Rules Manager dialog box.

12. From the Conditional Formatting Rules Manager dialog box, click New Rule to bring up the New Formatting Rule dialog box. Click the third button, All Cells Showing "Units Sold" Values for "SalesRegion" and "ResellerType," from the Rules Domain section, select Format Only Top or Bottom Ranked Values from the Rules Type section, type **3** (over the 10) in the Values field next to Top, and then choose Each Row Group in the % of the Selected Range For field. Click Format to bring up the Format Cells dialog box.

13. Check Bold from the Font Style pane, select Double from the Underline field, and then choose a green color in the Color field. Click OK to close the Format Cells dialog box and then OK again to close the New Formatting Rule dialog box.

14. From the Conditional Formatting Rules Manager dialog box, click New Rule to bring up the New Formatting Rule dialog box. Click the third button, All Cells Showing "Units Sold" Values for "SalesRegion" and "ResellerType," from the Rules Domain section, select Format Only Values That Are Above or Below Average from the Rules Type section, select Below from the Format Values That Are field, and choose Each Row Group in The Average for the Selected Range For field. Click Format to bring up the Format Cells dialog box.

15. Check Bold from the Font Style pane, select Double from the Underline field, and then choose a red color in the Color field. Click OK to close the Format Cells dialog box and then OK again to close the New Formatting Rule dialog box.

16. From the Conditional Formatting Rules Manager dialog box, click New Rule to bring up the New Formatting Rule dialog box. Click the third button, All Cells Showing "Units Sold" Values for "SalesRegion" and "ResellerType," from the Rules Domain section, select Format All Cells Based on Their Values from the Rules Type section, select Data Bar from the Format Style drop-down field, and then check Show Bar Only. Click OK to close the New Formatting Rule dialog box.

17. Using the Up and Down Buttons in the Conditional Formatting Rules Manager dialog box, set the rule precedence as Top 3, Below Average, and then Data Bar. Check the Stop If True box for the first two rules.

18. Verify that your Conditional Formatting Rules Manager dialog box looks like Figure 11-28, and then click OK.

19. Verify that your report looks like Figure 11-29.

Figure 11-28: Be sure to set the rule precedence as shown here.

	ProductCategory	SalesRegion	Specialty Bike Shop	Value Added Reseller	Warehouse	Grand Total
1	ProductCategoryDes (All)					
2						
3	UnitsSold		ResellerType			
4	ProductCategory	SalesRegion	Specialty Bike Shop	Value Added Reseller	Warehouse	Grand Total
5	Accessories	Australia	174	680	9	863
6		Canada	502	1,241	3,655	5,398
7		Central	231	1,032	882	2,145
8		France		150	1,654	2,046
9		Germany	102	244	1,190	1,536
10		Northeast	175	709	1,490	2,374
11		Northwest	259		1,389	2,474
12		Southeast	228	677	1,204	2,109
13		Southwest	353	1,716	2,976	5,045
14		United Kingdom	126	501	1,222	1,849
15						
16	Bikes	Australia	335	836	385	1,556
17		Canada	1,084	4,895	7,511	13,490
18		Central			2,023	7,490
19		France	424	995	2,875	4,294

Figure 11-29: Your report should look like this if you did everything right.

Reviewing What You Did

This example provides you with some more practice on some of the formatting material covered in this chapter, including how to display data in the compact, tabular form, apply conditional formats, and set conditional formatting rule precedence. Although this example covered just a small part of the available suite of formatting tools that are included in Excel 2007, it provides you with some additional perspective on how you might design a report in the real world.

Chapter Review

This chapter covered a lot of ground in PivotTable formatting. I started the chapter with a review of how PivotTable style templates could be created for rapidly applying preconfigured formats to numerous elements of the report. After that, I covered an array of available PivotTable formatting tools and features, including update options, field formatting options, and the various PivotTable forms. Next, I reviewed the robust suite of conditional formatting tools available in PivotTable reports, such as icons, data bars, and graded color scales. Here, I also reviewed the Conditional Formatting Rules Manager that can be used for managing numerous rules and setting rule precedence. I wrapped up the chapter with a review of the report printing options and tools that can be accessed for best laying out and managing your PivotTable report on paper.

CHAPTER 12

Managing PivotTable Data

Several tools are available in Excel 2007 for managing data in your PivotTable report. Using these tools, you can control how data is refreshed, utilized, and saved in your reports. For example, you can set up automatic data refreshes at specified intervals, toggle whether the underlying dataset is saved with the report, enable update queries to run in the background, configure multiple PivotTables to share the same source data, and define how PivotTable cells referenced outside the PivotTable are handled. This chapter covers all these data management features available with PivotTable reports and provides a perspective on how you can use these various features to simplify the management and operation of your reports.

I start this chapter by describing how you can use the various connection options available in the Connection Properties dialog box, including background refresh settings and automatic refresh options. After that I cover the data options under the Data tab of the PivotTable Options dialog box. Here, I review how you can control whether the underlying dataset is saved with the report and how PivotTable cells are referenced outside the report. Next, I show you how to copy PivotTable reports and configure them to either share the same dataset or use a separate dataset. I conclude this chapter with a real-world exercise that helps bring together some of the topics covered in this chapter into a realistic scenario that you might actually encounter in your own organization.

Before You Begin

All the examples in this chapter, including the "Trying It Out in the Real World" exercise, utilize the SQL query and PivotTable report outlined in this section. If you plan to follow along with the material and examples throughout this chapter, I recommend that you start by creating this PivotTable report that accesses the AdventureWorksDW database.

Complete these steps to create the PivotTable report and follow along with the examples used throughout this chapter:

1. From Excel, choose Data → From Other Sources → From Microsoft Query to bring up the Choose Data Source dialog box.

2. When the Choose Data Source dialog box appears, verify that Use the Query Wizard to Create/Edit Queries box is unchecked, select the AdventureWorks Data Warehouse data source, and click OK.

3. When the Microsoft Query program is launched, you are presented with the Add Tables dialog box. Close this dialog box and click the SQL button.

4. Paste or type the following query into the SQL dialog box, and then click OK:

```
SELECT tme.CalendarYear       AS [Year],
       tme.EnglishMonthName   AS [Month],
       cur.CurrencyName       AS [CurrencyName],
       fcr.EndOfDayRate       AS [EndOfDayRate]
FROM FactCurrencyRate fcr
INNER JOIN DimCurrency cur ON fcr.CurrencyKey = cur.CurrencyKey
INNER JOIN DimTime tme ON fcr.TimeKey = tme.TimeKey
WHERE tme.DayNumberofMonth = 1
  AND tme.CalendarYear > 2001
```

ON THE WEB You can download the ch12_example1.txt query file to your computer from the companion web site at www.wiley.com/go/ excelreporting/2007. **Look for this document in either the Chap12.zip file or Chap12 directory, depending on which .zip file you download.**

5. Click OK to acknowledge that the query cannot be displayed graphically.

6. Click the Return Data to Microsoft Excel button to return the data to Excel and continue.

7. When the Import Data Dialog box appears, choose PivotTable Report and click OK to create the PivotTable.

8. Drag CurrencyName to the Report Filter area, Month to the Row Labels area, Year to the Column Labels area, and EndOfDayRate to the Values area.

9. Left-click CurrencyName in cell B1 of the Report Layout area and choose EURO from the drop-down menu to show only the end-of-day rates for Euros.

10. Right-click the PivotTable and choose PivotTable Options from the pop-up menu to bring up the PivotTable Options dialog box. Click the Totals & Filters tab, uncheck the options Show Grand Totals for Rows and Show Grand Totals for Columns, and then click OK to close the dialog box and suppress the grand total calculation for rows and columns in the PivotTable report.

11. Verify that your PivotTable report looks like Figure 12-1.

	A	B	C	D
1	CurrencyName	EURO		
2				
3	Sum of EndOfDayRate	Column Labels		
4	Row Labels	2002	2003	2004
5	January	0.901225667	0.883158174	0.911161731
6	February	0.966463709	0.862887221	0.945537065
7	March	0.937646507	0.853606487	1.003210273
8	April	0.9046499	0.903342367	0.982511299
9	May	0.858000858	0.911078717	0.966930961
10	June	0.856164384	0.910580951	0.981065437
11	July	0.85999312	0.880126738	1.003814495
12	August	0.890234132	0.904077389	0.987654321
13	September	0.952018279	0.893894699	
14	October	0.92089511	0.870776733	
15	November	0.895575855	0.88269044	
16	December	0.887390185	0.87966221	

Sheet1 / Sheet2 / Sheet3

Figure 12-1: You use this PivotTable report for the examples in later sections of this chapter.

WATCH THE VIDEO To see how the PivotTable report shown in Figure 12-1 is created, watch the video **ch1201_video.avi at** www.wiley.com/go/excelreporting/2007.

Setting Connection Properties

You can configure the connection properties for a PivotTable from the Connection Properties dialog box. Click the PivotTable report to select it and then choose Pivot-Table Tools → Refresh → Connection Properties to bring up this dialog box. Alternatively, you can choose Data → Properties to bring up the Connection Properties dialog box shown in Figure 12-2.

This dialog box is separated into two tabs; Usage (see Figure 12-2) and Definition (see Figure 12-4). The Usage tab is used to configure refresh operations for PivotTable reports that access OLTP and OLAP data sources. There are also sections in this tab of the dialog box for controlling how formatting and drill-through features are handled for OLAP cubes. The connection file, the connection string, and the SQL query are all stored in the Definition tab of the Connection Properties dialog box. Buttons for changing and exporting the Connection File, accessing the Microsoft Query program, and configuring the authentication settings for Excel Services are also available from this tab of the dialog box.

Figure 12-2: Data Refresh options and OLAP formatting and drill-through functions are all controlled from this dialog box.

CROSS-REFERENCE Read the online OLAP chapter for more information about OLAP Formatting, Drill Through, and Language options in the Connection Properties dialog box.

Configuring Usage Options

The data options in the Usage tab of the Connection Properties dialog box in Figure 12-2 are separated into four sections: Refresh Control, OLAP Server Formatting, OLAP Drill Through, and Language. Only the first section, Refresh Control, applies to OLTP data sources. The remaining three sections all apply to OLAP data sources and are covered in the online OLAP chapter.

The options under Refresh Control are used to configure how queries are executed, how often data is refreshed, and whether the PivotTable report is automatically updated when the Excel workbook with the PivotTable report is initially opened. Table 12-1 provides brief a description of each option under Refresh Control.

Table 12-1: Explanation of Refresh Control Options

OPTION NAME	DESCRIPTION
Enable Background Refresh	Toggles whether the data refresh halts all Excel operations in the Excel worksheet until the refresh is completed or whether the user can continue working in Excel while the refresh query runs in the background.
Refresh Every	Automatically refreshes the report every *n* minutes.
Refresh Data When Opening the File	Toggles whether the report is immediately refreshed when it is first opened.

Enable Background Refresh

If you are importing a large dataset and/or accessing the data source through a remote connection, such as a Virtual Private Network (VPN), the data refresh might take a while to complete. While the new dataset is being loaded into your report, you cannot perform any operations in Excel, because the refresh operation halts all activities until the refresh has fully completed. You can work around this constraint by checking the Enable Background Refresh option (see Figure 12-2). Checking this option configures the refresh operation to run in the background so that you can go on about your report operations while the dataset is being updated.

WARNING Refresh operations that are running in the background may not be noticed by PivotTable report users who are not familiar with the Enable Background Refresh option. Be sure to review how this setting works in order to ensure that the report user understands that the report hasn't yet been refreshed.

Report Updating

Once the dataset is fully loaded into Excel, the PivotTable report is updated. During this update, Excel adds any new items to report fields, recomputes Calculated Field and Calculated Item formulas, and refreshes fields in the Report Layout area and Pivot-Table Field List dialog box. This update also freezes the Excel session, and unlike the refresh operation, it cannot be run in the background. However, this period is typically brief, so it's unlikely that it will negatively affect the report user.

TIP Keep in mind that the report update processing time is closely related to the size of the dataset and the number of Calculated Fields and Calculated Items.

Checking Refresh Status

A spinning globe appears in the Status Bar, located at the bottom-left of the Excel workbook, whenever a background refresh operation is running. Clicking the spinning globe opens the External Data Refresh Status dialog box (see Figure 12-3), where you can view all the queries and associated PivotTable reports that are being updated.

You can also bring up the External Data Refresh Status dialog box by choosing PivotTable Tools → Refresh → Refresh Status.

CROSS-REFERENCE Read Chapter 4 to learn more about using the External Data Refresh Status dialog box.

Refresh Every

The Refresh Every option schedules the report to be refreshed every *n* minutes. The value for minutes must be an integer between 1 and 999. This option is useful for reports designed to regularly monitor transactions or statistics. For example, a data entry processing manager might want to monitor the total number of transactions processed throughout the day and the average transaction processed each hour. Using this option, the report can automatically be updated every 15 minutes to show the updated transactions processed by the data entry staff.

Refresh Data When Opening the File

Check the Refresh Data When Opening the File option to automatically refresh the PivotTable report when the Excel workbook containing the PivotTable is first opened. This feature can be useful when the report user has no experience with PivotTable reports, because it doesn't require the user to take any action to refresh the report. When this option is checked, a refresh operation is automatically triggered for the report.

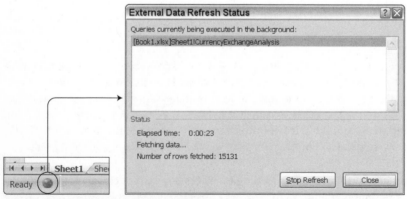

Figure 12-3: Click the spinning globe to open the External Data Refresh Status dialog box, where you can view data refresh progress.

The Refresh Data When Opening the File option should not be checked when a report user needs to keep archived copies of the report data prior to it being automatically refreshed, because report users are likely to forget to save a copy of the report before the new data becomes available. This can happen when the report data is archived at month-end, for example. You should also carefully evaluate the use of this option when the PivotTable report takes a long time to refresh.

WARNING **Keep in mind that it is possible that a malicious query could update or delete rows from the database tables. So be sure the query is verified to be safe and that you trust the source of this report before enabling the automatic refresh feature.**

I suggest that you use this option when:

- The report user is not familiar with PivotTable technology.
- The PivotTable report can be refreshed in a short period of time.
- It's important for the report user to view the most current information in the report.
- The data in the PivotTable report is never archived.

Configuring Definition Options

Several connection settings can be adjusted from the Definition tab of the Connection Properties dialog box. Looking at Figure 12-4, you can see that there are numerous components in this tab of the dialog box that are comprised of panes, buttons, fields, and check boxes.

The Connection Type label displays the type of external data source connection being used. Clicking the Browse button enables you to change the connection file for the report (changing this connection file enables you to utilize a different connection string and SQL query for the report). The Connection String pane contains the connection string information for the external data source. The Command Text pane contains the table name or SQL query being used for the PivotTable report. Clicking Authentication Settings brings up the Excel Services Authentication Settings dialog box, where you can configure the PivotTable report security for Microsoft SharePoint 2007. Clicking the Edit Query button starts the Microsoft Query program, where you can edit an SQL query for the external data source.

Looking at the Connection Information

The connection information for the data source is stored in a connection file. This file contains information on the type of data being accessed, the location of that data, the authentication information (if applicable), and the object or data to extract (for example, the database table or SQL query). The connection information is stored in the Connection String pane. Here, you can manually change the server connection, the default database, and the password. Clicking the Export Connection File button creates an Office Data Connection (*.odc) file that contains the connection information and the SQL query that is being used for the PivotTable report.

Figure 12-4: The connection string, SQL query, and the connection file are all accessed from this dialog box.

CROSS-REFERENCE Read Chapter 4 for detailed explanations of the connection string information that is stored in the Connection String pane.

Save Password

The Save Password option toggles whether the password to the external data source is saved with the report. Although this option may be accessible, it is only relevant when the PivotTable accesses an external data source where a password is actually required. For example, if the PivotTable report uses an SQL database as its data source, and the database uses an SQL Server security authentication type, this option toggles whether the password is saved along with the user login. Keep in mind that if Windows Authentication is used instead of SQL Server authentication, this Save Password option has no effect on the PivotTable, even though it is still accessible.

Uncheck this option if you want the user to specify a password in order to refresh the report or to edit the SQL query. You can also uncheck this option when you want to change the data source.

WARNING In Excel 2007, the password for an SQL login is automatically saved with the report, even if the Save Password option is checked. Until this software bug is remedied, you can check the Save Password option and then enter in a dummy password if you want the password to be specified whenever the report is refreshed.

Configuring PivotTable Data Options

You can set the PivotTable data options from the Data tab of the PivotTable Options dialog box. Right-click the PivotTable report, choose PivotTable Options from the pop-up menu, and click the Data tab to bring to bring up this view of the dialog box. Alternatively, you can choose PivotTable Tools → Options and then click the Data tab to bring up the dialog box view shown in Figure 12-5.

The Data tab of the PivotTable Options dialog box is separated into two sections. In the first section, PivotTable Data, there are options for saving the source data with the file, enabling detail to be expanded, and refreshing the data when the Excel workbook containing the PivotTable report is initially opened. The section Retain Items Deleted from the Data Source provides tools for caching the number of unique items for each field. This feature is very important for controlling how current field items in the PivotTable are handled.

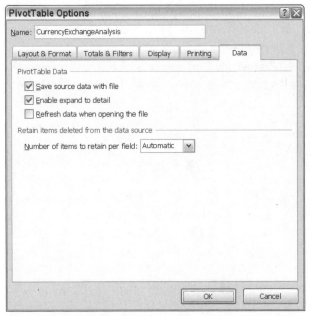

Figure 12-5: The connection string, SQL query, and the connection file are all accessed from this dialog box.

Saving Source Data with File

Unchecking the Save Source Data with File option removes the underlying dataset from the worksheet when the report is saved and closed. This can be useful if you need to email the report to a programmer for troubleshooting or to another user who can refresh it. This feature is also especially helpful when the PivotTable report is several megabytes in size. Rather than trying to send a huge file, you can just send the Pivot-Table report shape with the SQL query and DSN connection information. The report looks exactly the same with this option checked; it's just that the underlying data is not available, so changes to the report cannot be made until the report is refreshed.

Purging Ghost Values

Sometimes items that once appeared in the PivotTable drop-down list continue to appear in the drop-down list even though the item no longer exists in the dataset. I refer to these old items that are no longer valid as *ghost* items. These ghost items appear when previous items in a field are no longer valid. For example, if you are importing the calendar day and calendar month as fields in your report, you may still see the items 28, 29, and 30 as valid items of the Day drop-down list, even though you're halfway into a new month and you're only importing the last five days of transactions into your PivotTable report.

You can clear these items by setting the field Number of Items to Retain per Field (see Figure 12-5) to None and refreshing the report.

To see how ghost values can appear in your PivotTable report, follow these steps:

1. Starting with the PivotTable report in Figure 10-1, click the PivotTable report to select it and choose PivotTable Tools → Refresh → Connection Properties to bring up the Connection Properties dialog box.

2. Click the Definition tab of the Connection Properties dialog box, and then paste in this new SQL query over the previous SQL query in the Command Text pane:

```
SELECT tme.CalendarYear                    AS [Year],
       UPPER(LEFT(tme.EnglishMonthName,3)) AS [Month],
       cur.CurrencyName                    AS [CurrencyName],
       fcr.EndOfDayRate                    AS [EndOfDayRate]
FROM FactCurrencyRate fcr
INNER JOIN DimCurrency cur ON fcr.CurrencyKey = cur.CurrencyKey
INNER JOIN DimTime tme ON fcr.TimeKey = tme.TimeKey
WHERE tme.DayNumberofMonth = 1
  AND tme.CalendarYear > 2001
```

ON THE WEB You can download the ch12_example2.txt query file to your computer from the companion web site at www.wiley.com/go/ excelreporting/2007. Look for this document in either the Chap12.zip file or Chap12 directory, depending on which .zip file you download.

Notice that the only difference between this SQL query and the SQL query in the "Before You Begin" section of this chapter is that the month is now upper-cased and abbreviated to three positions.

3. Click OK to close the Connection Properties dialog box and refresh the Pivot-Table report.

4. Verify that the months in the Row Labels area are now three positions in length and are uppercased (see Figure 12-6).

The report looks just like you should expect; the months have been abbreviated as defined in the SQL query. However, try clicking the Row Labels drop-down arrow in the Report Layout field to see a list of valid values for Month. Notice that the old month names are still listed, as shown in Figure 12-6.

Referencing Cells in the PivotTable Report

There are two ways to reference PivotTable cells outside of the report. These two methods can be switched by checking or unchecking the Generate GetPivotData option. Click the PivotTable report to select it and choose PivotTable Tools → Options → Generate GetPivotData to toggle this option on or off.

The first and default method (Generate GetPivotData checked) references the cell formula, which is basically the associated value in the Values area of the PivotTable report for some Row Labels item, Column Labels item, or Row Labels and Column Labels item combination. If new items are inserted into the PivotTable report, a filter is applied, or the cell value changes, the referenced cell could be moved to a completely new location in the PivotTable. However, the referenced cell value does not change because you are specifying the mapped or referenced formula of the report, instead of just a cell in the worksheet. This is a very helpful feature when you are referencing particular cell values in the PivotTable report and you don't want to be bothered with having to change all your formulas as the PivotTable report shape changes.

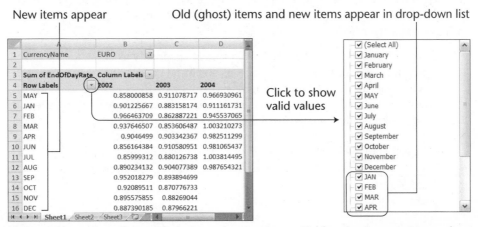

Figure 12-6: Unless the Number of Items to Retain per Field option is set to None, ghost values can appear in the drop-down list when old items are no longer valid in a field.

The second method is to reference the PivotTable cell value as if it were simply a regular worksheet cell. This method is helpful when you are copying and pasting formulas down a worksheet column or across a row.

CROSS-REFERENCE Read Appendix B for more information and tips about using the Generate GetPivotData option.

Managing Data Sources

Sometimes it's necessary to change the PivotTable report to use another database or database server. This section outlines the various methods available for changing the report to use another data source. It also covers how to configure reports to share the same dataset, thereby reducing the size of the Excel workbook and the amount of memory required to open the reports in the workbook.

Changing a Data Source for a PivotTable Report

Changing a data source for a PivotTable report can mean different things to different people. For example, it might be interpreted as pointing the PivotTable report at a Production database instead of a Test database area. Or, perhaps, it might be interpreted as configuring the report to connect to a Text File data source instead of a Database data source. It could even mean changing the table or the SQL query while still referencing the same database.

Changing Data Source Types and Data Source Locations

The first two examples, changing databases (for example, Production to Test) and changing data source types (for example, Text File to Database), were covered in the "Using the Change Data Source Button for PivotTable Reports" section of Chapter 4. The basic steps are as follows:

1. Create a connection — or verify that a connection already exists — for the new data source. For example, if the report uses a Test database, then create or verify that a connection to the Production database has already been created and can be accessed from the Existing Connections dialog box. You can bring up the Existing Connections dialog box by clicking off the PivotTable report and choosing Data → Existing Connections. Read the "Adding an External Data Source Connection to the Workbook" section of Chapter 4 if you need a refresher on how to create or access data sources from the Existing Connections dialog box.

2. Click the PivotTable report for which the data source must be changed and choose PivotTable Tools → Change Data Source → Change Data Source to bring up the Change PivotTable Data Source dialog box.

3. Click the Choose Connection button, click the new data source in the Existing Connections dialog box, and then click Open.

4. Click OK to close the Change PivotTable Data Source dialog box and change the data source for the PivotTable report.

CROSS-REFERENCE Read Chapter 4 for a detailed review of the Change Data Source button and more information on the Existing Connections dialog box.

Modifying the SQL Query for a PivotTable Report

If you want to edit the SQL query or change the table name for a PivotTable report that accesses an SQL database, you can bring up the Connection Properties dialog box and edit the query. Follow these steps to edit an SQL query for a PivotTable report:

1. Click the PivotTable report to select it and choose PivotTable Tools → Change Data Source → Connection Properties to bring up the Connection Properties dialog box.

2. Click the Definition tab in the Connection Properties dialog box to display this tab of the dialog box.

3. Paste or type in the new query in the Command Text pane of the Connection Properties dialog box (see Figure 12-7) or click the Edit Query button to edit the SQL query in the Microsoft Query program.

4. Once the changes are made, click OK to close the Connection Properties dialog box and apply the SQL query changes.

WARNING Earlier versions of Excel required that the Microsoft Query program be started in order to edit or change the SQL query for a PivotTable report. Don't fall into the trap of following steps that you used to perform in earlier versions of Excel. If you're a skilled SQL programmer, there's probably no reason to click the Edit Query button to start the Microsoft Query program. Instead, simply paste in the updated SQL query over the previous SQL query in the Command Text pane of the Connection Properties dialog box. This is a much quicker alternative to using the Microsoft Query program to change the SQL query.

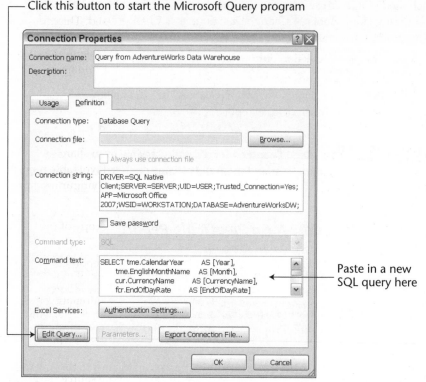

Figure 12-7: You can type or paste in a new query into the Command Text pane of this dialog box, or click the Edit Query button to bring up the Microsoft Query program.

If you selected a table using the Data → From Other Sources → From SQL Server, you'll see a qualified table name in the form of `"Database"."Owner"."Object"`. So, for example, the DimGeography table in the AdventureWorksDW database appears as follows in the Command Text pane:

```
"AdventureWorksDW"."dbo"."DimGeography"
```

You can change the table name by simply editing the last part of the table. So, if you wanted to change the table name from DimGeography to DimEmployee, for example, you would replace the previous string with this:

```
"AdventureWorksDW"."dbo"."DimEmployee"
```

When you click OK to apply the changes for this dialog box, an Excel dialog box will notify you that the link to the external connection file will be removed. This message simply tells you that the connection file that was saved when this connection was initially created is no longer going to be synchronized with the PivotTable report. Click Yes to acknowledge this message, close the Excel dialog box, and update the table name for the PivotTable report.

Configuring a PivotTable to Share Source Data

Multiple PivotTable reports that exist in the same Excel workbook can share the same source data. This can be particularly useful when there are several PivotTable reports that all use the same query but have a different layout or view. This configuration provides the following benefits:

- Reduced file size and memory requirements because only one copy of the source data has to be stored.

- Refreshing one PivotTable report refreshes the data for all the reports that share the same source data.

- Changes made to the SQL query in one PivotTable report are automatically applied to all reports that share the same source data.

- Changes to Data Options in one PivotTable report are automatically applied to all reports that share the same source data.

In order to configure another PivotTable report to share the same source data, just insert a new PivotTable report and choose an existing connection already in the workbook. Note that you can also choose Edit → Move Or Copy Sheet to copy the entire worksheet. This latter method works best when you want to copy everything in the worksheet, including the PivotTables, formats, titles, and printer settings.

Using the Existing Connections Dialog Box

Follow these steps to create a new PivotTable report using the Existing Connections dialog box that shares the same source data as the PivotTable created in the "Before You Begin" section of this chapter.

1. Verify that your PivotTable report looks like Figure 12-1 and click cell A20 of Sheet1; this is where the new PivotTable report will be inserted.

2. Choose Insert → PivotTable → PivotTable to bring up the Create PivotTable dialog box. Click Use an External Data Source and click the Choose Connection button, as shown in Figure 12-8.

Figure 12-8: Click the Choose Connection button to select an existing connection in the workbook for the new PivotTable report.

CROSS-REFERENCE Read Chapter 4 to learn more about managing external data source connections.

3. Double-click the Query from AdventureWorks Data Warehouse connection under the "Connections in This Workbook" section of the Existing Connections dialog box, as shown in Figure 12-9.

4. Click OK when you are returned to the Create PivotTable dialog box (see Figure 12-6) to create the PivotTable report that shares the same data source as the selected PivotTable report in step 1.

Figure 12-9: The existing connections in the workbook appear under the "Connections in This Workbook" section of the Existing Connections dialog box.

Using the Move or Copy Sheet Function

Follow these steps to create a new PivotTable report that shares the same source data as the PivotTable created in the "Before You Begin" section of this chapter by copying the existing worksheet:

1. Right-click the worksheet tab, in this example Sheet1, at the bottom of the workbook and choose Move or Copy from the pop-up menu.

2. Check the Create a Copy box (see Figure 12-10) and click OK to copy the new worksheet with the PivotTable report to a new workbook tab.

3. Double-click the worksheet tab Sheet1(2) to select it and type **PivotTable Copy** in the worksheet tab.

After you have completed these steps, you should now have a copy of the selected Excel worksheet along with any PivotTable report(s) that were on the worksheet.

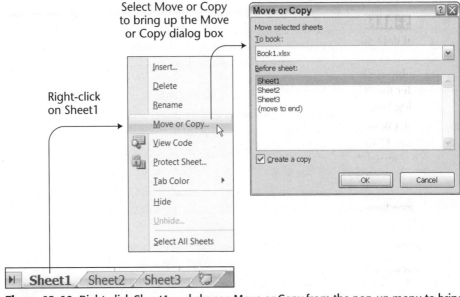

Figure 12-10: Right-click Sheet1 and choose Move or Copy from the pop-up menu to bring up the Move or Copy dialog box, where you can copy all the PivotTable reports to another worksheet tab.

Trying It Out in the Real World

You've been tasked with delivering a Currency Analysis PivotTable report to Laura Norman, the Chief Financial Officer at AdventureWorks. Laura needs this information for forecasting currency exchange risk, which is an important component of her five-year plan that is reviewed annually with the CEO. Laura is not familiar with PivotTable report technology, and as a busy executive she doesn't have the time or inclination to learn this technology. However, it's important that Laura has the most up-to-date information on currency exchange rates as new information becomes available. Laura's assistant, David Barber, who has attended some of your report training sessions and is more familiar with the technology, provided you with some helpful tips to ensure that your report is well-received by the CFO. First, David communicated that the report must have drill-down capability while it is connected to the network, but for security reasons, the data should not be available for drill-down when it is emailed or saved to the CFO's laptop. He also noticed that some PivotTable reports that have larger datasets take a long time to refresh, and during this refresh Excel is disabled. David expressed that Laura typically has several Excel worksheets open and that it's important that report updates do not freeze her sessions. Lastly, David said that Laura often copies and pastes columns and rows of data from her reports to other cells in the workbook.

Getting Down to Business

Starting with the PivotTable report in Figure 12-1 of this chapter, follow these steps to complete the real-world example:

1. Right-click the PivotTable report and choose PivotTable Options from the pop-up menu to bring up the PivotTable Options dialog box.

2. Click the Data tab of the PivotTable Options dialog box and uncheck Save Source Data with File to ensure that the dataset is removed when the Pivot-Table report is saved.

3. Check Refresh Data When Opening the File to configure the PivotTable report to automatically refresh when the Excel workbook is opened.

4. Click OK to apply the changes and to close the PivotTable Options dialog box.

5. Click the PivotTable report to select it and choose PivotTable Tools → Refresh → Connection Properties to open the Connection Properties dialog box.

6. Check Enable Background Refresh to enable the SQL query to run in the background, and then click OK to close the Connection Properties dialog box.

7. Uncheck the GetPivotData option by choosing PivotTable Tools → Options → Generate GetPivotData. Unchecking this option from the PivotTable tab enables cells to be copied and pasted from the PivotTable report.

WATCH THE VIDEO To see how this example is completed, click the ch1202_video.avi file at www.wiley.com/go/excelreporting/2007 and watch the video.

Reviewing What You Did

This example provides you with some additional perspective on how you can configure PivotTable data options to meet important business requirements. In the real world, you may encounter an array of similar situations. For example, perhaps your organization has a strict limit on the size of incoming or outgoing email attachments. If the report utilizes a large dataset, you may have to remove the underlying data from the PivotTable report in order for it to be successfully transmitted or received. Likewise, you may have to configure a PivotTable report to automatically refresh every 10 minutes to show current production statistics without requiring the user to manually refresh the report to get the most recent report data.

I recommend that you review the PivotTable data options and examples throughout this chapter in order to become more familiar with the various types of data options that are available and how they might be used in real world.

Chapter Review

I started this chapter by describing how you can use the various connection options available in the Connection Properties dialog box. Following that, I covered the data options under the Data tab of the PivotTable Options dialog box. Next, I demonstrated how you can copy PivotTable reports and configure them to either share the same dataset or use a separate dataset. I concluded this chapter with a real-world exercise that helps bring together some of the topics covered in this chapter into a realistic scenario that you might actually encounter in your own organization.

Analyzing Data in a PivotChart

You've probably heard the expression that a picture is worth a thousand words. The same can also be said of reports. Rather than showing data in a numerical format, there can be situations in which a graphical portrayal provides a much better representation and description of the data. So, to cover this area and round out your reporting skills, I've included this chapter on how you can combine the innovative features of Pivot-Table reports with the powerful tools of Excel charts to produce a PivotChart.

I start this chapter by reviewing the steps for creating a new PivotChart from an external data source. Following that, I cover the major components of a PivotChart. I also draw out some of the similarities and differences between PivotTable and Pivot-Chart reports, covering new terminology and reviewing how these two report types relate to one another. Next, I outline the basic formatting functions available, including how to customize the chart type, use 3-D charts, and configure display settings. After that, I cover some of the basic presentation features, including how to set a chart title, display a chart legend, and add a data table. I conclude with a real-world exercise that ties together several of the topics covered into a realistic scenario that you might encounter in your own organization.

Before You Begin

Start this chapter by creating a new PivotTable and PivotChart report from an external data source that accesses the AdventureWorksDW database.

Complete these steps to create the PivotChart report and follow along with the examples used throughout this chapter:

1. From Excel, choose Data → From Other Sources → From Microsoft Query to bring up the Choose Data Source dialog box.

2. When the Choose Data Source dialog box appears, verify that Use the Query Wizard to Create/Edit Queries is unchecked, select the AdventureWorks Data Warehouse data source, and click OK.

3. When the Microsoft Query program is launched, you are presented with the Add Tables dialog box. Close this dialog box and click the SQL button.

4. Paste or type the following query into the SQL dialog box and click OK:

```
SELECT prod.EnglishProductName          AS [Product Name],
       fact.SalesAmount                 AS [Order Amount],
       fact.Freight                     AS [Freight],
       fact.OrderQuantity               AS [Quantity],
       catg.EnglishProductCategoryName  AS [Category Name],
       tmek.CalendarYear                AS [Year],
       tmek.EnglishMonthName            AS [Month],
        CASE
          WHEN prod.Status IS NULL
               THEN 'Discontinued'
               ELSE 'Current'
               END                      AS [Status]
FROM FactInternetSales fact
INNER JOIN DimProduct prod
        ON fact.ProductKey = prod.ProductKey
INNER JOIN DimProductSubcategory subc
        ON prod.ProductSubcategoryKey = subc.ProductSubcategoryKey
INNER JOIN DimProductCategory catg
        ON subc.ProductCategoryKey = catg.ProductCategoryKey
INNER JOIN DimTime tmek ON fact.OrderDateKey = tmek.TimeKey
```

ON THE WEB You can download the ch13_example.txt query file to your computer from the companion web site at www.wiley.com/go/ excelreporting/2007. **Look for this document in either the Chap13.zip file or Chap13 directory, depending on which .zip file you download.**

5. Click OK to acknowledge that the query cannot be displayed graphically.

6. Click the Return Data to Microsoft Excel button to return the data to Excel and continue.

7. When the Import Data dialog box appears (see Figure 13-1) choose PivotChart and PivotTable Report, and then click OK to create the PivotTable and the Pivot-Chart.

Figure 13-1: Select the PivotChart and PivotTable Report option to create a PivotChart.

8. Verify that the PivotTable report and PivotTable layout areas are both created and that the PivotTable Field List dialog box and the PivotChart Filter Pane also appear, as shown in Figure 13-2.

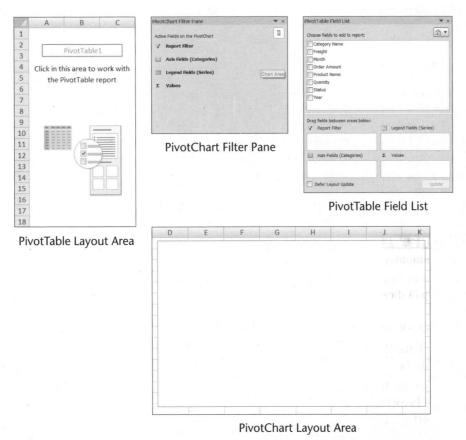

PivotChart Filter Pane

PivotTable Field List

PivotTable Layout Area

PivotChart Layout Area

Figure 13-2: These three components appear when a PivotChart is initially created.

Getting Familiar with a PivotChart

Entire books have been dedicated to Excel charts because there is so much material to cover. I don't try to review every feature, function, and tool associated with a Pivot-Chart. Instead, this chapter covers only the core chart features with an emphasis on the narrower topic of a PivotChart, and how this technology can be used to complement or even supplement a PivotTable report.

PivotTable and PivotChart Relationships

A PivotChart is always linked to a PivotTable; it cannot exist on its own. Thus, a change in a PivotTable (for example, adding or removing a field) results in a corresponding change to the PivotChart, and vice versa. Given the close relationship between these reporting tools, you shouldn't be surprised to learn that many of the concepts, terminology, and features of a PivotTable also apply to a PivotChart. Additionally, the same types of components of a PivotTable are also found in a PivotChart. The main difference is that PivotChart components are designed for managing the graphical chart display, whereas PivotTable components are designed for managing the numerical report display.

Creating a PivotChart

You can either create a PivotTable and PivotChart report at the same time or you can create a PivotChart from an existing PivotTable report. To create both reports at the same time, follow the steps outlined in the "Before You Begin" section, and at the last step, select PivotChart and PivotTable Report from the Import Data dialog box. Of course, it's just as easy to create a PivotChart later; simply select an existing PivotTable and click the Chart button in the PivotTable tab.

CROSS-REFERENCE Read Appendix B for more information about buttons under the PivotTable Tools tab.

Terminology and Display

A PivotChart uses much of the same terminology as a PivotTable. For example, in a PivotTable there is a Report Filter area, a Row Labels area, a Column Labels area, and a Values area. In a PivotChart, the same areas are applicable, except that the Row Labels area is referred to as the Category Axis area and the Column Labels area is referred to as the Legend Series area. The location is also different for these two types of fields. Legend Series fields are usually shown on the right, and Category Axis fields are usually shown at the bottom of a PivotChart (see Figure 13-3).

To see how this works with the PivotChart you created in the "Before You Begin" section of this chapter, follow these steps:

1. Click the PivotChart Layout area to select it (see Figure 13-2).

2. From the PivotTable Field List dialog box, drag Category Name to the Category Axis area, Status to the Legend Series area, Year to the Report Filter area, and Quantity to the Values area of the PivotChart.

3. Verify that your PivotChart looks like Figure 13-3.

As you can see in Figure 13-3, the data is graphically displayed in the PivotChart. Instead of showing numbers for the quantity sold by Status and Product Category, colored column bars are used to display this information. Though this is a very simple example, it's not hard to extrapolate how this graphical representation can be used to view percentage-shares, trends, and relationships in more sophisticated and robust datasets. You can probably also imagine how this type of reporting tool can be very useful for presentations or even for getting a first look at the data. After a preliminary understanding of the data is gleaned from a PivotChart, you could use the PivotTable report to dive in for a more detailed and quantitative analysis.

Now, take a look at how the PivotTable and PivotChart relate to one another by looking at both reports in Figure 13-4.

Notice how the items Current and Discontinued in the Column Labels area of the PivotTable report are displayed as items in the PivotChart's legend at the right of the PivotChart. Also notice how the Row Labels items Bikes, Accessories, and Clothing are displayed as Category Axis items at the bottom of the PivotChart. Now, try double-clicking Bikes in the PivotTable and in the PivotChart. Note how both of these reports respond in exactly the same way: by bringing up PivotTable Field List window where you can change the summary type. Adding or removing fields in one report also produces an immediate and corresponding change in the other report.

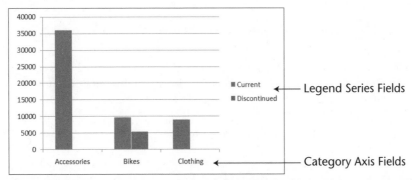

Figure 13-3: After you have completed the steps in this section, your PivotChart should look like this.

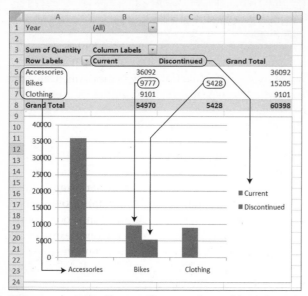

Figure 13-4: This diagram illustrates how objects in a PivotChart are linked to objects in a PivotTable.

Working with the PivotChart Components

Five components are made available when a PivotChart is created. You should already be familiar with the first two components, the Report Layout area and the PivotTable Field List dialog box, from reading earlier chapters in this book. The remaining three components are as follows:

- **PivotChart Filter Pane:** This component can be used to filter and sort data in the PivotChart.

- **PivotChart Layout Area:** This is where the PivotChart is displayed. You can right-click several sections of the layout area to bring up different pop-up menus for managing display options.

- **PivotChart Tab:** This component is used to control several types of display settings, including the location of the PivotChart.

I provide more detailed descriptions of each of these components in the following sections. I also briefly cover the PivotTable Field List dialog box, because there are some minor changes to this component for a PivotChart.

Using the PivotChart Filter Pane

The PivotChart Filter Pane is new to PivotChart reports in Excel 2007. Unless closed by the user, the PivotChart pane appears whenever a PivotChart is selected. It's similar to the PivotTable Field List dialog box, but only provides a subset of the functions. You can use the PivotChart Filter Pane to:

- Apply filters to Value or Label Fields
- Sort data
- Toggle the display of the PivotTable Field List dialog box

The PivotChart Filter Pane is shown in Figure 13-5 for the PivotChart example that I provided in the previous section (see Figure 13-3). Clicking the drop-down arrow next to a Report Filter field brings up a drop-down box where you can choose to display one or more items for the PivotChart. Clicking the drop-down arrow next to a Category Axis or Legend Series field brings up a drop-down box where you can sort items and apply filters. Clicking the Field List button in the top right of the dialog box toggles the display of the PivotTable Field List dialog box.

The PivotChart Filter Pane only appears when a PivotChart is selected. You can close this pane by clicking the X in the top right of the dialog box. Once closed, the dialog box will no longer appear when the PivotChart is selected. Keep in mind that there isn't a readily available option to bring this pane back up from a right-click menu; it can only be brought up again by selecting the PivotChart and choosing Analyze → Show/Hide → PivotChart Filter.

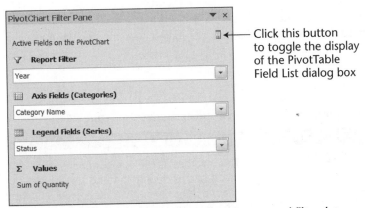

Click this button to toggle the display of the PivotTable Field List dialog box

Figure 13-5: Use the PivotChart Filter Pane to sort and filter data.

Operating in the PivotChart Layout Area

There are several areas and components in the PivotChart Layout area; right-clicking each one of them brings up different context-oriented pop-up menus for the selected area or component (note that this is similar to how PivotTable reports also work in Excel 2007). For example, right-clicking a gridline brings up a pop-up menu that includes items for formatting gridlines. Similarly, right-clicking a Data Series items brings up a pop-up menu with items for formatting the selected Data Series item. In order to help you better understand the different areas and components of a Pivot-Chart, I've assigned a number to each unique item in Figure 13-6. The descriptions of these items are provided in Table 13-1.

Table 13-1 identifies and provides a brief explanation of the various areas of the PivotChart shown in Figure 13-6.

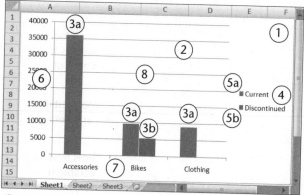

Figure 13-6: The various areas of a PivotChart are numbered here and described in Table 13-1.

Table 13-1: PivotChart Components (see corresponding numbers in Figure 13-6)

SECTION	ITEM	DESCRIPTION
1	Chart Area	This includes all the components of the PivotChart, including the Plot area, the Legend Series area, the Category Axis area, and the Data Series items. Right-clicking in this area brings up the Chart Area pop-up menu.
2	Plot Area	This is the area where the Values area items are graphically plotted. Right-clicking here brings up the Plot Area pop-up menu.

Table 13-1 *(continued)*

SECTION	ITEM	DESCRIPTION
3	Data Series	The Data Series items are represented graphically in the chart; 3a is the Sum of Quantity for Current product categories, and 3b is the Sum of Quantity for Discontinued product categories. This area is linked to the Values area of the PivotTable report.
4	Legend Series Area	This area includes a color code explanation of each color coded Data Series item (see 3a and 3b). This area is linked to the Column Labels area of the PivotTable report.
5	Legend Series Item	Each Legend Series item can be individually selected and formatted. The items in this area are the same as the items in the Column Labels area of the PivotTable report.
6	Chart Axis	This area includes tools for formatting the major and minor gridlines, and setting numerical scale options.
7	Category Axis Area	This area includes all the items from the Row Labels area of the PivotTable report Unlike the Legend Series area, individual items cannot be selected and formatted in this area.
8	Gridlines	Right-click any gridline to apply formatting options to all the gridlines in the chart.

Depending on the type of chart that you are using and the layout that you have selected, you may have more or less areas and components that are available for selection and formatting. I've just tried to highlight the basic components to give you a better idea of how a PivotChart works and help you understand the various formatting options that can be applied to each unique chart component.

TIP The available components and areas can vary based on the formatting and type of PivotChart being used. Don't forget to use the toolbar tips if you're unsure about which area or component is being selected (the toolbar tips automatically appear when the mouse pointer is held over a particular area for more than one second).

Examining the PivotChart Tools Tab

The PivotChart Tools tab has several readily available buttons for formatting your PivotChart. From this menu, you can change the chart type, apply a chart template or chart styles, and change the PivotChart location. You can access the PivotChart Tools tab by selecting a PivotChart and clicking the PivotChart Tools tab that appears above the Design tab, as shown in Figure 13-7. Keep in mind that this tab is only available when you click a PivotChart.

Once you click the PivotChart Tools tab, the PivotChart Tools tab is revealed, as shown in Figure 13-8.

Notice that the buttons in the PivotChart Tools tab are organized into five groups. In the Type group, buttons are available for setting a chart type and saving a modified chart type as a template. The Data group includes two buttons for rapidly switching fields between the Category Axis and the Legend Series axis (note that these buttons do not work for external data). The Chart Layouts group has a Quick Layout button that can be used to apply a predefined layout to the chart. Here, you can choose from eleven default layouts where chart titles, legends, Data Series labels and other chart elements are positioned differently on the chart. The Chart Styles group enables you to choose from a vast palette of colors for displaying Data Series items in the PivotChart. The Location group has a Move Chart button that enables you to set the location of the PivotChart. I've provided a more detailed description of each button in Table 13-2.

Click this tab to bring up
the PivotChart Tools menu

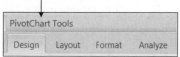

Figure 13-7: The PivotChart Tools tab appears above the Design tab whenever a PivotChart is selected.

Figure 13-8: The PivotChart Tools tab has several buttons for formatting the PivotChart.

Table 13-2: Summary of PivotChart Group Buttons

GROUP	BUTTON	DESCRIPTION
Type	Change Chart Type	Allows you to choose a chart type (for example, Column, Line, Pie, Bar, Area, Surface, Bubble, and so on).
Type	Save As Template	Enables you to save a customized chart layout for use as a template for future charts.
Data	Switch Row/Column	Swaps the fields in the Legend Series area with the fields in the Axis area.
Data	Select Data	Brings up the Edit Data Source dialog box for customizing the data range.
Chart Layouts	Quick Layout	Shows a selection of template chart layouts that can be applied to the selected PivotChart.
Chart Styles	Quick Styles	Provides options on template chart styles that can be applied to the selected PivotChart.
Location	Move Chart	Brings up the Move Chart dialog box where a selected PivotChart can be moved to a new or different worksheet.

Using the PivotTable Field List Dialog Box

The PivotTable Field List dialog box used for a PivotChart (see Figure 13-9) looks just like the PivotTable Field List dialog box used for a PivotTable report, except that the Row Labels area is replaced with the Axis (Categories) area and the Column Labels area is replaced with the Legend Fields (Series) area. Other than these small label changes, the dialog box works exactly the same way as it does for PivotTable reports.

NOTE You may find it odd that a PivotChart uses a dialog box that is labeled as Pivot*Table* Field List instead of Pivot*Chart* Field List. I'm not completely sure why Microsoft hasn't renamed this dialog box, except that any change you make to the PivotChart is simultaneously applied to the linked PivotTable.

Figure 13-9: The PivotTable Field List dialog box for a PivotChart should look familiar, because it's very similar to the one used for a PivotTable.

Formatting the PivotChart

Several types of charts and layout options are available for your PivotChart. In this section, I outline some of the core formatting tools that area available for customizing the display of your PivotChart. In this section, I cover the following topics:

- Selecting a chart type
- Using 3-D charts
- Formatting the Plot area
- Formatting the data series

Selecting a Chart Type

You can choose from several types of charts in the Change Chart Type dialog box shown in Figure 13-10. You can bring up this dialog box by right-clicking in the Chart area of the PivotChart Layout area and choosing Change Chart Type from the pop-up menu.

Several types of charts are available in the Change Chart Type dialog box. And once you select a chart type, you can typically choose from a list of several types of subcharts. Looking at Figure 13-10, note that there are 19 types of column charts and seven types of line charts. These charts are the same ones that are used to create a standard Excel chart. I suggest using Excel's Online Help if you need guidance in selecting an optimal chart type for your report data.

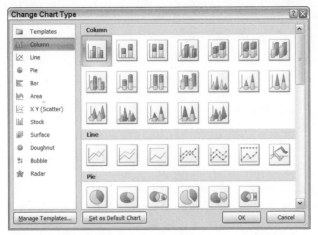

Figure 13-10: Choose a chart type for your PivotChart from this dialog box.

TIP You can set a default chart type by clicking a chart type in the Change Chart Type dialog box and clicking the Set as Default Chart button, located at the bottom of the dialog box.

Making a Chart Three-Dimensional

Making charts three-dimensional (3-D) can add some pizzazz to the presentation effect of your report data. And if you interested in that kind of thing, there are some great tools for managing the 3-D chart display. In this section, you see how you can convert a two-dimensional (2-D) PivotChart into three dimensions. In the following sections, you see some of the menus and tools that are available for controlling the 3-D display.

To configure your PivotChart to appear in 3-D and to follow along with the examples throughout this chapter, complete these steps:

1. Verify that the PivotChart looks like Figure 13-3, right-click in the Chart area, and select Change Chart Type to bring up the Change Chart Type dialog box.

2. Verify that Column is selected in the Chart Type pane (left side), and then, in the Sub-Chart pane, select 3-D Cylinder. Note that this is the eleventh chart sub-type in the pane, counting from left-to-right and then down. You can also use the toolbar tips to confirm that you've selected the correct sub-chart.

3. Click OK to change the chart type and to close the Change Chart Type dialog box.

4. Verify that your PivotChart now looks like Figure 13-11.

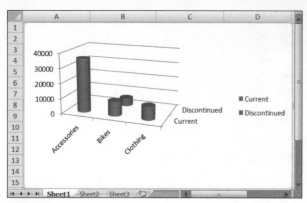

Figure 13-11: The data in the PivotChart should now be displayed in three-dimensional cylinders.

Rotating a Three-Dimensional Chart

You can customize the rotation and perspective of a chart from the 3-D Rotation tab of the Format Chart Area dialog box. You can bring up this dialog box tab by right-clicking either the Chart area or the Plot area of the PivotChart and selecting 3-D Rotation from the pop-up menu.

The 3-D Rotation tab of the Format Chart Area dialog box shown in Figure 13-12 provides several buttons and fields for setting the rotation, perspective, and scale of 3-D charts.

As settings are changed in the 3-D Rotation section, they are simultaneously applied to the PivotChart. You can either use the buttons to make discrete adjustments to the rotation and perspective, or you can type a specific value into the fields that are just left of each button. The Autoscale box can be checked to ensure that adjustments to the depth of the PivotChart are scaled with similar adjustments to the height, thereby maintaining the original chart scale.

TIP If you completely mess up the rotation of your PivotChart, you can reset it back to the default display by clicking the Default Rotation button, located at the bottom of the Format Chart Area dialog box.

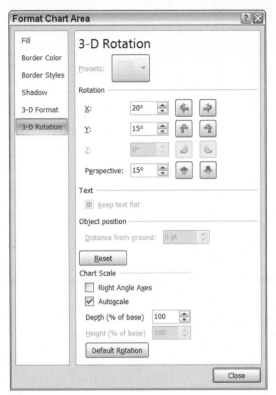

Figure 13-12: The rotation, perspective, and depth of a 3-D chart can all be controlled from this dialog box.

Formatting PivotChart Components

There are several components of a PivotChart that can be formatted; each type of chart and layout option provides different components that can be customized. Formatting options typically include the background fill, border color, border style, shadow effect, and 3-D format. And, if you're working with a 3-D chart, then a 3-D rotation option is also available for some chart components.

Right-clicking the Plot area of the PivotChart in Figure 13-11 and selecting Format Plot Area from the pop-up menu brings up the Format Plot Area dialog box shown in Figure 13-13.

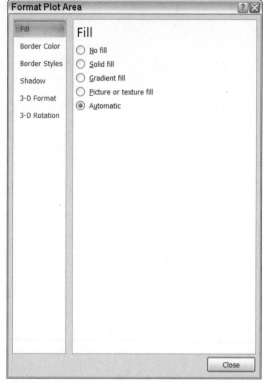

Figure 13-13: You can customize the background, patterns, and fill effects for the Plot area of the PivotChart in the Format Plot Area dialog box.

Looking at Figure 13-13, you can see that there are several tabs on the left side of the Format Plot Area dialog box that are available for formatting the plot area. This dialog box in Figure 13-13 is available for several other components and areas of your Pivot-Chart. All you need to do is right-click one of them and select the format item from the pop-up menu.

Formatting the Data Series

If you are following along with the example in this chapter, you can see that the Data Series items in Figure 13-11 are displayed in two different colors for each unique Legend Series item: Current in blue and Discontinued in red. You can format each of the two Data Series items by right-clicking one of the cylinders in the series and choosing Format Data Series from the pop-up menu. This brings up the Format Data Series dialog box where you can change the shape, color, pattern, texture, and border of the Data Series item in the PivotChart.

To format a Data Series item and to follow along with the example in this section, complete these steps:

1. Verify that your PivotChart looks like Figure 13-11, then right-click the 3-D cylinder for Accessories and choose Format Data Series from the pop-up menu.

2. Verify that the Format Data Series dialog box in Figure 13-14 appears.

3. Set the Gap Depth and the Gap Width both to 25% on the Series Options tab.

4. Click the Shape tab and choose Partial Pyramid as the shape.

5. Click the Close button to close the Format Data Series dialog box.

6. Verify that your PivotChart looks like Figure 13-15.

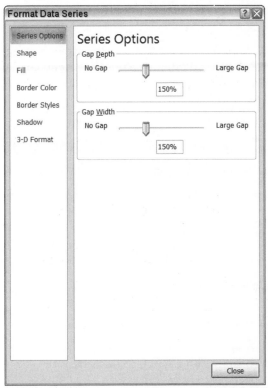

Figure 13-14: You can use the Format Data Series dialog box to format items in a Data Series.

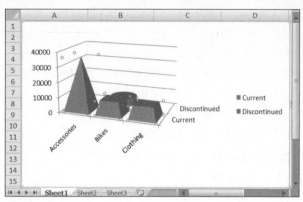

Figure 13-15: Each Data Series item can be represented as a different shape and uniquely formatted.

Notice that the Format Data Series dialog box in Figure 13-14 has seven tabs that you can use for formatting Data Series items. Table 13-3 provides a brief description of the functions that are available in each of these tabs.

Table 13-3: Explanation of Format Data Series Tabs

TAB	DESCRIPTION
Series Options	Configure the gap depth and width between Data Series items in the PivotChart.
Shape	Choose the type of shape to be displayed for a selected Data Series item.
Fill	Apply solid, gradient, picture, and texture fills for a selected Data Series item object in the PivotChart.
Border Color	Set a border line and color for the selected Data Series item.
Border Styles	Configure the border width and style for the selected Data Series item.
Shadow	Apply shadow options for the selected Data Series item object in the PivotChart.
3-D Format	Configure three-dimensional formatting options for the selected Data Series item in the PivotChart.

Labeling the PivotChart

Labels can help clarify and provide perspective to the data illustrated in a PivotChart. There are several types of components that can be labeled, including the following:

- Chart title
- Horizontal, vertical, and depth axes
- Legend
- Data Series labels
- Data Table

The labels for these PivotChart components can be accessed from the Labels group. You can access this group shown in Figure 13-16 by clicking the PivotChart to select it and clicking the Layout tab.

Table 13-4 provides a brief description of the functions that are available for each button in the Labels group.

Figure 13-16: The titles, labels, legend, and Data Table display options for a PivotChart are configured from this tab group.

Table 13-4: Explanation of Buttons in the Labels Group

TAB	DESCRIPTION
Chart Title	Sets the chart title as centered-overlay or above the chart
Axis Titles	Configures labels for the horizontal, vertical, and depth axes
Legend	Sets the position of the chart legend
Data Labels	Toggles the numeric display of the Data Series items in the PivotChart
Data Table	Toggles the display of a data table

Adding a Chart Title

Titles are often added to a chart to describe what type of data is being presented. This chart title can also be particularly important if the PivotChart is displayed by itself, because there are no worksheet cells that can be pulled in to describe the chart. You can add a chart title by selecting a predefined layout from the Chart Layouts tab (most of the predefined layouts include a chart title) or from the Chart Title button, accessed from the Labels group under the Layout tab. The Chart Title button has two options for adding a chart:

- **Above Chart:** Select this option to position the title above the chart and automatically resize the PivotChart to fit the newly added chart title and the Pivot-Chart within the Chart area. (See Table 13-1 for a more detailed explanation of the Chart area.)

- **Centered Overlay Title:** Select this option to position the chart title on top of the chart without resizing the PivotChart.

Once a chart title is added to the PivotChart, you can simply click in the Chart Title box to change the description. You can also right-click the Chart Title component and select Format Chart Title to format the chart title (this dialog box is similar to the one shown in Figure 13-14).

TIP You can remove a chart title from a PivotChart by selecting None from the Chart Title drop-down button.

Managing Axis Titles

Three types of axis titles can be added to a PivotChart from the Axis Titles button in the Labels group. These titles include a Horizontal axis title, a Vertical axis title, and a Depth axis title. The Horizontal axis title is used to label Category Axis items. In Figure 13-17, I labeled the category names as "Product Category." The Vertical axis title is used to label the numeric scale for the data being summarized in the Values area of a PivotChart. This title is usually a currency code, a description of the unit of measure, a description of the data being summarized, or some combination of these descriptions. In Figure 13-17, I labeled the Vertical title as "Gross Units Sold." The Depth axis title is used to label Legend Series fields. In Figure 13-17, I labeled the status codes as "Product Status."

There are many formatting options for each of the axis titles. You can change the font, add borders, and configure three-dimensional settings. There are also options for setting the alignment of axis titles for the Vertical axis and the Depth axis titles to rotated, vertical, or horizontal.

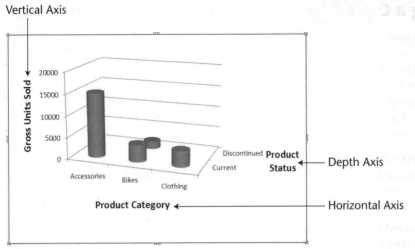

Figure 13-17: Three types of axis titles can be added to a PivotChart to label Category Axis items, Legend Series items, and summarized data in the Values area.

Configuring the Chart Legend

The Chart Legend provides highly visible information on how each Data Series color corresponds to a Legend Series item. The default chart layout positions the Chart Legend at the right of the chart (see Figure 13-15). You can change this position from the Legend button in the Labels group, located under the Layout tab. The Legend button enables you to position the legend above, below, to the right of, or to the left of the Pivot-Chart. There are also overlay options for the left and right of the chart. Selecting None from the Legend drop-down button turns off the legend display.

Toggling the Display of Data Labels

You can toggle the display of labels for the Values area data being summarized in a Pivot-Chart from the Data Labels button, located in the Labels group, under the Layout tab. If you choose to display the Data Labels, the numeric value for the Values area field being summarized appears above each Data Series icon.

Adding a Data Table

The Data Table button, located in the Labels group, enables you to add a Data Table below the PivotChart. This Data Table is essentially a grid that shows the cross-tabular Category Axis and Legend Series item values in a numeric format; just like what you'd see in a PivotTable report. There are even options for displaying the Data Table with legend keys. This feature can be useful when you want to quickly add a table of numeric values during a presentation, or when you don't want to quickly provide both the numeric and graphical data on one sheet.

To add a Data Table to the PivotChart and to follow along with the example in this section, complete these steps:

1. Verify that your PivotChart looks like Figure 13-15 and choose Layout → Data Table → Show Data Table with Legend Keys.

2. Choose Layout → Legend → None to turn off the display of the Chart Legend.

3. Verify that your PivotChart looks like Figure 13-18.

Changing the PivotChart Location

The default setting is to display the PivotChart as an object in the worksheet. In order to change the location of the PivotChart in its own worksheet tab, follow these steps:

1. Click the PivotChart to select it and choose PivotChart Tools → Move Chart to bring up the Move Chart dialog box shown in Figure 13-19.

2. Select the location to display the report and click OK to close the dialog box and set the new location.

In order to display the PivotTable and PivotChart report in the same worksheet, select that worksheet name from the Object In drop-down field list.

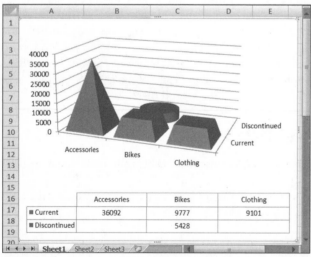

Figure 13-18: A Data Table can display a legend key along with the cross-tabular numeric data normally found only in a PivotTable report.

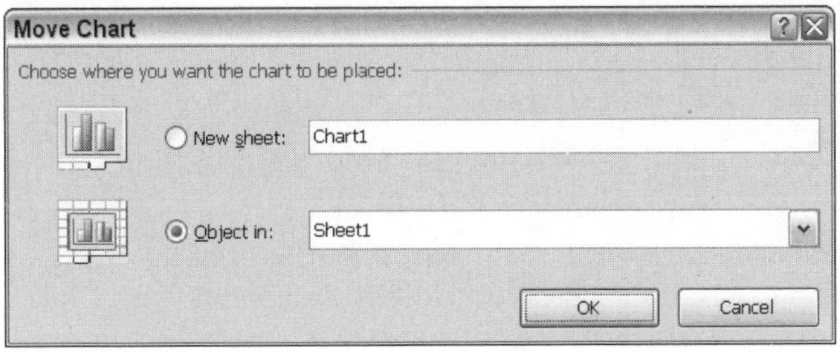

Figure 13-19: You can change the location of the PivotChart in this dialog box.

Trying It Out in the Real World

Brian Welcker, the Vice President of Sales at AdventureWorks, has asked for your assistance in presenting a major initiative to increase sales of AdventureWorks products. Brian's strategy is to provide significant discounts to customers in months where there is a significant sales drop. Brian only wants to offer these discounts to regions that experience a significant sales drop in a one-month span.

Brian has already contacted the company's database administrator to prepare the SQL query shown here to extract the necessary sales data from the AdventureWorks Data Warehouse database.

```
SELECT trty.SalesTerritoryRegion      AS [Region],
       fact.SalesAmount               AS [Order Amount],
       fact.OrderQuantity             AS [Quantity],
       tmek.CalendarYear              AS [Year],
       tmek.EnglishMonthName          AS [Month]
FROM FactInternetSales fact
INNER JOIN DimTime tmek ON fact.OrderDateKey = tmek.TimeKey
INNER JOIN DimSalesTerritory trty
       ON fact.SalesTerritoryKey = trty.SalesTerritoryKey
```

ON THE WEB You can download the ch13_rwe.txt query file to your computer from the companion web site at www.wiley.com/go/ excelreporting/2007.

You've been asked to create a PivotChart that graphically displays the annual sales by month and region in a graphical format. The sales team is not interested in looking at numerical figures right now; they only need to see the data trends by geographical region and month.

Getting Down to Business

Complete these steps to create the PivotChart report:

1. From Excel, choose Data → From Other Sources → From Microsoft Query to bring up the Choose Data Source dialog box.

2. When the Choose Data Source dialog box appears, verify that Use the Query Wizard to Create/Edit Queries is unchecked, select the AdventureWorks Data Warehouse data source, and click OK.

3. When the Microsoft Query program is launched, you are presented with the Add Tables dialog box. Close this dialog box and click the SQL button.

4. Paste or type the query from the previous section into the SQL dialog box and click OK.

5. Click OK to acknowledge that the query cannot be displayed graphically.

6. Click the Return Data to Microsoft Excel button to return the data to Excel and continue.

7. When the Import Data Dialog box appears, choose PivotChart and PivotTable Report, and click OK to create the PivotTable and the PivotChart.

8. Drag Region to the Legend Series area, Month to the Category Axis area, and Quantity to the Values areas.

9. Right-click the Chart area of the PivotChart and select Change Chart Type from the pop-up menu to bring up the Change Chart Type dialog box.

10. Click the Line tab and select the Stacked Line chart type (second chart from the left) and click OK to change the chart type and close the Change Chart Type dialog box.

11. Verify that the PivotChart looks like Figure 13-20.

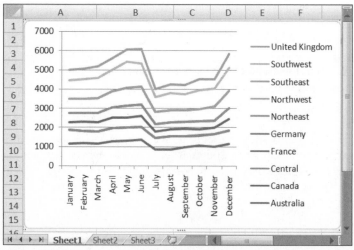

Figure 13-20: Line chart types are ideal for showing trends in data.

WATCH THE VIDEO You can watch the video ch1301_video.avi to see how this PivotChart is created at www.wiley.com/go/excelreporting/2007.

Reviewing What You Did

This real-world example demonstrated how you can use a PivotChart to illustrate trends in data. Looking at this chart, you can easily see that the United Kingdom and the Southwest regions experience the most significant sales drop-off from June to July. Although the other regions also experience a sales decline during this same period, it's easy to see from the PivotChart that the drop is not as severe.

Chapter Review

This chapter outlined the similarities and differences between a PivotChart report and a PivotTable report. I started by covering the terminology and major components of a PivotChart. Next, I provided information and examples on the various types of formatting functions and options available in a PivotChart report. This included chart type selection, 3-D functionality, and Data Table display. I concluded with a real-world example that helped tie together some of the material in this chapter.

Spreadsheet Reporting

Creating and Using Spreadsheet Reports

This chapter is the first of three chapters in Spreadsheet reporting. Here, I show you how to create professional-looking Spreadsheet reports using the powerful tools and functions that are included in Excel 2007. I assume that you have already read over the PivotTable report chapters and have a basic understanding of this technology, because I make some comparisons between these two types of reporting tools.

I start this chapter by providing some perspective on why you might use a Spreadsheet report in place of a PivotTable report. After that, I review all the buttons in each of the five groups of the Table Tools tab, which is only available for Spreadsheet reports. Next, I review how you can filter data in your Spreadsheet report using the numerous types of filter tools that are available with Spreadsheet reports. Following that, I show you how to sort data using the enhanced Sort dialog box in Excel 2007. I also demonstrate how Spreadsheet report columns can be moved and added in the report, and how you can convert the Spreadsheet report into a Range, so that the data can be subtotaled. I conclude with an example that helps tie some of the material in this chapter into a scenario that you might encounter in the real world.

Introducing Spreadsheet Reports

You can use Spreadsheet reports to organize data into the traditional columnar format, as opposed to the cross-tabular format of a PivotTable report. And despite its traditional roots, a columnar report is still quite powerful. You might have heard about or used report development programs such as Business Objects (formerly Crystal

Reports), Microsoft SQL Server Reporting Services, or Microsoft Access Reports. You can use any of these software applications to create cutting-edge reports and business forms from external data sources. Although Excel provides much more powerful functionality in the area of cross-tabular functionality with its PivotTable reports, it does not measure up to the columnar report features available in these other software programs. Nevertheless, Spreadsheet reports include several innovative features and tools that cover the basics and also offer some advanced functionality.

Looking at Some Features of Spreadsheet Reports

Spreadsheet reports let you access data from numerous types of external data sources, including databases, text files, and even web pages. With the exception of web page data sources, Spreadsheet reports use the Microsoft Query program, or the buttons in the Get External Data group, to access external data. Thus, you can import a table or file using the buttons in the Get External Data group (covered in Chapter 4), create a simple SQL query using the graphical tools included in the Query Wizard (covered in Chapter 7), build a more advanced SQL query in the Microsoft Query program (covered in Chapters 8 and 9), or just paste an SQL query created from a query development software application, such as Query Analyzer or SQL Server Management Studio (covered in Chapter 9). And, by using the Web Query dialog box (covered in Chapter 15), you can import specific text and table data into the Spreadsheet report from an Internet or Intranet web page.

Spreadsheet reports also support parameters that enable the report user to specify values that are mapped to conditions in the Where part of an SQL query or to variables in a stored procedure. These parameters can even store default values or reference particular cell values in the Excel workbook. And, if worksheet cells are used, the report can be configured to automatically refresh whenever the value in a referenced cell is modified.

CROSS-REFERENCE Review Chapter 15 to learn more about web queries and parameter queries, and review Chapter 16 to learn more about advanced formatting functions for your Spreadsheet reports.

Other innovative features of Spreadsheet reports include fill-down formulas, conditional formatting, and auto-refreshing. All these functions are covered in greater detail throughout this chapter and the following two chapters.

Comparing Spreadsheet Reports to PivotTable Reports

Consider using a Spreadsheet report in place of a PivotTable report when one or more of the following conditions are met:

- The report data should not be aggregated.
- The report has no numeric fields to summarize.
- The report data needs to be displayed in a columnar format.

Figure 14-1 shows an example of a report with extracted product information from the AdventureWorksDW database. (Note that the SQL query for this report is shown a little later in the "Before You Begin" section of this chapter.) This report includes the business type, the order frequency, the first order year, the number of sales units, and the sales revenue. Icon sets and data bars are also used to enhance the display of report data. Both data and icons are displayed in First Order Yr (the third column from the left in Figure 14-1) and Sales Revenue (the last column on the right in Figure 14-1), whereas only a data bar is shown for Sales Units. You can also see that Sales Revenue is subtotaled for each change in Business Type, whereas Sales Units (another numeric column) is not subtotaled. Additionally, the items in Business Type and Order Frequency are repeated multiple times and are not aggregated into a single unique value like they would be in a PivotTable report.

As you can see in Figure 14-1, the Spreadsheet report displays the dataset in a columnar layout, similar to how the dataset would be presented in the Microsoft Query program (see Chapters 8 and 9 for more information about the Microsoft Query program). Now, look at Figure 14-2, which shows how this same data might appear in a PivotTable.

	Business Type	Order Frequer	First Order Yr	Reseller Name	Sales Units	Sales Revenue
1	**Business Type**	**Order Frequer**	**First Order Yr**	**Reseller Name**	**Sales Units**	**Sales Revenue**
2	Specialty Bike Shop	Annual	2001	World Bike Discount		2,689.18
3	Specialty Bike Shop	Annual	2001	Some Discount Store		41.99
4	Specialty Bike Shop	Annual	2001	Yellow Bicycle Comp		41.99
5	Specialty Bike Shop	Annual	2002	Blue Bicycle Compan		1,530.80
6	Specialty Bike Shop	Annual	2002	Cash & Carry Bikes		1,376.99
7	Specialty Bike Shop	Annual	2003	Fitness Department S		445.41
8	**Specialty Bike Shop Total**					6,126.37
9	Value Added Reseller	Semi-Annual	2001	Modern Bike Store		65.99
10	Value Added Reseller	Semi-Annual	2001	Basic Bike Company		65.99
11	Value Added Reseller	Semi-Annual	2003	Wingtip Toys		209.97
12	Value Added Reseller	Semi-Annual	2003	Second Bike Shop		1,466.01
13	**Value Added Reseller Total**					1,807.96
14	Warehouse	Quarterly	2001	Major Cycling		1,466.01
15	Warehouse	Quarterly	2003	Outdoor Sporting Go		600.16
16	Warehouse	Quarterly	2003	Good Bicycle Store		1,466.01
17	Warehouse	Quarterly	2004	Sensational Discount		323.99
18	**Warehouse Total**					3,856.17
19	**Grand Total**					11,790.49

Figure 14-1: A typical Spreadsheet report displays data in a columnar format without aggregation.

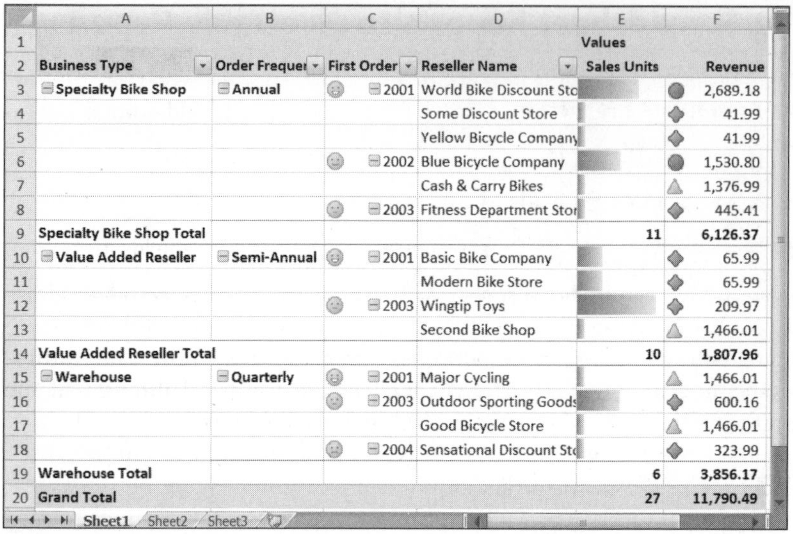

Figure 14-2: PivotTable reports are not suited for a columnar format, but it is possible to show Values area fields across columns rather than down rows.

Notice how the PivotTable report shows only the unique items in Business Type, Order Frequency, and First Order Year. Additionally, the items in the Values area (Sales Units and Revenue) are both subtotaled. Although it is possible to make Sales Units a field in the Row Labels area, it isn't possible to display a non-numeric field after Values area fields. For example, First Order Yr could not be moved after Revenue in the Pivot-Table.

Spreadsheet reports and PivotTable reports have many differences besides just the way the data is organized. Table 14-1 lists some of these differences.

Table 14-1: Differences between Spreadsheet and PivotTable Reports

SPREADSHEET REPORT	PIVOTTABLE REPORT
Organizes data into a columnar format.	Organizes data into a cross-tabular format.
Works only with OLTP data sources.	Works with OLTP and OLAP data sources.
Limited to about one million rows.	Limited only by the client computer's available memory.
Supports parameters that can be mapped to conditions in the `Where` part of an SQL query.	Does not support parameters.
Supports web queries.	Does not support web queries.
Includes Fill Down fields for adding formulas to report data.	Includes Calculated Field and Calculated Items for adding formulas and items to the report.

Table 14-1 *(continued)*

SPREADSHEET REPORT	PIVOTTABLE REPORT
Sorts the dataset by specifying a sort order in the SQL query or a sort order in the Spreadsheet report.	Sorts Items are within each field — not the entire dataset.
Subtotals can be applied to individual fields.	Subtotals are applied to all the fields in the Values area.

Don't worry if you don't understand all these differences right now. The features that pertain to Spreadsheet reports are explained in greater detail throughout the appropriate sections of this chapter as well as the next two chapters.

CROSS-REFERENCE Refer to Chapters 10–12 if you need more information on the features included with PivotTable reports.

Before You Begin

All the examples in this chapter, including the "Trying It Out in the Real World" exercise, utilize the SQL query and Spreadsheet report outlined in this section. If you plan to follow along with the material and examples throughout this chapter, I recommend that you start by creating this Spreadsheet report that accesses the Adventure-WorksDW database.

Complete these steps to create the PivotTable report and then follow along with the examples used throughout this chapter:

1. From Excel, choose Data → From Other Sources → From Microsoft Query to bring up the Choose Data Source dialog box.

2. When the Choose Data Source dialog box appears, verify that Use the Query Wizard to Create/Edit Queries is unchecked, select the AdventureWorks Data Warehouse data source, and click OK.

3. When the Microsoft Query program is launched, you are presented with the Add Tables dialog box. Close this dialog box, and then click the SQL button.

4. Paste or type the following query into the SQL dialog box and click OK:

```
SELECT res1.BusinessType                        AS [Business Type],
       CASE OrderFrequency
         WHEN 'A' THEN 'Annual'
         WHEN 'S' THEN 'Semi-Annual'
         WHEN 'Q' THEN 'Quarterly'
               ELSE 'Other'
               END                              AS [Order Frequency],
```

```
         res1.FirstOrderYear                          AS [First Order Yr],
         res1.ResellerName                            AS [Reseller Name],
      (SELECT SUM(OrderQuantity)
         FROM FactResellerSales fact
   INNER JOIN DimTime dtme ON fact.ShipDateKey = TimeKey
      WHERE fact.ResellerKey = res1.ResellerKey
        AND dtme.CalendarYear = '2004')               AS [Sales Units],
      (SELECT SUM(SalesAmount)
         FROM FactResellerSales fact
   INNER JOIN DimTime dtme ON fact.ShipDateKey = TimeKey
      WHERE fact.ResellerKey = res1.ResellerKey
        AND dtme.CalendarYear = '2004')               AS [Sales Revenue]
FROM DimReseller res1
WHERE res1.LastOrderYear = '2004'
  AND res1.AnnualRevenue >= 50000
  AND res1.OrderMonth IN (1,2,3)
```

ON THE WEB   You can download the **ch14_example1.txt query file to your computer from the companion web site at** www.wiley.com/go/ excelreporting/2007. **Look for this document in either the Chap14.zip file or Chap14 directory, depending on which .zip file you download.**

5. Click OK to acknowledge that the query cannot be displayed graphically.

6. Click the Return Data to Microsoft Excel button to return the data to Excel and continue.

7. When the Import Data dialog box appears (see Figure 14-3), choose Table and click OK to create the Spreadsheet report.

8. Verify that your Spreadsheet report looks like Figure 14-4.

Figure 14-3: Choose Table from the Import Data dialog box to create a Spreadsheet report.

	A	B	C	D	E	F
1	Business Type	Order Frequ	First Or	Reseller Name	Sales U	Sales Reven
2	Specialty Bike Shop	Annual	2003	Fitness Department Stores	1	445.41
3	Warehouse	Quarterly	2004	Sensational Discount Store	1	323.994
4	Value Added Reseller	Semi-Annual	2003	Wingtip Toys	5	209.97
5	Warehouse	Quarterly	2003	Outdoor Sporting Goods	3	600.156
6	Value Added Reseller	Semi-Annual	2003	Second Bike Shop	1	1466.01
7	Specialty Bike Shop	Annual	2001	World Bike Discount Store	4	2689.176
8	Specialty Bike Shop	Annual	2002	Blue Bicycle Company	3	1530.798
9	Specialty Bike Shop	Annual	2001	Some Discount Store	1	41.994
10	Specialty Bike Shop	Annual	2001	Yellow Bicycle Company	1	41.994
11	Warehouse	Quarterly	2003	Good Bicycle Store	1	1466.01
12	Value Added Reseller	Semi-Annual	2001	Modern Bike Store	2	65.988
13	Warehouse	Quarterly	2001	Major Cycling	1	1466.01
14	Specialty Bike Shop	Annual	2002	Cash & Carry Bikes	1	1376.994
15	Value Added Reseller	Semi-Annual	2001	Basic Bike Company	2	65.988

Sheet1 Sheet2 Sheet3

Figure 14-4: Your Spreadsheet report should now appear as shown here.

Working with the Table Tools Tab

The Table Tools tab (see Figure 14-5) provides many powerful tools for managing Spreadsheet report operations. Included in this component are several functions that are not available on any other report components, such as toggling display options and summarizing the data into a PivotTable. Of course, many of the functions in the Table Tools tab are also available in one or more report components. Thus, for example, you can often choose from a few different methods for refreshing the data, accessing the connection properties, and converting the Spreadsheet report to a range.

The Table Tools tab is only available when a Spreadsheet report exists and is selected in the workbook. You can access this toolbar by clicking the Table Tools button above the Design tab in the Excel workbook (see Figure 14-6).

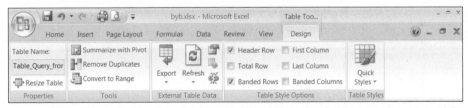

Figure 14-5: There are numerous buttons in the Table Tools tab for managing external data and formatting options for your Spreadsheet report.

Click this tab

Figure 14-6: The Table Tools tab only appears when a Spreadsheet report is selected. Click it to access the Tables Tool tab shown in Figure 14-5.

Looking at Groups in the Table Tools Tab

The various buttons for managing Spreadsheet report operations are organized into five groups under the Table Tools tab. These groups, along with a brief description of the functions, are summarized here:

- **Properties:** Setting the name of the Spreadsheet report and defining the report boundaries.

- **Tools:** Summarizing the report into a PivotTable, removing duplicate rows in the report, and converting the report to a range.

- **External Table Data:** Managing external data, including data refreshes, connection properties, exporting, and unlinking.

- **Table Style Options:** Toggling display options for first and last columns, header rows, total rows, banded rows, and banded columns.

- **Table Styles:** Applying a template table style to the Spreadsheet report.

The arrangement and the display width of the five groups of the Table Tools tab cannot be individually sized or arranged in a different order. And, depending on your display configuration (that is, pixel resolution and Excel window size), some of the toolbar groups may automatically be collapsed into smaller groups. Lower display settings provide a single-button shortcut to the full suite of buttons and available functions that are accessible in some of the collapsed PivotTable groups. Shrinking the screen size has a similar effect. I found that a 1600 x 1200 display setting is an easy way to fully display seven template styles in a row, under the Table Styles group.

Properties Group

The Properties group provides a field where you can enter the name of the Spreadsheet report and a Resize Table button that you can use for setting the report boundaries. As you can see from Figure 14-7, you can simply type in the name of your report right under the Table Name label.

If you have multiple reports in your workbook, it's a good idea to name each report. This enables you to readily associate connections with report names. These report names can also be helpful if you are creating macros or Visual Basic for Applications (VBA) code in the Excel workbook that reference these reports.

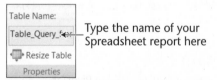

Figure 14-7: The Properties group enables you to name the Spreadsheet report and define the report range.

The Resize Table button enables you to define the boundaries for the Spreadsheet report. Using this button, you can remove or add columns from your Spreadsheet report. You can also add or remove rows from the report, although if you are working with external data sources, the boundary limits are not held as new rows become available.

Tools Group

The Tools group (see Figure 14-8) includes three buttons for summarizing the Spreadsheet report data into a PivotTable report, removing duplicate rows, and converting the Spreadsheet report into a range.

Summarize with Pivot

The Summarize with Pivot button enables you to create a PivotTable report from the Spreadsheet report data. When you click this button, the Create PivotTable dialog box appears with the Spreadsheet report table range input into the Table/Range field. This button can be useful if you need a one-time analysis of the data in a cross-tabular format.

CROSS-REFERENCE Read Chapter 2 for more information about the Create PivotTable dialog box and how a PivotTable report is linked to a data source within the Excel workbook.

Remove Duplicates

The Remove Duplicates button can be used to remove duplicate rows from the Spreadsheet report. A nice feature of this tool is that you can define which report fields constitute a duplicate. For example, you can specify all the columns in the report or choose a particular subset of the columns.

In addition to just removing duplicate rows, the Remove Duplicates button can be useful if you want to quickly view the unique items that comprise a certain column or a combination of columns. For example, you could quickly obtain a list of the unique business types, order frequency, and first order years for the Spreadsheet report example in Figure 14-4.

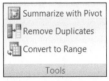

Figure 14-8: The Tools group includes tools for summarizing data into a PivotTable report, removing duplicates, and converting the Spreadsheet report into a Range.

To see how this works, start with the Spreadsheet report in Figure 14-4 and follow these steps:

1. Click the Spreadsheet report to select it and choose Table Tools → Remove Duplicates to bring up the Remove Duplicates dialog box (see Figure 14-9).

2. Uncheck Reseller Name, Sales Units, and Sales Revenue. Verify that the Remove Duplicates dialog box looks like Figure 14-9 and click OK.

3. When the Microsoft Office Excel dialog box appears with the message "6 Duplicate Values Found and Removed; 8 Unique Items Remain," click OK to acknowledge the message and close the dialog box.

4. Verify that the duplicate entries have been removed from your Spreadsheet report.

Convert to Range

The Convert to Range button transforms the Spreadsheet report into regular worksheet data. If the report was connected to an external data source, it is unlinked and the connection information is purged. The filter drop-down fields are also removed, and access to the Table Tools tab is no longer available from the report.

You may want to convert the Spreadsheet report into a Range for the following reasons:

■ You're sending the report to another individual or external party and you do not want to save the connection information along with the report.

■ You want to subtotal the data in the report.

WARNING Once a Spreadsheet report is converted to a Range, you cannot use the Undo function to reverse the transformation. The only way to restore the worksheet data back to a Spreadsheet is to re-create the Spreadsheet report or to restore the report from a saved backup file.

Figure 14-9: Use the Remove Duplicates dialog box to specify what columns in the Spreadsheet report constitute a duplicate entry.

External Table Data Group

The External Table Data group (see Figure 14-10) has five buttons for exporting data, refreshing data, setting connection properties, opening in a browser, and unlinking the data from an external data source.

The Export button includes two items under its drop-down arrow for exporting the Spreadsheet report to a SharePoint List and exporting the Spreadsheet report to a Visio PivotDiagram.

The Refresh drop-down button has five items that enable you to (1) refresh the selected Spreadsheet report (Refresh), (2) refresh all reports in the workbook including any PivotTable reports (Refresh All), (3) monitor the progress of refresh operations (Refresh Status), (4) cancel the current report refresh operation (Cancel Refresh), and (5) bring up the Connection Properties dialog box (Connection Properties).

The Properties button brings up the Connection Properties dialog box. This is the same dialog box that appears from choosing Refresh → Connection Properties. From the Connection Properties dialog box, you can configure options for refreshing data and view or modify both the SQL query and the connection string to the report's external data source. I cover this dialog box in more detail in Chapter 15.

The Open in Browser button enables you to view the Spreadsheet report in a browser program, although the report must be first published to a SharePoint server.

Clicking the Unlink button purges the connection information from the Spreadsheet report, but maintains the dataset as a Spreadsheet report and not a Range (see the previous section on the distinction between a Range and a Spreadsheet report). Clicking the Properties button brings up the External Data Properties dialog box (covered in Chapter 16).

Table Style Options Group

There are six buttons in the Table Style Options group (see Figure 14-11) that are mainly used for report formatting; the exceptions are the Header Row and Total Row options, which toggle whether the field header and grand total rows are displayed.

Figure 14-10: The External Table Data group includes several buttons for managing external data source connections.

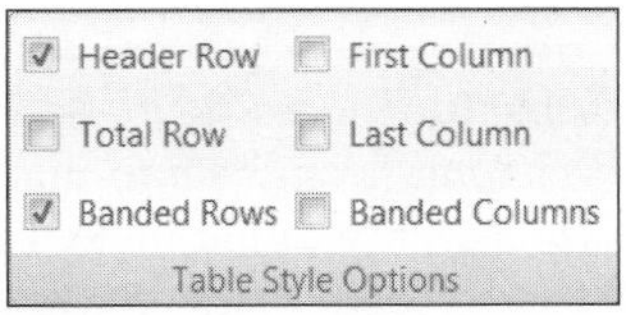

☑ Header Row	☐ First Column
☐ Total Row	☐ Last Column
☑ Banded Rows	☐ Banded Columns
Table Style Options	

Figure 14-11: Apply formatting options and toggle the header and total rows for a Spreadsheet report from this group.

Figure 14-12: You can apply a predefined style to your Spreadsheet report from this group.

The Banded Rows and Banded Columns options toggle whether alternating rows or columns are displayed in a single color band or dual-color bands. The two colors in the band vary based on the table style selected from the Table Styles group. The First Column and Last Column also include formatting options, such that the first or last column could be a different color or font style.

Table Styles Group

The Table Styles group (see Figure 14-12) includes numerous Table style templates from which you can select for your Spreadsheet report. You can also create your own Table Styles and make them available for future reports. This can be useful if you have a particular preference for formatting your Spreadsheet reports using specific fonts, font styles, borders, font colors, background color, and fill effects. There are also several components of the Spreadsheet report that can be formatted, including the headers, first and second rows (row banding), first and second columns (column banding), the total row, and the table frame.

Filtering Data in a Spreadsheet Report

Several types of filtering tools are available in Spreadsheet reports. You can filter data by manually checking or unchecking items in the field drop-down list. You can also use more advanced filtering tools for fields with hundreds or thousands of unique items; instead of checking or unchecking items, you can choose up to two numeric, text, or date operators per field to specify what rows to display in the report. You can also filter report data based on a selected cell value, cell background color, font color, or icon.

Understanding How Spreadsheet Report Filters Work

The filter drop-down arrows are automatically enabled when a new Spreadsheet report is first created. You can toggle the display of these filter field drop-down arrows by clicking anywhere in the Spreadsheet report and choosing Data → Filter.

Clicking a drop-down arrow on one of the fields in the Spreadsheet report displays the drop-down menu shown in Figure 14-13. This drop-down menu is organized into three sections. In the first section, there are three types of sorting functions (see the section on "Sorting Data in a Spreadsheet Report" later in this chapter for more information about sorting data). The second section provides access to advanced filtering tools and a menu item for removing the filter on a selected field. The third and last section displays all the unique items in the field. Each of these items can be manually selected or deselected to filter data in the Spreadsheet report. Checking the Select All item selects all of the items in the field and unchecking Select All deselects all of the items in the field.

Depending on the type of data in the selected field, you will see Text Filters, Number Filters, or Date Filters in the second section of Figure 14-13. Clicking this menu item brings up another submenu, where you can choose from a list of operators to use for the report filter. The list of available operators is different for each data type.

CROSS-REFERENCE Review Chapter 10 for a complete list of Filter operators for fields with a data type of text, number, and date.

Right-clicking any cell in the Spreadsheet report and choosing Filter from the pop-up menu brings up another submenu of filter choices (see Figure 14-14), where you can apply a filter based on that selected cell's value, background color, font color, or icon.

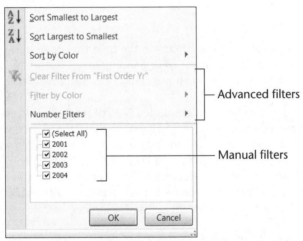

Figure 14-13: Clicking a drop-down arrow in a Spreadsheet report field header shows this menu, which enables you to sort and filter data.

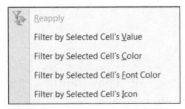

Figure 14-14: Right-click any cell in the Spreadsheet report and choose Filter to bring up this submenu of filter choices.

Examining Advanced Filtering Tools

The advanced filters shown in Figure 14-13 provide more sophisticated filtering capabilities. Using these types of filters, you can choose to select items based on some type of text, number, or date criteria. This kind of filter is more sophisticated than a manual filter, which only enables items in the drop-down list to be manually selected or deselected. Imagine how long that could take if you had several thousand unique items and you only wanted to display a few hundred items, scattered liberally throughout the item list. It could take you hours to apply the filter. In contrast, the advanced filter tools provide a more robust filtering capability that is delivered through a straightforward and easy-to-use dialog box. Using this type of filter, you can select from an extensive list of operators for choosing which items should be selected.

There are four types of advanced filters that you could see in the advanced filter section (see Figure 14-13):

- Color filters
- Text filters
- Number filters
- Date filters

The color filters are only enabled when there are items in the field that have more than one background or font color. Keep in mind that color banding is not considered a color for this type of filter; only cells that have been manually or conditionally colored are selectable for this kind of filter.

Depending on the type of data that you have in the selected field of the Spreadsheet report, you'll see Text Filter, Number Filter, or Date Filter in the drop-down menu. In the case of fields that have items with mixed data types (for example, 30 percent of items with a data type of Date and 70 percent of items with a data type of Text), the data type with the majority of items will appear in the drop-down list. And in the case of fields that have items with the same number of data types (for example, 50 percent text and 50 percent numeric), the hierarchy of data type assignment is Text → Number → Date.

WARNING If you want to maintain the filter settings for the Spreadsheet report, be sure that the Preserve Column Sort/Filter/Layout option is checked; otherwise the filter settings are removed when the Spreadsheet report is refreshed.

Applying Advanced Filters

You can apply an advanced filter to a field by left-clicking a drop-down arrow in the field header section of the Spreadsheet report and choosing Text Filters from the drop-down menu (note that Text Filters will be replaced with Date Filters or Number Filters if the field data type is date or numeric). However, regardless of the data type, each filter submenu has the Custom Filter item displayed at the bottom of this list.

Selecting this menu item brings up the Custom AutoFilter dialog box. I selected Filter → Custom Filter from Reseller Name to bring up the Custom AutoFilter dialog box in Figure 14-15. Here, you can specify up to two conditions for the filter. These conditions include a drop-down list of string, mathematical, or date operators on the left side of the dialog box, and a filter value on the right side of the dialog box. Clicking the Filter Value drop-down arrow reveals a list of unique items for the field. If you specify a second condition, it can be linked with an And or an Or operator.

To apply a filter and continue working along with the example, start with the original Spreadsheet report from the beginning of this chapter (see Figure 14-4) and follow these steps:

1. Click the Reseller Name drop-down arrow in cell D1 of the Spreadsheet report and choose Text Filters → Custom Filter to bring up the Custom AutoFilter dialog box.

2. Select Contains from the Filter Operator field and type **Bike** in the Filter Value field. Click Or and then select Contains in the second Filter Operator field and type **Bicycle** in the second Filter Operator field.

3. Verify that your Custom AutoFilter dialog box looks like Figure 14-16 and click OK to apply the filter and close the dialog box.

Filter Operator Field   Filter Value Field

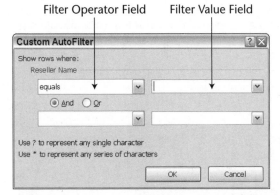

Figure 14-15: You can specify up to two conditions in the Custom AutoFilter drop-down box.

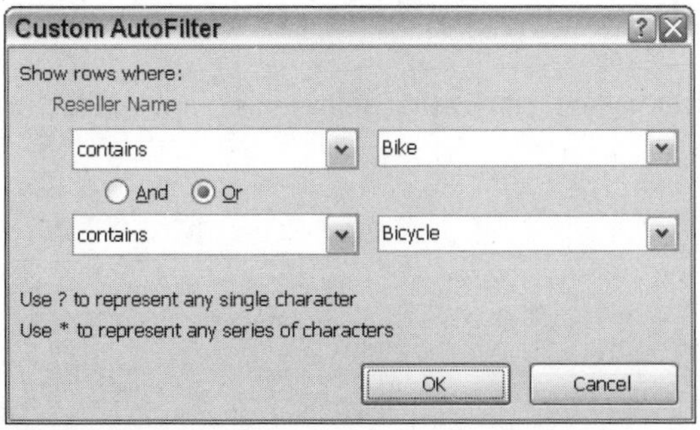

Figure 14-16: This filter selects all the rows that have Bike or Bicycle anywhere in Reseller Name.

4. Verify that only the rows with Bike or Bicycle in Reseller Name appear in the Spreadsheet report. Also notice that the row numbers in the Spreadsheet report are in a bolded blue font and that a filter icon appears in the Reseller Name field, as shown in Figure 14-17.

I already covered the various types of filter operators for text, numeric, and date fields extensively in Chapter 10. Review this chapter for more information about field operators and how they can be used to filter data in your report.

Filtering for Top n and Bottom n

You can apply a Top *n* or Bottom *n* filter by clicking a drop-down arrow in a report heading cell in the Spreadsheet report and choosing Number Filters → Top 10 from the pop-up menu. This brings up the Top 10 Filter dialog box where you can choose to display only the Top *n* or Bottom *n* items, percent, or sum of items (note that *n* denotes a number that you specify).

Filtering for Above and Below Average Items

You can apply a filter that shows only the rows that are above or below the average value of a selected column. This type of filter is applied by choosing Number Filters → Above Average (shows the rows that have an above-average value in the selected column) or Number Filters → Below Average (shows the rows that have a below-average value in the selected column).

Row numbers are skipped
and shown in a blue font

Filter icon indicates
that field has a filter on it

	A	B	C	D	E	F
1	Business Type	Order Frequ	First Or	Reseller Name	Sales U	Sales Reven
6	Value Added Reseller	Semi-Annual	2003	Second Bike Shop	1	1466.01
7	Specialty Bike Shop	Annual	2001	World Bike Discount Store	4	2689.176
8	Specialty Bike Shop	Annual	2002	Blue Bicycle Company	3	1530.798
10	Specialty Bike Shop	Annual	2001	Yellow Bicycle Company	1	41.994
11	Warehouse	Quarterly	2003	Good Bicycle Store	1	1466.01
12	Value Added Reseller	Semi-Annual	2001	Modern Bike Store	2	65.988
14	Specialty Bike Shop	Annual	2002	Cash & Carry Bikes	1	1376.994
15	Value Added Reseller	Semi-Annual	2001	Basic Bike Company	2	65.988

Figure 14-17: Row and field header indicators help signify that a filter has been applied to the Spreadsheet report.

Other Advanced Filtering Options

Don't forget that you can also create more advanced filters by customizing the Where part of the SQL query if you are accessing a database for your Spreadsheet report. And if the filters need to be interactive, you can use a parameter query to map user-input values to variables in the Where part of an SQL query or stored procedure.

CROSS-REFERENCE The various types of filter operators for text, numeric, and date data are fully described in Chapter 10 of this book. Using the Where clause to filter data is covered in Chapters 7–9. Parameter queries, used for interactive filtering, are covered in Chapter 15.

Filtering By Selection

Most of the filters that I have shown up to this point require that you either open a dialog box or navigate through a drop-down field list. These additional steps can make the process of filtering data more difficult when you're rapidly trying to select or deselect items in the Spreadsheet report. Routing through drop-down menus and dialog boxes can break your concentration and cause you to spend more time on applying filters than you'd like. Here's when Filtering By Selection can come in handy.

Filtering By Selection enables you to keep only the selected rows by selecting a cell in the Spreadsheet report. This filtering method provides a more rapid means for restricting data than navigating through drop-down lists, dialog boxes, and pop-up menus.

To see how Filtering By Selection works, start with the Spreadsheet report in Figure 14-4 and follow these steps:

1. Right-click 2003 in cell C5 of the Spreadsheet report and choose Filter → Filter By Selected Cell's Value.

2. Verify that only the items with First Start Year of 2003 are shown in the Spreadsheet report.

There are also tools for filtering by the selected cell's font color, background color, or icon (note that icons are covered in Chapter 16). Note that color banded cells are not selectable for this type of filter; cells must have a manual or conditional format applied in order for them to be selectable.

Viewing Applied Filters

Besides just seeing the filter icon next to fields in the Spreadsheet report, you can also view the filter details that have been applied to a field by moving your mouse pointer over the filter icon field. In Figure 14-18, you can see that only the items with 2003 under First Order Year are being selected.

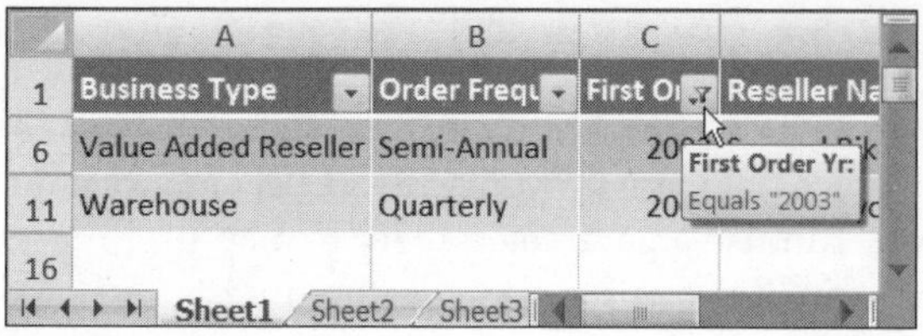

Figure 14-18: Drag your mouse on top of a filter icon to see what filter is being applied to the report field.

Clearing Filters

There are two options for clearing filters in a Spreadsheet report. The first option is to clear the filter on one field and the second option is to clear all the filters for all the fields in the Spreadsheet report. If you only want to clear a filter on a single field, click the drop-down arrow of the field header being filtered and choose Clear Filter From <Field Name> from the drop-down menu. If you want to clear the filters on all the fields in the Spreadsheet report, choose Data → Filter.

WARNING Choosing Data → Filter clears all of the report filters and removes the drop-down arrows next to each field. You might think that clicking this filter icon a second time would not only toggle the drop-down arrows to be displayed, but also restore the previous filter settings. However, that's not the case; though the drop-down arrows are displayed again, the previous filter settings are permanently removed.

Sorting Data in a Spreadsheet Report

In a Spreadsheet report, you can either specify the sort order in the SQL query (before the dataset is returned to Excel), or you can specify the sort order in the Spreadsheet report (after the dataset is returned to Excel). Specifying the sort order in the SQL query increases the time it takes to run the query, but results in faster overall processing time than sorting the data on the client computer running Excel. I recommend sorting the dataset in the query for a standard Spreadsheet report view, and then using the Sort features in Excel to apply additional interactive sorts as necessary.

After the data is in Excel, you can sort the data by selecting a field heading and clicking the A → Z or Z → A sort buttons under the Data tab (similar menu items also appear in the first section of each field header drop-down menu).

You can access more advanced sorts by clicking anywhere on the Spreadsheet report and choosing Data → Sort to bring up the Sort dialog box shown in Figure 14-19.

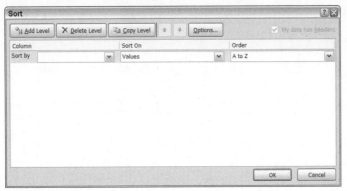

Figure 14-19: You can add multiple levels of advanced sorting instructions for your Spreadsheet report from this dialog box.

TIP The Sort dialog box enables you to specify up to 32 sorting levels.

In addition to sorting on field values, you can also sort on a font color, cell color, or icon. The sorting can be done in an ascending or descending order — and you can even create a custom list for more advanced sorting that does not follow an alphabetic or numerical rule.

WARNING If you want to maintain the sort order settings for the Spreadsheet report, be sure that the Preserve Column Sort/Filter/Layout option is checked in the External Data Properties dialog box, otherwise the sort order settings are lost when the Spreadsheet report is refreshed. Note that you can bring up the External Data Properties dialog box by clicking the Spreadsheet report and choosing Table Tools → Properties (see Chapter 16 for more detailed coverage of this dialog box).

To apply a sort order and continue working along with the example, follow these steps:

1. Starting with the Spreadsheet report in Figure 14-4, click anywhere on the report and choose Data → Sort to bring up the Sort dialog box.

2. Choose Order Frequency from the Sort By field, Values from Sort On field, and Custom List from the Order field.

3. When the Custom Lists dialog box appears, click in the List Entries pane and type **Quarterly** and then press Enter. Next, type **Annual**, press Enter, and then type **Semi-Annual**. Click Add and verify that your Custom Lists dialog box looks like Figure 14-20.

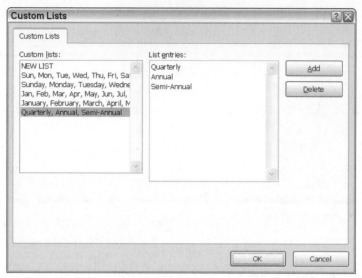

Figure 14-20: The Custom Lists dialog box enables you to add your own custom sort orders.

4. Click OK to close the Custom Lists dialog box and return to the Sort dialog box.

5. Click the Add Level button in the Sort dialog box to add another sorting level.

6. Select Sales Revenue from Then By, Values from Sort On, and Largest to Smallest from Order.

7. Verify that your Sort dialog box looks like Figure 14-21, and click OK to apply the sort and close the dialog box.

8. Verify that sort icons have been added next to the Order Frequency and Sales Revenue field headers and that the data has been sorted in the Spreadsheet reports, as shown in Figure 14-22.

Figure 14-21: Specify up to 32 levels of sorting instructions from this dialog box.

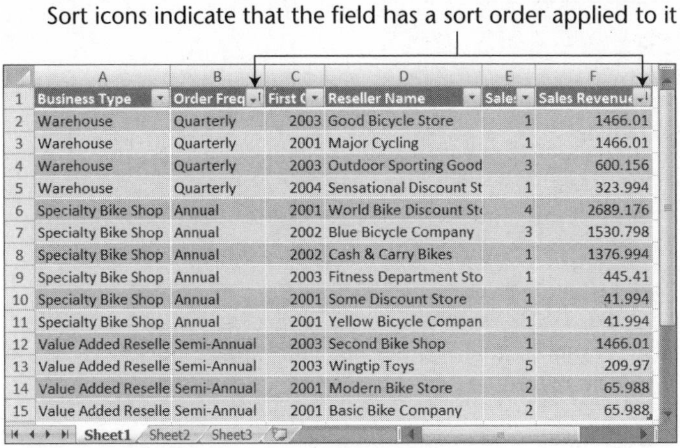
Sort icons indicate that the field has a sort order applied to it

	A	B	C	D	E	F
1	Business Type	Order Freq	First (	Reseller Name	Sale	Sales Revenue
2	Warehouse	Quarterly	2003	Good Bicycle Store	1	1466.01
3	Warehouse	Quarterly	2001	Major Cycling	1	1466.01
4	Warehouse	Quarterly	2003	Outdoor Sporting Good	3	600.156
5	Warehouse	Quarterly	2004	Sensational Discount St	1	323.994
6	Specialty Bike Shop	Annual	2001	World Bike Discount St	4	2689.176
7	Specialty Bike Shop	Annual	2002	Blue Bicycle Company	3	1530.798
8	Specialty Bike Shop	Annual	2002	Cash & Carry Bikes	1	1376.994
9	Specialty Bike Shop	Annual	2003	Fitness Department Sto	1	445.41
10	Specialty Bike Shop	Annual	2001	Some Discount Store	1	41.994
11	Specialty Bike Shop	Annual	2001	Yellow Bicycle Compan	1	41.994
12	Value Added Reselle	Semi-Annual	2003	Second Bike Shop	1	1466.01
13	Value Added Reselle	Semi-Annual	2003	Wingtip Toys	5	209.97
14	Value Added Reselle	Semi-Annual	2001	Modern Bike Store	2	65.988
15	Value Added Reselle	Semi-Annual	2001	Basic Bike Company	2	65.988

Sheet1 Sheet2 Sheet3

Figure 14-22: The Spreadsheet report first uses a custom sort under Order Frequency and then a descending sort under Sales Revenue.

Moving Spreadsheet Report Columns

When you first create a Spreadsheet report, the columns are displayed in the same order in which they are listed in the SQL query. Although it's possible to modify the query to change the column location, this only works when the report user has the technical capability and security privileges.

The best method for changing the column location is to cut and insert the report column. If you do not have any logos or report titles in the Spreadsheet report, just select the entire column, right-click it, and choose Cut from the pop-up menu, and then right-click the column where you want to paste the cut column and choose Insert Cut Cells from the pop-up menu. This inserts the cut column into the selected column.

To see how this works, try moving Order Frequency before Business Type in the Spreadsheet report from the "Before You Begin" section. To move Order Frequency before Business Type, complete these steps:

1. Starting with the Spreadsheet report in Figure 14-4, click the B column to select the entire Order Frequency column, right-click the highlighted area, and choose Cut from the pop-up menu. You should see a blinking dashed border around column B.
2. Right-click the A column to select the entire Business Type column and choose Insert Cut Cells from the pop-up menu to move Order Frequency before Business Type.
3. Verify that your Spreadsheet report looks like Figure 14-23.

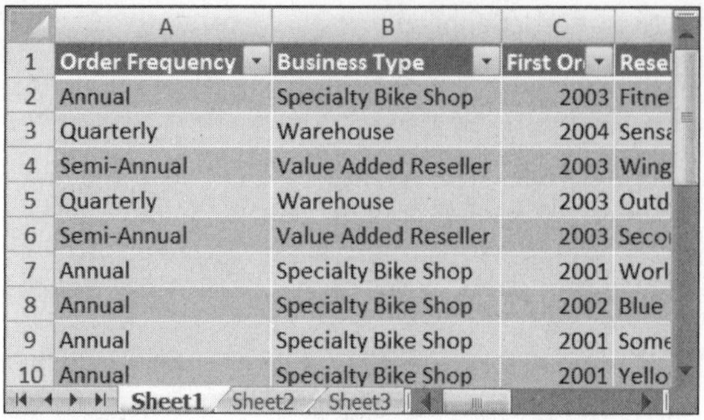

	A	B	C	
1	Order Frequency	Business Type	First Or	Resel
2	Annual	Specialty Bike Shop	2003	Fitne
3	Quarterly	Warehouse	2004	Sensa
4	Semi-Annual	Value Added Reseller	2003	Wing
5	Quarterly	Warehouse	2003	Outd
6	Semi-Annual	Value Added Reseller	2003	Seco
7	Annual	Specialty Bike Shop	2001	Worl
8	Annual	Specialty Bike Shop	2002	Blue
9	Annual	Specialty Bike Shop	2001	Some
10	Annual	Specialty Bike Shop	2001	Yello

Figure 14-23: In a Spreadsheet report, columns are cut and pasted, not dragged and dropped as they are in a PivotTable report.

Creating Fill-Down Formulas

Spreadsheet reports can use formula fields just like any Excel worksheet. The difference with Spreadsheet reports is that the formula can also be automatically filled down when the report is refreshed. This is akin to adding a Calculated Field in a PivotTable report. Essentially, the new formula field is automatically filled-down as it is also integrated as a new column in the Spreadsheet report.

To see how this works, start with the Spreadsheet report in Figure 14-4 and follow these steps:

1. Next to the Sales Revenue header, type **Net Profit** in cell G1 and press Enter. Notice that the new field is automatically integrated into the Excel report.
2. Type = **F2*0.45** in cell G2 and press Enter to calculate Net Profit as 45 percent of sales revenue. Notice that the cell formula is automatically copied down the column, as shown in Figure 14-24.

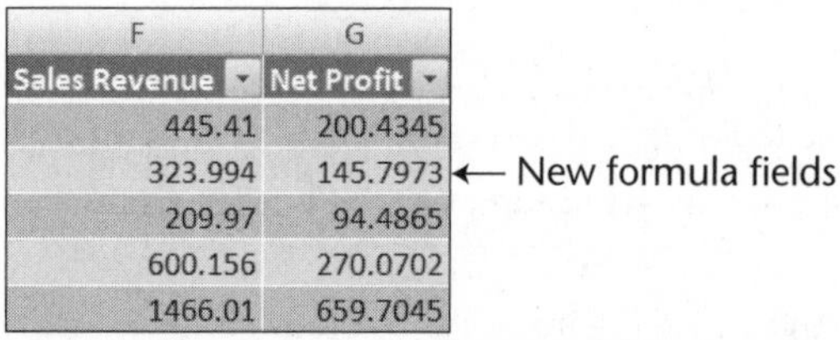

F	G
Sales Revenue	Net Profit
445.41	200.4345
323.994	145.7973
209.97	94.4865
600.156	270.0702
1466.01	659.7045

Figure 14-24: Formulas are automatically copied down the column for each row in the Spreadsheet report.

This feature is useful when the report user is not able to modify the underlying SQL query or when calculating the formula in the SQL query is not practical. An example of this situation is when the referenced column values are derived from complex, high-cost (that is, extensive CPU processing time) fields in the SQL query.

Calculating Subtotals

In earlier versions of Excel, subtotals could be calculated in a Spreadsheet report. However, there was a *slight* problem with the subtotal feature; each time the Spreadsheet report was refreshed, the subtotals were removed. Thus, the report user had to manually redefine the subtotals in order to get them back into the report. Unfortunately, instead of addressing the subtotaling shortcomings, Microsoft simply removed this feature for Spreadsheet reports in Excel 2007. Now, the only way to subtotal data your data is to first convert the Spreadsheet report into a Range, which is essentially a Spreadsheet report without an external data source connection. So, if you are trying to write a Spreadsheet report that subtotals data and relies on a connection to an external data source, you might try designing the report in a PivotTable or using SQL Server Reporting Services, Microsoft Access Reports, or Business Objects.

You can convert a Spreadsheet report to a range by clicking the PivotTable report and choosing Table Tools → Convert to Range. If you prefer using the right-click pop-up menu, you can choose Table → Convert to Range. Keep in mind that once the data is converted to a range, it can no longer be automatically refreshed from the external data source. (There is also no undo function for this action, so be sure to save a copy of your Spreadsheet report if you need to access it later.)

Applying Subtotals

Unlike PivotTable reports, where all of the fields in the Values area are subtotaled, you can choose which columns to subtotal in a Spreadsheet report. The subtotal calculation supports many functions, such as Count, Average, Min, Max, Sum, Product, Standard Deviation, and Variance. There are also options for adding page breaks between groups and displaying the subtotal at the bottom or the top of each group.

> **TIP** Before you apply a subtotal, you should verify that the data in the Range is properly grouped by sorting the data in the appropriate order. I also recommend that you arrange the report so that all the numeric columns are displayed on the right-most side of the report.

Starting with the Spreadsheet report in Figure 14-4, complete these steps to subtotal Sales Revenue by First Order Year:

1. Right-click the Spreadsheet report and choose Table → Convert to Range to convert the Spreadsheet report to a range. When the Microsoft Excel warning dialog box appears, click OK to acknowledge that query definition will be removed from the Spreadsheet report.

2. Click any cell in the first row of the Range and choose Data → Filter to define the first row as field headers and add drop-down boxes to each column heading.

3. Click the First Order Yr heading in cell C1 and click the A → Z button in the Sort & Filter group, under the Data tab.

4. Click Subtotal in the Outline tab to bring up the Subtotal dialog box. Choose First Order Yr for At Each Change In. Leave Sum in Use Function and Sales Revenue as checked. Verify that your Subtotal dialog box looks like Figure 14-25 and click OK to add the subtotals and close the Subtotal dialog box.

NOTE When the Subtotal dialog box is launched, the right-most numeric column in the Spreadsheet report is automatically checked for subtotaling.

In Figure 14-25, the check mark next to Replace Current Subtotals removes any current group subtotals and replaces them with the ones specified in this dialog box. You can check the Page Break Between Groups option to automatically insert page breaks after each group. Checking the Summary Below Data option toggles the display of subtotals at the end of each group. If this option is unchecked, subtotals are displayed at the start of each new group. Clicking the Remove All button removes all subtotal calculations for the group.

5. Verify that your Spreadsheet report looks like Figure 14-26.

Figure 14-25: Use this dialog box to subtotal data in a Spreadsheet report.

1 2 3		A	B	C	D	E	F
	1	Business Type	Order Freq	First Or	Reseller Name	Sales	Sales Rever
	2	Specialty Bike Shop	Annual	2001	World Bike Discount Sto	4	2689.176
	3	Specialty Bike Shop	Annual	2001	Some Discount Store	1	41.994
	4	Specialty Bike Shop	Annual	2001	Yellow Bicycle Company	1	41.994
	5	Value Added Reselle	Semi-Annual	2001	Modern Bike Store	2	65.988
	6	Warehouse	Quarterly	2001	Major Cycling	1	1466.01
	7	Value Added Reselle	Semi-Annual	2001	Basic Bike Company	2	65.988
	8			**2001 Total**			4371.15
	9	Specialty Bike Shop	Annual	2002	Blue Bicycle Company	3	1530.798
	10	Specialty Bike Shop	Annual	2002	Cash & Carry Bikes	1	1376.994
	11			**2002 Total**			2907.792
	12	Specialty Bike Shop	Annual	2003	Fitness Department Stor	1	445.41
	13	Value Added Reselle	Semi-Annual	2003	Wingtip Toys	5	209.97
	14	Warehouse	Quarterly	2003	Outdoor Sporting Goods	3	600.156
	15	Value Added Reselle	Semi-Annual	2003	Second Bike Shop	1	1466.01
	16	Warehouse	Quarterly	2003	Good Bicycle Store	1	1466.01
	17			**2003 Total**			4187.556

Sheet1 Sheet2 Sheet3

Figure 14-26: Adding a subtotal automatically groups the items and calculates the subtotal function (or functions) selected in the Subtotal dialog box.

After a subtotal is applied, the data is automatically grouped. The group tree appears in the Group pane (left-most section) of the Spreadsheet report, and includes nodes to show (+) or hide (–) the data in each group. If you uncheck the Summary Below Data option (refer to Figure 14-25), the nodes appear at the top of each group instead of at the bottom of each group, as shown in Figure 14-26. Clicking the 1, 2, or 3 icons displayed at the top of the Group pane shows just the report grand totals (1), the report subtotals and grand totals (2), or all of the detail in the Spreadsheet report (3).

Removing Subtotals

Once subtotals are applied, you can remove them by clicking anywhere in the Spreadsheet report to select it, and then choosing Data → Subtotal to bring up the Subtotal dialog box. Once the Subtotal dialog box appears, just click the Remove All button to remove the report subtotals and close the dialog box.

Trying It Out in the Real World

Jill Williams, a marketing specialist at AdventureWorks, is planning to launch a new targeted marketing campaign for resellers of AdventureWorks products. Jill has requested that you provide her with a list of resellers who have annual revenues of at least $50,000, a last order year of 2004, and a reorder period in the first quarter of the year. This report should include information about the reseller's name, business type, order frequency, first order year, and 2004 sales units and revenue. Jill would like to be able to switch between resellers with above and below average sales revenue. Additionally, she would like to see sales units and sales revenue subtotaled by year and grand totaled for the report. Lastly, she would like the resellers sorted first by sales year, and second by reseller type in the order of Warehouse, Specialty Bike Shop, and then Value Added Reseller. Once the data is loaded into the report, Jill will not need to refresh it, because the 2004 sales period has been closed.

Getting Down to Business

Follow these steps to complete this exercise:

1. Complete the steps in the "Before You Begin" section of this chapter to format the Spreadsheet report to look like Figure 14-4.

2. From the Spreadsheet report, right-click C to select the column and choose Cut from the pop-up menu.

3. Right-click A to select the column and choose Insert Cut Cells from the pop-up menu to move First Order Yr before Business Type.

4. Click anywhere on the Spreadsheet report to select the report and deselect the inserted column.

5. Choose Data → Sort to bring up the Sort dialog box, select First Order Yr in Sort By, Values from Sort On, and Smallest to Largest from Order.

6. Click Add Level to add another sort level, select Business Type in Then By, Values from Sort On, and Custom List from Order.

7. When the Custom List dialog box appears, type **Warehouse** and press Enter. Next, type **Specialty Bike Shop** and press Enter. After that, type **Value Added Reseller**, and then click Add to add the new custom sort.

8. Click OK to close the dialog box and return to the Sort dialog box.

9. Click OK to close the Sort dialog box and apply the sort.

10. Click Table Tools to bring up the Table Tools tab and check the Total Row option in the Table Style Options group to add a total row to the Spreadsheet report.

11. Click the Convert to Range button in the Tools group to convert the Spreadsheet report to a Range. Click OK to acknowledge the Microsoft Excel Office warning message that the query definition will be removed from the report.

12. Choose Data → Subtotal to bring up the Subtotal dialog box. Check the Sales Unit box without changing any other options in the dialog box.

13. Click OK in the Subtotal dialog box to calculate a Sum of Sales Units and Sales Revenue for First Order Yr.

14. Click in cell A1 to select a field header in the Range, and then choose Data → Filter to define the first row as field headers and create filter drop-down arrows in each field header cell.

15. Click the Sales Revenue Sort button in F1, and choose Number Filters → Above Average to show only the resellers with a higher than average sales revenue for the first quarter of 2004.

16. Verify that your Spreadsheet report looks like Figure 14-27.

WATCH THE VIDEO To see how this exercise works, click the ch1401_video.avi file from www.wiley.com/go/excelreporting/2007 and watch the video.

Reviewing What You Did

Starting with the Spreadsheet report in the "Before You Begin" section of this chapter, this exercise required that you move report columns, add sort instructions (including a custom sort), and apply an advanced numeric filter. The report was also converted to a Range in order to subtotal sales units and revenue by the reseller's first order year.

		A	B	C	D	E	F
	1	First Orde	Business Type	Order Freq	Reseller Name	Sales Un	Sales Rever
	2		2001 Warehouse	Quarterly	Major Cycling	1	1466.01
	3		2001 Specialty Bike Shop	Annual	World Bike Discount Sto	4	2689.176
+	8	2001 Total				5	4155.186
	9		2002 Specialty Bike Shop	Annual	Blue Bicycle Company	3	1530.798
	10		2002 Specialty Bike Shop	Annual	Cash & Carry Bikes	1	1376.994
–	11	2002 Total				4	2907.792
	13		2003 Warehouse	Quarterly	Good Bicycle Store	1	1466.01
	16		2003 Value Added Reseller	Semi-Annual	Second Bike Shop	1	1466.01
–	17	2003 Total				2	2932.02
+	20	Grand Total				11	9994.998

Figure 14-27: If you did everything right, your report should look like this.

Chapter Review

This chapter is the first of three chapters in Spreadsheet reporting. Here, I outlined the basic framework of Spreadsheet reporting. I started by providing a perspective on how Spreadsheet reports are used in the enterprise and helped you understand how this reporting technology compares to PivotTable reports. Next, I reviewed the Table Tools tab that is used to manage many Spreadsheet report operations and covered the core features of Spreadsheet reports, including sorting, filtering, and fill-down formulas. I also reviewed how you could convert the Spreadsheet report to a Range, so that you could add subtotals to the report.

In the next two chapters, I expand on some of the more sophisticated external data source and formatting options that you can use with Spreadsheet reports. Chapter 15 includes information on web and parameter queries, external data source connection tools, and data refresh options. Chapter 16 includes information on traditional and conditional formatting features that you can use to really enhance the presentation of your report data.

Building Report Solutions

This chapter continues to build on Spreadsheet report development techniques from the previous chapter. Here, I show you how to interweave reports, processes, and components into a larger report solution. Using this technology, you could, for example, build an invoice printing system where a data entry operator inputs an order number that automatically triggers Spreadsheet reports to import that customer's order line detail, order comments, and payment information. This information can even be derived from multiple external data sources, located on different servers.

I start this chapter by providing information about report solutions, how they are used in the enterprise, and what's involved in their development. After that, I review the Spreadsheet report data options, describing how they can be used to automate many of your report operations. Next, I cover how you can use parameters with your Spreadsheet reports to pull in only the data that meets the criteria specified by the report user. I also demonstrate how you can validate the parameters to accept only specific data ranges or items from another Spreadsheet report. Following that, I show you how to create custom messages and error handling routines to ensure that report users understand how each parameter is used and how to properly input a valid value. I conclude this chapter by tying in various sections of this chapter into a scenario that you might encounter in the real world.

Conceptualizing and Understanding Report Solutions

A report solution is merely an enhanced Spreadsheet report that doesn't require the report user to perform a refresh operation from the Table Tools tab of Excel. It can be something as simple as a Spreadsheet report that automatically refreshes whenever the Excel workbook is first opened to something as sophisticated as a collection of Spreadsheet reports that are interconnected and configured to perform automatic, cascading refreshes whenever a parameter value is modified. The solution may contain numerous components, such as report parameters, drop-down validation lists, worksheet formulas, custom icons, parameter input messages, and error alerts. The report solutions can be used to:

- Create a digital dashboard that provides different data perspectives, key performance indicators, and trends on important business data.

- Link one or more reports together to fulfill a larger goal, such as generating an invoice with order line detail.

- Add and link multiple reports that query different external data sources.

- Streamline and automate report operations.

Report solutions combine the powerful suite of Excel's spreadsheet tools with the innovative features of Spreadsheet reporting. You can, for example, import a single column of numeric values from an external database table that are averaged or summed using a formula in some other cell of the worksheet. You can also define a worksheet cell to be a parameter that is used in conjunction with a Spreadsheet report to return only a specific dataset. This variable could be a date range, a promotion code, a customer number, or anything else that can be used in the Where clause of an SQL query or the input variable of a stored procedure. Moreover, the worksheet cell that is defined as the parameter can be defined to only pull in the values for a certain numeric or data range that is interactively selected from a drop-down list by the report user.

In this chapter, I provide an example of a report solution that has the following features and components:

- A primary Spreadsheet report that returns the product category name, product name, product color, product safety stock level, product manufacturing days, and product stock reorder point information for a specified product color and product category.

- Two secondary Spreadsheet reports that automatically refresh when the Excel workbook is opened and feed their valid values for the product color and product category into the two parameter cells.

- Two parameters that trigger an automatic report refresh of the primary Spreadsheet report whenever one of their values are changed.

- A worksheet cell that calculates the average manufacturing days for the products in the primary Spreadsheet report.

■ Custom message handling and worksheet protection to ensure that the report user receives a streamlined interface.

■ Custom icons and dialog box messages that provide the user with a rich report experience.

An example of this report solution is shown in Figure 15-1. Keep in mind that the secondary Spreadsheet reports are typically hidden; I've only displayed them here so that you can see how they are integrated into the overall report solution.

As you can probably surmise from Figure 15-1, a report solution provides the user with a much richer experience than what can be achieved with a single Excel report (and this is a very simple report solution that only takes a few minutes to develop). This particular report solution utilizes six components that are briefly summarized here and described in greater detail throughout the various sections of this chapter.

The first component of the report solution is the primary Spreadsheet report — it's basically the same kind of report that I covered in Chapter 14. The main difference between the two reports is that the Spreadsheet report here utilizes a stored procedure with input parameters. These parameters can be used to return only the dataset for a user-specified product color and product category; the Spreadsheet report in the previous chapter did not allow the user to specify values for returning a more focused dataset.

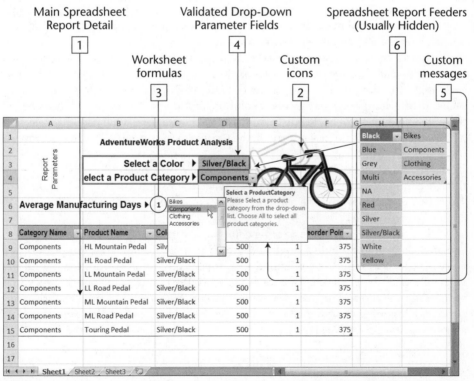

Figure 15-1: This report solution utilizes multiple Spreadsheet reports, parameters, and custom messages and icons to deliver a rich experience to the report user.

NOTE A report solution may have more than one primary Spreadsheet report. For example, if the report solution was designed to produce an invoice statement, there may be a primary Spreadsheet report for the order line detail and a primary Spreadsheet report for the payment detail.

The second component of the report solution in Figure 15-1 is an icon. I used a bicycle for this example, because this report is based on a business that sells bicycles and bicycle accessories. For your reports, however, this could be a corporate logo or some other type of artwork that describes the purpose of the report. Keep in mind that it isn't necessary to add an icon, but it can be a positive factor in the overall report presentation.

TIP Carefully evaluate the use of icons in your report solution. Although they can make the report look more professional, it can slow down printing and take up unnecessary space. Additionally, management may not appreciate the use of icons and pictures — preferring that report developers focus on delivering the important business data to decision-makers and avoid spending time looking for just the right report icon.

The third component calculates the average manufacturing days for the dataset returned from Column E of the Spreadsheet report. It uses the simple formula AVERAGE (E:E), and even though there is a non-numeric report header cell for the Spreadsheet report (cell E8), the formula still works.

The fourth component is comprised of two parameter cells that show a drop-down list of valid values for the product category and the product color. Whenever the user clicks in the Product Category parameter cell (see cell D4 of Figure 15-1), a helpful message (the fifth component of the report solution) automatically appears to describe the use of the field for the report user. In this case, the message tells the user that selecting All for the Product Category returns all the records in the primary Spreadsheet report, regardless of product category.

The sixth and last component is comprised of two secondary Spreadsheet reports that are configured to automatically refresh when the Excel workbook is first opened. These two Spreadsheet reports feed their values into the parameter cells (see cells D3 and D4 of Figure 15-1).

All the Spreadsheet reports and other components are closely related to one another, and are designed to provide a single, integrated report solution. For example, the primary Spreadsheet report is configured to automatically refresh. Additionally, all the valid values for the parameters are refreshed when the report is first opened. As you'll soon learn from the various sections of this chapter, there are many options for configuring and designing your own report solutions. This is just one simple example of how a report solution can be designed.

Developing a Report Solution

The first step in developing a reporting solution is to figure out what fields and variables are required for the primary Spreadsheet report. After that, the fields and parameters are integrated into a stored procedure or SQL query and linked to the primary Spreadsheet report. The report parameters can then be validated to ensure that the user only inputs a valid value.

Once all the parameters are working properly, the report data options are typically configured. This may involve configuring the secondary Spreadsheet reports to automatically refresh when the Excel workbook is first opened. After verifying that the report operations are working properly and that the report data is accurate, the final step is usually to add the icons, hide secondary reports, and protect the worksheet.

NOTE I provide some information and references about hiding columns and protecting the worksheet, so that you can build an impressive and bullet-proof report solution. However, these topics and many other general spreadsheet functions, features, and tools are covered in greater detail in books that review Excel from a broad perspective, instead of focusing on the reporting aspects like this one does. If you are interested in getting a broader understanding Excel 2007, consider purchasing John Walkenbach's *Excel 2007 Bible*.

I individually cover the various components of the report solution shown in Figure 15-1 throughout the remaining sections of this chapter. I also provide step-by-step examples on how to build a good deal of the report solution in the "Trying It Out in the Real World" section of this chapter. Good luck and remember to visit the www.exceluser.com and www.excelreportsolutions.com web sites if you need additional information, tips, or examples of report solutions.

Configuring Spreadsheet Report Data Options

Connection property settings are an important component of the report solution. These settings can be used to automate many of the report operations that would otherwise be manual or require Visual Basic for Applications (VBA) programming. For example, using these settings, you can configure reports to automatically refresh at specified intervals, refresh when the report is first opened, or not refresh at all. You can also set refreshes to either run in the background or halt all Excel operations until the update has completed.

Connection properties for Spreadsheet reports are configured from the Connection Properties dialog box. You can bring up this dialog box (see Figure 15-2) by clicking the report to select it and choosing Data → Connections or Table Tools → Refresh → Connection Properties.

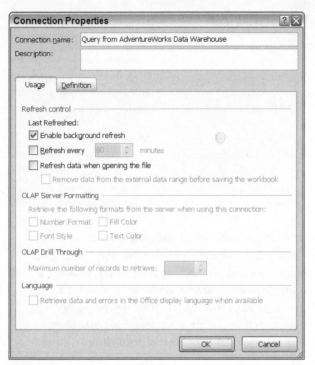

Figure 15-2: The data refresh options for Spreadsheet reports are controlled from this dialog box.

This dialog box is separated into two tabs: Usage and Definition. The Usage tab includes options for configuring refresh operations. The Definition tab includes tools for changing the connection file, managing the connection string, and accessing the SQL query. Buttons for changing and exporting the connection file, accessing the Microsoft Query program, and configuring the authentication settings for Excel Services are also available from the Definition tab of this dialog box.

Configuring Usage Options

The data options in the Usage tab of the Connection Properties dialog box shown in Figure 15-2 are separated into four sections: Refresh Control, OLAP Server Formatting, OLAP Drill Through, and Language. Only the first section, Refresh Control, applies to a Spreadsheet report. The remaining three sections all apply to PivotTable reports that access OLAP data sources and are covered in the online OLAP chapter.

The options under Refresh Control are used to configure how queries are executed, how often data is refreshed, and whether the Spreadsheet report is automatically updated when the Excel workbook with the Spreadsheet report is initially opened. Table 15-1 provides a brief description of each option under Refresh Control.

Table 15-1: Explanation of Refresh Control Options (See Figure 15-2)

OPTION NAME	DESCRIPTION
Enable Background Refresh	Toggles whether the data refresh halts all Excel operations in the Excel worksheet until the refresh is completed, or whether the user can continue working in Excel while the refresh query runs in the background.
Refresh Every	Automatically refreshes the report every *n* minutes (where *n* is defined as a number between 1 and 999).
Refresh Data When Opening the File	Toggles whether the report is immediately refreshed when it is first opened.

Enable Background Refresh

If you are importing a large dataset and/or accessing the data source through a remote connection, such as a Virtual Private Network (VPN), the data refresh might take a while to complete. While the new dataset is being loaded into your report, you cannot perform any operations in Excel, because the refresh operation halts all activities until the refresh has fully completed. You can work around this constraint by checking the Enable Background Refresh option (see Figure 15-2). Checking this option configures the refresh operation to run in the background so that you can go on about your report operations while the dataset is being updated.

WARNING Refresh operations that are running in the background may not be noticed by Spreadsheet report users who are not familiar with the Enable Background Refresh option. Be sure to review how this setting works in order to ensure that the report user understands that the report hasn't yet been refreshed.

Refresh Every

The Refresh Every option schedules the report to be refreshed every *n* minutes. The value for minutes must be an integer between 1 and 999. This option is useful for reports designed to regularly monitor transactions or statistics. For example, a data entry processing manager might want to monitor the total number of transactions processed throughout the day and the average transaction processed each hour. Using this option, the report can automatically be updated every 15 minutes to show the updated transactions processed by the data entry staff.

Refresh Data When Opening the File

Check the Refresh Data When Opening the File option to automatically refresh the Spreadsheet report when the Excel workbook containing the report is first opened. This feature can be useful when the report user has no experience with Spreadsheet reports, because it doesn't require the user to take any action to refresh the report. When this option is checked, a refresh operation is automatically triggered for the report when it is opened.

The Refresh Data When Opening the File option should not be checked when a report user needs to keep archived copies of the report data prior to it being automatically refreshed, because report users are likely to forget to save a copy of the report before the new data becomes available. This can happen when the report data is archived at month-end, for example. You should also carefully evaluate the use of this option when the Spreadsheet report takes a long time to refresh.

WARNING Keep in mind that it is possible that a malicious query could update or delete rows from the database tables. So be sure the query is verified to be safe and that you trust the source of this report before enabling the automatic refresh feature.

I suggest that you use this option when:

- The report user is not familiar with Spreadsheet report technology
- The Spreadsheet report can be refreshed in a short period of time
- It's important for the report user to view the most current information in the report
- The report data does not have to be archived

Configuring Definition Options

Several connection settings can be adjusted from the Definition tab of the Connection Properties dialog box. Looking at Figure 15-3, you can see that there are numerous components in this tab of the dialog box that are comprised of panes, buttons, fields, and check boxes.

The Connection Type label displays the type of external data source connection being used. Clicking the Browse button enables you to change the connection file for the report, which enables you to utilize a different connection string and SQL query for the report. The Connection String pane of the Connection Properties dialog box contains the connection string information for the external data source. The Command Text pane contains the table name or SQL query being used for the Spreadsheet report. Clicking the Authentication Settings button brings up the Excel Services Authentication Settings dialog box, where you can configure the Spreadsheet report security for Microsoft SharePoint 2007. Clicking the Edit Query button starts the Microsoft Query program, where you can edit an SQL query for the external data source.

Figure 15-3: The connection string, SQL query, and connection file are all accessed from this dialog box.

Looking at the Connection Information

The connection information for the data source is stored in a connection file. This file contains information on the type of data being accessed, the location of that data, the authentication information (if applicable), and the object or data to extract (for example, the database table or SQL query). The connection information is stored in the Connection String pane. Here, you can manually edit the server connection, the default database, and the password. Clicking the Export Connection File button creates an Office Data Connection (*.odc) file that contains the connection information, as well as the SQL query that is being used for the PivotTable report.

CROSS-REFERENCE Read Chapter 4 for detailed explanations of the connection string information that is stored in the Connection String pane of the Connection Properties dialog box.

Save Password

The Save Password option toggles whether the password to the external data source is saved with the report. This option is only relevant when the Spreadsheet report accesses an external data source where a password is actually required. For example, if the Spreadsheet report uses an SQL database as its data source, and the database uses an SQL Server authentication type, this option toggles whether the password is saved along with the user login. Keep in mind that if Windows Authentication is used instead of SQL Server authentication, this Save Password option has no effect on the report, even though it is still accessible.

Uncheck this option if you want the user to specify a password in order to refresh the report or to edit the SQL query. You can also uncheck this option when you want to change the data source.

WARNING In Excel 2007, the password for an SQL login is automatically saved with the report, even if the Save Password option is unchecked. Until this software bug is remedied, you can check the Save Password option and then enter in a dummy password if you want the password to be specified whenever the report is refreshed.

Removing External Data

Checking the Remove External Data from Worksheet Before Saving option in the Usage tab of the Connection Properties dialog box removes all external data retrieved by the Spreadsheet report when the Excel workbook is saved and closed. This option can be useful if you need to email the report to a programmer for troubleshooting or to another user who can refresh it. Rather than trying to send a huge file, you can send just the Spreadsheet report shell with the saved SQL query.

Using Parameter Queries

A well-designed report solution accounts for the user's level of expertise. If you are delivering the report to expert-level users, you can usually just give them an unformatted report with the necessary data that the user can later customize. However, if the report is being delivered to users with only limited Excel report experience, you might consider the use of parameter queries and validated lists that provide the user with a more streamlined and easily understood interface to the report and report data.

A parameter query enables the user to input parameter values into Excel for the Spreadsheet report. These values are mapped to variables in the Where clause of an SQL query or stored procedure. The parameter values are evaluated each time the report is refreshed, working at the server level and filtering data before it is even imported into the Spreadsheet report. This typically results in a compact dataset and fast query processing time, allowing the user to focus on a concentrated range of data, such as a particular period of time, a specific business segment, or any other data element (or elements) that can be specified in a stored procedure or an SQL query.

A few things to keep in mind with this technology:

- Parameters are intended to be used only in a Spreadsheet report (Microsoft states that this technology is not intended to be used in PivotTable and PivotChart reports)
- Parameters can be used only in an SQL query where the query can be graphically displayed
- Parameters can be integrated with stored procedures, even if the stored procedure query cannot be graphically displayed
- Parameters can be integrated with web queries, but only by creating an .isql file outside of Excel

Although parameters are not intended to be used in a PivotTable report, you can create a PivotTable report that is based on the Spreadsheet report. Keep in mind, however, that because the data is imported into a Spreadsheet report, you are limited to a maximum of about one million rows for the PivotTable report.

> **TIP** Later, in the "Integrating Parameters into Excel Reports" section of this chapter, I provide an example on how you can configure a PivotTable report and a web query to accept parameters.

Integrating Parameters into Excel Reports

On the surface, a parameter might appear similar to the AutoFilter function in the Spreadsheet report. However, though both filter data, they do so at different points in the process. With filters, you specify the criteria *after* the dataset is returned to Excel. In contrast, a parameter is mapped to a variable in the Where clause of an SQL query. Therefore, the dataset is filtered *before* it is returned to Excel — and usually on a server with more powerful CPU, memory, and disk resources than what's typically available on a client computer.

> **TIP** From a performance standpoint, parameters work best on fields that are indexed in the database table. Thus, try to make use of indexed fields or work with your database administrator to determine if fields can be indexed.

Parameters can be integrated into an SQL query or into a stored procedure. Keep in mind, however, that parameters work only with an SQL query that can be graphically displayed. (Read Chapter 9 if you are unfamiliar with the concept of graphically displaying an SQL query.) If the query cannot be displayed graphically, you'll need to transform it into a stored procedure or view.

TIP When the stored procedure or view is created, the query plan (that is, the instructions for how the database server calculates the most efficient path for obtaining the data) is also created and saved with the object. This model results in the query running faster than it would as a regular SQL query, because the query plan does not have to be computed at runtime.

Creating Parameters in an SQL Query

You can specify a parameter in a query by using a question mark (?) in the Where clause of an SQL query. For example, try entering the following query into the SQL window of the Microsoft Query program of a Spreadsheet report:

```
SELECT * FROM DimProductCategory WHERE ProductCategoryKey = ?
```

The Enter Parameter Value dialog box shown in Figure 15-4 comes up asking for a parameter value. Entering **1** in this box causes only a single row to appear for the Bikes product category.

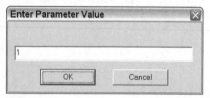

Figure 15-4: When a ? is used in the Where clause of an SQL query, the Enter Parameter Value dialog box appears, prompting the user to enter in the filter criteria.

Queries that cannot be displayed graphically do not allow parameter values to be accepted. For example, try using the SQL query shown here in the Microsoft Query program.

ON THE WEB You can download the ch15_example01.txt query file to your computer from the companion web site at www.wiley.com/go/excelreporting/2007. Look in the Chap15.zip file or Chap15 directory.

```
SELECT catg.EnglishProductCategoryName    AS [Category Name],
       prod.EnglishProductName            AS [Product Name],
       CASE
           WHEN prod.Color = 'NA'
               THEN 'No Color Choice'
               ELSE prod.Color
           END                            AS [Color],
       prod.SafetyStockLevel              AS [SafetyStockLevel],
       prod.DaysToManufacture             AS [Manufacture Days],
```

```
        prod.ReorderPoint                 AS [Reorder Point]
FROM DimProduct prod
INNER JOIN DimProductSubcategory subc
       ON prod.ProductSubcategoryKey = subc.ProductSubcategoryKey
INNER JOIN DimProductCategory catg
       ON subc.ProductCategoryKey = catg.ProductCategoryKey
WHERE catg.EnglishProductCategoryName = ?
```

When you attempt to execute this query, you see the dialog box shown in Figure 15-5.

Despite this restriction, it's easy to work around this limitation. You can either create a stored procedure or view for the SQL query. Once either of these objects is created on the database server, you will then be able to pass in parameters. This is because stored procedures provide native support of parameters and views transform what could otherwise be a sophisticated query into a basic query that can be graphically displayed.

Using Parameters in a View

A view is just like a virtual table, except that is doesn't contain any records like a regular database table. Instead, the view is essentially an optimized SQL query that is stored on the database server. The query can comprise particular fields in one or more database tables. The field names can also be renamed with more descriptive and easily understood names.

NOTE There's much more detail to the topic of views, but it is a bit outside the scope of this book. If you aren't familiar with how views work, you can read up on this subject in the SQL books online.

Creating a View

Creating a view from an existing SQL query is simple. All you need to do is add one line before the SQL query:

```
CREATE VIEW {ViewName} AS
```

Figure 15-5: Parameters cannot be used in queries that cannot be graphically displayed.

To create a view in the AdventureWorksDW database from the earlier SQL query, follow these steps:

WARNING In order to create a database view on the SQL Server, you must have the appropriate level of security. Work with your organization's database administrator if you need help or additional clarification about creating database views.

1. From Excel, choose Data → From Other Sources → From Microsoft Query to bring up the Choose Data Source dialog box.

2. When the Choose Data Source dialog box appears, verify that Use the Query Wizard to Create/Edit Queries is unchecked, select the AdventureWorks Data Warehouse data source, and click OK.

3. When the Microsoft Query program is launched, you are presented with the Add Tables dialog box. Close this dialog box, and then choose File → Execute SQL to bring up the Execute SQL dialog box.

4. Paste the following SQL query into the Execute SQL dialog box:

```
CREATE VIEW ProductInfo AS
SELECT catg.EnglishProductCategoryName    AS [Category Name],
       prod.EnglishProductName            AS [Product Name],
       CASE
            WHEN prod.Color = 'NA'
                THEN 'No Color Choice'
                ELSE prod.Color
                END                        AS [Color],
       prod.SafetyStockLevel              AS [SafetyStockLevel],
       prod.DaysToManufacture             AS [Manufacture Days],
       prod.ReorderPoint                  AS [Reorder Point]
FROM DimProduct prod
INNER JOIN DimProductSubcategory subc
       ON prod.ProductSubcategoryKey = subc.ProductSubcategoryKey
INNER JOIN DimProductCategory catg
       ON subc.ProductCategoryKey = catg.ProductCategoryKey
```

ON THE WEB You can download the ch15_example02.txt query file to your computer from the companion web site at www.wiley.com/go/ excelreporting/2007. Look in the Chap15.zip file or Chap15 directory.

5. Verify that the AdventureWorksDW database is selected in the database dropdown field (at the bottom of the Execute SQL dialog box) and click the Execute button to run the query and create the view.

6. Click OK to acknowledge that the query was successfully executed.

7. Click Cancel to close the Execute SQL dialog box.

NOTE The column names in the view are created from the names specified for each column in the AS part of the SQL query. For example, DaysToManufacture becomes Manufacture Days, and EnglishProductName becomes Product Name.

Executing a Parameter Query against the View

After the view is created on the SQL server, just paste this query into the SQL dialog box:

```
SELECT * FROM ProductInfo Where "Category Name" = ?
```

After you execute this query, the Enter Parameter Value dialog box appears, where you can enter a category name. Try typing **Bikes** or **Clothing** into the Enter Parameter Value dialog box to see how this works.

TIP When working with parameters, I prefer using a stored procedure to using an SQL query that accesses a database table or view. This is because conditional logic can be programmed into a stored procedure; adding conditional logic to an SQL query results in the query not being displayed graphically — and thus not able to accept parameters.

Using Parameters in a Stored Procedure

A stored procedure can perform several complex tasks. However, for the purposes of Spreadsheet reporting, think of a stored procedure as an SQL query that can accept variables. And like a view, a stored procedure is stored in the database and optimized for fast performance. Additionally, there are other benefits associated with using a stored procedure, including:

- Changes to the stored procedure query are automatically reflected in the Spreadsheet report when the report is refreshed.

- The stored procedure can accept numerous input parameters, and conditional logic can be programmed into the report to handle default values and potential errors.

Any changes to the stored procedure are automatically applied to the Spreadsheet and PivotTable reports. Fields added or removed in the stored procedure are automatically reflected in the Excel report, once it is refreshed. This enables you to modify the stored procedure in one place instead of modifying the queries in every Excel report.

In the stored procedure example (ch15_example03.txt, which is provided on the web site) used in the next section, I demonstrate one method for how a special value, such as All, can be used to pull the entire dataset instead of just the data for a particular product category name.

Creating a Stored Procedure

Creating a stored procedure from an existing SQL query is simple. All you need to do is add one line before the SQL query:

```
CREATE PROCEDURE {ProcedureName} AS
```

I've transformed the earlier query in this chapter into a stored procedure. I also added variables for the product color and for the product category. These variables are used in the `Where` clause of the stored procedure query and are mapped to parameters in the Spreadsheet report.

To create a stored procedure that has variables for Product Color and Product Category in the AdventureWorksDW database, and that you will use in future examples throughout this chapter, follow these steps:

WARNING In order to create a stored procedure on the SQL Server, you must have the appropriate level of security. Work with your organization's database administrator if you need help or additional clarification about creating stored procedures.

1. From Excel, choose Data → From Other Sources → From Microsoft Query to bring up the Choose Data Source dialog box.

2. When the Choose Data Source dialog box appears, verify that Use the Query Wizard to Create/Edit Queries is unchecked, select the AdventureWorks Data Warehouse data source, and click OK.

3. When the Microsoft Query program is launched, you are presented with the Add Tables dialog box. Close this dialog box and choose File → Execute SQL to bring up the Execute SQL dialog box.

4. Paste the following SQL query into the Execute SQL dialog box:

```
CREATE PROCEDURE AWProductInfo
(@Color VARCHAR(12),
 @Category VARCHAR(11))
AS
SELECT catg.EnglishProductCategoryName    AS [Category Name],
       prod.EnglishProductName            AS [Product Name],
       CASE
           WHEN prod.Color = 'NA'
               THEN 'No Color Choice'
               ELSE prod.Color
           END                            AS [Color],
       prod.SafetyStockLevel              AS [Safety Stock],
       prod.DaysToManufacture             AS [Manuf Days],
       prod.ReorderPoint                  AS [Reorder Point]
```

```
FROM DimProduct prod
INNER JOIN DimProductSubcategory subc
       ON prod.ProductSubcategoryKey = subc.ProductSubcategoryKey
INNER JOIN DimProductCategory catg
       ON subc.ProductCategoryKey = catg.ProductCategoryKey
WHERE prod.Color = @Color
  AND catg.ProductCategoryKey
      BETWEEN CASE
                 WHEN @Category = 'All'
                 THEN 0
                 ELSE (SELECT ctx.ProductCategoryKey
                        FROM DimProductCategory ctx
                       WHERE @Category = ctx.EnglishProductCategoryName)
              END
         AND
            CASE
                 WHEN @Category = 'All'
                 THEN 4
                 ELSE (SELECT ctx.ProductCategoryKey
                        FROM DimProductCategory ctx
                       WHERE @Category = ctx.EnglishProductCategoryName)
              END
ORDER BY 1, 2
```

ON THE WEB You can download the ch15_example03.txt query file to
your computer from the companion web site at www.wiley.com/go/
excelreporting/2007. **Look in the Chap15.zip file or the Chap15 directory.**

5. Verify that the AdventureWorksDW database is selected in the database drop-
    down field (at the bottom of the Execute SQL dialog box) and click the Execute
    button to run the query and create the view.

6. Click OK to acknowledge that the query was successfully executed.

7. Click Cancel to close the Execute SQL dialog box. Note that the Cancel button
    does not undo the action of creating the stored procedure; it simply closes the
    Execute SQL dialog box.

Executing Parameters in Stored Procedures

You can enter a stored procedure without variables into the SQL dialog box by simply
typing the stored procedure name into the SQL window. However, if the stored procedure has variables, you must also enter the values for each variable. If the variable is
defined as text, enter the variables in single quotes as shown here:

```
AWProductInfo 'Black','Accessories'
```

This query shows only the rows for products that have a black color and a product category name of Accessories. Now, if you want the user to interactively specify the values for these variables using report parameters, you should use the following *exact* format in the SQL window of the Microsoft Query program:

```
{Call AWProductInfo (?,?)}
```

WARNING There are many ways to run a stored procedure in the SQL dialog box of the Microsoft Query program (for example, Exec ProcedureName, Call ProcedureName, ProcedureName, and Execute ProcedureName), but you must use the *exact* format {Call AWProductInfo (?,?)} if parameters are specified.

Using Parameters in a Web Query

Spreadsheet reports include a *web query* feature that enables you to extract data from a web page. The process is similar to extracting data from a database, except that you specify a Uniform Resource Location (URL) address and an HTML table, instead of a database and database table name. Using this technology, you can extract information from web pages posted to an Intranet or Internet site. You can also use parameters with your web query to pull only the query results for a specified parameter(s).

CROSS-REFERENCE Read Chapter 5 for more information about using web queries in your Excel Spreadsheet reports.

There are few items that you should keep in mind when using parameters in a web query. First, the web page must support the use of a parameter, which is indicated by an equals sign (=) in the URL address. Second, the query and the parameters must be created outside of Excel, because there is no graphical user interface to integrate parameters for web queries within Excel.

To see how a web query with parameters works, follow these steps:

1. Open a Microsoft Internet Explorer session and type **www.Wiley.com** in the Address field.

2. Type **zapawa** in the Product Search field, choose By Author from the drop-down list of search types, and click the Go button (see Figure 15-6).

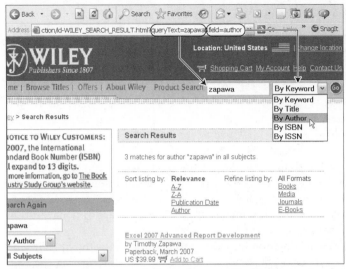

Figure 15-6: If the query information specified in the web page is translated into a URL segment, then a parameter can be used in the web query to enable the user to specify the string from an Excel report.

If you look at the URL in the address field of Microsoft Internet Explorer, you'll see that the address is as follows:

```
http://www.wiley.com/WileyCDA/Section/id-WILEY_SEARCH_RESULT
.html?queryText=zapawa&field=author
```

Note that the URL wraps into two lines, although it is only a single line. This is simply because I cannot fit all the information for the URL into a single line. Notice that the query text and search type specified in the second step are included in the URL. Additionally, I bolded the last part of the text, so that you can see how the information specified from the web page is translated into a URL.

Creating a Connection File for a Web Query

You only need to add two lines before the URL in order for it to work from a web connection file. You can also insert lines to set web formatting options. In the example here, I created a connection file using the SQL query from the previous section. I also added some lines to set web query formatting options, so that you can see how it all works. Keep in mind that I indented each line of the file with a number, because I provide more detailed information about each line.

```
1. WEB
2. 1
3. http://www.wiley.com/WileyCDA/Section/id-WILEY_SEARCH_RESULT.html?queryText=
   zapawa&field=author
4. Formatting=HTML
5. PreFormattedTextToColumns=True
6. ConsecutiveDelimitersAsOne=True
7. SingleBlockTextImport=False
8. DisableDateRecognition=False
9. DisableRedirections=False
```

The first two lines of the file simply tell Excel that a web query is being used. These lines are required for the web query to work properly. The third line (shown as two lines here, because it won't fit on a single line) is just the web URL that was used to conduct a search for books with an author name of *zapawa*. Lines 4–9 are optional and set the various web options that I covered in Chapter 5.

You can simply paste this information into Notepad and then save the file with the extension of ".iqy". Double-clicking the file now opens up Excel, returning the web data into your Excel report.

Adding Parameters to a Web Query

Adding a parameter to a web query is similar to how a parameter is added to an SQL query (explained later in the "Customizing the Prompt from Microsoft Query" section of this chapter). You simply put the name of the parameter in brackets. Thus, if you wanted to replace Zapawa with a parameter, you'd modify `queryText=zapawa` with `queryText=["AuthorName","Enter an Author Name to Search"]`. The first element is the name of the parameter (in this case, AuthorName) and the second element is the string that is presented to the user in the Enter Parameter Value dialog box. Thus, the modified query should appear as shown here:

```
1. WEB
2. 1
3. http://www.wiley.com/WileyCDA/Section/id-WILEY_SEARCH_RESULT.html?queryText=
   ["AuthorName","Enter an Author Name to Search"]&field=author
4. Formatting=HTML
5. PreFormattedTextToColumns=True
6. ConsecutiveDelimitersAsOne=True
7. SingleBlockTextImport=False
8. DisableDateRecognition=False
9. DisableRedirections=False
```

When you resave the .iqy file, and double-click the file to open it, Excel is automatically launched and you are presented with the Enter Parameter Value dialog box shown in Figure 15-7.

Figure 15-7: The parameter for the web query is specified in this dialog box.

Using Parameters in a PivotTable Report

Although parameters are not officially supported for PivotTable reports, there is at least one method that I know about for incorporating parameters into an Excel 2007 PivotTable report. Of course, I don't recommend building any permanent solutions on this technology, because Microsoft has said that this technology is not intended to be used in a PivotTable and it's possible that this method will no longer work in future service packs. But, if you're in a bind and you need something quick, you might try this method outlined here.

To incorporate parameters into a PivotTable report, follow these steps:

1. Develop a stored procedure or view with the required report parameters.

2. Create a PivotTable report that accesses the external data source that is required for the report. However, use a dummy query that can be graphically displayed, instead of the stored procedure or view.

3. Once the PivotTable report is created in Excel, right-click the report and choose Data → Properties to open the Connection Properties dialog box.

4. Click the Definition tab of the Connection Properties dialog box, delete the current SQL query from the Command Text pane, and paste in the stored procedure or SQL query with the parameters (note that the stored procedures that utilize parameters must be in the exact format outlined in the "Executing Parameters in Stored Procedures" section of this chapter).

5. Click OK to close the Connection Properties dialog box, and then enter in the parameter report values.

NOTE **I'm not sure why Microsoft has restricted the use of parameters to Spreadsheet reports. I've often had to develop VBA programs, build OLAP cubes, or create innovative solutions to restrict the dataset size for PivotTable reports. It would be much better for report users (and for the Excel application) to have this technology available for PivotTable reports.**

Naming Parameters

The parameters are initially named as Parameter *n*, where *n* represents the number in which the variable is first defined in the stored procedure. You can rename the parameters to use more meaningful names by editing the parameter in the Microsoft Query program.

Choose View → Parameters to bring up the Edit Parameter dialog box, shown in Figure 15-8, where you can rename the parameter.

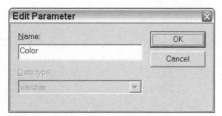

Figure 15-8: The Edit Parameter dialog box enables you to rename Parameter 1 with a more meaningful name.

NOTE Parameter names can be customized only in the Parameters dialog box for queries that are used with Spreadsheet reports, because this dialog box is accessible only from the Microsoft Query program.

In Figure 15-9, you can see how I renamed Parameter 1 to Color and Parameter 2 to Category Name.

Figure 15-9: You can rename parameters in this dialog box.

Working with Parameters in Excel Reports

After the parameters are successfully integrated into an SQL query or a stored procedure, you have three options for determining how to use the parameters in a Spreadsheet report:

- Prompt the user with a value each time the report is refreshed.
- Use a default value specified by the user.
- Fetch the data from a cell in the Excel workbook.

If you prefer to prompt the user for the values, you can customize the prompt that is presented to the user for report refreshes. If you choose to configure a default value, the default value is used as the parameter value each time the report is refreshed. If you choose to fetch the data from a particular cell value in the Excel workbook, you have the option to configure the Spreadsheet to automatically refresh whenever the cell value is changed.

TIP Each parameter can be customized to use a specific option; they do not all have to use the same one. For example, one parameter can use a default value, and another could fetch values from a particular worksheet cell. It's also easy to configure the parameter to use a different method.

These options are all controlled in the Parameters dialog box that you access from the Spreadsheet report. You can access this dialog box by right-clicking the Spreadsheet report and choosing Table → Parameters from the pop-up menu.

Customizing the Prompt for a Parameter

You can configure a parameter to prompt the user for the parameter value each time the report is refreshed. If you are using an SQL query, you can configure this prompt in the Microsoft Query program or in the Parameters dialog box. If you are using a stored procedure, you can configure the prompt only in the Parameters dialog box. This is because the changes are made in the Criteria pane, and that pane is not available for stored procedures because they cannot be graphically displayed in the Microsoft Query program.

Customizing the Prompt from Microsoft Query

You can customize the prompt for a parameter in the Microsoft Query program by entering a prompt string in brackets in the Value field of the Criteria pane. For example, try pasting this SQL query into the SQL dialog box:

```
SELECT *
FROM DimProductCategory
WHERE ProductCategoryKey = ?
```

After you click OK in the SQL dialog box and specify a value for the parameter, Microsoft Query adds closed brackets ([ ]) in the Value field of the Criteria section. Now, all you need to do is replace the closed brackets in Value with the string **[Enter a Category Key]**, as shown in Figure 15-10.

TIP This prompt can be customized only for parameters in an SQL query. Prompts for a stored procedure must be configured in the Parameters dialog box.

After you press the Tab key in Value (see Figure 15-10), the dialog box in Figure 15-11 appears with the prompt you just added.

Customizing the Prompt from the Spreadsheet Report

You can configure the prompt for a parameter in the Spreadsheet report by accessing the Parameters dialog box. This method works well for parameters in both queries and stored procedures.

Complete these steps to customize the prompt for a parameter field in the earlier stored procedure query and to follow along with the example in this section:

1. Verify that the AWProductInfo stored procedure has been created, as outlined in the "Creating a Stored Procedure" section earlier in this chapter.

2. Create a Spreadsheet report using the AWProductInfo stored procedure, specifying a product color of Black and a product category name of Clothing. Refer back to the "Creating a Stored Procedure" section of this chapter if you need a more detailed list of steps for creating a Spreadsheet report that uses the AWProductInfo stored procedure.

3. Right-click the report and choose Table → Parameters from the pop-up menu to bring up the Parameters dialog box.

4. Click Parameter 2 in the Parameter Name pane (on the left side of the Parameters dialog box), click the Prompt for Value Using the Following String button, and then type **Enter in a Product Category Name (select All for all Product Categories)** into the string prompt field, as shown in Figure 15-12.

Figure 15-10: The prompt can be customized for a parameter in the Microsoft Query program by adding brackets around the prompt string in the Value field.

Figure 15-11: A customized prompt is now displayed for the parameter.

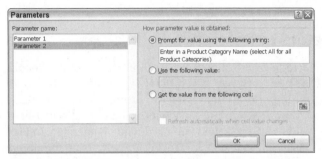

Figure 15-12: A prompt can be customized in the Parameters dialog box for parameters in a stored procedure or in an SQL query.

5. Click OK to modify the prompt for Parameter 2 (Category Name) and to close the Parameters dialog box.

Now, when you refresh the report, the Enter Parameter Value dialog box with the newly added prompt string appears for the Category Name parameter field, as shown in Figure 15-13.

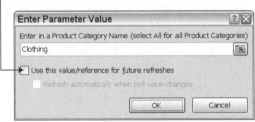

Figure 15-13: The prompt string now appears for the Category Name field whenever the report is refreshed.

Configuring Parameters to Use Default Values

A default value is useful when you want the flexibility of specifying a parameter value, but you don't want to be bothered with having to enter a value each time the Spreadsheet report is refreshed.

You can set a default value for a parameter in the Parameters dialog box by typing in the default value and checking the Use This Value/Reference for Future Refreshes option (see Figure 15-13). By checking this box, you are no longer prompted for the parameter value when the report is refreshed.

Configuring Parameters to Reference Cell Values

A parameter can be configured to fetch its value from a cell in the Excel workbook. (Note that this cell can be in the same worksheet or a different worksheet of the workbook.) This method enables you to build an impressive reporting solution in which users can select values from a drop-down list. You can even configure the Spreadsheet report to trigger a refresh operation whenever the referenced value is changed. In Figure 15-14, I demonstrate how this might look in a Spreadsheet report, using the stored procedure that was included earlier in this section (ch15_example03.txt).

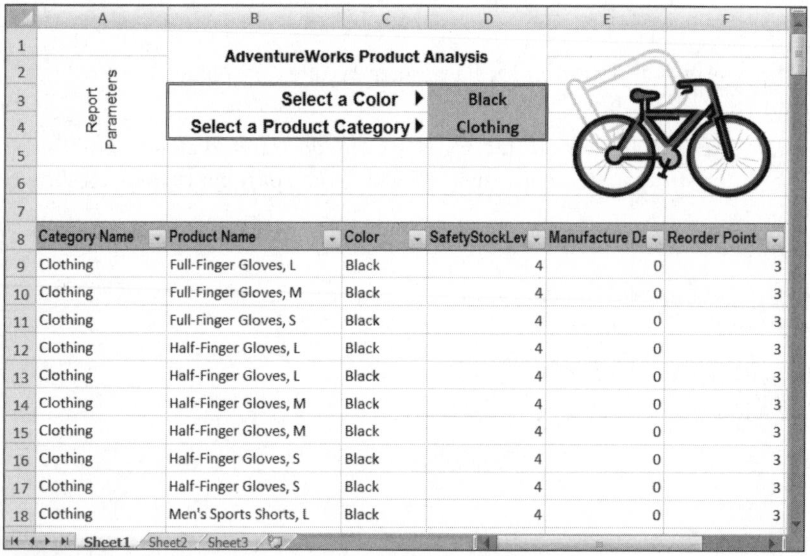

Figure 15-14: The parameter values for Color and Category Name are obtained in the worksheet cells D3 and D4, respectively.

ON THE WEB **You can download the ch15_ReportExample.xls Spreadsheet report to your computer from the companion web site at** www.wiley.com/go/excelreporting/2007. **Look in the Chap15.zip file or the Chap15 directory.**

I've configured the Spreadsheet report shown in Figure 15-14 to obtain the Product Color parameter value (Parameter 1) from cell D3 and the Product Category (Parameter 2) value from cell D4. I've also created a drop-down list for both fields, configuring these cells to accept only valid colors and product category names from the AdventureWorksDW database.

You can configure the parameters to use a worksheet cell in the Parameters dialog box by clicking the Get the Value from the Following Cell button and then typing the cell reference, as shown in Figure 15-15. Check the Refresh Automatically When Cell Value Changes option to configure the Spreadsheet report to automatically refresh whenever the value is changed in the referenced cell.

Validating Parameter Value Inputs

You can customize input cells to accept only a specific values, ranges, and formats. You can even set up a custom list that pulls values from another column or range in the worksheet. This validation creates a professional edge to the report and helps prevent errors that might confuse the report user.

You can define the validation for a particular worksheet cell by clicking a cell and choosing Data → Data Validation to bring up the Data Validation dialog box shown in Figure 15-16.

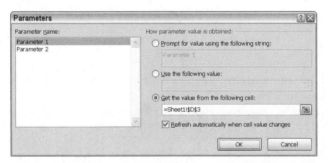

Figure 15-15: You can configure parameters to fetch data from any worksheet cell in the Excel workbook and to automatically refresh the Spreadsheet report whenever the cell value is modified.

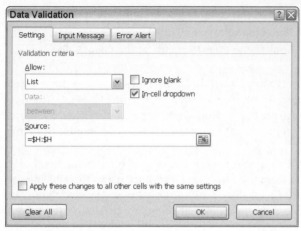

Figure 15-16: You can validate parameters from this dialog box.

From the Data Validation dialog box, you can configure a cell to accept only:

- Any value (no validation)
- Whole number in a particular range
- Decimal value in a particular range
- List of items in a range that can be defined in the worksheet
- Date value in a particular range
- Time value in a particular range
- Particular text length or text length range
- Custom formula

From the Data Validation dialog box, you can also create custom input messages when the cell is selected, and informational, warning, or error messages when the validation conditions you've set are not satisfied.

Complete these steps to customize the parameter values for Product Color and for Product Category and to follow along with the example in this section:

1. Click cell D3 to select it and choose Data → Data Validation to bring up the Data Validation dialog box for the Color parameter.

2. From the Settings tab, select List from the Allow drop-down list, uncheck Ignore Blank, and check In-Cell Drop-Down, click in the Source field, and then either type **=$H:$H** in the field or click the H column.

3. Verify that your Data Validation dialog box looks like Figure 15-16 and click OK to close the dialog box.

4. Click cell D4 to select it and choose Data → Data Validation to bring up the Data Validation dialog box for the Category Name parameter.

5. From the Settings tab, select List from the Allow drop-down list, uncheck Ignore Blank, and check In-Cell Drop-Down, click in the Source field, and then either type **=$I:$I** in the field or click the I column.

Creating a Validation Input Message

You can add an input message that is presented to report users whenever they click a validated cell from the Input Message tab of the Data Validation dialog box (see Figure 15-17). In the Title field, you specify the message header, which appears in a bold font. In the Input Message field, you can create a message that helps the user understand how the validated field works. For this example, I added a message that tells the user that selecting All results in records not being filtered based on a product category value.

To add the Input Message in Figure 15-17 and to continue following along with this example, complete these steps:

1. Continuing with the Category Name field, click the Input Message tab, verify that the Show Input Message When Cell Is Selected option is checked, type **Select a ProductCategory** in Title, and then type **Please Select a product category from the drop-down list. Choose All to select all product categories.**

2. Verify that your dialog box looks like Figure 15-17 and then click the Error Alert tab.

Creating a Validation Error Alert

You can add an Error Alert message, which is presented to report users whenever the value input does not meet the conditions of the data validation. This message is defined in the Error Alert tab of the Data Validation dialog box (see Figure 15-18). In the Style field, you choose from three types of error alert dialog boxes: Stop, Warning, or Information. In the Title field, you specify the message header, which appears in a bold font at the top of the Error Alert dialog box. In the Error Message field, you can create a message that helps the user understand that the field is validated. For this example, I added a message that simply tells users that a valid product category must be selected.

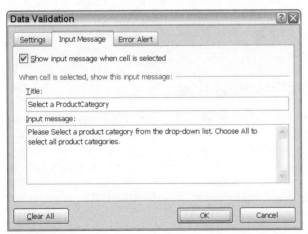

Figure 15-17: You can create a message box for the validated cell from this tab of the dialog box.

Figure 15-18: You can create a message box for the validated cell from this tab of the dialog box.

To add the Error Alert message in Figure 15-18 and to continue following along with this example, complete these steps:

1. From the Error Alert tab, select Stop from the Style drop-down list, type **Invalid Product Category** in the Title field, and type **You did not select a valid product category. Please try again!** in the Error Message field.

2. Verify that your dialog box looks like Figure 15-18, and click OK to add the validation rules and close the dialog box.

Now that the cells for product color and product category name are configured to pull the list of valid values from Columns H–I, you can either type in the valid values or create a Spreadsheet report to import them into the worksheet. The product color cell (D3) is now validated against Column H and the product category name cell (D4) is now validated against Column I. The next step is to either type in the list of valid values or create two more Spreadsheet reports in Columns H–I of the worksheet that automatically extract the list of valid product colors and product category names from the AdventureWorks database.

Creating and Hiding Validation Lists

When a cell is configured to use a list for its validated values (see Figure 15-16), you must specify a range in the worksheet. If there are only a few unique values for the range and the values are not expected to change, you can simply type the values into a column in the worksheet and hide the column. If there are numerous values that are accepted for the range and those values are expected to change, you might consider using a Spreadsheet report with only a single column to pull in the valid values for the parameters.

In the last section, I specified column H for the valid product colors and column I for the valid product category names. As illustrated in the earlier reporting solution example (see Figure 15-1), I used two Spreadsheet reports to pull the list of valid values. The queries that are used for these two Spreadsheet reports are configured differently. For column H (product color), I used the following SQL query for the Spreadsheet report:

```
SELECT DISTINCT Color [Black]
FROM DimProduct
WHERE Color <> 'Black'
```

Notice that the column name is labeled as Black, instead of Color. This is because, if I left the column header as Color, then I'd have to turn the header off and move the Spreadsheet report up one row — otherwise, the value Color would appear in the list of valid values. This method seems a little quicker to me — although it could be problematic if a new color like Azure appeared in the list, because the list of colors would then not be in alphanumeric order. So, you should only use this method when the sort order is not important or you're certain that new items will not be added to the column. Otherwise, you should try using the method that I outline in the second query.

For the second query in Column I (product category name), I used the SQL query here for the Spreadsheet report:

```
SELECT EnglishProductCategoryName
FROM DimProductCategory
```

Once this query is created, the field header EnglishProductCategoryName appears in the first row. This results in the value EnglishProductCategoryName appearing at the top of the list when you click the valid values for Category Name in cell D4 of Figure 15-1. In order to remove that item from the list of valid values, you need to uncheck the Header Row option from the Table Style Options group in the Table Tools tab. This removes the header from the Spreadsheet report, but leaves a blank value where the field header used to be located. In order to remove the blank value, I suggest that you just highlight all the rows in the single-column Spreadsheet report and then drag the report up one row.

Once the Spreadsheet reports are properly working, you'll want to configure them to automatically refresh whenever the report is first opened (refer back to the "Configuring Spreadsheet Report Options" section of this chapter if you need more information about how automatic refreshes work). Additionally, I suggest that you hide these columns because they are not data that you'd want the user to see or try to modify. The columns can be hidden by right-clicking the column header (in this case, the H or I), and choosing Hide from the pop-up menu. If for some reason you need to unhide the columns, just select one column to the left and to the right of the hidden columns, right-click the highlighted columns, and choose Unhide from the pop-up menu.

Working with Validated Parameters in the Report

After you have established the validations and the validation lists for the Spreadsheet report, you're ready to start working in the report solution. Looking at Figure 15-19, you can see how the Input Message that was set up in Figure 15-17 automatically appears when the Product Category parameter cell is selected.

Now try clicking the drop-down arrow for the Product Category cell. You should see a list of valid values (see Figure 15-20) that were populated from the Spreadsheet report in Column I. Additionally, each time the value in the list is changed (for example, from Components to Bikes), the report can be automatically refreshed with the most current data in the data source.

And, if the report user tries to enter an invalid value into the field, the dialog box type (Stop), dialog box title (Invalid Product Category), and the error message that you defined in Figure 15-18 are all displayed (see Figure 15-21).

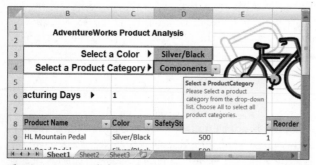

Figure 15-19: Clicking in the Product Category cell automatically displays the Input Message from Figure 15-17.

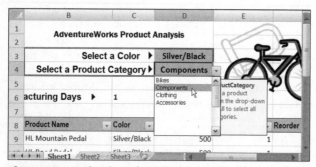

Figure 15-20: The drop-down list shows all values from the Spreadsheet report in Column I of the worksheet.

Figure 15-21: Selecting an invalid value displays the error message.

As you can see with this example, validations and parameters can help you build innovative and powerful reporting solutions using readily available functions that are included in Microsoft Excel.

Trying It Out in the Real World

Dan Bacon, an application specialist at AdventureWorks, has learned about your vast expertise with developing Excel reports and has requested that you provide him with an overview on how a report solution works. After some consideration about how to best deliver this type of training for Dan, you decide that the report solution example shown earlier in this chapter will provide Dan with the necessary insight as to how report solutions are created from the ground up. As part of this training session, you determine that the following components will be covered:

- A primary Spreadsheet report that returns the product category name, product name, product color, product safety stock level, product manufacturing days, and product stock reorder point information for a specified product color and product category

- One secondary Spreadsheet report that is used to feed its valid values for the product color into a parameter cell for the primary Spreadsheet report

- Two parameters that trigger an automatic report refresh of the primary Spreadsheet report whenever one of their values is changed

Getting Down to Business

Follow these steps to complete the real-world example:

1. Verify that the AWProductInfo stored procedure shown earlier in the "Creating a Stored Procedure" section of this chapter has been created in the Adventure-WorksDW database.

2. From Excel, choose Data → From Other Sources → From Microsoft Query to bring up the Choose Data Source dialog box.

3. When the Choose Data Source dialog box appears, verify that Use the Query Wizard to Create/Edit Queries is unchecked, select the AdventureWorks Data Warehouse data source, and click OK.

4. When the Microsoft Query program is launched, you are presented with the Add Tables dialog box. Close this dialog box and click the SQL button.

5. Type the following query into the SQL dialog box and click OK:

```
{Call AWProductInfo (?,?)}
```

6. Click OK to acknowledge that the query cannot be displayed graphically.

7. When the Enter Parameter Value dialog box appears for Parameter 1, type **Black** and click OK.

8. When the Enter Parameter Value dialog box appears for Parameter 2, type **Bikes** and click OK.

9. Click the Return Data to Microsoft Excel button to return the data to Excel and continue.

10. When the Import Data Dialog box appears, choose Table and click OK to create the Spreadsheet report.

11. Click cell H2, type **Black** and press Return to go to cell H3. Type **Bikes** in cell H3 and press Enter.

12. Right-click the Spreadsheet report and choose Table → Parameters from the pop-up menu to bring up the Parameters dialog box.

13. From the Parameters dialog box, select Parameter 1 from the Parameter Name pane, click Get the Value from the Following Cell Button, type **=Sheet1!$H$2** in that field, and check Refresh Automatically When Cell Value Changes.

14. From the Parameters dialog box, select Parameter 2 from the Parameter Name pane, click Get the Value from the Following Cell Button, type **=Sheet1!$H$3** in that field, and check Refresh Automatically When Cell Value Changes.

15. Click OK to close the Parameters dialog box.

16. Click in Cell H2 and choose Data → Data Validation to bring up the Data Validation dialog box.

17. Choose List from the Allow drop-down field, click in the Source field, type **=$K$2:$K$11**, and click OK to close the dialog box.

18. Click in cell K1 and choose Data → From Other Sources → From Microsoft Query to bring up the Choose Data Source dialog box.

19. When the Choose Data Source dialog box appears, verify that Use the Query Wizard to Create/Edit Queries is unchecked, select the AdventureWorks Data Warehouse data source, and click OK.

20. When the Microsoft Query program is launched, you are presented with the Add Tables dialog box. Close this dialog box and click the SQL button.

21. Type the following query into the SQL dialog box and click OK:

```
SELECT DISTINCT Color FROM DimProduct
```

22. Click the Return Data to Microsoft Excel button to return the data to Excel and continue.

23. When the Import Data Dialog box appears, choose Table and click OK to create the Spreadsheet report.

24. Right-click column K of the spreadsheet and choose Hide from the pop-up menu to hide the secondary spreadsheet report for product color.

WATCH THE VIDEO To see how this example is completed, click the ch1501_video.avi file at www.wiley.com/go/excelreporting/2007 and watch the video.

Reviewing What You Did

This example provides you with a quick overview of how two Spreadsheet reports can be linked together using parameters and data validation. The report solution is not as elegant as the example provided in Figure 15-1, but this example does cover the more difficult and crucial components. The icons and formatting shown in Figure 15-1 are the icing on the cake — and are best handled after the parameters, validation, and reports are all working properly. If you need additional practice, I suggest that you add another Spreadsheet report into the report solution for the Product Category field, and then try to provide a more finished look to the report solution, as illustrated in Figure 15-1.

Chapter Review

A lot of ground was covered in this chapter. I started by describing how several reports, components, and tools could be linked to one another for the development of a larger-scale report solution. After that, I covered the various parts of the reporting solution, starting with how the data options could be used to manage report refresh operations. Next, I showed how parameters could be integrated into Spreadsheet reports, such that users could interactively determine what data is loaded into the report. I also demonstrated how parameters could be validated, such that report users could choose from a list of valid values or be limited to specifying data in a specific range or format. As part of this validation, I provided examples of how validated lists could be populated from secondary Spreadsheet reports and how custom messages and error messages could be constructed to help guide user input.

CHAPTER 16

Spreadsheet Report Formatting

Excel provides several types of powerful formatting tools for customizing the display of your Spreadsheet report. Included in the toolkit are powerful tools for conditionally formatting data based on the data's value or particular characteristics. Using the conditional formatting tools, you can highlight important data in the Spreadsheet report using cell formats, icon sets, data bars, and graded color scales. Report developers who use Excel may also be interested in the new report styling features included in Excel 2007 that enable report formatting templates to be saved for later application to new Spreadsheet reports.

I start this chapter with a review of the Spreadsheet styles toolkit. Here, I review how you can add new report styles and select predefined report styles. Next, I cover the general formatting options that are included with Spreadsheet reports. After that, I show you how to use the conditional formatting tools. This includes cell highlighting, data bars, graded color scales, and icon sets. I also demonstrate how conditional formatting rules can be added, edited, and removed. I conclude this chapter with a real-world example on some conditional formatting using icon sets that you can use for additional practice.

Spreadsheet Styling

Instead of customizing each Spreadsheet report with specific font styles, borders, and background cell colors, you can rapidly apply a saved style template with all the settings already defined. This new table styling feature in Excel 2007 enables you to create and save custom formats for numerous elements of a Spreadsheet report. This is an especially helpful feature for report developers who customize their Spreadsheet reports with particular fonts, font colors, font styles, borders, and background fill colors.

Creating a New Style

You can create a new table style by clicking anywhere on the Spreadsheet report and choosing one of the following:

- Home → Format As Table → New Table Style
- Design → Table Styles → New Table Style

Either one of these methods brings up the New Table Quick Style dialog box shown in Figure 16-1.

The New Table Quick Style dialog box is where new table styles can be created for your Spreadsheet report. Here, you assign the name of the table style, and customize the formatting for particular elements of the table, such as the headings, grand total row, and first report column. The style name is important for associating the style with a meaningful description, especially when there are multiple styles defined. For example, a marketing report might be formatted differently than a finance report.

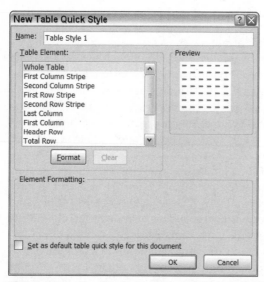

Figure 16-1: Use this dialog box to define a new Spreadsheet style with custom font styles, font colors, cell borders, and fill effects for each element of your spreadsheet.

Customizing Table Elements

Twenty-five elements can be customized for a Spreadsheet report style. These elements are available in the Table Element pane of the New Table Quick Style dialog box (see Figure 16-1). You do not have to define all the elements for a table style, however, because some elements cannot be used concurrently, and some element settings override other element settings. For example, setting the Whole Table element formats all the cells in the Spreadsheet report, but any other element setting overrides the Whole Table setting. So, if the Whole Table element is defined to use a Regular font style and the Total Row element is set to use a Bold font style, the cells in the Total Row would be set to a bolded font, because the Total Row setting overrides the Whole Table setting.

When you apply formatting options to an element by highlighting the element and clicking Format, the element becomes bolded in the Table Element pane. This feature is designed to help you readily identify which elements have formatting options applied to them. You can clear the format by highlighting an element in the Table Element pane and clicking the Clear button.

The Preview icon to the right of the Table Element pane (see Figure 16-2) provides a graphical depiction of how the Spreadsheet report will look once the style is applied. To use the new table style as the default table style for new Spreadsheet reports in the current workbook, check the Set as Default Table Quick Style for This Document option.

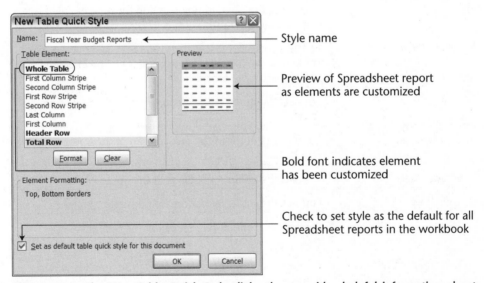

Figure 16-2: The New Table Quick Style dialog box provides helpful information about which elements have been customized and how they affect the Spreadsheet report.

> **NOTE** Styles are saved to a specific workbook and not globally to the general Excel application. If you want to make them global, you'll need to create a workbook template, or modify the default Excel template.

I provide a brief description for each element listed in the Table Element pane of the New Table Quick Style dialog box (see Figure 16-2) in Table 16-1.

Table 16-1: Spreadsheet Report Style Element Descriptions

ELEMENT	DESCRIPTION
Whole Table	Sets a default format for all the elements in a selected Spreadsheet report. Note that other option settings, if defined, override the options set up for this element.
First Column Stripe	Formats the first column stripe of a Spreadsheet report (note that the Banded Columns option must be enabled under the Design tab).
Second Column Stripe	Formats the second column stripe of a Spreadsheet report (note that the Banded Columns option must be enabled under the Design tab).
First Row Stripe	Formats the first row stripe of a Spreadsheet report (note that the Banded Rows option must be enabled from the Design tab).
Second Row Stripe	Formats the second row stripe of a Spreadsheet report (note that the Banded Rows option must be enabled under the Design tab).
Last Column	Formats the items in the last column of the Spreadsheet report.
First Column	Formats the items in the first column of the Spreadsheet report.
Header Row	Formats the column headings of the Spreadsheet report.
Total Row	Formats the totals row of the Spreadsheet report.
First Header Cell	Formats the top-left header cell of the Spreadsheet report.
Last Header Cell	Formats the top-right header cell of the Spreadsheet report.
First Total Cell	Formats the bottom-left total cell of the Spreadsheet report.
Last Total Cell	Formats the bottom-right total cell of the Spreadsheet report.

Applying and Clearing Styles

You can apply a specific style to your Spreadsheet report by clicking the Spreadsheet report to select it and choosing a style from the Table Styles group in the Design tab. You can also choose from a list of styles by clicking the Format As Table button in the Styles group, located under the Home tab.

You can clear the style from a Spreadsheet report by clicking it and choosing Design → Table Styles → Clear. This function removes all the Spreadsheet report formatting.

There are two ways to apply a style. The first method is to Apply and Clear Formatting. The second method is to Apply and Maintain Formatting. If you choose to Apply and Clear Formatting, the formats are cleared prior to the new format being applied. In contrast, if you choose Apply and Maintain Formatting, the existing formats are maintained and only formats defined in the new style are applied to the report.

Managing Styles

Numerous styles are provided with Excel. These styles are grouped into Light, Medium, and Dark. You can also create and save new styles that can be accessed under a Custom tab that appears at the top of this drop-down box. As you peruse the template styles, you may find some of them to be helpful for your Spreadsheet report formatting.

Once a style is added to the Spreadsheet Styles box, you can duplicate, remove, modify, and set the style as a default. The next few sections demonstrate how this is done.

Duplicating Styles

Duplicating styles is useful when you want to keep most of the existing formats from a selected style and customize just a few of the elements. You can duplicate a style by right-clicking a style under the Format As Table button (located in the Styles group under the Home tab) and choosing Duplicate from the pop-up menu. Duplicating a style results in all the settings from the selected style being copied over to the new style. The style name also has a "2" added to the end of the name to distinguish it from the original style.

Once the style is duplicated, you can customize the name and make any adjustments to the table elements settings that are necessary. Note that the new style appears under the Custom group.

Removing Styles

You can remove a style by right-clicking it under the Format As Table button (located in the Styles group under the Home tab) and choosing Remove from the pop-up menu. Note that default styles in the Light, Medium, and Dark groups cannot be deleted. Only the styles under Custom can be deleted.

TIP If you accidentally remove a custom style, you can use the Undo button (available from the Quick Access toolbar ribbon) to add it back to the Styles group.

Modifying Styles

You can modify a style by right-clicking it and choosing Modify from the pop-up menu. Note that default styles in the Light, Medium, and Dark groups cannot be modified, although you can always create a custom version of an existing style by first duplicating it and then making the necessary changes in the New Table Quick Style dialog box.

Setting the Style as a Default

New styles added to the Table Styles drop-down box are placed under the Custom group, located at the top of the box. Right-clicking a Style and choosing Set As Default sets the style as the default style for all new Spreadsheet reports in the workbook. Note that the style is saved to the workbook or the template file that you created. It is not saved globally to Excel.

Setting Report Formatting Options

The formatting options for a Spreadsheet report are configured from the External Data Properties dialog box, shown in Figure 16-3. Here, you can toggle the display of field headings and row numbers, and control whether report formatting changes are maintained each time the Spreadsheet report is refreshed. You can access this dialog box by either right-clicking the Spreadsheet report and choosing Table → External Data Properties from the pop-up menu or by clicking the Spreadsheet report and choosing Design → Properties.

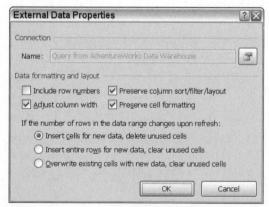

Figure 16-3: Several formatting functions are available from this dialog box.

The options in the External Data Properties dialog box are organized into two sections. In the first section, Connection, the external data source connection name is displayed. Clicking the icon next to this field brings up the Connection Properties dialog box (covered in Chapter 15). The options in the second section, Data Formatting and Layout, are used to toggle display settings and control how new rows resulting from a refresh operation are added into the Spreadsheet report. Table 16-2 provides a more detailed description of each option in this section of the dialog box.

The next few sections provide additional information about some of these formatting options.

Including Row Numbers

If the Include Row Numbers option is checked, a row number column is added to the Spreadsheet report. This column appears as the left-most column in the report and, by default, does not include a field heading. I find this option deficient in that the row numbers start at 0, instead of 1.

Table 16-2: Formatting Options in the External Data Properties Dialog Box

OPTION NAME	DESCRIPTION
Include Row Numbers	Toggles whether row numbers are included as a column in the report. (Note that the row number starts at 0, instead of 1.)
Adjust Column Width	Toggles whether the column widths are automatically adjusted (each time the report is refreshed) to display the best fit for the returned dataset.
Preserve Column Sort/Filter/Layout	Toggles whether the sort, filter, and layout are preserved when the Spreadsheet report is refreshed.
Preserve Cell Formatting	Toggles whether formatting changes are preserved each time the report is refreshed. Use this option in conjunction with Adjust Column Width.
Insert Cells for New Data, Delete Unused Cells	Enables you to insert cells for new data and delete unused cells.
Insert Entire Rows for New Data, Clear Unused Cells	Enables you to insert entire rows for new data and clear unused cells.
Overwrite Existing Cells with New Data, Clear Unused Cells	Enables you to overwrite existing cells with new data and clear unused cells.

Adjusting the Column Width

When the Adjust Column Width option is checked, the Spreadsheet report automatically adjusts each column width for a best fit. These column width settings are automatically applied each time the report is refreshed. Thus, the column widths vary based on the length of the data in each column of the report. This option is generally used in conjunction with Preserve Cell Formatting, because both of these options toggle whether the Spreadsheet report is automatically formatted each time a refresh operation is performed.

> **TIP** If you're going to change column width settings in the Spreadsheet report, be sure to uncheck the Adjust Column Width setting first. This will help ensure that you don't have to readjust the column width settings a second time.

Preserving Column Sort/Filter/Layout

The Preserve Column Sort/Filter/Layout option controls three settings in the Spreadsheet report:

- **Sort Order:** The specified sort instructions
- **Filter Settings:** The specified filter settings
- **Layout:** The order of columns (left to right)

If this option is unchecked, any changes made to the sort, filter, or layout in the Spreadsheet report are removed when the Spreadsheet report is refreshed.

> **NOTE** The sort, filter, and layout settings apply only to the changes specified in the Spreadsheet report. The sorting, filtering, and column order used in the SQL query are not controlled by this option unless you consider that the settings in the Spreadsheet report are actually overriding the sort order, the number of rows displayed, or the order of columns (left to right) specified in the SQL query.

Preserving Formatting Changes

The Preserve Cell Formatting option toggles whether formatting changes made in the Spreadsheet report are saved each time the Spreadsheet report is refreshed. This option applies to both the field headings and the report data. This option is generally used in conjunction with Adjust Column Width, because both of them impact whether the Spreadsheet report is automatically formatted each time a refresh operation is performed.

Conditional Formatting

You can create conditional formatting rules to highlight important data in your Spreadsheet report. These formatting rules can be applied to a specific column, to multiple columns, or to all the columns in the report. Some of the conditional formatting rules even provide options to replace the data. For example, with icon sets, you can display the icon in place of the data, or alternatively, you can display the icon alongside the data in the same worksheet cell. You can even configure the conditional formatting to run multiple times over the data, such that an icon, a data bar, and a color scale are all potentially applied to the same cell.

Adding Conditional Formatting Rules

Conditional formatting rules are added from the Conditional Formatting button, located in the Styles group under the Home tab. There are four ways to add a new conditional formatting rule to a Spreadsheet report:

- Click an icon under one of the Conditional Formatting button submenus.
- Choose Manage Rules under one of the Conditional Formatting button submenus.
- Choose New Rule from the Conditional Formatting button.
- Click the New Rule button from the Conditional Formatting Rules Manager dialog box.

Clicking an Icon

The first method, clicking an icon under one of the Conditional Formatting button submenus, is the fastest way to both create and apply a conditional format rule. This method is the fastest, because it does not require you to customize the settings for the conditional formatting rules. Instead, default rules (evenly distributed percentile range) are applied to the selected data range. Although this method does not provide the upfront capability to customize the conditional formatting rule settings, you can still modify them by bringing up the Conditional Formatting Rules Manager dialog box (explained later in the "Using the Conditional Formatting Rules Manager" section of this chapter).

If you choose this option, you should first select the range of data in the report that you want to format (see the section "Setting the Rule Domain" later in this chapter for more detailed information about how this works). Once the range is selected, click the Conditional Formatting button, choose the type of formatting that you want to apply from the drop-down menu, and then click an icon in the submenu. I demonstrate how this is done in Figure 16-4, by selecting the Green Data Bar icon, located in the Data Bars menu.

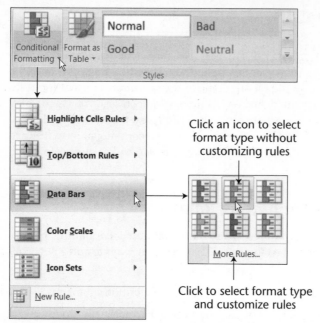

Figure 16-4: Choosing a conditional formatting option rapidly applies the selected formatting option to the Spreadsheet report.

Choosing Manage Rules

The second method, clicking Manage Rules under one of the Conditional Formatting button submenus, is the second fastest way to both create and apply a conditional format rule. This method is ideal when you already know the conditional format that you want to apply — and you need to customize how the rule is applied to the data.

If you choose this option, you should first select the range of data in the report that you want to format (see the section "Setting the Rule Domain" later in this chapter for more detailed information about how this works). Once the range is selected, click the Conditional Formatting button, choose the type of formatting that you want to apply from the drop-down menu, and then click Manage Rules in the submenu. I demonstrate how this is done in Figure 16-4.

Choosing New Rule

The third method for adding a conditional formatting rule in a Spreadsheet report is to click the Spreadsheet report and choose Home → Conditional Formatting → New Rule. This brings up the New Formatting Rule dialog box (see Figure 16-5). Use this method when you want to browse the types of conditional formatting options and select a rule type.

Clicking the New Rule Button

The fourth method for adding a conditional rule in a Spreadsheet report is to add the rule from the Conditional Formatting Rules Manager dialog box. I cover this dialog box in more depth in the "Using the Conditional Formatting Rules Manager" section of this chapter. For now, you should know that this option is best used when there are multiple conditional formatting rules in force, and you want to control how the new rule is going to be managed in the context of these other rules.

Creating a Conditional Formatting Rule

The New Formatting Rule dialog box is where new rules are created for a Spreadsheet report. The same view of this dialog box appears if you add a rule and later modify it; the only difference is that the title is changed from New Formatting Rule to Edit Formatting Rule. As you can see from Figure 16-5, this dialog box is organized into two sections. In the first section, Select a Rule Type, you select the type of rule being used. Here, you can choose from six different types of general rules for formatting the data. Once you choose a rule type, the Edit the Rule Description section in the bottom half of the dialog box is customized to accept more specific details that are associated with the selected rule type. Checking the Format Entire Row box formats all the columns in the selected row instead of just a single column.

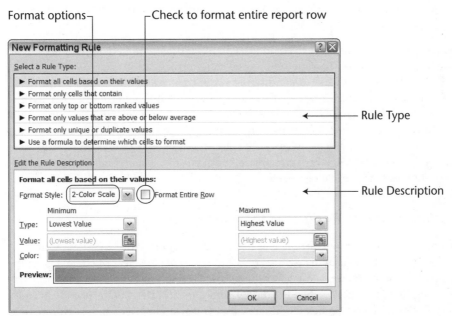

Figure 16-5: The New Formatting Rule dialog box is organized into two sections for a Spreadsheet report: (1) Rule Type and (2) Rule Description.

TIP The Format Entire Row option is only enabled when a single column range is selected. If the selection spans multiple columns, the Format Entire Row option is not available.

I provide more information about each section of the New Formatting Rule dialog box in the following sections.

Setting the Rule Domain

Conditional formatting rules are applied and evaluated on a range, or ranges, of data in a Spreadsheet report, which I refer to as a *rule domain*. This domain could be selected areas within the Spreadsheet report, a particular column, a group of columns (sequential or non-sequential columns), or the entire report. A few important items that you should keep in mind with applying conditional formatting to Spreadsheet reports:

- Select the range before creating the conditional formatting rule.

- If you want to apply the conditional formatting to the entire row in the Spreadsheet report, select only one column in the Spreadsheet report.

- Do not select the column heading in the Spreadsheet report unless you want to format it. (Highlighting the entire column of a Spreadsheet report generally does not work well.)

- Multiple ranges can be selected by holding down the Ctrl key while highlighting each range.

Although the rule domain can be defined after the rule is created, I recommend that you first select the range. This method works better on several fronts. For example, the first two methods for adding a conditional formatting rule ("Clicking an Icon" and "Choosing Manage Rules," covered earlier in the "Adding Conditional Formatting Rules" section of this chapter) require that the range first be selected. Also, the Format Entire Row option only appears when one column in the range is selected (see Figure 16-5). Additionally, it's generally easier to select the range, or ranges, of data prior to bringing up dialog boxes, which can impede both your vision and efficient navigation of the data ranges that must be selected.

Selecting a Single Range for the Rule Domain

Selecting only a single range for the rule domain can be performed by highlighting the cells with your mouse or by using the keyboard shortcuts to select the data. Using the mouse can be problematic, because scrolling down the screen to get to the last row can take a long time, especially when the dataset contains hundreds of thousands of rows. It's usually much faster to click the first cell that you want to select in the column, hold down the Shift key and press Ctrl and the Down Arrow key to go to the bottom of the dataset. Once the data is selected, you can click the Conditional Formatting button to format the data range.

TIP Do not select the column heading in the Spreadsheet report unless you want it to be formatted.

Selecting Multiple Ranges for the Rule Domain

Selecting multiple ranges is accomplished by holding down the Alt key while high-lighting the cells in each range. You can highlight the cells by using your mouse or by using the keyboard shortcuts (explained in the previous section).

Choosing a Rule Type

The first step in adding a new rule is to select a type of rule from the Select a Rule Type section of the New Formatting Rule dialog box. The type of rule that you select deter-mines the formatting options that can be used and how they are applied. Rule types enable you to format data based on the following:

- The cell value
- Cells that contain a specified value or contain values that fall within a particu-lar range
- A top or bottom ranked value or percentile range
- Values above or below a specified average
- Unique or duplicate values
- A custom formula that you can define

As you select different rules types, the rule description and formatting options in the New Formatting Rule dialog box change (bottom section of Figure 16-5). Each rule type provides different formatting options and criteria fields that can be used for spec-ifying the details of the selected rule type.

Formatting Cells Based on Their Values with Graphical Items

The first rule type, Format All Cells Based on Their Values, is the only option that enables you to display data bars, color scales, and icon sets. This option formats all the selected cells in the Spreadsheet report, so there are no operators needed for specifying conditions, such as *greater than* or *less than* a specific number. If you choose this option, skip to the sections on data bars, color scales, and icon sets in the "Formatting the Data" section for more information about how these graphical features are used in a Spreadsheet report.

Formatting Cells Based on a Value or Range

If you want to format cells based on a particular value or range of values, choose the Format Only Cells That Contain rule type from the Select a Rule Type section of the

New Formatting Rule dialog box. When this rule type is selected, the Edit the Rule Description section appears with these operator categories:

- **Cell Value:** Format report cells based on numeric, text, or date data that meet a specific mathematical condition (for example, *greater than*, *less than*, *equal to*).

- **Specific Text:** Format report cells based on text data that *contains*, *does not contain*, *ends with*, or *begins with* a specified text value.

- **Dates Occurring:** Format report cells based on date data that are in the previous, current, or next *day*, *week*, or *month*.

- **Blanks:** Format report cells based on the data being *blank*.

- **No Blanks:** Format report cells based on the data being *not blank*.

- **Errors:** Format report cells based on the data having *errors*.

- **No Errors:** Format report cells based on the date having *no errors*.

You can choose from one of these operator categories by clicking the Operator Category field drop-down arrow, as shown in Figure 16-6.

Additional information on these operator categories is provided in the following sections. Note that I grouped the last four Operator Category items (Blanks, No Blanks, Errors, and No Errors) into one category — Other Operators.

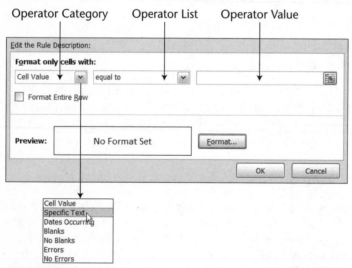

Figure 16-6: Cells can be conditionally formatted based on the different types of operator categories.

Cell Value

The Cell Value operator category provides mathematical operators that can be used with string, numeric, and date data. The following operators are included:

- Between or Not Between a specified range
- Equal To or Not Equal To a specified number or cell value
- Greater Than or Less Than a specified number or cell value

CROSS-REFERENCE **Read the section "Mathematical Operators" in Appendix A for more information about how these numeric operators can be used to filter data.**

Specific Text

The Specific Text operator category provides features for searching for string information. This operator category provides the following four operators:

- Containing or Not Containing a specified text string
- Beginning With or Ending With a specified text string

The Containing and Not Containing operators look for items that have the specified text anywhere in the field. For example, choosing either the Containing or Not Containing operators and specifying Bike in the Operator Value field would find "American Bike Shop", "Bikes and Accessories", "Bikers Anonymous", "Mike's Bike", and "LA Bikers & Rockers". In contrast, selecting the Beginning With operator only finds the field items that start with the string Bike. In this last example, that would include "Bikes and Accessories" and "Bikers Anonymous". Selecting Ending With only returns the field items that end with the string Bike; which in this example, would be only "Mike's Bike".

Keep in mind that there are no operators available for Not Beginning and Not Ending. You'll have to do your best with using the Not Containing operator to identify text that ends or starts with a particular text string, or use a custom formula (explained later in the "Formatting Data Using Custom Formulas" section of this chapter).

Dates Occurring

The Dates Occurring operator category provides features for searching on date information. This operator category provides the following operators:

- Yesterday, Today, or Tomorrow
- In the Last 7 Days
- Last Week, This Week, or Next Week
- Last Month, This Month, or Next Month

These date operators provide a means of dynamically filtering data that is in the previous, the current, or the next day, week, or month. This type of dynamic filtering doesn't require the filter to be regularly updated, because the range stays current with each new day, week, or month. For example, a static filter on today's date would need to be updated for each new day. In contrast, a dynamic filter that specified Today would continue to remain current as each new day passes.

If you do want to specify a particular date (for example, March 12, 2007), you should select the second rule type "Format Only Cells That Contain," specify an operator (such as Greater Than, Equal To, and so on), and input a cell reference into the Operator Value field that contains the date information. Do not type the date directly into the Operator Value field, because the Operator Value field does not recognize dates. (It automatically converts the date to a text string.)

Other Operators

The remaining four operator categories provide features for searching for values that include:

- Blanks
- No Blanks
- Errors
- No Errors

Choosing one of these operator categories suppresses the operator and operator value fields, because there are no conditions to specify for these categories.

Formatting Top or Bottom Ranked Values

You can conditionally format cells that are in the top or the bottom n or $n\%$ (where n is a number between 0 and 100 that you specify) by choosing Format Only Top or Bottom Rank Values from the Select a Rule Type section of the New Formatting Rule dialog box.

Formatting Above or Below Average Values

You can conditionally format cells that are above or below the average value by choosing Format Only Values That Are Above or Below Average from the Select a Rule Type section of the New Formatting Rule dialog box.

Formatting Only Unique or Duplicate Values

The Format Only Unique or Duplicate Values rule type provides you with a method for formatting data that has unique or duplicated values in the selected data range. You can choose either Unique or Duplicate from the Format All field (as shown in Figure 16-7) to format data that is either duplicated or not duplicated.

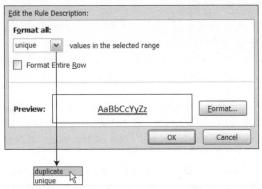

Figure 16-7: Conditional formatting can be applied to the Spreadsheet report based on whether the selected data range has duplicate or unique values.

Because this option uses a range of data, you can determine how many columns of the report should be included in the data range. So, for example, if you wanted to identify customers that purchased the same product on two different orders, you'd select the customer and product columns, but not the order column. This is because the order column would make the range unique.

CROSS-REFERENCE You can either hold down the Control key and click the ranges to select multiple ranges for the duplicate values or move columns in the Spreadsheet report to group them next to one another to make highlighting the range an easier operation. Read Chapter 14 for more information about moving Spreadsheet report columns.

Formatting Data Using Custom Formulas

You can conditionally format cells that are true for a custom formula that you create by choosing Use a Formula to Determine Which Cells to Format from the Select a Rule Type section of the New Formatting Rule dialog box. When you select this option, keep in mind that the formula must begin with an equals sign ("=") and the formula must return a True or a False.

Formatting the Data

Once the rule type and the rule description are set up, the next step is to define the type of formatting that should be applied to the data. There are four types of conditional formatting that you can choose to apply:

- Cell Highlighting
- Data Bars
- Graded Color Scales
- Icon Sets

Cell highlighting includes most cell formatting options, such as number format, font styles, font colors, borders, background cell color, and background cell patterns. This type of conditional formatting can be used with all the rule types except Format All Cells Based on Their Values. This rule type does not require any conditions and is specifically reserved for data bars, graded color scales, and icon sets. Note that if you want to apply cell highlighting to all the data in the report, you should either modify the table style (covered earlier in the "Spreadsheet Styling" section of this chapter) or create a rule under one of the other rules types that selects all the rows (for example, format all cells that are not blank when there are no blank cells in the Spreadsheet report).

Data Bars, Graded Color Scales, and Icon Sets are only available with the first rule type, Format All Cells Based on Their Values. When you select this option, conditions cannot be specified, and only the type of formatting can be controlled.

TIP All four types of conditional formatting can be applied to the entire row of the Spreadsheet report by selecting only one column for the rule domain and checking the Format Entire Row option in the New Formatting Rule dialog box.

I provide more information about each type of conditional formatting in the next few sections.

Highlighting Cells

The Cell Highlighting conditional formatting option applies to all the rule types except Format All Cells Based on Their Values. This formatting feature uses some aspect of the data to determine which cells should be formatted. For example, you could use this rule type to format cells based on the rule domain having values greater than a number that you specify.

The formatting options that can be applied using this rule type include:

- Number formats
- Font styles, colors, and effects
- Border styles and colors
- Cell background colors, patterns, and fill effects

Once you have defined the rule type and specified the rule criteria, just click the Format button in the New Formatting Rule dialog box to bring up the Format Cells dialog box. This enables you to specify the formatting options that you want to apply to the data.

Adding Data Bars

A data bar represents data using a bar that varies in length with the data value. It can only be used on columns in the Spreadsheet report that contain numeric or date information. It does not work on cells that have text data.

You can either use data bars as a substitute for the numeric or date data or configure them to appear in the cell background. By default, the lowest value appears as the shortest bar and the highest value appears as the longest bar. This display setting can easily be customized and even reversed.

You can bring up the Data Bar dialog box by selecting the rule domain in the Spreadsheet report and choosing Conditional Formatting → Data Bars → More Rules. This brings up the New Formatting Rule dialog box with the Data Bar section displayed in the Edit the Rule Description section of the dialog box (see Figure 16-8).

Check the Show Bar Only option to hide the numeric data and show just the data bar. The default setting for a data bar is to use Lowest Value for Shortest Bar and Highest Value for Longest Bar. However, you can change these settings by clicking the Type drop-down fields under Shortest Bar and Longest Bar. The other available types are:

- **Number:** Format the shortest or longest bar to be a specified number.
- **Percent:** Format the shortest or longest bar to be a specified percent.
- **Percentile:** Format the shortest or longest bar to be a specified percentile.
- **Formula:** Format the shortest or longest bar based on a formula.

These other options are useful when the smallest or highest value in the dataset should not represent the shortest or longest data bar, or when the data should not necessarily be represented in a completely discrete manner. For example, perhaps the longest data bar could represent salespersons that are in the top 90th percentile.

You can change the color of the data bar by clicking the Bar Color field. The Preview field, next to Bar Color, shows how the data bar will appear in the Spreadsheet report.

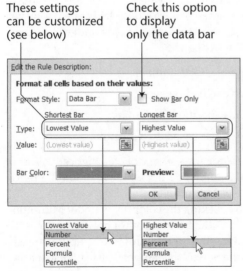

Figure 16-8: Data bars vary with the value of the numeric or date data in the rule domain.

Applying Graded Color Scales

A graded color scale represents data using a color spectrum that changes in color with the value of the data. It can only be used on columns in the Spreadsheet report that contain numeric or date information. It does not work on cells that have text data. This formatting option is something like data bars, except that the cell color varies, instead of the length of the bar. You can choose from a two-color or three-color spectrum. If you choose to use two colors, then colors are specified for the minimum and for the maximum. If you choose three colors, then colors are specified for the minimum, the midpoint, and the maximum. You can also specify each one of these points to utilize a number, a percent, a percentile, or a formula.

NOTE Unlike data bars, color scales cannot be configured to replace the data; they simply highlight the data with a varying spectrum of color.

You can bring up the Color Scales dialog box by selecting the rule domain in the Spreadsheet report and choosing Conditional Formatting → Color Scales → More Rules. This brings up the New Formatting Rule dialog box with the 2-Color Scale section displayed in the Edit the Rule Description section of the dialog box. You can change this to a three-color scale by clicking the Format Style field arrow and choosing 3-Color Scale from the drop-down list. Selecting this option displays Minimum, Midpoint, and Maximum fields in the Edit the Rule Description section of the dialog box, as shown in Figure 16-9.

The Minimum, Midpoint, and Maximum fields are used to indicate what colors should be used to represent the data. The default setting for a three-color scale is to use a red accent for the Lowest Value under Minimum, a yellow accent for 50 percent under Midpoint, and a green accent for the Highest Value under Maximum. However, you can change these settings by clicking the Type drop-down fields under Minimum, Midpoint, and Maximum. The other available types are:

- **Number:** Format cell color based on a specified number.
- **Percent:** Format cell color based on a specified percent.
- **Percentile:** Format cell color based on a specified percentile.
- **Formula:** Format the shortest or longest bar based on a formula.

These other options are very useful when the lowest, middle, or highest values in the dataset are not represented evenly. For example, perhaps yellow should be represented as 30 percent, instead of 50 percent (see Figure 16-9).

You can change the color of the data bar by clicking the color fields under Minimum, Midpoint, and Maximum. The Preview field at the bottom shows how the color scale will appear in the Spreadsheet report. Checking the Format Entire Row option applies the graded color scale to all the columns in the Spreadsheet report, instead of just a single column.

You can vary the midpoint ─

Choose a
two or three
color scale

Check
to format
entire row

Specify
a value,
a percent,
a percentile,
or a formula

Color
spectrum
preview

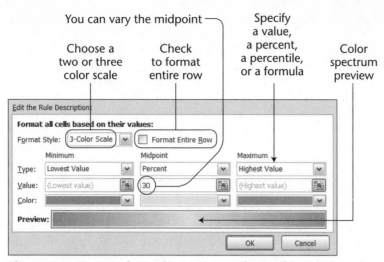

Figure 16-9: You can choose from a two- or three-color scale from the Color Scales view.

Using Icon Sets

You can choose from a library of icon sets to represent your data. These icons can either replace the numeric text altogether or appear to the right of the numeric data. The default icon set is three unrimmed traffic lights. However, you can choose from a list of several icon sets that range from three icons to five icons. The order of these icons can be configured to display in ascending or descending order.

You can bring up the Icon Set dialog box by clicking the Spreadsheet and choosing Conditional Formatting → Icon Sets → More Rules. This brings up the New Formatting Rule dialog box with the Icon Sets section displayed in the Edit the Rule Description section of the dialog box (see Figure 16-10).

Click to format
entire row

Specify a value, a percent,
a percentile, or a formula

Choose from a library
of icon sets that have
3-5 icons each

Reverse the order
of the icons

Click to show
icon only

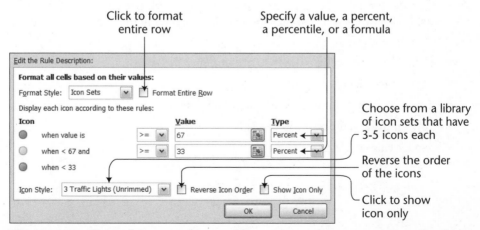

Figure 16-10: Choose from several types of icon sets to enhance or represent the display of numeric data.

For each icon in the selected icon set, you specify an operator, a value, and a type. You can choose from two operators: Greater Than (>) or Greater Than Or Equal To (>=). You can either input a value or a cell reference into the Value field. The available types include Number, Percent, Percentile, and Formula. Notice that the icon rules are displayed from highest to lowest. As you define each level in the icon hierarchy, the icon below it starts with either a Less Than (<) or a Less Than Or Equal To (<=) operator. As you experiment with the rules, you'll notice that changing an operator from Greater Than (>) to Greater Than Or Equal To (>=),or vice versa, changes the operator description directly below it. The same is also true for any number that you type into the Value column. These changes are made to ensure that the rules do not overlap and that all the possible values are evaluated by the rule. For example, in Figure 16-10, the green traffic light (the top light shown in grayscale under Icon) is >= 67 and the yellow traffic light description (the second light shown in grayscale under Icon) is <67. Changing the operator to > and the value to 50 for the green light (the top light), automatically changes the yellow light description from <67 to <=50. If this change hadn't been automatically applied, the rules could have overlapped. This feature eliminates most conflicts, although it's still possible to make a mistake. However, if any of the rules do overlap, you'll get a message box stating that one or more icon data ranges overlap, requiring the error to be fixed before the rule can be created.

Clicking the Reverse Icon Order box reverses the order of the icons, although the values are still specified from highest to lowest. Checking the Show Icon Only option hides the numeric data and shows just the icon. Checking the Format Entire Row option shows icons in all the rows of the Spreadsheet report, instead of just a single column. However, unlike the graded color scales, which generally display well across all the columns of the Spreadsheet report, showing the icons in all the report columns typically looks strange and should probably be avoided, except in rare instances.

Using the Conditional Formatting Rules Manager

The conditional formatting rules are managed from the Conditional Formatting Rules Manager dialog box (see Figure 16-11). Here, you can choose to apply a filter that shows the rules for only a specified domain, such as a worksheet, a PivotTable report, a Spreadsheet report, or selected cells in the worksheet. From this dialog box, you can also:

- Add, delete, and edit conditional formatting rules
- Set rule precedence
- View rule formats for data bars, color scales, and icon sets
- View the area where a rule is applied
- Manage rule conflicts

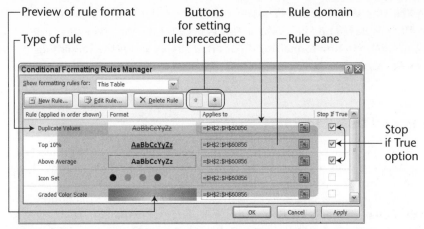

Figure 16-11: Conditional formatting rules are managed from this dialog box.

All the rules in force for the workbook appear in the Conditional Formatting Rules Manager dialog box. You can use the Show Formatting Rules For drop-down field to filter the rules to a particular rule domain, such as the selected Spreadsheet.

The rules in force for the selected rule domain are shown in the Rule pane of the Conditional Formatting Rules Manager dialog box. The rules could be cell formats, data bars, graded color scales, or icon sets. The selected rule format also appears next to each rule in this dialog box. So, for example, if you choose to use a specific icon set or graded color scale, the selected configuration appears in this dialog box. The rule domain, that is, the area where the rule is being applied, appears next to the Format column.

Setting Rule Precedence

The number of conditional formatting rules that can be added to your Spreadsheet report is limited only by your imagination and your computer's available memory. Keep in mind, however, that only one type of unique format rule can be applied. Additionally, the first rule that does the formatting is the rule that prevails when multiple rules are set up. For example, if Rule A formats cells with a green font for field values over 100 and Rule B formats cells with a yellow font for field values over 50, then a cell value of 175 would be formatted in a yellow font, if rule B was first applied. Thus, the ordering of the rules is very important whenever two types of formats are the same or overlapping.

You can set the rule precedence from the Conditional Formatting Rules Manager dialog box (see Figure 16-11). Choose Conditional Formatting → Manage Rules to bring up this dialog box. Once this dialog box is opened, highlight a rule and click the up or down arrows to move the rule up or down in the rule hierarchy. Clicking the Stop If True box halts all formatting to the selected cell, should the cell meet the specified criteria defined for the rule.

> **NOTE** The Stop If True option is not enabled when the rule type is set to Format All Cells Based on Their Values. This is because this rule type does not utilize any criteria to turn formatting on or off; it simply varies the formatting based on the cell value.

Changing and Deleting Rules

Rules can be added, changed, or deleted from the Conditional Formatting Rules Manager dialog box (refer back to Figure 16-11). You can bring up this dialog box by choosing Conditional Formatting → Manage Rules. To modify a rule, open the Conditional Formatting Manager dialog box, select the rules, and click the Edit Rule button. This brings up the Edit Formatting Rule dialog box, which is exactly the same dialog box as the New Rule Formatting dialog box, except that the title is different. To delete a rule, select the rule in the Conditional Formatting Manager dialog box, and click the Delete Rule button.

Trying It Out in the Real World

Dan Bacon, an application specialist at AdventureWorks, was exceptionally pleased with your training on developing Spreadsheet report solutions (from Chapter 15). Dan has already developed several reporting solutions for various department managers. However, Dan has run into a stumbling block with using icons in his report. Dan has requested that you help customize his report with icons.

Getting Down to Business

Follow these steps to complete the real-world example:

1. Verify that the AWProductInfo stored procedure from Chapter 15 has been created in the AdventureWorksDW database.

2. From Excel, choose Data → From Other Sources → From Microsoft Query to bring up the Choose Data Source dialog box.

3. When the Choose Data Source dialog box appears, verify that Use the Query Wizard to Create/Edit Queries is unchecked, select the AdventureWorks Data Warehouse data source, and click OK.

4. When the Microsoft Query program is launched, you are presented with the Add Tables dialog box. Close this dialog box and click the SQL button.

5. Type the following query into the SQL dialog box and click OK:

   ```
   {Call AWProductInfo (?,?)}
   ```

6. Click OK to acknowledge that the query cannot be displayed graphically.

7. When the Enter Parameter Value dialog box appears for Parameter 1, type **Black** and click OK.

8. When the Enter Parameter Value dialog box appears for Parameter 2, type **All** and click OK.

9. Click the Return Data to Microsoft Excel button to return the data to Excel and continue.

10. When the Import Data Dialog box appears, choose Table and click OK to create the Spreadsheet report.

11. Select cells E2 to E130 by clicking cell E2, holding down the Shift key and pressing the Ctrl and the Down Arrow key to select all the cells under the Manufacture Days column.

12. With the Manufacture Days cells being selected, choose Home → Conditional Formatting → Icon Sets → More Rules to bring up the New Formatting Rule dialog box with the Icon Sets option selected for the Format Style field.

13. Choose 5 Ratings from the Icon Style dialog box, and replace Percent with Number from the four drop-down fields under Type.

14. Check the Reverse Icon Order and the Show Icon Only options.

15. Starting with the first icon, type 4, then 3 for the next icon, 2 for the third icon, and 1 for the last icon under Value.

16. Verify that the bottom section of the New Formatting Rule dialog box looks like Figure 16-12, and click OK to create and apply the conditional formatting rule to the Spreadsheet report.

17. Verify that your Spreadsheet report looks like Figure 16-13.

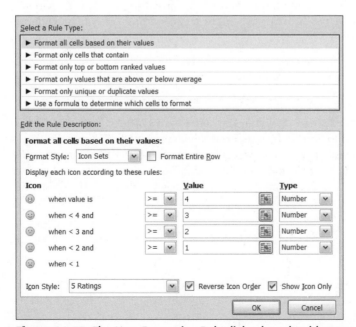

Figure 16-12: The New Formatting Rule dialog box should appear as shown here.

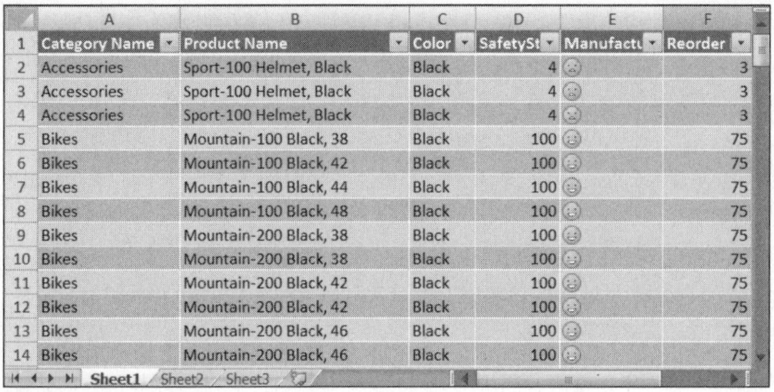

	Category Name	Product Name	Color	SafetySt	Manufactu	Reorder
2	Accessories	Sport-100 Helmet, Black	Black	4		3
3	Accessories	Sport-100 Helmet, Black	Black	4		3
4	Accessories	Sport-100 Helmet, Black	Black	4		3
5	Bikes	Mountain-100 Black, 38	Black	100		75
6	Bikes	Mountain-100 Black, 42	Black	100		75
7	Bikes	Mountain-100 Black, 44	Black	100		75
8	Bikes	Mountain-100 Black, 48	Black	100		75
9	Bikes	Mountain-200 Black, 38	Black	100		75
10	Bikes	Mountain-200 Black, 38	Black	100		75
11	Bikes	Mountain-200 Black, 42	Black	100		75
12	Bikes	Mountain-200 Black, 42	Black	100		75
13	Bikes	Mountain-200 Black, 46	Black	100		75
14	Bikes	Mountain-200 Black, 46	Black	100		75

Figure 16-13: The icons now appear in place of the data under Manufacture Days.

WATCH THE VIDEO **To see how this exercise works, click the ch1601_video.avi file from** `www.wiley.com/go/excelreporting/2007` **and watch the video.**

Reviewing What You Did

This example provided you with a quick overview of how conditional formatting can be used on a Spreadsheet report. It demonstrated how icons could be reversed in the icon set, and how icons could substitute for report data. If you need additional practice, I suggest that you create some more conditional formatting rules in the Conditional Formatting Rules Manager dialog box and practice setting the rule precedence with the Stop If True option.

Chapter Review

I started this chapter with Spreadsheet styles, where I demonstrated how table styles can be added and applied to Spreadsheet reports. Next, I reviewed the general formatting options that are included with Spreadsheet reports. After that, I covered conditional formatting tools, including cell highlighting, data bars, graded color scales, and icon sets. I also showed how conditional formatting rules can be added, edited, and removed.

PART

V

Appendices

SQL Reference

Understanding how to use SQL is important for developing powerful and innovative reports from external data sources. Although there are several functions available in the Microsoft Query program and numerous tools included with Excel's reports, you must hone your SQL programming skills to really take your report development capabilities to the next level. I've included this brief appendix to help get you started. I provide instructions, examples, and guidelines to help you understand and immediately begin using SQL in your Excel reports. It is not meant to be a comprehensive manual, but rather a basic instructional guide and reference.

This appendix starts by outlining how a basic query is structured and shows you the fundamental elements of the `Select`, `From`, and `Where` parts of a query. It also provides an example of a more sophisticated query, breaking apart each section of the query into separate components that are then covered in more detail. Here, string functions, Case logic, aggregate functions, table joins, operators, and sorts are all reviewed.

The queries in this appendix, like the queries throughout this book, use the AdventureWorksDW database and are designed so that you can adjust various lines of the code to see how changes affect the resulting dataset. You can use the information in this appendix, along with the code and examples provided throughout the various chapters, to start writing your own SQL queries.

Dissecting a Basic SQL Query

If you are just learning SQL, it's important that you first learn about the basic structure of an SQL query, as outlined here:

```
SELECT  <Column Name>
FROM    <Object Name>
WHERE   <Conditions>
```

You can select one or more fields (also called *columns*) in the Select part of the SQL query. If you are selecting from multiple tables, I recommend that you specify the table name or the table alias before each field. In the From part of the SQL query, the object name is typically a database table name or a database view name. The conditions in the Where statement are used to restrict the number of rows that are returned from the data source.

Working in the Select

If you put in an asterisk (*) after the Select statement, you will pull all the columns from the database table or the database view identified in the From part of the query. If you want only a specific column, type the column name after the Select.

The following query pulls from the AdventureWorksDW database all the rows from the DimProduct table:

```
SELECT * FROM DimProduct
```

In order to select just one field, say EnglishProductName, use this query:

```
SELECT EnglishProductName FROM DimProduct
```

If you want to label EnglishProductName as something different, say Product Desc, add AS [New Name] after the column, like this:

```
SELECT EnglishProductName AS [Product Desc] FROM DimProduct
```

If you want to select multiple columns from the table, just separate each column with a comma, as shown here:

```
SELECT EnglishProductName AS [Product Desc], Color AS [Color] FROM DimProduct
```

TIP If you are new to SQL programming, watch out for missing or extra commas after column names. This is one of the most frequent problems that users new to SQL seem to experience.

You can also add text in the SQL query by placing it within single quotation marks (' '). For example, I could add a date to indicate when the product was last extracted from the table:

```
SELECT EnglishProductName AS [Product Desc],
       Color              AS [Color],
       '01-01-2007'       AS [Extract Date]
FROM   DimProduct
```

In this example, I labeled the new column as Extract Date, but it could be any name that you choose. I also put each field in the query on its own line. The extra lines make the query easier for me to read and understand and should be a help to others who might have to read or adjust it.

Working in the From

A table name or a view name is used after the From in an SQL query. In the previous section, the table name was DimProduct. If you are selecting from multiple tables, you must assign the table name to any fields that have the same name in the Select part of the query. For example, the following query does not work because the database server doesn't know which table to pull ProductSubcategoryKey from:

```
SELECT ProductSubcategoryKey
FROM DimProduct, DimProductSubcategory

Msg 209, Level 16, State 1, Line 1
Ambiguous column name 'ProductSubcategoryKey'.
```

If the table name is specified before the field name (in the format tablename.field name), the database server is able to run the query because it now knows which table to pull SupplierID from:

```
SELECT DimProduct.ProductSubcategoryKey
FROM DimProduct, DimProductSubcategory
```

Of course, putting the table name before each field seems like a lot of work. So you could simply put an alias after the table name and then use that alias before each field name, as shown here:

```
SELECT prd.ProductSubcategoryKey
FROM DimProduct prd, DimProductSubcategory sub
```

CROSS-REFERENCE In this example, the tables are Cross-joined, producing a Cartesian product from the records of each table. Read Chapter 9 for more information about using table joins.

Working in the Where

The results returned from a query can be restricted by specifying the filter conditions in the Where part of an SQL query. For example, to limit the rows returned from the DimProduct table to just the records with a ProductSubcategoryKey of 2, simply add that condition to the query as shown here:

```
SELECT * FROM DimProduct WHERE ProductSubcategoryKey = 2
```

NOTE Filters based on aggregated data must be put in the Having part of the SQL query.

Working with More Sophisticated SQL Queries

The basic SQL query described in the preceding section shows you how to extract data from a single database table or database view. However, it does not provide any instruction on how to extract data from multiple database sources, use aggregate functions, program Case logic, or incorporate string functions. This section provides a concise reference on these topics that you can use as a guide or a reference.

Dissecting a Sophisticated SQL Query

This section provides an example of a more sophisticated SQL query. I recommend that you retype the query into your SQL development software program to get a better idea of how it works. In order to help you with some of the functions, I break the query apart into more easily understandable components that are covered in detail throughout the remaining sections of this appendix. Here's the query:

```
SELECT UPPER(prd.EnglishProductName)          AS [Product Desc],
       CASE
            WHEN prd.ProductLine = 'M'
              THEN 'Mountain'
            WHEN prd.ProductLine = 'R'
              THEN 'Road'
            WHEN prd.ProductLine = 'S'
              THEN 'Sport'
            WHEN prd.ProductLine = 'T'
              THEN 'Touring'
              ELSE 'Other'
                END                           AS [Product Line],
          SUM(sls.OrderQuantity)              AS [Units Sold]
FROM FactInternetSales sls
INNER JOIN DimProduct prd ON prd.ProductKey = sls.ProductKey
WHERE sls.SalesTerritoryKey IN ('1','3','10')
```

```
GROUP BY prd.EnglishProductName,
         prd.ProductLine
HAVING SUM(sls.OrderQuantity) > 250
ORDER BY 2,3
```

You may not always need to use all the parts listed in this query. However, if you do need to use all of them, you must specify them in this order: Select, From, Join, Where, Group By, Having, and then Order By.

You should specify the fields and conditions common to both tables in the Join (tables) and On (conditions) parts of the query. Although Join...On are not required, it is the ANSI programming standard, and I recommend that you follow it.

Specify the conditions that should be used to restrict the rows returned in the Where part of the SQL query. If the filter conditions are based on aggregated data, such as a Sum or Count, the conditions must be specified in the Having part of the SQL query.

If you are using an Aggregate function, you must include all non-aggregated fields in the Group By part of the SQL query. Otherwise, the following error message is produced:

```
Server: Msg 8120, Level 16, State 1, Line 1
Column 'prd.EnglishProductName' is invalid in the select list ⊃
because it is not contained in either an aggregate function or the ⊃
GROUP BY clause.
```

The Order By part of the SQL query is used to sort the data. You can either specify the column number or the column name. If you specify a column number instead of a column name, be careful to remember that any change to the field order (left to right) or to the number of fields included in the Select part of the SQL query could impact the Order By instructions.

TIP **If you are just learning SQL programming, try to start with a basic query that you can understand and successfully execute. After that, introduce only one new step at a time and verify that each new component works before moving to the next. It's much easier to diagnose a problem when you know where it exists in the SQL query. Adding multiple components at one time can quickly lead to confusion and frustration for beginner-level SQL programmers.**

Using String Functions

String functions are typically used in the Select part of an SQL query to format the results in a particular way. Table A-1 lists some of the String functions available in SQL and the results they produce. You can see how these functions work by replacing the text UPPER(pro.EnglishProductName) (used in the query shown earlier in this section) with the function listed in the first column of this table.

Table A-1: String Functions

FUNCTION	RESULT	EXPLANATION
LOWER(English ProductName)	ml mountain tire	Displays the field in lowercase.
UPPER(English ProductName)	ML MOUNTAIN TIRE	Displays the field in uppercase.
LEFT(English ProductName,4)	ML M	Displays the first four positions of the field.
RIGHT(English ProductName,4)	Tire	Displays the last four positions of the field.
SUBSTRING (EnglishProduct Name,4,5)	Mount	Displays five positions of the field, starting at position four.
REVERSE(English ProductName)	eriT niatnuoM LM	Displays the field in reverse order.
LEN(English ProductName)	16	Displays the length of the field.
STUFF(English ProductName, 14, 2, 're')	ML Mountain Tree	Deletes two positions of the current field, starting at position 14, and replaces it with 're'.
REPLICATE('*',8)	********	Displays eight asterisks.
SPACE(8)		Displays eight spaces.
LTRIM(Field)		Removes the leading spaces from a field.
RTRIM(Field)		Removes the trailing space from a field.

You can also combine multiple String functions to achieve a particular format, and use the + operator to concatenate fields and expressions. Here's a query that uses multiple String functions and concatenates fields. Try experimenting with this query and the functions in Table A-1 to get a better idea of how String functions can be used in your own queries:

```
SELECT   'I am '
       + REVERSE(' eht bmilc ot gniog')
       + LOWER(SUBSTRING(EnglishProductName, 4,8))
       + REPLICATE('!',4)                         AS [MESSAGE]
FROM DimProduct
WHERE ProductKey = '536'
```

```
MESSAGE
-----------------------------------
I am going to climb the mountain!!!!
```

Using Case Logic

Case logic adds a powerful dimension to your reports. Using this function, you can create new fields and new values in the field name. Here's the `Case` statement that was used in the SQL query shown earlier in this appendix:

```
CASE
     WHEN prd.ProductLine = 'M'
        THEN 'Mountain'
     WHEN prd.ProductLine = 'R'
        THEN 'Road'
     WHEN prd.ProductLine = 'S'
        THEN 'Sport'
     WHEN prd.ProductLine = 'T'
        THEN 'Touring'
        ELSE 'Other'
          END                            AS [Product Line],
```

The logic used in this `Case` statement was simple enough. I evaluated ProductLine in order to assign a full description of the one-position value. For records that do not have a value of M, R, S, or T, the Product Line is set to Other.

With a `Case` statement, I have the capability to evaluate multiple conditions, tables, and fields. For example, for product lines not equal to M, R, S, or T, I could have chosen to use the product category for finished goods and the product subcategory for unfinished goods. In that case, I'd evaluate the FinishedGoodsFlag (in the DimProduct table) in the `When` part of the `Case` statement and use the ProductSubcategoryKey or ProductCategoryKey in the `Then` part of the `Case` statement. The possibilities are limited only by your imagination.

When working with Case logic, it's important for you to keep in mind that the first True condition is always used. Be sure to arrange the order of the `When` statements with this understanding in mind.

Try experimenting with this query to get a better idea of how Case logic can be used in your own queries:

```
SELECT EmployeeKey                    AS [Employee Num],
       CASE
         WHEN Gender = 'F'
         AND MaritalStatus = 'M'
         THEN 'Mrs. ' + LastName
       WHEN Gender = 'F'
          THEN 'Ms. '  + LastName
          ELSE 'Mr. '  + LastName
          END                         AS [Employee Name]
FROM DimEmployee
```

```
Employee Num Employee Name
------------ -------------
1            Mr. Gilbert
2            Mr. Brown
3            Mr. Tamburello
4            Mr. Walters
5            Mr. Walters
```

In this example, I created a new field called Employee Name and used multiple When statements to determine how to set the title of courtesy based on marital status and gender. The Case logic could be written many different ways. Here's another example that produces the same results:

```
SELECT EmployeeKey                AS [Employee Num],
       CASE
         WHEN Gender = 'M'
           THEN 'Mr. '  + LastName
         WHEN MaritalStatus = 'M'
           THEN 'Mrs. '  + LastName
           ELSE 'Ms. '   + LastName
           END                    AS [Employee Name]
FROM DimEmployee
```

Notice that I was able to reduce the amount of code by moving the gender test for males to the beginning of the Case statement. Because all other genders must be female, subsequent tests can simply be performed on marital status, instead of both marital status and gender.

When you write your own Case statements, try to organize them in a logical and efficient way, meaning that evaluation of field values should be grouped together whenever possible. Also, don't include unnecessary evaluations in your When statements (for example, gender does not need to be tested again in the second Case example).

Using Aggregate Functions

Aggregate functions compute a single value result for a particular column (or columns). In the query used earlier in this section, I summed the quantity of units sold as shown here.

```
        SUM(sls.OrderQuantity)             AS [Units Sold]
```

If you decide to use an aggregate function in your query, keep the following items in mind:

- All non-aggregated fields must be included in a Group By statement of the SQL query.

- If filters are based on aggregated data, the filter must be specified in the Having part of the SQL query, not the Where part.

In this example, there were two non-aggregated fields in the SQL query, so I had to include them both in the Group By statement as shown here:

```
GROUP BY prd.EnglishProductName,
         prd.ProductLine
```

In order to filter the dataset to only the rows with a total quantity sold greater than 250, I specified the criteria in the Having part of the SQL query, as shown here:

```
HAVING SUM(sls.OrderQuantity) > 250
```

Try modifying the query by placing the filter instructions in the Where part of the SQL query. The query still runs, but the quantity is evaluated *before* the data is aggregated (Where clause), giving you much different results than it does when the quantity is evaluated *after* the data is aggregated (Having clause).

Joining Tables

Tables are joined to one another using fields or conditions common to both tables. If you are just beginning to learn SQL programming, I recommend that you start with the Microsoft Query program to join tables because this is one of the most difficult topics for beginner-level SQL users to understand. You can use the program's graphical tools to build the table joins while the SQL query with the table joins are automatically created in the background.

NOTE Microsoft Query does not create the table joins using the ANSI standard, it applies its own style (explained in Chapter 9). However, it does work, and you can use it as a template or starting point for your SQL query.

Several types of table joins are available. Read Chapter 9 for more information about the meaning of each type of table join and the effect each one has on the resulting dataset.

In the query shown earlier, I created an Inner join between the FactInternetSales table and the DimProduct table using the ProductKey field that is common to both tables, as shown here:

```
FROM FactInternetSales sls
INNER JOIN DimProduct prd ON prd.ProductKey = sls.ProductKey
```

It does not matter whether you use prd.ProductKey = sls.ProductKey or sls.ProductKey = prd.ProductKey in the ON part of the join. However, I do recommend that you be consistent in whatever method you decide to use. Also, keep in mind that the field names do not necessarily have to be the same on each table, and that you might have to specify multiple conditions for the join to work properly.

Using Operators

Several operators are available for you to use in the Where or Having parts of your SQL query to filter data. This section covers the ones you are most likely to use, including the following:

- Mathematical operators
- Comparison operators
- Logical operators

You can read the SQL Books Online (accessed from the Query Analyzer program by choosing Help → Transact SQL Help) if you need more information or examples for other available operators. If you are using SQL Server 2005, select the function that you need additional help with in the query window and then press the <F1> key to bring up the online help.

Mathematical Operators

Table A-2 provides a list of the mathematical operators. These operators perform mathematical functions on numeric data and are typically used in the Select part of the SQL query to compute some type of value, or in the Where or Having parts to build an appropriate filter.

Comparison Operators

Table A-3 provides a list of the comparison operators. You use these operators in the Where or Having parts of an SQL query to filter data.

Table A-2: SQL Mathematical Operators

SQL OPERATOR	EXPLANATION
+	For addition
−	For subtraction
*	For multiplication
/	For division
%	For a modulus (remainder value)

Table A-3: SQL Comparison Operators

SQL OPERATOR	EXPLANATION
=	Equals the specified value
<>, !=	Does not equal the specified value
>	Is greater than the specified value
>=	Is greater than or equal to the specified value
<	Is less than the specified value
<=	Is less than or equal to the specified value
!>	Is not greater than the specified value
!<	Is not less than the specified value

TIP You can use the operators in Table A-2 only to evaluate a single condition. You cannot use these operators to evaluate multiple values like you can with a logical operator, such as IN.

Logical Operators

Logical operators evaluate whether a particular condition is true. Some logical operators such as IN and NOT IN are not limited to a single value, as comparison operators are. In the Where part of the SQL query shown earlier, I used the logical operator IN to select the products with a SalesTerritoryKey of 1, 3, or 10, as shown here:

```
WHERE sls.SalesTerritoryKey IN ('1','3','10')
```

You cannot use a comparison operator for multiple values. In other words, the following query does not work because multiple values are attempting to be evaluated:

```
WHERE sls.SalesTerritoryKey = ('1','3','10')
Server: Msg 102, Level 15, State 1, Line 10
Incorrect syntax near ','.
```

Table A-4 provides a list of logical operators that you can use in the Where or Having parts of your SQL query. Keep in mind that any of these operators accept a preceding NOT to reverse the specified conditions (for example, NOT IN or NOT LIKE).

Table A-4: SQL Logical Operators

SQL OPERATOR	EXPLANATION	EXAMPLE
IN	Contains one of the specified values.	IN ('A','B','C')
LIKE	Used in conjunction with the % wildcard to evaluate whether a text string starts, contains, or ends with the specified text.	Starts with an A: LIKE 'A%' Contains the text Red: LIKE '%RED%' Ends with the text eld: LIKE '%eld'
BETWEEN	Between two values.	BETWEEN 10 and 20
NULL	Has a null value. Fields with a data type of Datetime either have a specific date or a null value (note that a Null value represents that the datetime field does not have a value).	IS NULL

Sorting the Result Set

You can sort one or more columns of the result set by specifying the column name or column number reference in the Order By part of the SQL query. By the column number, I mean the order in which it appears in the Select part of the SQL query. For example, in the Order By part of the SQL query shown earlier, I used the column numbers 2, and then 3, as shown here:

```
ORDER BY 2,3
```

If you decide to use the column number, instead of the column name, keep a close eye on the Order By statement whenever fields are ever added, moved, or rearranged in the query. Inserting a new field between Product Description and Product Line requires that you adjust the Order By to maintain the original sort order. Alternatively, if field names are used instead of field numbers, you no longer have to remain concerned if fields are added or removed. This is what the Order By statement looks like with column names instead of column numbers:

```
ORDER BY prd.ProductLine, SUM(sls.OrderQuantity)
```

An ascending or descending sort order can also be specified after the field name. If no sort order is specified, the database server assumes an ascending sort order. Here's the Order By statement with a descending sort on OrderQuantity and an ascending sort order on ProductLine:

```
ORDER BY prd.ProductLine, SUM(sls.OrderQuantity) DESC
```

Appendix Review

This appendix covered the basics of SQL programming. It started with a review of the basic query structure (Select, From, and Where). After that, I showed you a more sophisticated SQL query and reviewed each part in detail. Keep in mind that this appendix was meant only as a reference or starting point for readers new to SQL programming. As you know if you have some experience with SQL, there are often several ways to accomplish a particular task, and there are many more advanced topics that I simply could not cover in these few pages. Nonetheless, I hope you found this appendix a useful reference and that it inspires you to learn more about SQL.

Pop-Up Menus, Clicking Actions, and Tab Functions

As part of the Excel 2007 redesign, Microsoft made significant improvements and changes to the reporting tools. In this latest Excel version, a new section and a plethora of new functions have been added to the PivotTable Field List dialog box. The previously diminutive PivotTable toolbar has been transformed into a formidable Excel tab that spans the entire length of the workbook. The right-click pop-up menus in the Report Layout area have also been enhanced to provide context-specific functions.

All these changes got me thinking that it would be nice to summarize the various pop-up menus, tab functions, and clicking actions into a single appendix that could easily be referenced. So, instead of searching through several chapters for what's available across the various PivotTable components, you can obtain a centralized list of functions and actions in this appendix.

I start this appendix with a summary of double-click actions and right-click pop-up menus in the Report Layout area. After that, I review each group of the PivotTable tab, providing brief explanations of each button. I wrap up with a summary of the left- and right-click functions in the PivotTable Field List dialog box.

Working in the Report Layout Area

The PivotTable report is displayed in the Report Layout area. Here, you can double-click several types of report components to bring up dialog boxes or perform report actions. You can also right-click various parts of the PivotTable to bring up context-specific pop-up menus. In this section of the appendix, I describe the resulting actions of double-clicking different areas of a PivotTable report and summarize the various types of right-click pop-up menus that are available in the Report Layout area. Keep in mind that explanations are typically brief (because this is an appendix), so be sure to refer to the appropriate chapters for more information about particular terminology, functions, and features.

Understanding Double-Click Actions

There are several areas of a PivotTable report for which items can be double-clicked. These double-clicking actions are shortcuts to functions that are also available in the right-click pop-up menus. The available double-click actions are summarized in Table B-1 and illustrated in Figure B-1.

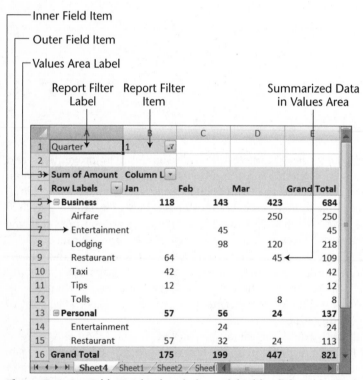

Figure B-1: See Table B-1 for descriptions of double-click actions in the various areas of this PivotTable report.

Table B-1: Double-Click Actions in the Report Layout Area

ITEM	DOUBLE-CLICK ACTION DESCRIPTION
Report Filter area label	Brings up the Field Settings dialog box with the Subtotal and Filters tab displayed.
Report Filter area item	Brings up a Microsoft Excel dialog box error message stating that detail cannot be shown or hidden for this area.
Values field label	Brings up the Data Field Settings dialog box with the Summarize By tab displayed.
Summarized data in the Values area	Brings up a new worksheet with the underlying data that comprises that cell's summarized value.
Outer-field in the Row Labels or Column Labels area	Collapses or expands the detail of all the inner fields. [†]
Inner field in the Row Labels or Column Labels area	Brings up a list of fields not already in the PivotTable report that can be displayed. [‡]

[†] If specific items at lower levels in the hierarchy are collapsed by the report user, these settings are retained and not displayed when the selection is later expanded.

[‡] Fields that are only in the Values area of the PivotTable are summarized as a new field (for example, Sum of Amount) and are therefore available to be displayed as an inner field.

Looking at Right-Click Pop-Up Menus

Right-click pop-up menus are useful for quickly accessing PivotTable design and management functions. Using these pop-up menus, you can rapidly perform report functions such as refreshing a report, sorting data, applying filters, and changing summary types. In this section, I review the following five types of pop-up menus that can be accessed from an Excel PivotTable report:

- Report Filter label or item
- Report Layout area
- Column Labels items or Row Labels items
- Values area
- Grand Total

These pop-up menus are illustrated in Figure B-2 and are described in greater detail throughout the new few sections of this appendix.

CROSS-REFERENCE These pop-up menus are shown only for OLTP data sources. If you are accessing an OLAP data source, the pop-up menus are displayed differently. Read the online OLAP chapter for more information on OLAP pop-up menus.

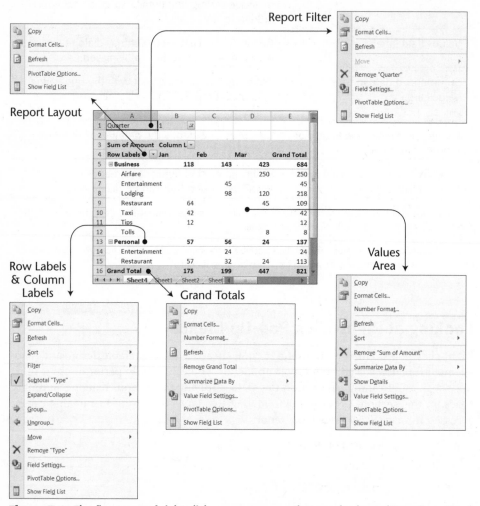

Figure B-2: The five types of right-click pop-up menus that can be brought up from Excel for non-OLAP data sources.

Report Filter Area Pop-Up Menu

The Report Filter pop-up menu shown in Figure B-3 can be accessed by clicking any field or field item in the Report Filter area. This pop-up menu provides functions for copying data to the clipboard, toggling the display of the PivotTable Field List dialog box, moving and removing fields, and accessing the Table Options and Field Settings dialog boxes.

The menu items in this pop-up menu are summarized in Table B-2.

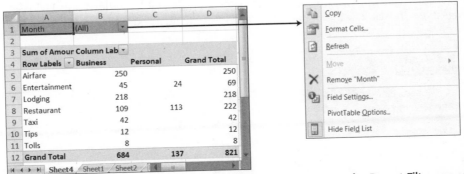

Figure B-3: Right-clicking cells in the Report Filter area brings up the Report Filter pop-up menu.

Table B-2: Report Filter Area Pop-Up Menu Items

MENU ITEM	DESCRIPTION
Copy	Copies the value in the selected cell to the clipboard.
Format Cells	Brings up the Format Cell dialog box where items or labels can be formatted.
Refresh	Refreshes the PivotTable report.
Move	Enables you to move the selected field up or down in the list of available fields in the Report Filter area.
Remove	Removes the field from the Report Filter area.
Field Settings	Brings up the Field Settings dialog box.
PivotTable Options	Brings up the PivotTable Options dialog box.
Hide (Show) Field List	Hides or shows the PivotTable Field List dialog box.

Report Layout Pop-Up Menu

The Report Layout pop-up menu can be accessed by clicking any heading in the Row Labels or Column Labels areas. In Figure B-4, this is the cell range B3:D3 and cell A4. Keep in mind that a number of variables determine the exact size and location of the label area, such as the number of items in the Column Labels area, the location of the PivotTable report in the worksheet, the number of items being summarized in the Values area of the report, and whether field headers are displayed.

The Report Layout pop-up menu provides a short list of functions for refreshing the PivotTable report, formatting labels, and accessing the Table Options and Field Settings dialog boxes. The menu items in this pop-up menu are summarized in Table B-3.

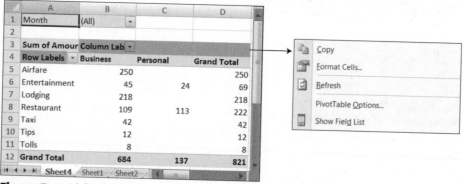

Figure B-4: Right-click Row Labels or Column Labels headings to bring up the Report Layout pop-up menu.

Table B-3: Report Layout Area Pop-Up Menu Items

MENU ITEM	DESCRIPTION
Copy	Copies the value in the selected cell to the clipboard.
Format Cells	Brings up the Format Cell dialog box where labels can be formatted.
Refresh	Refreshes the PivotTable report.
PivotTable Options	Brings up the PivotTable Options dialog box.
Hide (Show) Field List	Hides or shows the PivotTable Field List dialog box.

Row Labels and Column Labels Pop-Up Menus

The pop-up menus for the Row Labels or Column Labels areas can be accessed by clicking any field label or item in either the Row Labels or the Column Labels areas, as illustrated in Figure B-5.

These Row Labels and Column Labels pop-up menus contain many of the same types of functions that are accessible from the pop-up menus in the PivotTable Field List dialog box. There are some functions in this menu, however, that are not accessible from the PivotTable Field List dialog box. This includes copying data to the clipboard, grouping and ungrouping data, collapsing and expanding fields, subtotaling data, and refreshing the PivotTable report. The menu items in this pop-up menu are summarized in Table B-4.

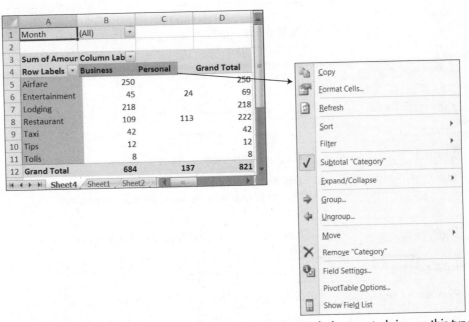

Figure B-5: Right-click cells in the Row Labels or Column Labels areas to bring up this type of pop-up menu.

Table B-4: Row Labels and Column Labels Pop-Up Menu Items

MENU ITEM	DESCRIPTION
Copy	Copies the value in the selected cell to the clipboard.
Format Cells	Brings up the Format Cell dialog box where items or labels can be formatted.
Refresh	Refreshes the PivotTable report.
Sort	Sorts the items in the selected field in ascending or descending order. The Sort dialog box (where more advanced sorting options are located) can also be accessed from this pop-up menu by choosing Sort → More Sort Options.
Filter	Provides several tools for filtering the field labels or field items. The Filter dialog boxes can also be launched from here.
Subtotal	Toggles subtotaling of inner fields for a selected outer field.
Expand/Collapse	Expands or collapses the detail for an outer field.
Group	Groups selected items into a new PivotTable field.
Ungroup	Ungroups selected items from a PivotTable field.
Move	Enables you to move the selected field up or down in the list of available fields in the Row Labels or Column Labels areas.
Remove	Removes the selected field from the Row Labels or Column Labels area.
Field Settings	Brings up the Field Settings dialog box.
PivotTable Options	Brings up the PivotTable Options dialog box.
Hide (Show) Field List	Hides or shows the PivotTable Field List dialog box.

Values Pop-Up Menus

The Values pop-up menu can be accessed by clicking any cell in the Values area of the PivotTable, as illustrated in Figure B-6.

The Values area pop-up menu provides several useful functions for summarizing and formatting summarized fields in the Values area of the PivotTable report. There are also functions for drilling-down on the data, sorting data, and refreshing the PivotTable report. The Data Field Settings and Table Options dialog box can also be accessed from this pop-up menu. The menu items in this pop-up menu are summarized in Table B-5.

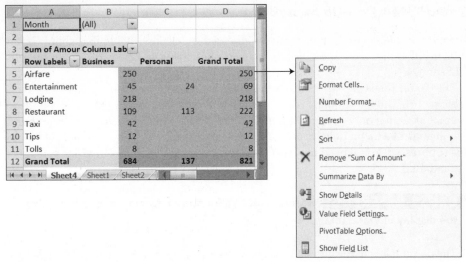

Figure B-6: Right-click cells in the Values area to bring up this pop-up menu.

Table B-5: Values Pop-Up Menu Items

MENU ITEM	DESCRIPTION
Copy	Copies the value in the selected cell to the clipboard.
Format Cells	Brings up the Format Cells dialog box where items or labels can be formatted across six available tabs.
Number Format	Brings up the Format Cells dialog box with just the Number Format tab displayed and available.
Refresh	Refreshes the PivotTable report.
Sort	Sorts the items in the selected field in ascending or descending order. The Sort dialog box (where more advanced sorting options can be accessed) can also be accessed from this pop-up menu by choosing Sort → More Sort Options.
Remove	Removes the selected field from the Values area.
Summarize Data By	Provides a list of aggregate functions for summarizing the selected field.
Show Details	Brings up the underlying dataset that comprises the selected cell in a new worksheet tab.
Value Field Settings	Brings up the Data Field Settings dialog box.
PivotTable Options	Brings up the PivotTable Options dialog box.
Hide (Show) Field List	Hides or shows the PivotTable Field List dialog box.

Grand Totals Pop-Up Menus

The Grand Totals pop-up menu can be accessed by clicking fields that show Grand Total in either the Row Labels or the Column Labels areas. In Figure B-7, these are cells A12 and D4.

The Grand Totals pop-up menu also operates on fields in the Values area of the Pivot-Table report. Thus, it contains many of the same functions as the Values area pop-up menu. In fact, the only new pop-up menu item is Remove Grand Total. Keep in mind that there isn't a menu item on any of the pop-up menus to display a grand total once it is suppressed. You'll need to access the Table Options dialog box in order to display a grand total.

CROSS-REFERENCE Read Chapter 11 for more information about toggling the display of grand totals.

The menu items in the Grand Totals pop-up menu are summarized in Table B-6.

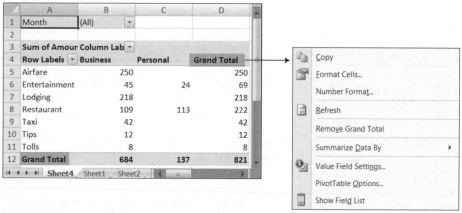

Figure B-7: Right-clicking Grand Total for either the Column Labels or Row Labels area brings up this pop-up menu.

Table B-6: Grand Totals Pop-Up Menu Items

MENU ITEM	DESCRIPTION
Copy	Copies the value in the selected cell to the clipboard.
Format Cells	Brings up the Format Cells dialog box where items or labels can be formatted across six available tabs.
Number Format	Brings up the Format Cells dialog box with just the Number Format tab displayed and available.
Refresh	Refreshes the PivotTable report.

Table B-6 *(continued)*

MENU ITEM	DESCRIPTION
Remove Grand Total	Removes the Grand Total for the selected field from the Row Labels or Column Labels area of the PivotTable.
Summarize Data By	Provides a list of aggregate functions for summarizing the selected field.
Value Field Settings	Brings up the Data Field Settings dialog box.
PivotTable Options	Brings up the PivotTable Options dialog box.
Hide (Show) Field List	Hides or shows the PivotTable Field List dialog box.

Working with the PivotTable Tab

The PivotTable tab is useful for managing many types of report operations. Included in this component are several functions that are not available on any other report components, such as changing the data source, toggling display options, creating an associated PivotChart, and accessing dialog boxes for managing Calculated Fields and Calculated Items. There are also many functions that are available in one or more report components, such as sorting and grouping data, collapsing and expanding details, and refreshing data.

Accessing the PivotTable Tab

The PivotTable tab (see Figure B-8) is only available when a PivotTable report exists and is selected in the workbook. You can access this tab by clicking the PivotTable Tools button above the Options menu in the Excel workbook.

CROSS-REFERENCE Read Chapter 3 for more information about accessing the PivotTable tab.

Figure B-8: The PivotTable tab includes eight groups for accessing functions to manage PivotTable reports.

Looking at the PivotTable Tab Groups

The buttons on the PivotTable tab are organized into the following eight groups:

- **PivotTable:** Accessing the PivotTable Options dialog box, changing the Pivot-Table report name, showing Report Filter pages, and toggling the Generate Get PivotTable option

- **Active Field:** Expanding and collapsing fields, changing field names, and accessing the Field Settings dialog boxes

- **Group:** Grouping and ungrouping data

- **Sort:** Basic and advanced sorting operations

- **Data:** Refreshing report data, configuring access options, and changing the data source

- **Actions:** Clearing filters, removing all fields from the PivotTable report, selecting PivotTable areas, and moving the PivotTable report

- **Tools:** Creating a PivotChart, managing Calculated Fields, Calculated Items, and accessing OLAP tools

- **Show/Hide:** Toggling the display of the PivotTable Field List dialog box, expansion buttons (+/−), and Field Headers

The arrangement and the display width of the eight groups of the PivotTable tab cannot be individually sized, and depending on your display configuration (from 1024×768 to 1900×1200), some of the tab groups may automatically be collapsed into smaller sections. Lower-resolution settings provide a single-button shortcut to the full suite of buttons and available functions that are accessible in some of the collapsed PivotTable groups. Shrinking the screen size has a similar effect.

PivotTable Group

The PivotTable group is shown in Figure B-9. It includes an Options button for accessing the PivotTable Options dialog box, showing the Report Filter area pages, and toggling the Generate Get PivotData setting. The name of the PivotTable also appears in the top left of this PivotTable tab group.

CROSS-REFERENCE You can see the PivotTable name is displayed in the Report Layout field when there are no fields in the PivotTable. Though it was mainly used for VBA programming in earlier versions of Excel, it has become more important in Excel 2007, because external data source connections can be readily traced to PivotTable report names. Review the "Viewing Where Connections Are Used in the Workbook" section of Chapter 4 to see how this works.

Figure B-9: Modify the PivotTable report name and change PivotTable option settings from this tab group.

The Options button includes the following menu items:

- **Options:** Brings up the PivotTable Options dialog box.

- **Show Report Filter Pages:** Creates new worksheet tabs for each unique item in a specified Report Filter area.

- **Generate GetPivotData:** This item can be toggled, such that references to cells in the PivotTable use the cell reference (unchecked) or use the GetPivotData function (checked).

TIP The Generate GetPivotData item is a very useful tool when you are looking up or referencing cells of a PivotTable report. If the report shape is expected to be static (meaning that the shape is not expected to change), uncheck the GetPivotData option to reference the cell location instead of the PivotTable location. This makes it easy to copy and paste multiple cell references in the PivotTable. By contrast, if the report shape is expected to be dynamic and you need the specific cell value for a particular intersection of a specific Row Labels and Column Labels item, check the GetPivotData option. This setting ensures that you pull the correct value for a specified intersection, regardless of how the PivotTable shape is changed.

Active Field Group

The Active Field group shows which field is selected in the PivotTable. It includes buttons for expanding and collapsing details and accessing the Field Settings dialog box for the selected field. In Figure B-10, Type is the selected field.

The buttons and associated functions for each button in the Active Field group of the PivotTable tab are summarized in Table B-7.

Figure B-10: You can expand and collapse field hierarchies and access the Field Settings dialog box from this group of the PivotTable tab.

Table B-7: Buttons and Descriptions for the Active Field Group

BUTTON	DESCRIPTION
Field Settings	Opens the Field Settings dialog box for the selected field.
Expand Entire Field	Shows the inner field(s) for a selected outer field.
Collapse Entire Field	Hides the inner field(s) for a selected outer field.

Group Section

The Group section shown in Figure B-11 includes three buttons for grouping and ungrouping fields in the PivotTable report.

The Group Selection button creates a new group from items that you select in either the Row Labels or the Column Labels areas. You can group items that are in sequential order by highlighting the items with your mouse and then clicking the Group button. You can also group non-sequential items by holding down the Control key while left-clicking each item of a particular field to select it. Once all the items are selected, click the Group button to bind the selected fields into a new group. The Ungroup button simply ungroups items that have already been grouped into a new field. Just select the group field name and click the Ungroup button to remove the group and the associated field from the PivotTable report.

TIP Ungrouping items in a grouped field is the only way to remove the group from the list of available fields in the PivotTable Field List dialog box.

The buttons and associated functions for each button in the Group section of the PivotTable tab are summarized in Table B-8.

Figure B-11: You can group and ungroup items in the PivotTable report from this group of the PivotTable tab.

Table B-8: Buttons and Descriptions for the Group Section

BUTTON	DESCRIPTION
Group Selection	Groups the selected items for a field into a new field in the PivotTable report.
Ungroup	Ungroups a selected field and removes the grouped field from the list of available fields in the PivotTable Field List dialog box.
Group Field	Used for grouping and ungrouping numeric and date fields. As of this writing, Microsoft hadn't fully enabled the Group Field button yet.

Sort Group

The Sort group shown in Figure B-12 includes three buttons for sorting items in the Values, Row Labels, and Column Labels areas of the PivotTable report. The A → Z button sorts items in ascending order, and the Z → A button sorts items in descending order. Clicking the Sort button brings up either the Sort dialog box (for non-aggregated data in the Row Labels or Column Labels areas) or the Sort By Value dialog box (for aggregated data in the Values area), where more advanced sorting options can be applied.

The buttons and associated functions for each button in the Sort group of the PivotTable tab are summarized in Table B-9.

Figure B-12: Apply basic and advanced sorts from this group of the PivotTable tab.

Table B-9: Buttons and Descriptions for the Sort Group

BUTTON	DESCRIPTION
A → Z	Sorts items in ascending order.
Z → A	Sorts items in descending order.
Sort	Brings up the Sort or Sort By Value dialog box for applying more advanced sorting functions.

Data Group

The Data group shown in Figure B-13 includes two buttons for refreshing data and changing the source data connection.

The Refresh drop-down button includes menu items for refreshing a selected Pivot-Table report, refreshing all the PivotTable reports in the workbook, monitoring the refresh operation(s) status, canceling a refresh operation, and accessing the Connection Properties dialog box. Clicking the main Refresh button simply refreshes the selected PivotTable report.

The Change Data Source button has two menu items under its button: Connection Properties and Change Data Source. The Connection Properties item performs the same function as the Connection Properties item under the Refresh button; it simply brings up the Connection Properties dialog box. Selecting the Change Data Source item or clicking the Change Data Source button brings up the Change PivotTable Data Source dialog box, where you can change the PivotTable source data to a different location. This works for both internal and external data sources, including OLTP and OLAP data sources.

The buttons and associated functions for each button in the Data group of the Pivot-Table tab are summarized in Table B-10.

Actions Group

The Actions group shown in Figure B-14 includes three buttons: one for clearing filters and removing all the fields from the Report Layout area (Clear button), one for selecting different areas of the PivotTable report (Select button), and one for moving the Pivot-Table report to a different location (Move PivotTable button).

Figure B-13: Refresh or change the source data location of a PivotTable report from this group of the PivotTable tab.

Table B-10: Buttons and Descriptions for the Data Group

BUTTON	DESCRIPTION
Refresh	Refreshes a PivotTable report(s), monitors and cancels refresh operations, and accesses the Connection Properties dialog box.
Change Data Source	Changes the data source for a PivotTable report and accesses the Connection Properties dialog box.

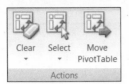

Figure B-14: The Actions group of the PivotTable tab includes tools for clearing filters and fields from the PivotTable report, selecting PivotTable components, and moving the PivotTable report to another worksheet.

The Clear button has two items in the drop-down menu. The first option, Clear All, clears all the filter settings and removes all the fields from the Report Layout area. This is a useful function for rapidly starting a new report using the same source data. The second option, Clear Filters, simply clears all the field filters that are applied in the Report Filter, Row Labels, and Column Labels areas of the report. This is another useful function for maintaining the report layout while clearing all the filter settings.

The Select button can be used to select Labels or Values areas of a PivotTable report. Once an area is selected, you can format, copy, or make changes to the selection. The Enable Selection item under the Select button can be toggled on or off to enable selection of individual cells, all instances of a single item, subtotals, and totals.

The Move PivotTable button enables you to move the selected PivotTable report to a new location, either in the same workbook (in a new cell or worksheet tab) or in a new workbook. Note that there are no options for transferring the PivotTable to another existing workbook; you'll need to use the Move Sheet function to do that.

The buttons and associated functions for each button in the PivotTable Actions group of the PivotTable tab are summarized in Table B-11.

Tools Group

This tab group shown in Figure B-15 lists three buttons that perform very different functions. The PivotChart button at the top of the list provides a handy means of rapidly adding a PivotChart to the selected PivotTable report. Clicking this button brings up the Create Chart dialog box where you can select a chart type for your Pivot-Chart. The Formulas button, located under the PivotChart button, includes functions for creating a Calculated Item or a Calculated Field. You can also list formulas and view the formulas for Calculated Items from this button. The OLAP Tools button at the bottom of the list has three functions for viewing field properties, creating and toggling the connection to an OLAP cube, and converting OLAP data to MDX formulas.

Table B-11: Buttons and Descriptions for the PivotTable Actions Group

BUTTON	DESCRIPTION
Clear	Removes filter settings and/or clears all fields from the Report Layout area.
Select	Enables selection of Labels or Values areas of a PivotTable report.
Move PivotTable	Moves a PivotTable report to a new location in the workbook or to a new workbook.

The buttons and associated functions for each button in the Tools group of the Pivot-Table tab are summarized in Table B-12.

Show/Hide Group

The Show/Hide group shown in Figure B-16 includes three buttons: one for toggling the display of the PivotTable Field List dialog box, one for expansion (+/−) buttons, and one for the Row Labels and Column Labels field headers.

The display of the PivotTable Field List dialog box can be toggled by clicking the Field List button. The +/− Buttons button controls whether expansion buttons appear for outer fields when there is more than one field in the Row Labels or Column Labels areas. The Field Headers button controls whether field headers are displayed in the PivotTable report. Unless renamed, the default field header names simply show the name of the area: Row Labels or Column Labels. Of course, these field headers can be renamed to something more meaningful. For example, if you dropped the City, Province, and Country fields in the Row Labels area, you might set the field header name to Geographical Region.

The buttons and associated functions for each button in the Show/Hide group of the PivotTable tab are summarized in Table B-13.

Figure B-15: The Tools group of the PivotTable tab includes tools for creating a PivotChart, managing Calculated Fields, and accessing OLAP tools.

Table B-12: Buttons and Descriptions for the Tools Group

BUTTON	DESCRIPTION
PivotChart	Brings up the Create Chart dialog box for creating a PivotChart from the PivotTable.
Formulas	Enables you to manage Calculated Fields and Calculated Items.
OLAP Tools	Enables you to show properties, manage offline OLAP, and convert OLAP data to MDX formulas.

Figure B-16: Display settings for the PivotTable report can be toggled from this group of the PivotTable tab.

Table B-13: Buttons and Descriptions for the Show/Hide Group

BUTTON	DESCRIPTION
Field List	Toggles the display of the PivotTable Field List dialog box.
+/– Buttons	Toggles the display of expansion buttons when two or more items are in the Row Labels or Column Labels area of the PivotTable report.
Field Headers	Toggles the display of field headers in the Row Labels and Column Labels areas of the PivotTable report.

Clicking in the PivotTable Field List Dialog Box

The Fields and Areas sections of the dialog box each provide a unique set of functions. The Fields section includes functions for sorting data, configuring filters, and setting field locations. The Areas section includes tools for moving fields up or down in the hierarchy, switching field locations, and accessing the Field Settings dialog box, where more advanced tools and options can be used. Right-clicking and left-clicking fields in each of these two sections of the PivotTable Field List dialog box brings up different pop-up menus where you can access these commonly used functions for managing the PivotTable report. I've summarized the functions and pop-up menu items in Table B-14.

Table B-14: Left- and Right-Click Functions in the PivotTable Field List Dialog Box

ACTION	FIELDS SECTION	AREAS SECTION
Right-click field	Brings up a pop-up menu where the field can be added or moved to a selected PivotTable report area.	No action.
Left-click check box	Adds (checked) or removes (unchecked) the field from the PivotTable.	Not applicable because fields in the Areas section do not have a check box.

(continued)

Table B-14 *(continued)*

ACTION	FIELDS SECTION	AREAS SECTION
Left-click drop-down arrow next to field	Brings up filter dialog boxes.	Brings up a pop-up menu where the field can be moved to a different report area, removed from the report, or moved up or down in the hierarchy of fields in the selected area. The Field Settings dialog box can also be launched from here.

Fields Section

Fields in the Fields section of the PivotTable Field List dialog box can either be left-clicked or right-clicked. Right-clicking a field brings up the pop-menu shown in Figure B-17, where you can move or add a field to a selected location in the PivotTable.

Left-clicking a field brings up a filter dialog box where you can sort items and apply filters to items and labels. Note that fields already in the Report Filter area of the Pivot-Table show a simplified filter dialog box, where items can only be checked or unchecked.

Areas Section

Fields in the Areas section of the PivotTable Field List dialog box can only be left-clicked. Double-clicking and right-clicking fields in the Areas section do not invoke any function or action. The left-click pop-up menu shown in Figure B-18 provides a list of functions that enable you to move the field up or down in the hierarchy of fields in the particular PivotTable area or to another area of the PivotTable report.

The items for this pop-up menu are summarized in Table B-15.

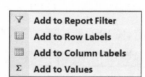

Figure B-17: Right-click a field in the Fields section of the PivotTable Field List dialog box to add or move it to a particular location in the PivotTable report.

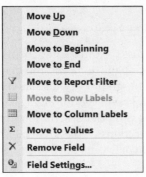

Figure B-18: Left-click a field in the Areas section of the PivotTable Field List dialog box to set the field location or remove it from the PivotTable report.

Table B-15: Left-Click Pop-Up Menu Items for the Areas

MENU ITEM	DESCRIPTION
Move Up	Moves the selected field one level up in the hierarchy of fields in the selected PivotTable area.
Move Down	Moves the selected field one level down in the hierarchy of fields in the selected PivotTable area.
Move to Beginning	Moves the selected field to the top of the hierarchy of fields in the selected PivotTable area.
Move to End	Moves the selected field to the bottom of the hierarchy of fields in the selected PivotTable area.
Move to Report Filter	Moves the selected field to the Report Filter area of the PivotTable.
Move to Row Labels	Moves the selected field to the Row Labels area of the PivotTable.
Move to Column Labels	Moves the selected field to the Column Labels area of the PivotTable.
Move to Values	Moves the selected field to the Values area of the PivotTable.
Remove Field	Removes the selected field from the PivotTable report.
Field Settings	Brings up the Field Settings dialog box.

Appendix Review

This appendix covered all the functions that are available across the three components of a PivotTable report. I started with a review of double-clicking actions and the five types of pop-up menus in the Report Layout area, providing graphical illustrations and brief descriptions of each pop-up menu item. After that, I reviewed the eight sections of the PivotTable tab, where I provided screen captures and brief descriptions of each tab button. I concluded with a review of the clicking actions in the PivotTable Field List dialog box. Given all the changes in this new version of Excel, I hope you find this to be a useful reference!

Index